The forgotten French

MANCHESTER
UNIVERSITY PRESS

For Claire, Charlotte and Benjamin

The forgotten French
Exiles in the British Isles
1940–44

NICHOLAS ATKIN

Manchester University Press
Manchester and New York

distributed exclusively in the USA by Palgrave

Published by Manchester University Press
Oxford Road, Manchester M13 9NR, UK
and Room 400, 175 Fifth Avenue, New York, NY 10010, USA
www.manchesteruniversitypress.co.uk

Distributed exclusively in the USA by
Palgrave, 175 Fifth Avenue, New York,
NY 10010, USA

Distributed exclusively in Canada by
UBC Press, University of British Columbia, 2029 West Mall,
Vancouver, BC, Canada V6T 1Z2

British Library Cataloguing-in-Publication Data
A catalogue record for this book is available from the British Library

Library of Congress Cataloging-in-Publication Data applied for

ISBN 0 7190 6438 4 *hardback*

First published 2003

11 10 09 08 07 06 05 04 03   10 9 8 7 6 5 4 3 2 1

Typeset in Minion
by Action Publishing Technology Ltd, Gloucester
Printed in Great Britain
by Bell & Bain Ltd, Glasgow

Contents

Figures and maps

Figures

Maps

Preface

It is sometimes easier to explain what a book is not about before stating its purpose. This is very definitely not another study of de Gaulle, the Free French and the troublesome relations they enjoyed with their British hosts, although inevitably the name of the general appears repeatedly in the text. Countless words have already been spilt on these subjects, and it is likely that more will follow, if only to satiate the curiosity of a British public which, astonishingly, still seems surprised that Churchill and the Free French leader were not always the best of allies.[1] Nor is this another account of those secretive and murky relations that the Vichy government conducted with the Foreign Office during 1940–42. This, too, has been an overworked topic, maybe in an effort to counter those disingenuous and tedious arguments continuously peddled by unreconstructed Pétainists in France who claim their hero was involved in a double game with the Germans, outwardly proclaiming his adherence to collaboration while secretly negotiating with Churchill to shield the French people from greater suffering, thus deserving to be counted among the pioneers of resistance. It should be further stressed that this is not primarily an examination of those writers and thinkers, most notably Raymond Aron and André Labarthe, who made London their temporary home in 1940. To be fair, we still await a synthesis of French intellectual activity in wartime London, just as we need an overall account of exiled intellectuals in Britain's capital. We are, though, well served by the autobiographies of the protagonists themselves, and there is no shortage of biographical studies of the most prominent exiled figures, French and otherwise. And, finally, this is not an attempt to write the response of British public opinion to events in France. So dramatic were the ups and downs of the Vichy regime that the reactions within Britain have been amply mapped out, their subsequent course well plotted, and their importance recorded at every twist and turn. All this the book is not. It is instead an exploration of the lives of those French men, women and children who discovered themselves, usually by happenstance ahead of design, on British shores in May–June 1940. These communities constitute what I have termed the 'forgotten French', repeatedly ignored by historians who have preferred to concentrate on de Gaulle and other more visible exile groups whose experiences have been deemed of greater significance. Crudely speaking, the 'forgotten French' comprised the following: some 4,000 refugees jostled out of northern France by the battering of Guderian's Panzers; maybe 12,000 stranded servicemen, principally sailors, survivors of Narvik and Dunkirk and those unlucky enough to be arrested in British ports at the time of Mers-el-Kébir, who would not be returned home until the close of the year; an indeterminate number of Vichy officials, possibly 200 or so consular and mission staff, together with their wives and families, left behind to keep the wheels of petty bureaucracy turning, despite the breaking off of diplomatic relations between Britain and Vichy; and a French colony of 12,000 strong, which decided to stay put on British soil, despite the fact that maybe 18,000 *colons* chose to return home with the outbreak of war or at some point during the *drôle de guerre*.

The objective of this book is, then, to lift these groups out of obscurity – to scrutinise their existence, to assess the material conditions in which they lived and to probe their concerns, which were as much to do with social issues as they were to do with political ones. An underlying aim is also to monitor how the British government and public reacted to these strangers in their midst, foreigners who, unlike the Norwegians, Poles and Belgians, did not possess a government-in-exile, thus raising doubts about their loyalty to the Allied cause.

If there exists any burning need to depose the myth that Britain was a welcoming haven for those retreating from Nazi oppression on the Continent, then much evidence may be uncovered in the pages that follow. While the public often displayed charity and sympathy, even if it was only doling out a cup of tea, a beverage the French did not take kindly to, government officials at all levels were far less indulgent, and at times it is difficult not to avoid the conclusion that Whitehall would much have preferred it if the 'forgotten French' had stayed in France, or at least had joined their cousins in North America, where there existed a huge colonist community, and where they would have been out of view, their incomprehensible arguments a concern for the State Department rather than the Foreign Office. More fundamentally, this book helps lay the myth, cultivated by de Gaulle at the time and believed by many since, notably a British public that readily identified itself with the general's courage and isolation in 1940, that the French in Britain, notwithstanding some obvious exceptions, constituted a homogeneous group who had quickly rallied to the cause of the general and, as such, deserve to be counted among the 'resisters of the first hour'. This book demonstrates that this explanation will simply not do. The 'forgotten French' were extremely varied in their response to events and displayed a strong wariness of de Gaulle himself. In this respect, this study mirrors the approach that historians have increasingly adopted in their research into occupied France. No longer are the key concerns the high politics of Vichy–German relations, the ins and outs of collaborationist politics at Paris, the interminable intrigues of the corridors of power at Vichy and the workings of the Resistance movements; instead, historians have chosen to look at the history of the Occupation from the bottom up. Just as historians of Nazi Germany have become obsessed with *Alltagsgeschichte*, 'the history of daily life', *la vie quotidienne* has likewise become the central concern for researchers into Vichy France.

Viewed through these prisms, the 'forgotten French' constitute far more than a footnote in the history of the Second World War. An examination of their lives reveals much about of the splintering of French opinion during the war. Many of the attitudes that have been identified in metropolitan France, in the different zones created by the Germans, may also be found among the exiles in Britain. Pétainism, in particular, crossed the Channel alongside the refugees and servicemen, while Gaullism struggled to put down roots, even among communities one might have thought indulgent and sympathetic to the general, and it is not difficult to perceive similarities between the popular anti-Gaullism of the Fourth and Fifth Republics and that articulated in wartime Britain. The experiences of the 'forgotten French' also reveal much about the business of exile, something the French especially have never warmed to, even though they have regularly made Britain their temporary home at moments of crisis in their country's history, for instance in the aftermath of the Massacre of Saint Bartholomew, the Revocation of the Edict of Nantes, the Revolution of 1789, and those upheavals of 1830, 1848 and 1871. As David Thomson observed in his 1951 profile of de Gaulle, 'Exiles, even those who have courageously sought voluntary exile in order to continue the battle for their country's honour and liberation, have usually acquired a mentality which, though completely understandable and humanly forgivable, calls for constant patience and imaginative sympathy on the part of their hosts.'[2]

Such a mentality was indeed adopted by the 'forgotten French', men, women and children who generally had not chosen to advance the fight by settling in Britain, and who were not well cut out for life abroad, even in a country as geographically close to France as Britain, thus contributing to an uncomfortable mix of cultures. It was fortunate both for the 'forgotten French' and their British hosts that, often unbeknown to one another, they shared a set of common values, and appreciated that these could only be fulfilled with the ultimate defeat of Nazism.

Notes

1   S. Berthon, *Allies at War* (London, Collins, 2000).
2   D. Thomson, *Two Frenchmen. Pierre Laval and Charles de Gaulle* (London, The Cresset Press, 1951), p. 168.

Acknowledgements

Paradoxically for a book that takes issue with much of the wartime mythology of Gaullism, the origins of this study lie in the centenary commemorations of the general's birth when I gave papers, first, at the Maison Française, Oxford, in 1988 and two years later at UNESCO, Paris, at the international *colloque* sponsored by the Institut Charles de Gaulle, 'De Gaulle en son siècle'. It was during the research for these contributions that my curiosity about the French in wartime Britain was ignited. It was fuelled further by a chance to contribute to the volume edited by François Poirier, of the University of Nanterre, on London at war. Subsequent invitations to deliver academic papers allowed me to sharpen my ideas. I should especially like to thank Dr Martin Conway of Balliol College, Oxford, together with the Wiener-Anspach Foundation, Brussels, for a chance to speak at the 1998 conference on 'Europe in Exile'. Thanks also extend to Maurice Vaïsse, Director of the Centre d'Etudes d'Histoire de la Défense, Vincennes, for the opportunity to contribute to a volume on the French defeat of 1940 as viewed by foreign historians. Segments of the research for my earlier essays, listed in the bibliography, reappear in the present volume, and I am grateful to repeat material already in print.

In the course of my research I have visited several libraries and should like to thank the staff of the following institutions: University College, London; Royal Holloway and New Bedford College, London; the Institute of Historical Research, London; Senate House Library, University of London; the British Library; and the British Newspaper Library, Colindale.

I further owe a tremendous debt to those archivists who have made my task that much easier: Rhys Griffiths of the London Metropolitan Archives; Stephen Walton of the Imperial War Museum; Dorothy

Sheridan and the Trustees of Mass-Observation, University of Sussex; the staff of the LSE archives; Mike Bott of the University of Reading; Geoff Winner of the BBC Written Archives, Caversham; Rachel Lloyd at Churchill College, Cambridge; and Father Ian Dickie of Westminster Diocesan Archives, who was an excellent lunch companion. I must especially thank Lady Toulson of the Women's Royal Voluntary Service for granting me permission to consult WRVS holdings, Megan Keble for taking me through the inventories and Siobhan Abbott for driving over to Wallingford to give me access to the papers themselves. In Paris, Audrey Bonnery took time out of her own important research into the BBC's wartime role to check materials for me in the Ministère des Affaires Etrangères. Matthew Peaple undertook a similar task in Berlin. At the Public Records Office, Kew, many archivists offered their assistance, but I should like to record a debt of friendship to Dr David Leitch, now Director of Corporate Affairs, an old friend from student days in Paris, who was another welcome lunch partner.

I am additionally grateful to the PRO for enabling me to reproduce Crown Copyright materials. All efforts have been made to trace copyright holders, and the publishers would welcome any further information in this regard. To protect the identity of individuals who played little direct role in the dramatic events of wartime exile, I have cited their initials in place of their full names. Mass-Observation material is reproduced with the permission of Curtis Brown Group Ltd, London, on behalf of the Trustees of Mass-Observation Archive. Copyright of the Mass-Observation Archive.

For their offers of advice and information, I wish to thank, among others, Katie Lingard, Marie-Laure Clausard, Joan Delin, Professor Jim Knowlson and the Earl of Bessborough. My postgraduate students David Smith, Fraser Reavell and Richard Carswell were also at hand with suggestions. Thanks further extend to colleagues and friends who have all worked to make this a better book: Dr Tom Buchanan, Professor John Keiger, Professor Julian Jackson, Professor Rod Kedward, Dr Richard Vinen, Lord Williams of Elvel, and Professor Mike Heffernan. Above all, I am indebted to Matthew Buck, now at the Museum of the Royal Woolwich Arsenal, whose work into Belgian refugees was an inspiration. All mistakes are naturally my own contribution.

Over the years, I have had the chance to interview some remarkable people who lived through the war years. In particular I should like to thank Mrs Helen Long, Monsieur Jacques Veydert of the Amicale de

Mauthausen, Monsieur Léon Wilson, and Monsieur Georges Le Poittevin, President of the Association des Combattants Volontaires in the UK.

A book such as this is also a chance to acknowledge long-standing intellectual debts. I wish to thank in particular Professor Douglas Johnson, who did much to nurture my early interest in French history; Professor Martin Alexander, who read through an early draft and who has always been supportive of my many projects; and Professor Michael Biddiss who likewise read the text and who, nearly twenty years ago, along with Professor Olwen Hufton, appointed me to a temporary lectureship, which helped launch my career. I must also thank my colleague at the University of Reading, Dr Frank Tallett, who is always a source of good humour and advice. The School of History at Reading was an especially convivial place to write this book and I am grateful that in the last two years I was given time to finish the research.

Alison Whittle and the staff at Manchester University Press carefully saw this book through to production and were supportive throughout. The copy-editor was Susan Womersley.

As always, family played a great part in the making of this book, my wife Claire, and children Charlotte and Ben whose knowledge of things French as yet extends little beyond buying cakes from Maison Bertaux in Greek Street. Although I wasn't initially aware, the 'forgotten French' have long been with me. For years, on a Saturday afternoon after the football is over, I have made my way along Pembury Road, Tottenham, little realising that in 1940–41 this street was the home to several displaced Boulogne and Breton fishermen.

Nicholas Atkin
Windsor

Abbreviations

AN	Archives Nationales
AVF	Amis des Volontaires Français
BBC	British Broadcasting Company
BCRA	Bureau Central de Renseignements d'Action
CCC	Churchill College Cambridge
CEAF	Comité d'Entr'Aide aux Français
CEGES	Centre d'Etudes et de Documentation Guerre et Sociétés Contemporaines
CFR	Committee on Foreign (Allied) Resistance
FBAF	Fédération Britannique de L'Alliance Française
FFL	Forces Françaises Libres
FGB	Français de Grande Bretagne
FL	*La France Libre*
FNFL	Forces Navales Françaises Libres
IWM	Imperial War Museum
LCC	London County Council
LMA	London Metropolitan Archives
LSE	London School of Economics
MAE	Ministère des Affaires Etrangères
MCC	Middlesex County Council
M-O	Mass-Observation
NS & N	*New Statesman and Nation*
PAC	Public Assistance Committees
PRO	Public Records Office
RAF	Royal Air Force
RUL	Reading University Library
RVPS	Royal Victoria Patriotic School
SOE	Special Operations Executive

UAGBF	United Associations of Great Britain and France Solidarity Committee
UFOM	Union des Français d'Outre Mer
WDA	Westminister Diocesan Archives
WRVS	Women's Royal Voluntary Service (Archives)
WVS	Women's Voluntary Service

1

The context of exile: communities, circumstances and choices

Quitter la France est, pour un français, une situation funèbre.
(Honoré de Balzac, *Le Cousin Pons*)[1]

An independent-minded people, with a strong cultural awareness and attachment to region, if not always to nation, the French have generally made unhappy exiles. It has been their misfortune that the many crises punctuating French history have compelled them to take refuge abroad, especially in Britain, a land that is so 'alike' France yet so 'different'.[2] In the sixteenth and seventeenth centuries, religious persecution was the spur. The Massacre of Saint Bartholomew in 1572 and Louis XIV's Revocation of the Edict of Nantes in 1685 banished Protestants aplenty: soldiers, lower nobility and, crucially, artisans and craftsmen, men whose skills came to be missed in France and resented among rival workers in Britain.[3] In the eighteenth century, it was the turn of the *philosophes*, Voltaire and Rousseau, hounded out by the ideological intolerance of absolutism, the latter spending much of his time, miserably, in the mists and rain of Derbyshire, the source of the following piece of doggerel:

> At Wootton-under-Weaver,
> Where God came never![4]

The *philosophes* were themselves succeeded by some 100,000–150,000 *émigrés* of all kinds – soldiers, priests, sailors, peasants and pastry cooks, significantly not just aristocrats as is sometimes claimed – fleeing the excesses of the Revolutionary and Napoleonic regimes.[5] Most of these unwilling exiles, maybe up to two-thirds, had returned to France by 1801, when Napoleon signed a Concordat with the Pope and made overtures to appease the nobility, although a handful of die-hard monarchists bided their time and did not re-establish themselves in

their homeland until the restoration of the Bourbons in 1814–15.[6]
Paradoxically, it was not long before French kings were travelling in the
opposite direction. Both Charles X and Louis-Philippe took refuge in
Britain following the revolutions of 1830 and 1848; and, in 1870, there
came a Bonaparte, Napoleon III, who had already spent some of his
earlier life in London enrolling, in 1848, as a special constable at the
time of the Chartist demonstrations in Hyde Park. After the collapse of
the Second Empire in 1870, he set up an ersatz court at Chislehurst in
Kent, where he died in 1873, not so far from Petts Wood, the temporary home of General de Gaulle in autumn 1940. For many years
afterwards, the Orpington Museum proudly displayed a copy of de
Gaulle's bill for coal deliveries.[7]

The upheavals that toppled kings and emperors also uprooted revolutionaries and artists. The political activists Godefroy Cavaignac,
Louis Blanc, and Alexandre Ledru-Rollin all took shelter in London, as
did the writer and painters Victor Hugo, Camille Pissarro and Claude
Monet, the latter pair seeking to escape the upheavals of the Paris
Commune of 1871, which had seen their homes occupied by Prussian
troops.[8] They were accompanied by several Communard insurgents,
the most notorious being the journalist Jules Vallès, who wrote extensively, and very critically, of his time in London; most of these exiles
returned after an amnesty was declared in 1878, although a small
number remained to settle in Soho, for example the Bertaux family
who set up a patisserie in Greek Street, an establishment that survives
to this day, albeit under new Anglo-French ownership.[9] In the following decade, the ideological battles of the Boulanger Affair brought forth
the general himself, together with one of his most committed champi-
ons, the writer Henri Rochefort. During the 1890s, the Dreyfus Affair
led to a fresh round of exiles, notably that of the novelist Emile Zola,
who lived a clandestine existence in Weybridge where he largely kept
himself to himself, taking photographs of the neighbourhood and
following events in France.[10] Ironically Esterhazy, the man who had
sparked off the whole scandal by selling secrets to the Germans, probably to finance his mistresses and gambling debts, also escaped French
justice by hiding in London. Men and women of a very different moral
calibre – monks and nuns belonging to religious orders dissolved by
the so-called *lois d'exception* of 1901 and 1904 – followed in the foot-
steps of Esterhazy, discovering Protestant Britain a far more tolerant
refuge than the secular and purportedly liberal-minded Third
Republic.[11] It was a symbolic act when the convent at Montmartre,

dedicated to the English martyrs and set up by religious originally expelled at the time of the Reformation, was transferred to Tyburn in the centre of London. As Aidan Bellanger records, history seemed to 'have turned full-circle'.[12]

Ideological intransigence, religious persecution and revolution had thus been the principal factors driving the French across the Channel. In the early years of the twentieth century commercial factors became the key. Although the stagnation in French population growth did not necessarily create a ready band of economic exiles, the downturn in the European economy in the 1880s, the allure of London as a business centre and the growing diversification of commercial activities attracted several large businesses to Britain. On the eve of the First World War, there were 30,000 or so French living in the British Isles, the third largest group of European exiles. What is astonishing is that such an important group of immigrants should have been constantly overlooked by historians who have tended to concentrate on German, Russian and Italian arrivals.[13] Something of the reasons for this neglect are addressed in Chapter 5, but it might well stem from the fact that sources on the French are hard to come by, as they were for this present study.

War, that defining feature of the twentieth century, also drew the French to Britain, although it should be stressed that the vast majority of Continental refugees in 1914–18 stemmed from Belgium, a country whose low-lying and watery lands had become an ever-moving battle-ground.[14] The foreign ways of the Belgians, their alleged low standards of hygiene and supposed indiscipline were not remembered with fondness in 1940 when Britain again welcomed Europe's 'unwanted', although the swift advance of Hitler's armies ensured that their numbers (perhaps 20,000) were never as great as in 1914 when some 250,000 had taken refuge in the British Isles. This was the largest influx of foreigners into the UK since the 1790s, and many had to be housed in religious houses of Southern Ireland. Initially, the French government had only been too happy that such displaced persons should be dispatched across the Channel, yet already by 1915 the strains of war meant that Belgians were a welcome addition to the French work-force.[15] At the start of the First World War, Joffre's ability, or luck, in holding the Germans at the Marne, enabled the mass of France's own refugees to retreat into metropolitan territory where they were at least among their countryfolk; negligible numbers came to Britain. The withdrawal inland was imitated by their government, which set up a temporary home at Bordeaux in 1914, the resting place for some ministries for the duration of the war.

In the summer of 1940, France once again became a country of entrances and exits. On 10 May, German forces, having conquered much of eastern Europe, turned westwards and began their simultaneous assault on Belgium, the Netherlands and Luxemburg. Their advance was so fast that they soon reached Sedan, the cornerstone of French defences, which fell on 13 May. Two days later, the Dutch army surrendered; within a fortnight, the Belgians had followed suit. On 28 May, trapped by the German manoeuvre, the British Expeditionary Force (BEF) started the evacuation from the beaches of Dunkirk, accompanied by bedraggled elements of the French army. As the soldiers retreated, the politicians also departed. On 10 June, the same day as an opportunist Mussolini entered the war against France, Reynaud's government left Paris for Bordeaux. Holding a series of makeshift meetings along the châteaux of the Loire valley, on 11–13 June, the French Cabinet discussed whether to leave and fight on from North Africa or to sue for an armistice, an option favoured by General Weygand, Gamelin's recent replacement as commander-in-chief, and Marshal Pétain, who had been appointed deputy prime minister on 18 May in a desperate attempt to shore up morale. On 16 June, two days after the Germans occupied Paris, the government reached Bordeaux where a dispirited Reynaud resigned and recommended Pétain as his successor. The next day, this ancient soldier, some eighty-four years of age and best known for his victory at Verdun in 1916, announced to a stunned nation that he was in the process of negotiating an armistice. Signed on 23 June, the terms of this agreement divided France into two principal zones, the larger area comprising the northern and western territories, which were to be occupied by the Germans. Still in flight, the French government eventually retired to the little spa town of Vichy, often likened to an English Harrogate, Cheltenham or Tunbridge Wells, where on 10 July the National Assembly voted itself out of existence and granted full powers to Pétain.[16] Politically ambitious and naive of true German intentions, he quickly used his new-found authority to promote a policy of collaboration abroad and a reactionary programme of renewal at home. Few dared defy the leadership of this old man whose patriotism seemed unquestionable. One exception was his former protégé General de Gaulle who, on 5 June, had been appointed under-secretary of war and who, on 17 June, quit France for London in disgust at the Armistice and the defeatism of the marshal. The day after his arrival, he broadcast to his countrymen on the BBC urging them to continue the fight.[17]

In 1940, the success in repeating the retreat to Bordeaux (though not the victory of the Marne) guaranteed that far more French than in 1914 reached the relative safety of Britain, although it should be stressed that most still retreated inland. Some, notably civilians and soldiers, had little choice in their destination, squeezed out at Dunkirk by the pincer-movement of Guderian's tanks, and ferried across the Channel in the 'little boats'. Others such as de Gaulle deliberately chose London as it was in the thick of the fighting and the nerve centre of resistance to Nazism. In an interview of October 1990, Maurice Schumann, de Gaulle's broadcaster, admitted that he was happy in London as he felt he was at the front.[18] As Maurice Agulhon remarks, London was also a place from where radio messages could be transmitted to the Continent.[19] Yet few initially heeded the calls on the BBC; only a handful listened to de Gaulle's now famous broadcast of 18 June.[20] To the general's disgust and frustration, several prominent intellectuals who had arrived in London at the same time as himself were soon repacking their bags, destined for the safer shores of North America. It was with some justification that Elizabeth de Miribel acerbically observed, 'In June 1940 London was not a town where you arrived, but one from which you left.'[21] Likewise, Ronald Tree, one of Churchill's close associates, recalls how, in the wake of the fall of Sedan, London University's Senate House, the wartime home of the Ministry of Information, was deluged with prominent French figures, all desirous to secure passage to New York.[22] And, finally, there were the existing colonists, descendants of Huguenots and nineteenth-century revolutionaries, together with economic immigrants, who looked with sadness and bewilderment at what was happening to their homeland.

The Gaullist legacy

Apart from General de Gaulle and his supporters, who have generated what one historian has described as an 'intimidating' literature,[23] those French exiles who sheltered in Britain during the 'dark years' of 1940–44 have largely been forgotten by historians. Why this neglect? Part of the answer lies in the fact that the French in wartime Britain constituted a small, self-contained community, or rather communities, who left few traces of their existence, and who were all too eager to return to France, some seeking repatriation while the Germans still occupied their lands.[24] When I was engaged in a fruitless search for the papers of a now-disbanded French charity, one archivist in the London Metropolitan Archives compared the French in wartime London to the present-day Chinese community: both sets of people determined to keep themselves to themselves, conscious of their privacy, anxious to assert their independence of spirit, and extremely wary of any meddling from the outside. This might explain why the French remain invisible in social histories of Britain during the Second World War, and earn little more than a footnote in most accounts of wartime London, the city where a majority of them congregated; indeed, they are hidden in most survey histories of the capital.[25] Piecing together fragments of the lives of these exiles was thus no easy matter, with sources elusive and scattered in out-of-the-way places; those scraps of evidence that do survive often pertain to such mundane matters as billeting allowances and unemployment relief, testimony to the prudent housekeeping and Victorian spirit of self-help that pervaded the British state at war.

It is also apparent that the French have been overshadowed by other more prominent groups of foreigners who arrived in wartime: Jews, Germans and American GIs. The abominations that were perpetrated in the death camps of central and eastern Europe have rightly focused attention on what Britain, and France, could have done for the victims of Nazi persecution in 1939–45. Far more is surely the answer.[26] Attention has also centred on those politically suspect groups whose loyalty was called into question in 1940. Italian economic immigrants, long settled in this country and well integrated into London life, found themselves serving *espressos* in Soho coffee bars one minute and brewing tea in rusty canteens in an Isle of Man internment camp the next. German arrivals in the 1930s fared no better, becoming immediate objects of suspicion, even if they had originally fled their homeland to escape Nazi racial persecution.[27] And, of course, there were the Allies, principally the Americans, who, in the so-called 'friendly invasion', brought with them hope, fresh faces, nylon stockings, cigarettes and candy bars, leaving behind plenty of women holding unwanted babies.[28] By contrast, French exiles never had the same impact on British culture, although outraged citizens in the garrison towns of Camberley and Aldershot complained bitterly about the loose morals and libidinous behaviour of Gaullist troops stationed there,[29] reflecting the widely held notion that French men were sexual athletes ready to prey on the virtuous womanhood of Albion. Gender issues aside, the reasons why the French had such a minimal impact on British culture are not hard to fathom: their numbers were small, especially compared to the Americans; their traditions were different; and, ultimately, they were dependent on their British hosts for virtually everything. Tereska Torrrès, who at nineteen took the brave decision to quit her homeland in order to enrol in the Corps Féminin des Forces Françaises Libres, the women's wing of La France Libre, relates how she and her colleagues wore British uniforms until these were distinguished by the addition of French insignia, thus providing a separate identity.[30]

It is also possible that French exiles in Britain have been neglected in favour of their cousins in North America. The French communities in the USA and Canada, especially, were always much larger than their counterparts in London. It is calculated that, in 1939, the French-speaking population in the USA was approximately 1,400,000, the majority being of Canadian or Louisiana extraction. Some 30,000 French expatriates were located in Washington and New York alone; London could boast no more than 7,000 *colons*. Given these numbers, it was inevitable that the American French communities took a keen interest in what was happening to their compatriots over the Atlantic. As de Miribel remarked, the safety of American shores ensured that their numbers were further swelled by many prominent politicians and artists.[31] While George Bernanos, the Catholic author, and Charles Corbin, the former ambassador to Britain, headed for South America, such luminaries as Henri Bernstein, Camille Chautemps, Jules Romains, André Maurois, Claude Lévi-Strauss, Jean Monnet and Henry Torrès, father of Tereska, all took up residence in New York. To be fair to these men, their courage in reaching America was often considerable. Not all of them had quickly forsaken London, expecting Britain to be the next domino to fall in Hitler's game of conquest. Rather than travelling in relative safety from English ports on board US-registered vessels, their journey often involved a difficult passage through Spain and Portugal, and from Lisbon across treacherous seas to Liberty Island, avoiding German submarines en route as well as the patrols of the Royal Navy, which, in the aftermath of the shelling of the French fleet at Mers-el-Kébir on 3 July 1940, was prepared to stop, board and sink any craft sailing under the tricolour lest it fell into Hitler's clutches. Once on American soil, the significant numbers of intellectuals ensured that New York, together with Montréal, became the French cultural capital overseas. London could never make the same claim, this to the disappointment perhaps of British writers such as Raymond Mortimer, Cyril Connolly, Kathleen Raine and Stephen Spender who, according to Arthur Koestler, suffered from 'French flu', all too ready to abandon their normal prudence whenever they saw a line of French verse or prose, especially if it was written by Vercors, André Gide or Louis Aragon.[32]

While the French in Britain might well have been eclipsed by other groups, de Gaulle at least has attracted intense interest, and herein lies the principal reason why the French communities have been overlooked. All too often, the general and his supporters have been seen as synonymous with all French exiles in London. This tendency even existed in the war itself. Robert Mengin, a former member of the Mission Naval Française and later a writer for the British-run Resistance journal *Courrier de l'Air*, remembers how his English friends were extremely perplexed when he explained that he was not a Gaullist. This caused consternation, and a belated and hesitant question as to whether he was a Pétainist. To overcome such social embarrassments, Mengin feigned eccentricity: 'The easy way was to pass oneself off as a little mad. A touch of madness is quite well considered in England.'[33]

Although it is not correct to believe French exiles and the Free French were one and the same, such misguided ideas are at least understandable. De Gaulle was a truly remarkable figure whose importance in the history of the Second World War and subsequent evolution of France cannot be overstated.[34] In 1940, all the odds appeared stacked against him. Here was a two-star general, the author of some overlooked books on tank warfare, and a minor member of Reynaud's last Cabinet, who was defying the authority of Marshal Pétain, the most celebrated of France's soldiers, the 'Victor of Verdun', a man whose authority and patriotism seemed unchallengeable.[35] Here, too, was a rebellious officer whose claims to incarnate French sovereignty rested on some highly dubious criteria. Although his legal expert René Cassin was soon put to work in demonstrating that it was Vichy that was the unconstitutional regime,[36] even the British refused to confer on de Gaulle the status of a leader of a government in exile, merely acknowledging him on 28 June 1940 as the head of the Free French. The general was always reliant on British backing, just as Tereska Torrès was dependent on the British for her uniforms. Initially, this support came from Churchill himself, who was impressed by de Gaulle's courage and who was eager to rein in the pro-Vichy sympathies of the Foreign Office; later, it was the Foreign Office that became de Gaulle's principal supporter, keen to dampen Churchill's enthusiasm for the

Americans.[37] For their part, Roosevelt and the State Department retained an outright hostility to the general, the president being unable to understand how any man could compare himself to Joan of Arc, and being irritated, as Churchill bemoaned, that he could not get his own bishops to burn him.[38] Yet, against these odds, de Gaulle played what few cards he had skilfully, building up his support in the colonies, outwitting potential rivals in the shape of Admiral Muselier and General Giraud, nurturing his contacts with the Resistance in metropolitan France, and retaining an extreme suspicion of both British and American intentions. Such behaviour ensured that, in 1944, he was acknowledged as the undisputed leader of the French Resistance both inside and outside of France, although such status did not ensure the political settlement he craved. For that, he would have to wait until 1958.

Aside from de Gaulle's obvious political importance, memory has also played its part in the close identification of French exiles with the general. To explain why this is so in the case of the British, it is necessary to reflect on the extraordinary and unpropitious circumstances of June 1940. On his arrival, the general was an 'unknown' and received little publicity: his broadcast of 18 June was not widely reported and there was little information readily available on his past.[39] *The Times*, which on 7 June 1940 had published a short biographical sketch of the new under-secretary of state for war, was one of the few papers to publish his *appel* in full.[40] Major-General Spears, who became the liaison officer between the British and the Free French, claimed there was only one copy of de Gaulle's *Army of the Future* in the War Office whose pages had not even been cut.[41] Churchill was so troubled by this state of affairs that he employed a public relations consultant, Richmond Temple, to boost the general's appeal, a gesture that led to a deterioration of personal relations between the two leaders.[42] De Gaulle complained bitterly that the prime minister would sell him like a brand of soap, and preferred to keep himself to himself.[43] According to Spears, he regularly used the following phrase in conversation with staff officers, 'I do not want to be made a film star by the press.'[44] The historian Douglas Johnson tells the astonishing story of bumping into Geoffrey de Courcel, de Gaulle's right-hand man who had boarded the same aircraft on 17 June 1940, wandering around Frognal looking for the house in which his hero had once lived, never having visited there during the war.[45]

Yet it remains questionable whether de Gaulle needed to be

marketed by Churchill. The romantic image of this lonely soldier, defying the menace of Nazism and the cowardice of Vichy, appealed to a nation that had few enough heroes at the height of the Blitz. His striking presence, and enormous height, was quickly noted in the streets of London. When one of the characters, the rather seedy and paedophile uncle, in Mary Wesley's wartime novel *The Camomile Lawn* remarks how he saw de Gaulle that morning, and had saluted him, this was far from fiction.[46] The general was a familiar sight in metropolitan life, and quickly become enmeshed in the British legend of a heroic and steadfast nation determined to resist the German onslaught at whatever cost. 'Good old de Gaulle', cried workers when he visited a munitions factory.[47] As the populist newspaper the *Daily Sketch* observed in imagery that might well have appealed to the general himself, 'He is like Robinson Crusoe washed up on his island and anxious to save as much as possible that may be useful to him.'[48] Listening in Notting Hill to one of his first broadcasts on the BBC, the nurse and little-known diarist Vere Hodgson noted on 28 June 1940, 'Magnificent personality he sounds ... His voice is thrilling, and his answer made me shiver in my chair. Such tragedy too in his tones.'[49] Although public opinion was often exasperated by de Gaulle, especially by his high-handed methods and rudeness, which could not always be concealed from the press, and entertained doubts about his political ambitions,[50] it remained impressed by his heroism and determination. The diplomat Harold Nicolson, who himself had despaired at the general's rudeness in the war,[51] caught this mood perfectly when reviewing the first volume of the *Mémoires de guerre* in 1955 for the *Observer*:

> For all his rigid ways his potent nationalism gave him charm. We in this country always have an affection for lost causes and in 1941 the cause of France did in fact seem lost. De Gaulle inspired us with a glow of wonder that he should be positive, that he could lead his people out of the abyss by the force of his dreams and theirs.[52]

Some fifty years after his flight to London, his voice of defiance still echoed. Commemorating the centenary of his birth in 1990, the Institut Charles de Gaulle conducted a *sondage* among the British public.[53] Of those interviewed, the overwhelming majority recalled that he had been the leader of the Free French in London. Far fewer recalled his presidency of the Fifth Republic and, maybe surprisingly in these Eurosceptic times, the fact that he said *non* to Britain's request to join the Common Market in 1963.

Within France, too, there has been a tendency to view the Free French and French exiles as one and the same. This is understandable given the way in which both Germany and Vichy rigorously censored both press and radio reports and the manner in which the Free French often dominated BBC broadcasts to France, even though the organisation was only supposed to enjoy half-an-hour early evening slots in the schedules.[54] It is, though, de Gaulle himself, the supreme myth-maker, who ensured that all French expatriates in Britain were identified with his cause. To admit that he had not been able to win over the entire French community in Britain would have been an admission of failure, and might well have dented his already precarious position yet further. It would certainly have undermined his claims to embody the sovereignty of the French people and the legitimacy of the republican tradition both of which, he argued, Vichy had illegally usurped. He returned to these themes in his memoirs written in the 1950s, a time when he was desperate to keep his political options alive given the difficulties of the Fourth Republic. In recalling how, on 18 June 1940, his 'irrevocable words flew out upon their way', urging his countrymen, both on metropolitan and British soil, to join him in London, he readily acknowledges that only 'isolated volunteers' reached England: 'They mostly came from France, brought by the last ships to have left there normally, or escaping in small boats which they had managed to seize, or, again, having with great difficulty got across Spain, evading its police which shut up in the camp at Miranda those it caught.'[55] That more did not sail from France, and that many servicemen stranded in England did not rally, are conveniently attributed to Mers-el-Kébir. For de Gaulle, this was 'a lamentable event' and 'a terrible blow for our hopes'.[56] Thereafter, he makes little mention of the French community in Britain, other than to imply that he commanded their loyalty, something that was simply not true. Rather, his memoirs emphasise his own role in the Resistance, 'the man of June Eighteenth' who, as Henry Rousso writes, personified the sovereignty of the French people and who single-handedly took 'under his wing' the forty million French men and women on metropolitan territory, turning them into a 'nation of resisters'.[57] For a set of memoirs written about his time in London, there is remarkably little about the city itself, the manner in which the Free French settled there, and their relations with the British and wider French communities. Just as de Gaulle passes over Jews and Paris collaborators – two other embarrassing groups of his countrymen, albeit embarrassing for different reasons – he largely overlooks the many other French citizens in Britain.

Figure 1   De Gaulle's words immortalised in stone on the front of Carlton
Gardens

Since the general's death in 1970, much work has been conducted into disassembling Gaullist 'resistancialist' mythology, unveiling the complex nature of the Resistance, both inside and outside of France.[58] This work has conclusively demonstrated that Vichy was far from being an aberration in French history, as de Gaulle always claimed. Instead, it drew on existing political and ideological traditions, most embarrassingly a potent anti-Semitism, which has recently resurfaced in the shape of Jean-Marie Le Pen's extreme rightist Front National.[59] The same research has further demonstrated that the Resistance was principally the work of a minority; one historian has calculated that the number of active resisters was no more than 400,000, in other words, less than 2 per cent of the population, a claim that will always be impossible to substantiate.[60] The divisions within the Resistance have also been exposed, not just those between de Gaulle and the far left, which the general was all too ready to acknowledge in his attempts to condemn the Communists as revolutionaries, but the deeper personal and ideological clashes that threatened his overall control. That de Gaulle was able to take charge of the transitional government in France in 1944 owed much to his diplomatic and political skills, which had to be at their sharpest in outwitting the Americans who had plans to put their own people into position.[61]

While historians of Vichy France have shown great creativity in developing new lines of enquiry, the one area where they have not displayed the same kind of imagination is in uncovering the life of exiles in Britain. Here, the concerns of scholars have unquestionably been extensive, but they have also been very traditional, focusing largely on diplomacy and high politics, the sort of issues that de Gaulle himself tackles in his memoirs: the uneasy bond between the general and Churchill;[62] the curious triangular relationship that existed between London, the Free French and Vichy;[63] the growth of the Free French movement itself;[64] the squabbles among its leading figures, especially those with Admiral Muselier;[65] the emergence of anti-Gaullism as an intellectual movement;[66] the quarrels over BBC broadcasts to France;[67] the role of intelligence gathering;[68] the power struggle that took place with General Giraud in 1942–43;[69] the ambiguous legacy of Jean Moulin, de Gaulle's close lieutenant on metropolitan soil and a visitor to England in 1942;[70] and the evolution of the Free/Fighting into an embryonic government, which eventually settled in Algiers rather than in London.[71] Generals, admirals, politicians and professors thus dominate the history of France in Britain to the exclusion of those other émigrés – the refugees, non-Gaullist soldiers, Vichyite officials and colonists, the 'forgotten French' – who also sought refuge here in 1940.

Communities and circumstances

The aim of this book, then, is not to write another account of La France Libre. Nor is it to recount in detail the quarrels between de Gaulle, the Anglo-Saxons and the Americans. Although this study touches upon the

French intellectual community in London, these men and women also have their historians. Several good accounts on all these issues already exist, and anyone seeking a conspectus on French resistance overseas would be advised to look elsewhere, notably to Jean-Louis Crémieux-Brilhac's exhaustive and magisterial history of La France Libre, which is broader than its title suggests.[72] The concern of the present book is the 'forgotten French': to lift them out of obscurity and to dissect their existence. It would be disingenuous to suggest that these people were politically more important than de Gaulle's own supporters; this would be to stretch revisionism too far. Nonetheless, the book serves as a corrective in that it displays the majority of French men and women were not enamoured of the general; in many ways, the lure of Pétain was stronger, even across the Channel. Most exiles were embarrassed and confused by the political decisions that they had to make, choices that were shaped by the same factors that confronted their compatriots on occupied metropolitan soil: the *exode*; defeat; national humiliation; the future place of France in Europe and the world; German repression of relatives, friends and compatriots; and the growth of resistance within France itself. In this way, the book asks many of the questions that historians have recently asked about public behaviour in Vichy France, and it is striking that many of the responses are the same.[73]

The terrible choices and constraints that dominated the lives of the 'forgotten French' constitute a central strand of this study, yet the book is as much a social and cultural history of exile as it is a political one. In the social domain, it is interested in the backgrounds of the exiles themselves. Where in France did they come from, and for what reasons did they cross the Channel? How did they survive in Britain? Where did they settle, and why? In cultural terms, it examines how they adapted to a new country, alien customs and a new way of life, one that was being constantly buffeted by the circumstances of conflict. Many felt that they had escaped one war only to discover another, especially at the time of the *Luftwaffe*'s remorseless pounding of British cities. Refugees, in particular, were resentful that they had been housed in London, which had quickly become the front line. Indeed, the 'forgotten French' had to adopt several positions in regard to their hosts; in this regard, the book is not solely concerned with all things French. Throughout, it keeps a close watch on how both the British government and public catered for and responded to these strange communities in their midst, communities that often seemed to be at odds with one another.

The organisation of the book revolves around the dual themes that dominated the lives of the 'forgotten French': community and circumstance. In the midst of my research, it became clear that while many of the groups often intermixed – for instance, Gaullist troops sought passport advice from Vichyite consular officials in Bedford Square, intellectuals and refugees rubbed shoulders in Soho restaurants, and servicemen seeking repatriation frequently read anti-Pétainist propaganda devised by the general's headquarters in Carlton Gardens – they also kept their distance from one another, and retained separate identities. The distinct nature of these communities was reinforced by the manner in which they were catered for. Within a few weeks of the Franco-German Armistice, there existed a wide range of different organisations, British and French, dealing with specific groups. This often resulted in the replication of effort and endless quarrels over responsibility, necessitating the creation of Lord Bessborough's French Welfare, a sub-committee of the Foreign Office, whose remit was, in large measure, to keep the peace among competing charitable bodies.

Circumstance further helped demarcate these communities. The manner of arrival always overshadowed the lives of the 'forgotten French', determined their futures and curtailed their choices. Refugees could never escape the fact that they had been forced to flee their homes, and had been pushed towards the Channel. Most had come to Britain not out of design – out of a wish to fight on, whether with de Gaulle or the British – but by chance, without money, friends and English contacts. So it is that an initial chapter examines the 'misfortune' of exile, the pitiful story of the 3,500 French refugees whose lives were dominated by hardship, sorrow and alienation. The ensuing chapter investigates 'the conflict of exile': the experiences of those soldiers and sailors who were marooned in Britain at the time of the Armistice and Mers-el-Kébir. These comprised some 2,500 wounded soldiers, convalescing at Crystal Palace and White City, approximately 100 merchant seamen, also at Crystal Palace, and some 6,500 sailors billeted in makeshift barracks-cum-detention centres, located well away from London, generally in the Midlands and north of the country: Aintree, Haydock, Arrowe Park, Trentham Park, Doddington, Oulton Park and Barmouth. The 'conflict' of their exile was whether to fight on, either alongside de Gaulle or the British, or to opt for repatriation. While the Free French expended much energy proselytising among these troops, the British authorities were less anxious to recruit their services, fearful that they might prove to be fifth columnists or

Figure 2   Carlton Gardens, the headquarters of the Free French

German spies. The allegiance of the many French communities was always in question. To whom did they owe their loyalty? To Pétain? To de Gaulle? To the British? To Vichy? To General Weygand who, in September 1940, became High Commissioner in North Africa and distanced himself from the policy of collaboration that the marshal was pursuing with Berlin?[74]

Such dilemmas ensured that both the British and the Gaullists kept a close watch on the French communities in Britain, on the scent for any whiff of treachery. In the event, fifth columnists never formed a significant, or readily identifiable community, yet it is clear that they gravitated to one group of men and women who did: the Vichy consuls and legations, which had been left in Britain at the time of the Armistice. Although Britain had cut off diplomatic relations with Vichy, it permitted a skeleton consular staff to remain in order to handle administrative matters and to tidy up the economic agreements that had been concluded between London and Paris in the course of the war. The lives of these men and women constitute a third chapter – 'the surveillance of exile'. The remaining chapter focuses on the French community in Britain.[75] As already noted, in 1914 this community was the third largest European immigrant group in Britain, numbering approximately 30,000. The call-up of French nationals into the army in 1939 reduced numbers to around 12,000, 7,000 of whom lived in London; the remainder were largely concentrated in the Home Counties. Even so, they still ranked as a significant immigrant group and were naturally perplexed about what was happening across the Channel. Some might have wished to keep their heads down, adopting an *attentiste*, or wait-and-see approach. Yet this was not possible. It was inevitable that the new arrivals would seek out their countryfolk, if only as a point of reference in a strange land that observed curious habits. Driving on the left, orderly queues at the bus stop, the totality of the blackouts, the good manners of London motorists who observed traffic lights even during a bombing raid, and the mysteries of the Underground – these were all unfamiliar sights to the exiles and required explaining.[76] Moreover, it was inevitable that the more politically active exiles would attempt to mobilise the support of the colonists. Significantly, intellectual exiles would quickly integrate with the colonists, often making it difficult to distinguish them apart. The British also kept an eye on these colonists and, although it was quickly decided that they did not pose any real threat, the deterioration of London-Vichy relations during 1941 brought with it the prospect of general internment.

Misfortune, conflict, surveillance and tradition: these, then, were the

circumstances in which the communities of the 'forgotten French' –
refugees, servicemen, Vichyite officials and colonists – lived, worked,
talked, dined and argued, never quite able to patch up their differences,
thus presenting an elaborate mosaic of responses to the war, responses
that echoed positions adopted on metropolitan soil, although, Britain,
unlike their homeland, never became subject to the jackboot.

Piecing together the fragments

Overlooked by historians, eclipsed by other exile communities and
dwarfed by Gaullist mythology, the literature that touches on the lives
of the 'forgotten French' does not take long to survey. Admittedly,
there are titles that promise much, notably Pierre Accoce's *Les Français
à Londres* and Jean-Paul and Michèle Cointet's *La France à Londres*, yet
the former is more or less another history of the Free French, de Gaulle
appearing on every page, while the latter concentrates on the reconstruction of the French state abroad, a process that, once again, came
to be dominated by the Gaullists.[77] A broader picture is drawn in André
Gillois's *Histoire secrète des français à Londres*, one of those books that
sits awkwardly on the cusp of being both a primary and secondary
source.[78] Having helped coordinate the efforts of the three principal
partisan movements in the unoccupied zone – Combat, Libération Sud
and Franc-Tireur – Gillois fled to Britain in 1942, and his work stands
almost as a memoir of these momentous times. Yet having arrived late
in the day, Gillois was forced to recreate the atmosphere and events of
1940–41. In the words of Emile Delavenay, a journalist working for the
BBC and a resident in London throughout the war, the book is thus,
'un ramassis de rapports, rapportés sans le moindre sens de la critique
historique'.[79] This reservation aside, Gillois still dwells on the high
politics and the key personalities of the day, saying little about the
everyday experience and culture of exile.

This, then, is a study assembled almost entirely from primary
sources. Just as virtually every member of the Pétain Cabinet chose to
make public their recollections of the Occupation, most prominent
exiles, both Gaullist and anti-Gaullist – Jacques Soustelle, René Cassin,
Maurice Schumann, Jean-Pierre Bloch, François Coulet, Elizabeth de
Miribel, Robert Mengin, to name but a few – have all left their
memoirs.[80] While these allude to some of the experiences of exile, they
are, for the most part, the stories of an educated and articulate elite,
newly arrived in Britain. Hence, they focus principally on high politics

and the wider events of the war; de Gaulle often constitutes the context in which they articulate their memory. An exception to this pattern are the articles that Georges Blond wrote for the collaborationist newspaper, *Je Suis Partout*, and that were collected together in his *L'Angleterre en guerre. Récit d'un marin français* published in both French and German during 1941.[81] A naval engineer, an ardent Anglophobe and associate of Robert Brasillach, in 1940 he was interned in Britain along with other French sailors and did not hide his disgust at the manner in which he was treated. Repatriated to France, he made his mark as a right-wing journalist, was sentenced to 'dégradation nationale' in 1949, before resuming his literary career in the 1950s, writing an apologia for Marshal Pétain in 1966.[82]

Given the limitation of memoirs, wherever possible this study has drawn on unpublished diaries of lesser-known figures, together with interviews conducted among former exiles and their British associates. Newspapers also proved of value, not so much the British press, but the many French journals that sprang up in London. For the most part, British journalism provides few clues to the fact that not all French expatriates were supporters of de Gaulle, the obvious exception being the *Observer*. Under the proprietorship of the Astor family, who had enjoyed close contact with the French ever since June 1940 when large numbers of sailors disembarked at Portsmouth where Lord Astor was mayor, in 1943 the *Observer* launched a strenuous campaign against the authoritarian tendencies of the general, siding with the anti-Gaullist intellectuals who were making similar complaints in London. Among the French journals, which often ran off the Fleet Street presses, the newspaper *France* was widely perceived as a piece of Ministry of Information propaganda, and contains little other than reporting of events in occupied Europe, while *La Marseillaise* peddled the Gaullist line, supplemented by *Les Documents,* which drew together the general's speeches and proclamations. Of greater value for this particular study was *La France Libre*, the journal of André Labarthe and Raymond Aron (not a Gaullist publication despite its title), which reveals something about the social and political conditions of life in exile, providing helpful information about British customs and traditions, for instance how the London pub differed from the Paris *café*.[83] It is a pity these essays are few and far between. Labarthe himself, however, bitterly complained that he received far too many articles from the French colony in London – cooks, hairdressers and the like – who were eager to recount their personal experiences of wartime rather than getting down to the real business of attacking Vichy and debating schemes for post-war renewal.[84]

The bulk of the material, however, has emanated from archival sources, materials to be found chiefly in Britain rather than in France or in Germany. Given MI5 and Free French concerns that Vichy consuls in Britain were secreting information out of the country to both Berlin and the Pétain regime, use was made of the surviving files of the Buro des Staatssekretars of the German Foreign Office, as well as reports emanating from the German embassy in Paris. The documents selected dealt with Franco-British negotiations, yet nothing came to light to substantiate the spying allegations, although this is not to say that evidence cannot be found elsewhere in the enormous bureaucracy of the Nazi state. Papers pertaining to the Ministère des Affaires Etrangères, held both in Nantes and in Paris, were also consulted, but these largely dealt with the pre-1940 period. Having, in an earlier study, perused the personal *fonds* of the prominent Socialist exile André Philip, it was tempting to go through the voluminous *archives privées* of prominent Free French officials and other noted exiles based in London, but this would have resulted in me writing a very different book, the focus shifting immediately to high politics and matters Gaullist. In Britain, too, I wished to avoid an over-reliance on the papers of 'les grands et les bons'; yet with an empty hour to fill in a particular depot, it was difficult to resist ordering materials of individuals who seemingly had little connection with the 'forgotten French'. For instance, at Churchill College, Cambridge, I unexpectedly uncovered a good deal about refugees and soldiers in the personal letters of the then Labour MP for Derby, Philip Noel Baker, later the minister Lord Noel Baker, information that proved far more helpful to this particular study than that on the Special Operations Executive (SOE) preserved in Hugh Dalton's archive at the London School of Economics. Among private documentation, it was unquestionably the Spears material at Churchill and the Astor Papers, held at Reading University Archives, that proved most revealing.

For the most part, this book utilised holdings not normally associated in any shape or form with French history. Olive Anderson, in her research into British social history, once remarked that she had deployed a highly unusual reference work in the shape of the London *Yellow Pages* when tracking down the location of nineteenth-century pubs in the capital. This study cannot claim to have shown quite the same initiative, but it did delve in several nooks and crannies. Much on the lives of servicemen, refugees and expatriates was gleaned from the holdings of the London Metropolitan Archives, Westminster Diocesan Archives, Mass-Observation Archives, Reading University Archives and the Women's Royal Voluntary Service Archives, which, at the time of researching, were housed in a Pickfords depot outside Wallingford, Oxfordshire, interestingly a place de Gaulle himself travelled and where Free French troops went for picnics by the Thames. The BBC Written Archives at nearby Caversham were also visited, although arguments about BBC broadcasts to France largely concerned newly arrived intellectuals and Gaullists, not the 'forgotten French'. While the world of broadcasting to both France and Europe still requires further attention, it does not figure prominently in this particular study.

Of most use were the copious holdings of the Public Records Office at Kew. In line with most other authors who have written about de Gaulle, I made much of the General Correspondence (France) of the Foreign Office, series FO 371. Although not always well catalogued, this critical source unveiled much about British policy towards the French in this country, as well as revealing much about the day-to-day existence of refugees and others. FO 371 also contains the important minutes of the Committee on Foreign (Allied) Resistance, which met throughout the period 1940–42 and which reported directly to the War Cabinet. The CFR had begun life as the Vansittart Committee, an inter-departmental committee created at the time of the Armistice, whose remit was to look into all matters French.[85] Conducting some twenty-two meetings between 21 June and 8 July 1940, this committee, initially comprising Vansittart, Spears, Morton and the Foreign Office apparatchiks Strang and Speaight, became so unwieldy that something more formal was required, and hence the CFR was born.[86] Keeping an extremely close watch on the activities of French exiles in Britain, in April 1942 the CFR was retitled the Committee on French Resistance, looking at the wider developments in Syria, North Africa and elsewhere.[87] It is at this point that the minutes become less helpful for this particular study, although by 1941 it was already the case that more attention was being devoted to matters overseas than to developments within the French communities in Britain. Nonetheless, the material was certainly sensitive, and an unholy row broke out in 1941 when one of Spears's entourage absent-mindedly left a copy of CFR minutes in the smoking room of the Air Force Club.[88]

Also of value were two other series that have largely been overlooked in previous studies of wartime France. FO 1055 contains the papers of

Lord Bessborough's Committee on French Welfare. It is a pity that, at some point, these papers have been carefully weeded, leaving material pertaining essentially to servicemen and refugees. This is why the Home Office Aliens Department series, HO 213, proved of such worth; maybe it was unexpected that a historian of wartime France would take much interest in nationality files, buried amid applications for naturalisations and arguments over work permits. Yet here were discovered detailed records of the numbers of French in Britain, important as the national census scheduled to take place in 1941 was cancelled because of the war. It would be myopic to cite all the other PRO series consulted during this study. A full listing of all these papers, together with other archival depots, is to be found in the bibliography.

Tentative conclusions

On 1 January 1940, R. E. Balfour, a leading member of the Ministry of Information's Foreign Publicity Department, in liaison with the British embassy in Paris and the Commissariat Général à l'Information, drew up a very full report on the press reporting of the Franco-British war effort and how this should be conducted. In this, he observed:

> For as long as we can foresee, England and France will be bound together. We are nations of very different temperament, we do not easily understand each other, and we often disagree. It is safe to say that the ordinary Englishman with a slight knowledge of the Continent finds the Germans easier to get on with than the French. It is only those who have time and opportunity for lengthy travel or residence abroad who discover that deeper acquaintance with the two nations reverses the position; it reveals the deep cleavage between the English and German mentality, despite their superficial resemblance, and it shows how the English and French so different in everyday life and in apparent approach, do believe in the same fundamental values.[89]

Predicting an Allied victory, Balfour could not have foreseen how his observations would be put to the test by the enforced residence of thousands of French men, women and children in Britain. That these people retained an anathema for Nazi values cannot be doubted. As the war dragged on, their hostility towards Vichy also became readily apparent, although a lingering respect for Pétain endured, just as it did in metropolitan France where public opinion quickly distinguished between the marshal and his government. Indeed, the story of the 'forgotten French' is not a edifying tale of a heroic people, embracing the Republican tradition, to defy both Vichy and the German occupier by deliberately choosing to continue the struggle from abroad, from the one European country that had not fallen prey to Hitler's insatiable greed and ambition. Most of the French in Britain, with the exception of the *colons*, were there by chance, not by design, and were not wholly convinced that they should stay. While some were undeniably courageous in their opposition to Vichy and Hitlerism, the majority adopted a variety of positions; few initially were Gaullist. Only when the war looked truly won did they begin to rally around the general, and even then doubts remained. Yet if the 'forgotten French' do not emerge from this study with their reputations unscathed, neither do the British. While many ordinary people were generous in the help and sympathy they extended to refugees and other exiles, government officials could often be uncaring and critical, unable to understand the culture of another people and unable to hide their prejudices, prejudices that had been hardened by the bitter political squabbles that had broken out among the French themselves.

This, then is the history of the 'forgotten French'. It is a tale of several communities: communities that struggled to acclimatise to life abroad; communities that kept their distance from one another; communities that were often internally divided; and communities that frequently exasperated, irritated and bemused the British government and public.

Notes

1 (For a Frenchman, leaving France is a terrible business.) I am grateful to K. Carpenter, *Refugees of the French Revolution. Emigrés in London, 1789–1802* (Basingstoke, Macmillan, 1989), p. xiv for this reference.

2 Most of these examples of eighteenth- and nineteenth-century exiles have been taken from J.-A. Lesourd, 'Refugees, exiles, émigrés', in D. Johnson, F. Bédarida and F. Crouzet (eds), *Britain and France. Ten Centuries* Folkestone, Dawson, 1980), pp. 117–29. See, too, the accompanying essay by Maurice Hutt on British emigration to France, which was never of the same intensity (pp. 130–6).

3 On the Huguenots, see especially R. Gwynn, *The Huguenot Heritage. The History and Contribution of the Huguenots in Britain* (London, Routledge & Kegan Paul 1985). Their example was invoked, in 1942, by the leading French intellectual journal, *La France Libre*. See L. Tillier, 'Un Huguenot français à Londres', in *La France Libre* (hereafter *FL*), vol. 3, no. 13, 15 novembre 1941, pp. 83–9.

4 I am grateful to Michael Biddiss for this quotation.

5 See Carpenter, *Refugees*, and K. Carpenter and P. Mansel (eds), *The French Emigrés in Europe and the Struggle against Revolution, 1789–1814* (Basingstoke, Macmillan, 1999).

6 Carpenter and Mansel, *French Emigrés*, p. 179.

7 See H. Long, *Change into Uniform. An Autobiography, 1919–1946* (Lavenham, T. Dalton, 1978) for a facsimile of this bill.

8 There exists a vast literature on the Communards; far less is written on the exiles of 1830 and 1848. See P. K. Martinez, 'Paris Communard Refugees in Britain, 1871–1880', unpublished University of Sussex D.Phil, 1981, and S. Hutchins, 'The Communard Exiles in Britain', *Marxism Today*, March 1971, April 1971, June 1971.

9 In 1883, Vallès published his reminiscences of exile in *La Rue à Londres*, reprinted in R. Beller (ed.), *Oeuvres*, Vol. 2, *1871–1885* (Paris, Gallimard, 1989).

10 Among the many works on Zola, see F. Brown, *Zola. A Life* (New York, Macmillan, 1996).

11 See, especially, P. F. Anson, *The Religious Orders and Congregations of Great Britain and Ireland* (Worcester, Stanbrook Abbey Press, 1949) and D. A. Bellanger, *The French Exiled Clergy in the British Isles after 1789* (Bath, Downside Abbey, 1986).

12 A. Bellanger, 'France and England. The English Female Religious from Reformation to World War', in N. Atkin and F. Tallett (eds), *Catholicism in Britain and France since 1789* (London, Hambledon, 1996), pp. 10–11.

13 See especially C. Holmes, *John Bull's Island. Immigration and British Society, 1871–1971* (Basingstoke, Macmillan, 1988) for an overview of emigration to Britain.

14 See P. Cahalan, *Belgian Refugee Relief in England during the Great War* (New York/London, Garland, 1982).

15 *Ibid.*, pp. 83–4 and pp. 264–7.

16 See J. Jackson, 'Etrange défaite française ou étrange victoire anglaise', in M. Vaïsse (ed.), *Mai-juin 1940. Défaite française, victoire allemande sous l'oeil des historiens étrangers* (Paris, Autrement, 2001), pp. 177–213, and A. Roberts, 'Hitler's England. What if Germany had invaded Britain in May 1940?', in N. Ferguson (ed.), *Virtual History. Alternatives and Counterfactuals* (London, Papermac, 1997), pp. 281–320.

17 See especially H. Amouroux, *Le 18 juin 1940* (Paris, Fayard, 1980) and M. Schumann, *Un certain 18 juin 1940* (Paris, Plon, 1980).

18 Cited in O. Wieviorka (ed.), *Nous entrerons dans la carrière de la Résistance à l'exercice du pouvoir* (Paris, Seuil, 1993), p. 141.

19 M. Agulhon, *The French Republic, 1879–1992* (Oxford, Basil Blackwell, 1993), pp. 262–3.

20 E. Branca, 'Les Oreilles du 18 juin', *Espoir*, no. 71, juin 1990, 11–13.

21 Quoted in J. Lacouture, *The Rebel* (London, Harper Collins, 1986), p. 238.

22 R. Tree, *When the Moon was High. Memories of War and Peace, 1897–1942* (London, Macmillan, 1975), p. 111.

23 A. Shennan, *De Gaulle* (London, Longman, 1993), p. 167.

24 On this point, it is worth comparing the reasons why the Belgians in the First World War have been overlooked. See Cahalan, *Belgian Refugee Relief*, p. 2 *et seq.*

25 On Britain during the Second World War, see especially A. Calder, *The People's War. Britain, 1939–1945* (London, Pimlico, 1992 edn) and his *The Myth of the Blitz* (London, Jonathan Cape, 1991), S. Bridges, *The Home Front. War Years in Britain, 1939–1945* (London, Weidenfeld & Nicolson, 1975) and N. Longmate, *How We Lived Then. A History of Everyday Life during the Second World War* (London, Hutchinson, 1971). For London during the war years, see J. Mack and S. Humphries, *The Making of Modern London, 1939–1945. London at War* (London, Sidgwick & Jackson, 1985), F. Sheppard, *London. A History* (Oxford, Oxford University Press, 1998), J. White, *London in the Twentieth Century. A City and its People* (London, Viking, 2001) and P. Ziegler, *London at War, 1939–1945* (London, Sinclair Stevenson, 1995). See, too, the excellent study by P. Ackroyd, *London. The Autobiography* (London, Chatto & Windus, 2000).

26 See B. Wasserstein, *Britain and the Jews of Europe, 1939–1945* (Oxford, Oxford University Press, 1979) and L. London, *Whitehall and the Jews, 1933–1948. British Immigration Policy and the Holocaust* (Cambridge, Cambridge University Press, 2000). On France, see the many things by Vicki Caron, notably, *Uneasy Asylum. France and the Jewish Refugee Crisis, 1933–42* (Stanford, Stanford University Press, 1999). On the general experience of being 'unwanted', see M. Marrus, *The Unwanted. European Refugees in the Twentieth Century* (Oxford, Oxford University Press, 1985).

27 M. Berghahn, *German-Jewish Refugees in England. Continental Britons* (Oxford, Berg, 1988), G. Hirschfeld (ed.), *Exile in Great Britain. Refugees from Hitler's Germany* (Leamington Spa, Berg, 1984), D. Cesarani (ed.), *The Internment of Aliens in Twentieth-Century Britain* (London, Frank Cass, 1993) and A. J. Sherman, *Island Refuge. Britain and the Refugees from the Third Reich, 1933–1945* (London, Frank Cass, 1994, 2nd edn). Just as France lost out through the expulsion of the Huguenots, Germany lost out through its expulsion of Jews. See D. Snowman, 'How Germany's Loss was Britain's Gain', in *History Magazine*, vol. 1, no. 4, August 2000, 42–5, and his *The Hitler Emigrés. The Cultural Impact on Britain of Refugees from Nazism* (London, Chatto & Windus, 2002).

28 On the Americans, see M. Debouzy, 'L'amical invasion', in F. Poirier (ed.), *Londres, 1939–1945. Riches et pauvres dans le même élan patriotique, derrière la légende* (Paris, Autrement, 1995), pp. 108–19, J. Gardiner, *'Overpaid, Oversexed and Over Here.' The American GI in World War II Britain* (London, Abbeville Press, 1992), E. R. W. Hale and J. F. Turner

(eds), *The Yanks are Coming* (Tunbridge Wells, Hidus, 1983), N. Longmate, *The GIs. The Americans in Britain, 1942–1945* (London, Hutchinson 1975), G. Smith, *When Jim Crow met John Bull. Black American Soldiers in World War 2 Britain* (London, Tauris, 1987), P. Winfield, *Bye Bye, Baby. The Story of the Children the GIs Left Behind* (London, Bloomsbury, 1992), and D. Reynolds, *Rich Relations. The American Occupation of Britain, 1942–1945* (London, Phoenix Press, 2000).

29 Public Records Office (hereafter PRO) FO 1055 1, letter of Jean Hesse, Amis des Volontaires Français, to Lord Bessborough, 29 May 1941, to which are attached several reports on the Free French at Camberley.

30 T. Torrès, *Une française libre. Journal, 1939–1945* (Paris, Phébus, 2000), p. 92.

31 On the French communities in North America, see J. Hurstfield, *America and the French Nation, 1939–1945* (Chapel Hill, University of North Carolina Press, 1986), W. Crisham, *Divided Island. Faction and Unity of Saint Pierre* (Cambridge, Harvard, MA, University Press, 1969), C. Nettelbeck, *Forever France. Exiles in the United States, 1939–1945* (Oxford, Berg, 1991), and the forthcoming study by K. Munholland.

32 D. Johnson, 'Aragon and the British', *Times Literary Supplement (TLS)*, 10 December 1999. See too A. D. Harvey, 'Gide, Forster and HMG', *Times Literary Supplement*, 8 November 1996.

33 R. Mengin, *No Laurels for de Gaulle* (London, Michael Joseph, 1967), p. 103.

34 H. R. Kedward, 'The French Resistance', *History Today*, June 1984, Special Supplement, pages not numbered.

35 On the Pétain myth, see especially P. Servent, *Verdun, ou le mythe des tranchées* (Paris, Payot, 1988).

36 The legality of Vichy is neatly discussed in J. Jackson, *The Dark Years. France, 1940–1944* (Oxford, Oxford University Press, 2001). It also figured prominently in early editions of *La France Libre*.

37 See especially R. T. Thomas, *Britain and Vichy, 1940–1942* (London, Macmillan, 1979).

38 See R. Aglion, *De Gaulle et Roosevelt. La France Libre aux Etats-Unis* (Paris, Plon, 1984) and G. E. Maguire, *Anglo-American Relations with the Free French* (Basingstoke, Macmillan, 1995).

39 See N. Atkin, 'De Gaulle et la presse anglaise, 1940–1943', *Espoir*, no. 71, juin 1990, 39–45, P. M. H. Bell, 'L'opinion publique en Grande Bretagne et le général de Gaulle', *Guerres Mondiales et Conflits Contemporains*, 190, 1998, 79–101 and M.-L. Clausard, 'De Gaulle et la presse anglaise en 1940. Du ministre inconnu au célèbre homme d'Etat', *Mémoire de maîtrise*, Université de Paris X-Nanterre, 1997.

40 *The Times*, 7 June and 19 June 1940. The *Daily Telegraph* of 19 June published the text of his broadcast beneath the uninspiring headline, 'Call

by French General'.

41 PRO FO 371 24346 C13242/7328/17, Memorandum by Major-General Spears, late autumn 1940.

42 PRO FO 371 24340 C8211/7328/17, note by Richmond Temple, 24 September 1940.

43 R. Tournoux, *Pétain et de Gaulle* (Paris, Plon, 1966), p. 230.

44 Churchill College Cambridge (hereafter CCC) SPRS 1/134, 'General de Gaulle: The Man', by Spears, n.d., in which Spears also remarks that de Gaulle was reticent about his family.

45 Private letter to the author, 26 April 1994.

46 M. Wesley, *The Camomile Lawn* (London, Macmillan, 1984), p. 252.

47 F. Coulet, *Vertu des temps difficiles* (Paris, Plon, 1967), p. 116.

48 *Daily Sketch*, 25 June 1940.

49 V. Hodgson, *Few Eggs and No Oranges. A Diary Showing how Unimportant People in London and Birmingham Lived Through the War Years, 1939–1945, Written in the Notting Hill area of London* (London, Dobson, 1976), p. 31.

50 See Mass-Observation (hereafter M-O) FR 541, 'December 1940: Feelings about various racial groups'.

51 H. Nicolson, *Harold Nicolson's Diaries* (London, Flamingo, 1996), especially pp. 198–9.

52 CCC SPRS 1/137, press cutting from the *Observer*, 30 October 1955.

53 J. and M. Charlot, 'Le général de Gaulle dans la mémoire des Britanniques', in Institut Charles de Gaulle, *De Gaulle en son siècle. Sondages et enquêtes* (Paris, Institut Charles de Gaulle, 1992), pp. 297–319.

54 P. Laborie, *L'Opinion publique sous Vichy* (Paris, Seuil, 1990) is invaluable for understanding what people believed, whereas the quarrels over the BBC broadcasts are related in A. Briggs, *The History of Broadcasting in the UK*, vol. 3, *The War of Words* (London, Oxford University Press, 1972).

55 C. de Gaulle, *The Call to Honour, 1940–1942* (London, Collins, 1955), p. 95.

56 *Ibid.*

57 H. Rousso, *The Vichy Syndrome. History and Memory in France since 1944* (Cambridge MA, Harvard University Press, 1991), p. 245.

58 On the historiography of the regime, see S. Fishman *et al.* (eds), *France at War. Vichy and the Historians* (New York, Berg, 2000), which also demonstrates the current concerns of historians.

59 See especially M. Marrus and R. O. Paxton, *Vichy France and the Jews* (New York, Basic Books, 1981).

60 R. O. Paxton, *Vichy France. Old Guard and New Order, 1940–1944* (New York, Alfred A. Knopf, 1972).

61 See H. Footit and J. S. Simmonds, *France, 1943–45* (Leicester, Leicester University Press, 1986).

62 See F. Kersaudy, *Churchill and de Gaulle* (London, Collins, 1981).
63 See E. Barker, *Churchill and Eden at War* (New York, Macmillan, 1978), P. M. H. Bell, *A Certain Eventuality. Britain and the Fall of France* (London, Saxon House, 1974), P. M. H. Bell, *France and Britain* (London, Longman, 1996–97) 2 vols, R. Frank, 'Vichy et les britanniques, 1940–1941. Double jeu ou double langage?', in J.-P. Azéma and F. Bédarida (eds), *Vichy et les français* (Paris, Fayard, 1992), pp. 144–61, and Thomas, *Britain and Vichy*.
64 See especially J.-P. Cointet, *La France Libre* (Paris, Presses Universitaires de France, 1976), H. Michel, *Histoire de la France Libre* (Paris, Presses Universitaires de France, 1980 4th edn), and most importantly J.-L. Crémieux-Brilhac, *La France Libre de l'appel du 18 juin à la liberation* (Paris, Flammarion, 1995).
65 See Aglion, *De Gaulle et Roosevelt*, and Maguire, *Anglo-American Relations with the Free French*.
66 J. Jackson, 'General de Gaulle and his Enemies. Anti-Gaullism in France since 1940', *Transactions of the Royal Historical Society*, 6th series, vol. IX, 1999, 43–65.
67 See Briggs, *History of Broadcasting*, Vol. 3 and H. Eck (ed.), *La Guerre des ondes* (Paris/Lausanne, Armand Colin, 1986).
68 M. R. D. Foot, *SOE in France, 1940–1944* (London, HMSO, 1966), P. Paillole, *Services spéciaux, 1939–1945* (Paris, Laffont, 1975), and D. Stafford, *Britain and European Resistance, 1940–1945* (London, Macmillan, 1980).
69 See especially G. de Charbonnières, *Le Duel Giraud-de Gaulle* (Paris, Plon, 1984) and A. Funk, *The Politics of TORCH* (Lawrence, University Press of Kansas, 1974).
70 See especially D. Cordier, *Jean Moulin. L'Inconnu du panthéon* (Paris, Lattès, 1989) 3 vols, and P. Péan, *Vies et morts de Jean Moulin* (Paris, Fayard, 1998).
71 See Fondation Charles de Gaulle, *Le Rétablissement de la légalité républicaine, 1944* (Paris, Plon, 1996).
72 Crémieux-Brilhac, *La France Libre*.
73 See especially the essay by J.-M. Flonneau 'L'Evolution de l'opinion publique', in Azéma and Bédarida (eds), *Vichy et les français*, pp. 506–22 for a good introduction to these issues. R. Gildea, *Marianne in Chains. In Search of the German Occupation, 1940–1945* (London, Macmillan, 2002) is a brilliantly original interpretation of life during wartime.
74 It is now known that Weygand was, in no sense, preparing the French army in North Africa for a possible conflict with Germany, despite the sympathetic portrayal of the general in the most recent biography, B. Destremau, *Weygand* (Paris, Perrin, 1989). See C. Levisse-Touzé, *L'Afrique du Nord dans la guerre, 1939–1945* (Paris, Albin Michel, 1998) for a more rounded view.

75 There is virtually no literature whatsoever on the French colony. It is telling that the most recent studies are R. Faber, *French and English* (London, Hutchinson, 1925), H. Goiran, *Les Français à Londres. Etude historique, 1544–1933* (Pornic, Editions de la Vague, 1933) and G. R. Sims (ed.), *Living London* (London, Cassell, 1901) 3 vols. Some further information may be gleaned from P. Morand, *Londres* (Paris, Plon, 1933). An influential author, in 1940 Morand chose the path of active collaboration rather than a return to London where he had spent a considerable time as a journalist. Fortunately, some of the gaps in the literature on French expatriates are being filled by Fraser Reavell in a University of Reading Ph.D. thesis entitled 'French Exiles in Britain during the Third Republic, 1870–1914'.

76 J.-P. Bloch, *Londres, capitale de la France Libre* (Paris, Editions Carrère/Michel Lafon, 1986), p. 13, and interview between the author and Mrs Helen Long, 19 April 1994.

77 P. Accoce, *Les Français à Londres* (Paris, Balland, 1989) and J.-P. and M. Cointet, *La France à Londres. Renaissance d'un état* (Bruxelles, Editions Complexe, 1990).

78 A. Gillois, *Histoire secrète des français à Londres de 1940 à 1944* (Paris, Hachette, 1972).

79 E. Delavenay, *Témoignage d'un village savoyard au village mondial, 1905–1991* (Aix-en Provence, Diffusion Edisud, 1992), p. 195.

80 See the bibliography for full details.

81 G. Blond, *L'Angleterre en guerre. Récit d'un marin français* (Paris, Grasset, 1941). The articles originally appeared in *Je Suis Partout* in the following 1941 editions: 2 May, 12 May, 19 May, 26 May, and 9 June. I am grateful to David Smith for these references. See his 'La Perfide Angleterre. *Je Suis Partout* and Britain, 1941–44', University of Reading MA thesis, 2002.

82 G. Blond, *Pétain* (Paris, Presses de la Cité, 1966).

83 See the article on 'Angleterre', by A. Cohen in *FL*, vol. 2, no. 8, 20 June 1941, pp. 114–23, for instance.

84 Imperial War Museum (hereafter IWM) 63/34/1, diary of M.-L. Touchard.

85 PRO FO 371 31936 Z73/73/17, Minute of 11 December 1941.

86 CCC SPRS 1/136, Vansittart Committee, 'Terms of Reference', no date (June/July 1940?).

87 PRO FO 371 31936 Z73/73/17, Minute of 11 December 1941.

88 CCC SPRS 1/137, various correspondence of January 1941.

89 Balfour's report of 1 January 1940 quoted in R. Carswell, 'The British Press and France, 1940–1944', unpublished paper, January 2000, written in preparation for a Reading University Ph.D. on the same topic.

2

The misfortune of exile: refugees

The Frenchman cannot forgive the English, in the first place, for not speaking French, in the second, for not understanding him when he calls Charing Cross Sharon-Kro or Leicester Square Lessetair Square.

(Alexander Herzen, *My Past and Thoughts*)[1]

On 1 June 1940, as the first Allied troops trickled back from Dunkirk, George Orwell toured the London railway stations of Waterloo and Victoria in search of news of a family friend, the eminent surgeon Laurence O'Shaughnessy, who was attached to the Royal Army Medical Corps in Flanders. On the platforms, he observed 'few' British and French soldiers, 'but great numbers of Belgian and French refugees'.[2] While the waiting crowd frequently 'cheered' the servicemen, the evacuated civilians only evoked 'silence', maybe because they constituted such a pitiful sight and conjured up images of what might befall the British should Hitler's armies ever cross the Channel. Up until now, the 'phoney war' had largely sheltered the public from the suffering that had blighted the peoples of Eastern Europe and, more recently, those of France and the Low Countries. Henceforth, refugees were in the public midst, and could no longer be hidden from view. This 'silence' might also have emanated from a fear of fifth columnists. As John Anderson, Viscount Waverley, the Home Secretary and Minister of Home Security, confessed to his father on 2 March 1940, 'the newspapers are working up feeling about aliens. I shall have to do something about it, or we may be stampeded into an unnecessarily oppressive policy.'[3] At around the same time, the Council of Austrians in Great Britain protested that such reporting, especially prominent in the *Daily Mail*, would 'only make matters worse'.[4] Admittedly, the anxiety about a fifth column sprang from the notion that Belgian and Dutch refugees, rather than French, contained large numbers of Nazi sympathisers, and would subside in July when the number of incomers dried up,[5] yet in summer 1940 it is not difficult to believe that the British public suspected anyone with a foreign accent, despite the fact that on 11 September 1940 Count Ciano could confide to his diary, 'It seems incredible, but we do not have a single informant in Great Britain.'[6]

In all probability, the unfortunate citizens witnessed by Orwell would have been bussed to various reception centres dotted around London's suburbs, where they would have been processed, fed, and examined medically, before being distributed to a variety of lodgings in the capital, their homes for the remainder of the war, with their stories to be forgotten by history. To a degree, the retelling of their experiences involves an analysis of the administrative machinery that was put into place to assist their welfare, a chronicle culled from travel permits, ration books, food coupons and billeting allowances, documents that have survived because they relate to the spending of public monies, and have thus been retained for reasons of government accountability. Reconstructing the lives of the refugees further entails an examination of the emotions that ruled their lives – fear, boredom, alienation and uncomfortable personal choices – a history that is far more difficult to recreate, as such feelings rarely communicate themselves through the faded red and blue lines of ledger books. It is fortunate that those charged with looking after refugees – principally officials belonging to French Welfare, the Ministries of Health and Information, the volunteers of the Women's Voluntary Service (WVS) and Mass-Observation – frequently recorded interviews with those they met, and kept detailed records of refugee life. Such observations monitor the initial despondency felt by many arrivals in May–June 1940 and something of their expectations as the war drew to a close. There was a cruel irony in the events of summer 1944, when many of the French looked forward to going home only to find repatriation delayed by a fresh batch of refugees, principally children, rescued from the battlefields of Normandy.

Preparing to receive

In 1947, Mrs de l'Hôpital, one of the leading lights of the WVS, composed a report on 'The Story of the War Refugees in Great Britain, 1940–1947',[7] a detailed study on government preparations for the arrival of citizens from France and the Low Countries, and a first-hand account of how her 'ladies in green' assisted Europe's 'unwanted'.[8] For the historian, this document is a treasure trove of information, one of those meticulously prepared dossiers that helpfully brings together a mass of confusing and tiresome administrative circulars and memoranda to make the whole picture that much clearer. It is, though, worth examining in detail those other documents, confusing as they may be, for they suggest de l'Hôpital's report is misleading in two vital regards. To begin with, she paints a picture of orderliness in Whitehall's arrangements for refugees. The whole business is described in the manner of a precise military campaign, with the relevant officials standing at the ready, like benign sergeant majors, dispensing discipline and good humour among those who passed through their hands. Although the handling of refugees did not get out of hand, and never matched the chaos that was to be witnessed in France, Belgium and Holland where officials simply fled their posts to join the retreating flood of humankind,[9] the reception in Britain was hardly the smooth operation she depicts. Moreover, the impression she conveys is of a gentle and tolerant Britain, a land where the values of forbearance, assimilation and generosity prevailed, a view that was repeated in the first official histories of welfare during the Second World War: throughout the 1930s, it was maintained, brave Albion had constituted a safe haven for those fleeing Nazi oppression.[10] In the same way that Vicki Caron has dispelled notions that France was a welcoming retreat for German Jews and others,[11] Bernard Wasserstein, Louise London and Colin Holmes have demonstrated that Britain likewise constituted a 'reluctant asylum'.[12] The work by Matthew Buck on the treatment of Belgian refugees in 1939–40 confirms these findings,[13] as does an examination of the reception of the French. At best, British plans for the welcoming of refugees of all nationalities in 1940 were tardy, ill-conceived, lacking in goodwill and badly implemented.

These preparations had begun reluctantly in 1936 when mounting international tension concentrated government minds on the possibility of a general European war. Given the experiences of the First World War, it was widely appreciated that any handling of refugees could not be left solely in the hands of philanthropic bodies, yet beyond this there was little agreement on what to do.[14] Although it was quickly decided that the Ministry of Health was the most appropriate department to handle the arrival and accommodation of large numbers of friendly aliens, this was not a task that Health officials particularly warmed to, complaining on several occasions that their time would be taken up dealing with the evacuation of British civilians, a recognition of how aerial bombardment would seriously disrupt the rhythm of urban life.[15] Foreign refugees, it was argued, would consume precious resources and disrupt home defence. It took the advent of the 'phoney war' to speed up matters, various government departments coming together to pool information and resources. Recalling events in 1914–18, when 250,000 refugees had arrived in Britain from the Low Countries, an untitled Home Office document of 18 January 1940 anticipated that a staggering 500,000 civilians, mainly Dutch and Belgian, might make their way to British shores, an indication that London understood how Allied strategy, a rapid advance into Holland, would displace thousands of civilians and how these evacuees could not easily be returned home.[16] Although the figure of 500,000 was later reduced to under 200,000, the possibility of Britain taking in French refugees never entered the equation; it was naturally assumed that these unfortunates would be looked after by their own government and, in any case, would retreat into metropolitan territory just as they had done in 1914. After all, it was thought that the Allied advance into Holland and Belgium, together with the protection afforded by the Maginot Line, would more or less make French territory inviolable.

It had been further hoped that France would accept the majority of French-speaking Belgians, yet Paris argued that it only possessed the resources to cater for its own evacuees, and was anxious that its strategic plans were not compromised by large numbers of refugees who would clutter up the roads and railways. In January 1940, General Gamelin, the commander-in-chief, without consultation with his allies, announced his army's intention of conveying all Belgian refugees to Channel ports for subsequent transfer to Britain. The French embassy at London was, subsequently, instructed to repeat this stance to the Foreign Office.[17] Not surprisingly, this unilateral decision went down badly in Whitehall, where privately it was wondered whether Gallic concerns also hinged on the fact that Belgian refugees, or at least the Flemish-speaking ones, had not been warmly welcomed in France during the First World War. (Interestingly, nor had their experiences in Britain been especially happy.)[18] Nonetheless, not wishing to upset Franco-British relations at such a delicate juncture, and recognising the logic of French strategic concerns, London exerted little pressure on Paris over the refugee question, and busily sought out other solutions. So began an unsuccessful dialogue with the Irish Republic in which it became plain that Dublin no more wanted foreign evacuees than did London or Paris. In conversation with the Duke of Devonshire, the

High Commissioner for Eire explained that his government had no wish to compromise its neutrality, and recalled that in 1914–18 many Belgians, albeit Catholics, 'had proved to be of unsatisfactory character and undesirable influence in the religious houses in which they had been received'.[19] Distinctly uncomfortable and clutching at straws, the Commissioner even suggested that Britain was 'short of foreign currency' and was thus exaggerating the possibility of a German invasion of Western Europe in order to 'depress Dutch and Belgian securities' which London would then buy 'in large quantities' and unload 'at a substantial profit', an allegation so outrageous that it left officials in Whitehall dumbfounded.

Resigned to accepting significant numbers of Dutch and Belgian civilians, and unwilling to argue any further with either the French or the Irish, in March 1940 the Ministry of Health issued Memorandum WR1, along with Circular 1983, to local government authorities in London and coastal areas, that is those regions most likely to receive refugees. Going into considerable detail about the arrangements for the reception and treatment of refugees, these confidential guidelines were augmented by Memorandum WR2 and Circular 1984.[20] As de l'Hôpital recalled in her report of 1947, 'Landing places were to be organised at South and South East Coast resorts and at Mersey, Belfast Lough and the Clyde. Until the moment of the landing the refugees were to be the responsibility of the Admiralty. Thereafter, the Ministry of Health would take over.'[21] It is interesting to note that, well aware of their duties come the arrival of refugees, WVS officials closely studied French plans for the evacuation of Paris and Alsace Lorraine, and were greatly impressed by what they saw.[22] WVS observers were especially struck by the cooperation of private and public organisations, the revision of evacuation plans since the advent of the 'phoney war', and the strength of the French family unit, which was deemed stronger than its British equivalent and which would assist in the orderly withdrawal of civilians of all ages. No one had foreseen how the tactics of *Blitzkrieg* would pay little respect to elaborate government procedures and familial ties.

Arriving: 'We of this country wish to offer you our great sympathy'

As the *exode* of civilians gathered momentum in France and the Low Countries, with possibly some eight million people on the roads, the first refugees started to arrive in Britain, not in droves as originally feared, but in dribs and drabs, and not in orderly convoys to Northern Ireland and Scotland as anticipated, but at strategically important southern ports such as Southampton and Portsmouth.[23] From there, they made their way not to the provinces, as originally planned, but by train to London. As Buck relates, it had initially been the aim to keep refugees away from the capital, which was likely to suffer aerial bombardment, yet, on 10 May, the Ministry of Health instructed London County Council (LCC) to assist in the reception of refugees, a decision that surprised more perceptive members of the public.[24] As J. W. Dodgson, a lecturer in the Department of Chemistry at the University of Reading, observed in his wartime diary: 'What a desperate bit of foolery. If London is a dangerous area it is a doubtful kindness to stock it with refugees, if it is a safe area why remove Londoners? So while civil servants are having tennis parties, dances, concerts in the health resorts selected for their comfort, it is good enough for terrorised victims of Nazi bombing to go to the place from which these pampered civil servants have been sent. Either London is safe or it is not.'[25]

To be fair, officials at County Hall, the headquarters of the LCC, remained put and set about the arrangements for the handling of the expected influx of refugees.[26] Within a short space of time, nine reception centres had been established in the capital. There refugees were 'fed, bathed and medically examined' before being transferred to the twenty 'cooperating' borough councils for billeting.[27] Once settled in their new homes, the Local Assistance Boards (LABs) then took charge of refugee needs. Some effort was also made to explain these complicated arrangements to the refugees themselves. Middlesex County Council (MCC) quickly drafted an address to be read out by interpreters at the key reception centres. Delivered in Dutch, Flemish and French, it began, 'First of all, we of this country wish to offer you our great sympathy in the bitter trials you have had to face, and to assure you that we will do all we can to help you until the time comes for you to return once again to your country.'[28] Depending on which version was being relayed, it ended, 'Long Live Queen Wilhelmina', 'Long Live King Leopold', and always 'God save King George'. There was no 'Vive, la France'; nor later was there 'Vive, le maréchal Pétain', or for that matter 'Vive, le général de Gaulle'.

Reading the minutes of the local government authorities in London, it seems that the reception of refugees went without a hitch. 'An intimation from the Ministry of Health that about 1,200 refugees will be expected this weekend beginning on Friday', wrote in confident words the Director of Public Assistance of the MCC to his town clerks on 14 May.[29] Eye-witness accounts, however, suggest that refugees had exchanged one sort of administrative chaos in France for another in Britain. As the first trains, brimming with refugees, steamed into London, officials struggled to cope, especially in late May when immigration procedures were tightened up, following scares about fifth columnists. On the 23rd of that month, Mrs N—, a high-ranking figure in the WVS, filed a report on meeting a train of refugees at Waterloo. In this, she complained that, 'We were only told at 3 pm that a train was due at Waterloo station at that same hour.' A small party of WVS volunteers thus rushed to meet the coaches, which had arrived by the time they got there. On board were 150 refugees, half of whom were British. This was to create problems:

> There was no differentiation of treatment for British or foreigners. They were all herded like cattle, many of the women, young and old, were in the last stages of exhaustion. They all waited one-and-a-half hours before the buses came into the station, and though the ambulances were in the station, they were not allowed to go before the buses arrived.[30]

Bemoaning the lack of consideration shown by immigration officers towards British nationals, Mrs N— was also troubled by the behaviour of the refugees themselves, 'I was thoroughly ashamed to see such bad organisation, and even when the buses had come into the station, the extremely rough and pushing refugees were allowed to push their way in front of our nationals, and were allowed to get in before women, children and old folk.'

Although such behaviour was not typical of all refugees and betrayed something of the xenophobic attitudes of the time, it was understandable given the harrowing circumstances that the former had endured. The scenes in France were chaotic, and have since been vividly evoked both by novelists, among them Jean-Paul Sartre, and by film-makers, such as René Clément.[31] Yet it is the eye-witness accounts that are often the most harrowing. The following is an extract from the unpublished diary of a Monsieur Vila, a man of Franco-British citizenship and a former employee at the French Railways Office in Piccadilly. Enlisted into the French army in 1939, he recounts the scene in Montreuil on 13 June 1940:

> Once in Montreuil, we very soon realised the tragic panic situation and the full extent of the upheaval which the war had brought to France.

Normal life was completely upset and as we moved along the road leading out of the town we were shocked at the transformation which the deteriorating position had caused. Everywhere crowds of refugees were on the move in cars, lorries, on bicycles and most on foot taking with them only whatever they were able to transport in clothing and bedding. More people were watching from their houses uncertain whether they should join the exodus or remain and hope for the best when the Germans arrived. There was no further doubt that nothing could be done to stop the progress of the invaders since the Army was moving south with the civilians. It was a difficult decision to make for the people watching on their door steps, but those who remained at home were in the end more fortunate than the millions who took to the roads, abandoning their possessions to the bands of looters who followed the crowds.[32]

For those civilians who were forced off the roads and on to one of the ships bound for England, the voyage across the Channel was no less frightening. Buried amid the Middlesex County Council archives is the following press report, which, through its very terseness and lack of hyperbole, manages to convey something of the discomfort and danger that journey entailed:

> Most of the refugees have lost everything. Several had not slept for days. During the twenty-hour journey to an East Coast port, mother and babies slept on straw in the holds. One baby was born during the voyage.[33]

Once disembarked on English soil, it was small wonder that most refugees were fatigued and confused. Those who arrived in the West Country were characterised by one observer as 'profoundly pessimistic', believing that the food offered them by the local authorities was merely a publicity stunt.[34] The following is a WVS interview, written up in the language of the time, with one new arrival:

> The WVS spoke to a Belgian man with a dash of the tar brush, who got out of the train looking dazed.
> 'Can I help you?'
> 'Help!' he said turning on her almost savagely.
> 'Can we do anything for you; have you friends? Come and have some tea.' After he had tea, he mellowed very much, seemed grateful and went off to some address he knew.[35]

The refugee was fortunate in that he at least had an address to go to. From the Empress Hall Refugee Centre was posted a pathetic letter by a French refugee, albeit a rather curious individual who was pursuing theophilosophical science and looking forward to the age of Aquarius,

who admitted to the Foreign Office that he had desperately looked
through the phone book in order to write to anybody who shared his
name in case they were a distant relation, but with no success.[36] The
result, in his pidgin English, was that he had to endure 'sleeping among
people, ill-breeded enough, talking, smoking and spitting even at
night.'

The pathetic nature of the refugees' plight is further evoked by the
lists of lost luggage filed with the British authorities. Typical of these
was that lodged by a Mme L— who had arrived from Boulogne on 22
May, and who had since been billeted at Our Lady's Priory in Haywards
Heath. In a letter to the Commanding Officer of the Crystal Palace
Reception Centre, where she had briefly been housed, she asked after
'one travelling bag of dark grey material checked dark blue, no address
attached owing to the extreme haste of our departure'.[37] Apart from an
expensive fox fur, worth some 2,000 francs, which she had managed to
hang on to, the remainder of her belongings testified to the desire to
recover some dignity by reclaiming what few possessions were still hers.
The bag comprised:

One lady's mantle, grey mixture	200 frs
One pair lady's shoes	200 frs
One pair snow boots	50 frs
One pair black stockings (new)	50 frs
Lady's underclothing	300 frs

In a similar case, a Mlle Le— enquired after a 'small chromium watch
with a waistband of yellow leather' that she had entrusted to a Mme
Lefebvre en route to England from Le Havre.[38]

While some refugees managed to hang on to some of their most
treasured possessions (Orwell observed one with a parrot in cage),[39]
their lack of material goods testified to the unexpected speed of the
German advance and lack of prior thought civilians had given to the
question of flight. This was a trend picked up by Mass-Observation in
a series of interviews it conducted with sixty-two refugees (French,
Dutch, Belgian, Polish and one Czech) at the Camberwell and Fulham
Road Reception Centres.[40] Among this number, 60 per cent had no
plans about their flight, 4 per cent had 'plans to a point', 16 per cent
had unsuccessful plans, 4 per cent successful plans, 3 per cent were
unsure how to judge the success of their plans, and 13 per cent gave
'irrelevant answers'.

What the British had not been counting on was the large number of bicycles that the refugees brought with them. Two-thirds of the refugees questioned by Mass-Observation at Camberwell and Fulham had possessed a bicycle on the Continent or had access to a car.[41] One man (nationality not given) remarked, 'I had a bicycle which I used for about 1,200 km and my trousers were still whole. I didn't know where to go, I just rode on with the Germans on my heels.'[42] It was not long before the reception centres in Britain were clogged up with such vehicles of all shapes and sizes. In a report of 25 May 1940, the WVS complained, 'Another trouble which is arising very energetically is the fact that practically everybody is bringing over a bicycle. For instance, on a train carrying 642 men, women and children, there were 175 bicycles. Our people view this with alarm. The number of bicycles coming into the country is, I am told, fantastic.'[43] The archives of individual reception centres bear out these stories and frequently contain lengthy handwritten ledgers detailing the descriptions, serial numbers and ownership of bicycles, testimony to the wishes of the refugees to cling on to one of their most valued possessions, a mode of transport that, more than likely, had helped them evade danger,[44] as it had in the case of some soldiers. Léon Wilson, one of the very first (if not *the* first) French soldier to enlist with the British army in the summer of 1940, recalls how he and a small band of colleagues retreated to Dunkirk. Some kilometres outside the town, they stumbled across a bicycle shop, by then deserted, where they appropriated the bikes to speed their journey.[45] Some sixty years later, when revisiting the area, Monsieur Wilson was astonished to discover that the same shop existed; even after that period of time, he still felt guilty about taking the bikes, even though the desperate circumstances had necessitated their acquisition.

While the reception of refugees might not have passed off smoothly – bogged down by the registering of property and thrown off course by the erratic arrivals of trains ferrying civilians from the ports – it is only fair to say that the British authorities were never overwhelmed and were frequently touched by the harrowing stories refugees brought with them. Despite the 'silence' that Orwell observed among the public, and despite a general wariness about foreigners and fifth columns, there was a general sympathy with their plight. At a café in Waltham Cross, Mass-Observation overheard a conversation between the sixty-year-old proprietress and two of her younger customers, in which all agreed it 'must be terrible' for the refugees.[46] There were also many spontaneous charitable gestures. The WVS recalls how, in May–June 1940, it was overwhelmed with offers of interpreters and assistance.[47]

At the main London stations, the porters, in the politically incorrect words of one WVS official, 'all worked like blacks, without any tips'.[48] The suspicion must remain, however, that things would have been very different if the 200,000 or so refugees that the government had originally been envisaging had actually arrived.

Late arrivals: The Royal Victoria Patriotic School

With hindsight, what is surprising is the laxity of immigration formalities pursued in May–June 1940, especially given the fear of a fifth column. While these were toughened up, in part on the recommendation of the Vansittart Committee,[49] they were not foolproof. After the official declaration of welcome, there might have followed much form-filling, undoubtedly extended in the course of May, and possibly some rudimentary interrogation at one of the reception centres, yet it was not difficult to wander away from these makeshift depots. In an interview with André Gillois, Henri Beausaire, an early recruit for the Free French, recalled his time at Camberwell, incidentally the same place that had processed Gilbert Renault-Roulies (later known by his *nom de guerre* Colonel Rémy), who was to become one of the most daring of resisters:

> We were not questioned there. In principle we were locked up, but almost every evening I threaded my way through a hole in the wall in order to live it up in London. One morning the hole was blocked up. A baker happened to deliver some cakes by the main door. I took a plate into the van, and the sentries mistook me for a deliveryman.[50]

Such laxity was not long-lived. With places in reception centres becoming scarce, and with the declaration of the Franco-German Armistice and the creation of the Vichy regime, from July 1940 new arrivals – whether refugees, volunteers for de Gaulle or even British citizens fleeing the Continent – were likely to discover themselves incarcerated in prisons until their bona fides could be vouched for. Such was the case of the writer Arthur Koestler who arrived in Britain from France at the close of the Blitz after a difficult journey via Marseille, Casablanca and Lisbon. 'The last stage of this long trek to freedom was Pentonville Prison', he writes, 'where I spent six peaceful weeks in solitary confinement'. Conditions were not good:

> Most of the time – on the average fifteen to sixteen hours a day – the cell was pitch dark, because the alert usually came with the fading of daylight,

and the lights in the cell were then switched off to prevent us presumptive
fifth columnists from signalling to the raiders.[51]

Deprived of matches, Koestler learned how to ignite cigarettes via the
cotton wool of the filters through which was inserted a slither of silver
paper, the makeshift contraption then inserted into a light socket in the
hope of causing a short circuit: 'Average duration until success is
achieved: one hour.'[52] Through a Frenchman, he also learned Marseille
chess, a fiendish game in which a player made two moves instead of
one, and was not allowed to check the king by his first move. Philippe
Barrès and Jean Fayard, two ardent anti-Nazis who had quit France on
board a Polish vessel, were less stoical in the face of Pentonville: one
bath a week, one hour of exercise per day, and thrown in among
common criminals.[53] Barrès soon left for the USA.[54] Equally outraged
was Hélène Terré, a French Red Cross official, who was detained at the
woman's prison of Holloway, which also housed a group of young
students from a boarding school near Dunkirk.[55] Like Pentonville, this
Victorian jail was close to the railway stations of King's Cross and
Euston, prime bombing targets for the *Luftwaffe*. Before long, the
inside of the prison came to resemble Bedlam as the inmates screamed
throughout the air raids. Unwittingly, Terré had come to London
accompanied by a Vichy agent, a Mlle Nicole, whom we shall meet in a
later chapter.

Recognising the unsuitability of prisons, and aware of the withdrawal of the reception centres, which were increasingly required for
the accommodation of Londoners who had been bombed out of their
houses, in late 1940 the government sought out alternative venues for
the processing of Continental arrivals. An early choice was the Oratory
School, Brompton, today the school of Tony Blair's son, yet this also
proved too cramped.[56] After further searching, the Royal Victoria
Patriotic School (RVPS) in Wandsworth, a former school for the sons
of military officers, was made available to the Security Services.
Capable of holding some 300 residents, the RVPS fell under the aegis of
BS Department in the Home Office, which had hitherto been
concerned with civil internment camps. It was further decided that the
new establishment should be exclusively concerned with men. Women
were to be sent to a new reception centre at 101 Nightingale Lane,
Balham.

As early as March 1941, the Home Office was singing the praises of
the RVPS and the speed that new French entries into Britain were now
being dealt with. It was acknowledged, however, that there had been a

Figure 3   The Royal Victoria Patriotic Buildings, Wandsworth – today
an arts, restaurant and office complex; in 1940 an interrogation centre
for all refugees entering the UK

number of teething problems, especially in respect to the way in which
French volunteers for de Gaulle had been handled, not so much at
Wandsworth, but at Liverpool. In a trenchant letter to the Home
Office, Spears complained that 'the worst impression' was being given
'to enthusiasts who had forfeited everything to come to this country
and continue the fight'.[57] On arrival at the port, there was no liaison
officer to handle matters; the French were simply bundled into a Black
Maria and taken off to a transit camp. There, officers had to share a
dormitory with their men and refugees, and suffered the indignity of
having to wash their cutlery and plates after each meal. It would not be
difficult, concluded Spears, to rectify matters and to ensure that some
word of encouragement was passed on to the volunteers.

   To be fair, the Home Office was alarmed to hear of the procedures at
Liverpool, which were allegedly being replicated at Glasgow. A series of
promises were thus made to Spears. To begin with, it was made clear
that the practice of driving volunteers to transit camps in prison vans
had been abandoned; as we shall see, it is doubtful it ever existed in the
first place.[58] Next, the Home Office promised to ease entry regulations.
If warning of any new arrival was given beforehand, and if this person
could be vouched for by de Gaulle, then the volunteer would be
excused the ordeal of the RVPS. This exemption, it was pointed out,
had recently been made in the case of Colonel Vallin, later to take

charge of the Free French Air Force. In a fictional setting, it is the intervention of Carlton Gardens that saves the young pianist and her opera-singing companion from a spell in Liverpool gaol, and then presumably Nightingale Lane, in the 1991 film *L'Accompagnatrice*.[59] Should a French national arrive by plane, or at any other place than a controlled port, and so long as they did not seek to conceal their identity, the Home Office promised that they would be subject to only a short spell at Wandsworth, although reading between the lines it appears that one Frenchman who had landed thus, a certain A— C—, had still been questioned at length by MI5.[60] Later, in May 1941, the Home Office agreed that British representatives could issue visas to 'vouched for' Free French volunteers in order that they did not have to attend the RVPS.[61]

In a further gesture to ease procedures, the Home Office accepted that the police should adopt a more conciliatory approach when handling arrivals and, on 5 June 1941, a circular was issued to chief constables in which local police forces were instructed to reassure de Gaulle's volunteers 'that they are being escorted to the Centre (ie the RVPS) not because they are personally suspect but in accordance with security measures'.[62] Arrangements were also made for the distribution of leaflets carrying a personal message of welcome from de Gaulle. And, finally, the Home Office agreed to seek out further information on the manner in which French nationals were being dealt with at their point of arrival.

In some places, it appears the authorities went out of their way to offer support. The Immigration Officer in Poole replied that it was, on average, necessary to send one person a week up to Wandsworth.[63] Most arrived not by sea, but by plane, and were of 'the superior type', not refugees, but 'senior officers and men of means'. It had thus been deemed inappropriate to lock them up in the cells; rather, given their wealth, they had been able to put themselves up in a hotel where they had been supervised by an NCO before departing to London the next day. In the West of England, immigration officers recorded no complaints at Avonmouth, Whitchurch and Bristol. Instead of putting new arrivals into prison, they were kept on board their vessels overnight and then sent on to London the next day.[64] At Cardiff, the authorities also claimed that 'every consideration' was given to French nationals.[65] As Spears alleged, it appears that the trouble spots were indeed Glasgow and Liverpool, the places where, after summer 1940, most refugees and volunteers for de Gaulle landed. From Scotland, the police claimed that every effort was being made to dispatch arrivals to Wandsworth on the overnight train to London.[66] Yet, depending on the time of disembarkation, this was not always possible, and so they had to be held overnight. This was the only way in which these people could be prevented from making contact with the French community in the city. In future, however, the immigration officers promised to follow the Bristol practice of keeping arrivals on their ships overnight until a train was ready to depart.

If the Immigration Office at Glasgow was irritated at the intervention of Whitehall, its counterpart at Liverpool was positively fuming.[67] Complaining that the city's constabulary was already overstretched, it was angry that police had to be used for the processing of French nationals. As to the question of housing, the only way to prevent 'wanderings around the city', and to maintain proper surveillance, was to use prison cells rather than boarding houses and hotels. Maybe in the light of what we know about the behaviour of the nearby French consulate this was a sensible precaution (see Chapter 4). Moreover, the immigration officer in overall charge could never remember an occasion when a Black Maria had been used, but conceded that buses might be employed in future; indeed, a separate enquiry by the Committee to the RVPS discovered that no prison vans had been deployed, merely 'charabancs or taxis'.[68] The officer also promised to look into the possibility of keeping arrivals on board ship overnight, and requested that the Ministry of Shipping be put in charge of these arrangements, and that a representative of the RVPS be sent up to meet vessels when docking. In a subsequent letter of April 1941, the Liverpool Immigration Office made known that future French arrivals were now held overnight on the Free French vessel *La Volontaire* until arrangements could be made to escort the men to London.[69] However, this meant that arrivals, sometimes in groups as large as twenty-five, could not be kept in a state of incommunicado. This troubled the Home Office, which urged the police in Liverpool to billet them in hotels or the Liverpool Scottish Drill Hall rather than *La Volontaire*,[70] a change that was indeed implemented.[71] It remains unclear whether the overworked and irritable Liverpool police complied with other Home Office recommendations; the fact that the Spears Mission was still complaining about the modes of transport in September 1941 suggests not or, more likely, that the Free French remained very sensitive about the way in which potential recruits were handled.[72]

Carlton Gardens was unquestionably the most strident critic of the

RVPS. There was intense dissatisfaction that arrivals to Britain were issued with a letter of welcome from de Gaulle, but were then not allowed to keep it.[73] The Français de Grande Bretagne (FGB), the self-appointed civil wing of the Free French, was also irritated that it could not distribute its own personal letter of welcome, a move scuppered by Downing Street, which thought an additional message unnecessary and likely to upset those who were not for de Gaulle.[74] Certainly, the official welcoming at Wandsworth was hardly cordial. After a very correct address, in which the School's Commandant offered his greetings, the internees were presented with a set of the rules, which must have gone down badly with men who had already broken a whole series of regulations to get to Britain in the first place:

1 This Reception Centre has been established with the purpose of offering temporary lodging to allied and neutral subjects who arrive in Great Britain.

2 It is duly the duty of the Centre's officers to assist you in proving your identity and, to this effect, of seeing all the documents to be found in your possession, and to ask you for all the information that they will judge necessary.

Your interest is therefore to reply in a frank and explicit manner to the questions that are put to you.

3 As soon as your identity and good faith have been established, you will be sent to the representatives of your country in Great Britain, and every help will be given to you in order that you can reach your destination. In waiting, you will understand that, for reasons of security, no communication will be permitted with the outside, either by message, letter, telephone or any other means.[75]

To the annoyance of the Free French, 'residents' at Wandsworth were further required to sign a document to say that they understood all the rules and that they would observe them during their stay.

A further grumble concerned conditions within the RVPS. In a letter of September 1941, MI5 revealed that the Free French were especially disgruntled about the food, the quality not the quantity: 'We gathered that something a little more continental would be appreciated! I doubt whether the Mecca Cafés, or whoever they are, can rise to it, but perhaps you would like to consider the point.'[76] It later transpired the real problem was the prices in the canteen, which the inmates had to afford out of their pocket money.[77] Across in Nightingale Lane, French internees appear to have kicked up a fuss about sleeping arrangements, although this was contemptuously dismissed by the welfare officer, 'I

can appreciate that continental women, more especially the tempera-
mental French who normally spend much of their time in well
furnished bed-sitting rooms, may feel rebuffed and disheartened by an
array of army blankets', but the other nationals were content.[78] The
presence of armed guards was, however, thought disconcerting by both
men and women, yet this was insisted upon by the War Office.[79] A
further fuss blew up as to who among the French should be sent to
Wandsworth, despite the earlier attempts of the Home Office to deter-
mine which groups needed to pass through the RVPS. It transpired that
some French signed the *acte d'engagement* abroad, and were thus
exempted from the RVPS; yet, on arrival in Britain, they proved either
unsuitable for service with de Gaulle, or simply changed their minds
and claimed to be mere refugees.[80]

Just as French arrivals had not anticipated a stay in a Victorian
boarding school, they had certainly not bargained on the nature of
their questioning. Gillois cites the example of Joseph Kessel and his
nephew, Maurice Druon, who, with the help of smugglers, had crossed
the Pyrenees to make their way to London via Lisbon.[81] At
Wandsworth, Kessel was interviewed for some 48 hours in total, sometimes in 8- to 10-hour stretches. In the interrogation itself, his
interviewers displayed an intimate knowledge of French geography,
asking him about his mother and how she had travelled through
Luchon on her way to the southern zone; had she gone by train or by
bus. When he replied 'by train', his interviewer congratulated him,
remarking that there was no bus through Luchon. When it was the turn
of the aviator Henri Schutz, his inquisitors asked him where he was
born and where he had spent his adolescence; on discovering he had
studied at a particular *lycée* in Marseille, he was quizzed on teachers
past and present. These questions he could answer; he was genuinely
stumped when asked about the location of a nearby war memorial. This
gap in his local knowledge ensured that his stay at Wandsworth lasted
over a month. Even well-known figures were subject to prolonged
holding. Claudius Petit, a member of the Conseil National de la
Résistance (CNR) and a deputy of the Algerian Assembly, had the
misfortune to land in England with a camera.[82] In the ten days' wait for
a plane to ferry him out of France, he had indulged his hobby for
photography, snapping the local scenery. This raised the suspicions of
his MI5 officers, who developed his film, although quite what they
made of photographs of trees and hedges remains unknown; Petit only
secured his release after his travelling companion, General de Lattre de

Tassigny, who himself had arrived disguised in beard and civilian clothes, vouched for him.

Maybe the greatest grumble of those held at Wandsworth was not so much the conditions or the intensive questioning, which interrupted community life, and on one occasion prematurely ended a football match as there were not enough players left on the pitch since one after another was called away for questioning.[83] Rather the greatest frustration was the delay in reaching freedom. As the Welfare Officer of the RVPS observed, 'The dominating idea is to get out; the guests after many vicissitudes are on the threshold of liberty, impatient to step across. They are like the passengers of a big liner which, after a rough passage, has docked in port, who are told they will not be allowed to land for a number of days.'[84] This was certainly the sentiment of Georges Le Poittevin who, in 1943, had escaped solitary confinement in a Pétainist jail in North Africa, and who is now president of the London-based Association des Combattants Volontaires. On reaching Gibraltar, he boarded a cargo vessel for Liverpool, which arrived only after being bombed by both the Luftwaffe and U-Boats, taking a direct hit from a 250 kilogram bomb, which thankfully did not explode. 'When I arrived in Liverpool, I took a breath and thought, freedom at last.'[85] In the event, he was handcuffed and sent immediately to Wandsworth where he soon learned he was under detention; although he had arrived in good faith, he was naturally troubled by stories doing the rounds among other detainees that some individuals had been shot as spies.

However unsatisfactory conditions were at Wandsworth, it should be stressed that the British were only taking prudent precautions. This was wartime, and after the initial influx of refugees had crossed the Channel in the summer of 1940, it was certain that later arrivals would be looked upon with suspicion, even if they had signalled their desire to join de Gaulle. Moreover, Wandsworth was not the Hôtel Terminus in Lyon where the SS man, Klaus Barbie, regularly tortured and murdered resisters, including Jean Moulin. MI5 officers might have deployed gruelling interviewing techniques, but they were not breaking people's arms or using terror tactics. As the former deputy for the Aisne Jean Pierre-Bloch, an arrival in London in 1942, acknowledged, some French recognised this.[86] For his part, Monsieur Le Poittevin recalls how he was questioned at length, with 'a very bright light shining in my eyes', yet the 'tone of the voice questioning me was always friendly, even when I was erring slightly in my explanations'.[87]

On leaving, he was given a warm handshake by the colonel in charge and given 50 pounds sterling, the largest sum of money he had ever had in his possession, some of which was spent on a 'wonderful' steak-and-chips lunch in Soho and a gold wrist watch that never ever worked. It should be further stressed that it was principally the Free French that complained most about Wandsworth, ironical given the scandal that surrounded their own holding centres at Duke Street and Camberley where rough tactics, if not torture, were frequently used, and where the principle of habeas corpus was blatantly disregarded.[88] In truth, what really irritated Carlton Gardens about the RVPS was the fact that the British were getting hold of French arrivals before Gaullist officials. In this way, MI5 collated valuable intelligence on French matters. In his exhaustive history of British intelligence, F. H. Hinsley reveals how vital information in the preparation for D-Day was culled from Wandsworth[89] something vouched for by Monsieur Le Poittevin who was questioned extensively about his native Normandy, questions which at the time seemed utterly futile.[90] Information about conditions in occupied Europe was also passed on to the BBC for its broadcasts to France.[91] The British could also recruit prospective agents for SOE, before the BCRA (Bureau Central de Renseignements d'Action) could get their hands on them. In his memoirs, de Gaulle betrays this particular grievance about the 'Patriotic School':

> As soon as a Frenchman arrived in England, unless he was somebody well known, he was confined by Intelligence ... and invited to join the British Secret Services. It was only after a whole series of remonstrances and requests that he was allowed to join us. If, however, he had yielded, he was kept away from us and we would never see him.[92]

Such quarrels about the RVPS were, however, nothing compared to the squabbles that broke out over who should look after refugees once in the wider community.

Les pauvres types

How many refugees, especially French, did Britain receive? This is no easy question to answer. Refugees of all nationalities arrived at different times, at different places in the country; and were processed in different ways, some being quickly repatriated. In her report of 1947, de l'Hôpital records that on 17 May 1940 alone, WVS canteens fed some 8,500 French refugees at a cost of £100,[93] a figure repeated in older histories,[94] although as we shall see detailed breakdowns, collated from a variety of sources, suggest for July–August a total French refugee population of about half this size, an indication that many civilians were immediately returned to their homeland, alongside the majority of French troops rescued at Dunkirk. Another problem in counting heads lies in the bureaucracy that was assembled to register their presence. Despite the eventual imposition of strict immigration and registration procedures, several refugees failed to complete the necessary forms, and openly defied restrictions on their freedom of movement. It is possible that some simply did not understand what information was being asked of them, especially as official inter-preters were scarce and were frequently of a poor standard. Others may have left London to escape the Blitz, or perhaps to seek out jobs beyond the capital. Such was the case of one Frenchman investigated by the WVS, 'P.R-D, French, formerly billeted in Islington. Local Authority stated that he had "left Islington". Further enquiry showed that he had gone to work in Ripon. Ripon police stated they had no trace. Scotland Yard stated they had no trace; and there the matter rests since 3rd December.'[95] There was also the case of nine Frenchmen at the Norwood Centre who had subse-quently vanished without any forwarding address.[96]

WVS reports suggest that the French were among the worst of all nationalities at keeping the authorities informed of their whereabouts. It is possible that this was a characteristic defiance of authority, or possibly a churlish snub to the British. It is more likely to have been prudent behaviour. It was well known that the Vichy consulate, housed in London's Bedford Square, was on the look-out for French nationals living in Britain, giving rise to fears that retaliatory action might then be initiated against their families on metropolitan soil. As early as September 1940, the Home Office was instructing police authorities not to disclose any information about French civilians.[97] In the case of the Dutch, Poles, Norwegians and Greeks, such warnings were nowhere near as strict. In May 1941, the Home Office repeated the advice and the 'necessity of special care in enforcing the general rule in respect of enquiries which might be received about French citizens from officials of the Vichy Consulate'.[98] It might also be that French refugees wanted to keep their heads down in order to escape the atten-tions of Carlton Gardens, which, as we shall see in Chapter 5, was known to be pressing both the Home Office and Foreign Office for a full list of French nationals resident in Britain, purportedly for propa-ganda purposes yet, in truth, for a recruitment drive.

Despite the above difficulties, it is still possible to arrive at a reasonably accurate figure for the number of French refugees. Statistics from four separate sources suggest a sum of 2,500–4,000, roughly a tenth of all refugees, that came to Britain during May–June 1940. All available evidence suggests that the French were the second largest group after the Belgians, who numbered approximately 20,000.[99] Interestingly, government figures are the least detailed, suggesting how willing Whitehall was to farm out refugees to local authorities and charitable bodies. In August 1940, the Committee on Foreign (Allied) Resistance (CFR) recorded 2,564 French refugees arrived since May 1940.[100] WVS totals for October 1940 are astonishingly similar, putting the estimate at 2,550.[101] For its part, the LCC reported that, by the close of October 1940, 2,905 French refugees had passed through its reception centres.[102] Maybe the most accurate breakdown comes from the Comité d'Entr'Aide aux Français (CEAF), a charitable organisation whose remit was the welfare of all French nationals in Britain.[103] It counted 2,046 refugees with addresses and 1,693 without addresses, an overall total of 3,739. It remains possible that both the WVS and the government had failed to take this latter body of non-addressees into their own calculations, or that these elusive refugees had been repatriated. It is known that over 500 refugees were sent home in the course of 1940–41 in circumstances of great secrecy, partly to protect them from patrolling U- and E-boats, which had already torpedoed a vessel carrying French sailors for repatriation, and partly not to upset the already fragile relations with de Gaulle's headquarters. Few files on refugee repatriation appear to have survived.

It is not hard to ascertain why so few French nationals arrived on these shores and, for that matter, why the large numbers of Belgian and Dutch failed to materialise.[104] To begin with, the suddenness of the German victory severed the escape routes on the northern coastline, forcing civilians to retreat inland, not that they had necessarily put plans in place for their flight. The questioning of Mass-Observation as to refugees' plans for flight will be recalled.[105] As the columns of civilians retreated into the heart of France, towns in the south swelled in size.[106] Rod Kedward cites the following examples: 'Cahors in the Lot grew from 13,000 to an estimated 60–70,000, Brive in the Corrèze from 30,000 to 100,000, and Pau in the Basses-Pyrénées, a major centre of exile from the north in 1914–18, from 38,000 to 150,000.'[107] Retracing the steps of those caught up in the *exode*, Kedward has further shown how many civilians, confused and without any real knowledge of where they were going, believed that they might be positively welcomed in those southern resort towns, which they had first encountered after the introduction of paid holidays by the Popular Front, only to discover their sojourn was a far less pleasant than the one they had experienced during the *avant guerre*.[108] Interestingly, some Continental refugees, at least well-heeled ones, might well have travelled to British seaside resorts, such as Bournemouth, having spent holidays there in peacetime.[109] It was the British government's belief that French refugees were trying to reach North Africa.[110] The initial impact of Pétainism may also have stemmed any attempted flight to Britain. As Kedward has again demonstrated, the appeal of the marshal effectively cast a trance over the demoralised peoples of France; here was the saviour who would rescue his people from the abyss.[111] Why, then, attempt the hazardous journey to Britain, a country responsible for the shelling at Mers-el-Kébir, and a country soon to constitute another piece in Hitler's European empire? Such events only fuelled a growing Anglophobia among the French public, which, throughout the 'phoney war', had questioned Britain's contribution to the war effort. It is not hard to believe that something of this Anglophobia travelled across the Channel with the refugees; certainly, many retained an admiration for Pétain, believing that he was doing his best in difficult circumstances.

While it is possible to account for the paltry numbers of French refugees, it is harder to ascertain their social complexion. As regards age and gender, WVS statistics highlight two key groups: children and women born before 1922.[112] There is little of surprise here. More interesting is the high proportion of young men. CEAF figures include 740 males between the ages of 17 and 35.[113] Why so many young males should have figured is uncertain. How had they evaded conscription? It may be that they belonged to reserved occupations, especially since many stemmed from the industrial heartlands of northern France. Being young, healthy and without family ties, it might also be that they were best placed to flee. It is further possible that they were fearful of what fate might await them when the Germans arrived. In its interviews with refugees, Mass-Observation uncovered several reasons why civilians had taken to the roads, yet among young non-Jewish men the most frequent answer was their desire not to work for the Nazis.[114] Whatever the case, in the eyes of the Home Office and MI5, these males were a real nuisance.[115] Resisting calls to join either the Free French or the British armed services, they were deemed parasitical and a disturbing influence in that their morale was low. Maybe it would have been better if some effort had been made to find them employment in their existing fields of expertise; as we shall see, the government shied away from such proposals, fearing that refugees would be accused of stealing British jobs.

Unsurprisingly, most refugees appear to have come from the districts of the Nord-Pas-de-Calais, that is those areas that felt the squeeze of Guderian's grip as German armour swung towards the coast to encircle the hapless BEF. Among the addresses of refugees processed by the LCC, it is the names of towns and villages of northern France that predominate: Berck-sur Mer; Dunkerque; Boulogne; Armentières; Calais; Chimay; Sainte Marie Kerque; Lille; Abbeville (the scene of de Gaulle's tank triumph); Port de Briques; Albert; Bruay; and Cauchy (the birthplace of Pétain himself).[116]

As to profession and social class, no real statistics appear to have survived, and might never have been obtainable in the first place. In August 1940, WVS complained that its office only possessed professional details of 950 of the 2,550 French refugees on its books.[117] For its part, Mass-Observation did a statistical tally of refugees at Camberwell and Fulham, yet it was acknowledged that the samples were not truly representative as they included too many middle-class elements.[118] Contemporary observations about the wealth of the refugees are also ambiguous. Having escaped France in 1940, the British journalist Neville Lytton watched newsreel of the *exode* in British cinemas:

> Since my arrival in England I have seen some films of these refugees and none of them get the atmosphere quite right. In these films the refugees seem to be drawn from the poorer classes only, whereas in fact all classes were on the road. You saw high powered Hispano-Suiza cars jammed in between farm wagons drawn by horses.[119]

It appears, however, that those with money and influence were best placed to evade the German advance by escaping into metropolitan France; the majority of those who came to Britain appear, in the words of Orwell, to have been 'middling people of the shopkeeper-clerk type … in quite good trim',[120] an observation supported by Jean-Louis Crémieux-Brilhac, who describes such refugees as 'les humbles'.[121] Yet whatever their position in France, most refugees arrived in England penniless and without means of support.

Despite the above ambiguities, two groups of refugees do stand out. In its statistical profile, the CEAF counted some 50 priests and novices. Other accounts of refugees also point to the presence of both regular and secular clergy.[122] One French woman, evacuated on 22 May 1940, found herself on a boat of 41 persons, of whom 4 were Sisters of

Charity.[123] While the evidence may be piecemeal, it tends to support W. D. Halls's observation that the Catholic Church was the one body, unlike local and national government French organisations, that remained alongside the refugees in France, tending for their needs, only for its own members to be swept up in the general mêlée.[124] Interestingly, in all the reports compiled by British agencies handling French refugees, little mention is made of Jews although, in its interviews with refugees during June 1940, Mass-Observation did uncover small numbers.[125] Unsurprisingly, these men, women and children had left France and the Low Countries fully aware of the fate that awaited them when the Nazis arrived. Later in the war in 1942, shocked at Vichy's anti-Semitism, London gave some consideration to taking in some 1,000 Jewish orphans from unoccupied France, resettling them in either Britain or Palestine.[126] As Wasserstein has shown, the shortage of accommodation, the continued threat of invasion, early preparations for D-Day and the November 1942 Allied landings in North Africa effectively scuppered what was, in any case, a very limited humanitarian gesture.

The other readily identifiable body among French refugees was the large number of French fishermen and their families who made their home in the West Country. The presence of Breton fishermen has always been well known. In his memoirs, de Gaulle observes, 'In the last days of June a flotilla of fishing boats reached Cornwall, bringing over to General de Gaulle all the able-bodied men from the island of Sein.'[127] Crémieux-Brilhac suggests that, in September 1940, such Breton fishermen constituted the bulk of the Free French Navy.[128] It is

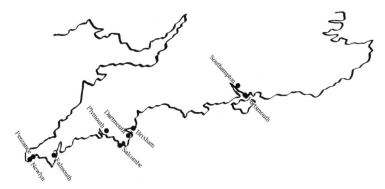

Map 1   Principal ports visited by French refugee fishermen and their families in 1940

true that many of these seamen enlisted with Carlton Gardens, but not all, some arriving as late as October 1940 without any real prior knowledge of de Gaulle.[129] In conversation with a Mr Matthews, the representative of the French consulate at Penzance, Henry Astor of French Welfare learned that French fishing boats, principally from Boulogne and the Breton Coast, had begun to arrive after 19 June, 'having left France at a moment's notice in a panic', making their way to the Cornish coast where many had fished before the war and, perhaps in the case of the Breton sailors, to a place where they recognised a cultural affinity.[130] In early July, the Foreign Office recorded seven fishing boats at Penzance alone, all carrying large numbers of human cargo: *Souvenir du Monde* (Boulogne), 67 people; *Ma Gondole* (Boulogne), 52; *Notre Dame de Montligeon* (Boulogne), 92; *Velleda* (Audierre), 45; *Espérance* (Boulogne), 52; *Corbeau* (Carmaret), 19; and *Maris Stella* (no port given), 23.[131] The writer Ian Hay recalls that one Boulogne boat arrived at Brixham with 70 passengers on board, each one with the name 'Duval'.[132]

While the families and friends of the fishermen were allowed on shore, the crews themselves, along with their vessels, were initially treated as 'captives', hardly surprising perhaps given that maritime relations between Britain and France, never that warm at the best of times and even cooler at the moment of Mers-el-Kébir, were far from cordial. Bobbing up and down in Newlyn and Penzance harbours, and likely to be sunk by the Royal Navy if they attempted to set sail into the Atlantic, the crews had faced starvation, and owed their survival to Matthews who, on his own initiative, spent some £400 to feed these men.[133] It remains unclear whether the money was Matthews' own or, more likely, that of the French consulate. According to Astor, the Ministry of Health's representative at Truro, a Mr Kirby, had been given permission by Whitehall to repay the amount, yet in late October 1940 Matthews was still waiting for his money.

Just how many French boats, their crews and families, crossed the Channel to relative safety in England remains unclear. British reports compiled for the Home Office and the CFR all suggest different figures. Some of the problems in ascertaining precise figures for this category of refugees were outlined in a report of E. Ashley Dodd of the Ministry of Information.[134] At the start of August 1940, he travelled down to Cornwall and Devon, visiting 'every likely port in the two counties', no mean feat given that he was unfamiliar with the localities and was short of petrol. He reported no French fishermen settled on the northern coast but some fifty men and women at Penzance, another thirty at Salcombe, along with other groups of uncertain numbers at Falmouth and Plymouth. Clearly this was a shifting community. Some men, having offloaded their human cargo on the Cornish coast, had quickly headed back for France before the British authorities could impound their boats; others had journeyed up to London to be registered or to enlist with de Gaulle; a small band of men were reportedly travelling up and down the coast to discover a suitable port to make their home; and a small number had been interned. Their numbers, however, were inferior to those of the Belgians, as Hay suggests,[135] and as the following police statistics for Newlyn and Brixham in 1940 attest (see table).[136]

	Male	Female	Children	Total
French	45	30	20	95
Belgian	224	169	135	528

In their work on Belgian refugees, utilising the CEGES archives in Brussels, Buck and Bernado y Garcia have suggested that the overall numbers of Belgians in the region might even have been higher, closer to 1,000, dwarfing the figures for the French, an impression borne out by contemporary observers.[137] It is also recalled that relations between the Dutch and Belgians were not that harmonious. This may be because the Belgians possessed more boats, and boats of a better quality, than the French.[138] As will be seen, the quality of these craft was later to become a source of real friction between the fishermen themselves and the Mission Economique Belge (MEB), part of the Belgian government-in-exile.

Catering for the refugees

As the *exode* gathered momentum, French refugees were caught up with other nationalities and were processed in much the same way, notably through the Central Committee for War Refugees from Holland, Belgium and France, the local War Refugee Committees, and the London reception centres, which were often aided by such charitable bodies such as the WVS, the Catholic Women's League and the British Red Cross. What is striking is that, as early as June 1940, a number of specifically French organisations were emerging to cater for their own nationals. In part, this reflected a strong sense of patriotic pride, and the impressive organisational skills of a long-established French colony in London. It also signalled that the refugees were about to become part of the political infighting that bedevilled the 'forgotten French', and which partially necessitated the setting up of Bessborough's French Welfare.

Foremost among these organisations was the CEAF. As an undated Foreign Office memo recalled, it had been founded in the first week of August 1940 to deal with the welfare of refugees and was part of the many bodies that fell under the aegis of the Comité Central Permanent de la Colonie Française de Londres.[139] Its objectives, outlined in an open letter to members of the French colony in Britain, were to provide French refugees with financial and material assistance, shelter and lodging, meals at reduced prices, medical and hospital services, offers of employment, education, help with communications to France, and even advice on repatriation. Although French in origin, it soon had an English chairwoman, Lady Warwick, the sister of Antony Eden, and enjoyed good relations both with French Welfare and with the French consulate in Bedford Square, urging all French nationals to make contact with this Vichy outpost. As the war progressed, Lady Warwick's organisation took on broader responsibilities, looking after men demobilised from de Gaulle's forces, civilians of the *colonie française* and the employment rights of French nationals in this country. Following the D-Day landings, it held glorified bring-and-buy sales at the Grosvenor House to help the needy across the Channel.[140]

Because of its links with both the Foreign Office and the Vichy consulate, the CEAF soon fell foul of the Français de Grande Bretagne (FGB), which was also doing battle with the Catholic Women's League and the French Red Cross, organisations that allegedly harboured Pétainist sympathies.[141] As the self-appointed civil wing of the Free French, founded shortly before the famous broadcast of 18 June, the FGB was eager to recruit as much support as possible. It argued that the 98-year-old Société de Bienfaisance was the most appropriate body to handle French refugees, partially because this body exuded respectability and maybe because it was in such a state of disrepair that it seemed ripe for a Gaullist takeover.[142] As the WVS noted, much of the Société's funding was frozen in the French War Loan compelling it to ask the Treasury for assistance. Interestingly, the CEAF was also subject to WVS criticism, although the nature of the complaints were very different to those of the FGB. 'General impression was very hole in the corner', remarked WVS visitors of the CEAF headquarters, 'Not calculated to give any one confidence; though very earnest they don't appear to have any initiative.'[143]

The competition and sniping among the above agencies eventually forced the government to act. In a memorandum of early August 1940, the Foreign Office admitted there was 'urgent necessity in coordinating all the many voluntary committees, both British and French, which have been set up in this country' in order to expedite the administration of aid.[144] The political quarrels among the French organisations, alongside the personal rivalries that existed among the English involved in handling the refugees, were also thought damaging for propaganda. So it was that Duff Cooper, at the Ministry of Information, asked Bessborough to handle the new department of French Welfare.[145]

In many ways, Vere Ponsonby, the ninth Earl of Bessborough, was the right man for the job.[146] He had already witnessed at close hand several fratricidal quarrels: in 1917, after action at Gallipoli, he had travelled to Russia as part of the Milner Mission; in 1920, he had been forced to quit the family seat in Kilkenny, Ireland, because of the civil war. Bessborough subsequently settled at Stanstead House on the Sussex/Hampshire border in 1924 and married Roberta de Neuflige, the daughter of a French banker. During the interwar years, he sat as chairman of numerous companies, served as governor-general of Canada and took a keen interest in amateur dramatics. In 1940, he had displayed an early concern for the fate of the French, and put aside Stanstead for the billeting of troops from Dunkirk.[147] Here, then, seemed to be the man who possessed the necessary authority, diplomatic skills and knowledge of things French to sort out the Gallic quarrels that irritated both the Foreign Office and Ministry of Information.

The remit of Bessborough's French Welfare was large. It was to oversee Gaullist propaganda and to be responsible for all social and welfare work associated with:

- General de Gaulle's movement
- French civilians and refugees
- Those members of the French armed forces who are either undecided as to whether to remain to continue the struggle or return to France, including the wounded, and those who have definitely decided to be repatriated, and who, it seems, may have to be retained for some time in this country owing to shipping difficulties.[148]

Situated in the Savoy Hotel, in rooms vacated by the Friends of the French Forces Fund, he soon discovered his work cut out. At the end of August, he complained that 'chaos' reigned among the many committees handling refugees, which were 'launching out in every conceivable direction', partly because they were unaware that his new body had been set up to coordinate their actions.[149] It was thus agreed to announce the emergence of French Welfare in the press, and on the radio on at least two or three 'different occasions'.[150] If the annual report filed by Bessborough for French Welfare during 1941 is to be believed, some semblance of order was established during that year; as we shall see, various of the charitable bodies were designated different groups to look after.[151] Nonetheless, the impression is that infighting continued apace. In early October, Sir Desmond Morton joked that Bessborough was 'nearly suffering from a nervous breakdown owing to the appalling time he is having with these Frenchmen, I don't wonder'.[152] That his work was cut out is testified by the sheer range of agencies catering for French refugees and civilians.

So many agencies were there that, in late 1940, the Foreign Office even published a booklet, listing names, addresses and responsibilities of the different societies.[153]

Comité d'Assistance aux Familles
   des Soldats Français
CEAF
FGB
Hôpital Français
Institut Français
Société de Bienfaisance
Société des Anciens Combattants
   Français de Grande Bretagne
Union des Mutilés Français,
   Anciens Combattants, et
   Victimes de la Guerre
British Committee for the French
   Red Cross and other French
   War Charities
French War Charities Society
British Red Cross: Foreign
   Relations Department, French
   Section
Army Welfare
Catholic Women's League

All Nations Voluntary Service
   League
British Council
Catholic War Refugees Spiritual
   Welfare Committee
Central Committee for War
   Refugees from Holland,
   Belgium and France
Foster Parents' Plan for War
   Children
YMCA
Salvation Army
Seven Seas Club
International Commission for
   War Refugees in Great Britain
WVS
British Empire Union
British War Relief Society
Merseyside Council for
   Hospitality [154]

Despite Bessborough's good efforts, bickering among the welfare agencies continued throughout the war. To begin with, this was a turf war – a struggle to win public and private monies and extend influence – rather than an ideological battle. In October 1940, Lady Warwick complained that the statutes of the Société de Bienfaisance were contrary to the War Charities Act and thus the organisation should desist from performing its current activities, a charge that proved wholly spurious.[155] In mid-November, Lady Warwick visited the Foreign Office itself where she vented her anger at the Société, telling one official that they 'were an entirely bad lot, that they were in debt and wanted to collar any refugee money which they could'.[156] When the hapless official looked into the matter, he was told by Lord Bessborough, 'that Lady Warwick worried him daily about questions, and he was not anxious to encourage her'.[157] Not to be outdone, the FGB also moaned regularly about the CEAF, particularly the contacts it maintained with the Vichy consulate. Eventually, in 1941 some sort of truce was established when Bessborough decided that, in future, the venerable Société de Bienfaisance would cater for all those French who came to Britain before 10 May 1940, that is before the German invasion of Western Europe. All those who arrived after this date – mainly refugees – would receive help principally from the CEAF.[158]

This, of course, did not please the FGB, which considered it had been denied a valuable source of recruits. Nor did it please the Free French, which, in early 1942, attempted to muscle in on the care of refugees, turning the question of welfare into a more overtly political issue. On 27 January, Colonel Tissier criticised existing welfare arrangements on the grounds that they 'helped Vichy nationals too much' and did not 'do enough' for the Free French.[159] Interestingly, he also reproached the FGB. While Gaullist, it was 'a commercial opportunist movement', which had taken organisations under its wing that were part Vichy-funded, notably the Comité d'Assistance aux Familles des Soldats Français. To remedy the situation, the Free French had accordingly established the Assistance Sociale, under the direction of Pleven and Tissier himself. Linked to the Forces Féminines de la France Libre (FFFL), its role was to visit and report on the welfare of French nationals in the UK, although it was admitted that the training of its female recruits was meagre.

If Tissier had hoped that the women of the Assistance Sociale would monopolise the caring for all French refugees in Britain, and no doubt win some extra recruits in the process, he had not counted on the irrepressible spirits of Lady Warwick and Madame de l'Hôpital whose timeless sense of patrician and middle-class philanthropy was not going to pushed aside by such blatant politicking. By March 1942, both the WVS and the CEAF were becoming agitated at the behaviour of the forty ladies belonging to the Assistance Sociale.[160] A furious row soon broke out over the care of the unfortunate Madame I—, an elderly lady, unable to speak English, suffering from paranoia, and with a ten-year-old grandson to look after, who had been in the care of the Camberwell Borough British War Refugee Committee.[161] This body had arranged for the grandmother and child to be transferred to a convent at Baldock in Hertfordshire. In the meantime, two ladies of the Assistance Sociale had taken matters into their own hands, collecting the clothes of Madame I—while she was in hospital, but failing to give these to her, thus leaving the poor lady with nothing to wear when the time came for her move to the north of London. When the CEAF investigated the case, it was learned that the same two ladies had regularly called on the grandson every Thursday, taking him to a school in Victoria, despite the fact that the local War Refugee Committee had found him a place at a Roman Catholic school in Camberwell itself.

Before long, Lady Warwick had unearthed further cases of Assistance Sociale meddling, leaving several no doubt unwanted notes on Lord Bessborough's desk. From the West Country emerged the story of Mlle L— who had apparently visited refugees in Taunton, St Ives and Penzance making 'a nuisance of herself, stirring up ill-feeling and misinterpreting facts'.[162] From the north-west, it was learned that the Assistance Sociale were setting up *foyers* for refugees in the Manchester district, which had turned into political forums, and a quarrel had broken out over who should be responsible for transferring a refugee from Warrington for a three-week holiday in Torquay.[163] On the south coast, the Assistance Sociale had apparently promised refugees much, but had then failed to deliver.[164] Indeed, this became the focal point of Lady Warwick's criticisms. In April 1942, she reported that the Gaullist ladies of the Assistance Sociale had caused tremendous disappointment among refugees, and was alarmed to hear that the organisation was now in the hands of Capitaine Terré who had been originally earmarked for a post in the colonies.[165] Colonial conditions, the CEAF chief continued, were not the same as those as in England. Terré had clearly inflamed the situation by suggesting that French women preferred to be visited by French women. This was not the case, thundered Lady Warwick. They disliked 'women in uniform, spying in an authoritative manner', asking political questions, forcing people to join the FGB and selling the Croix de Lorraine. French refugees, she concluded, much preferred her own visitors, many of whom were, in any case French, belonging to the Sisters of Saint Vincent de Paul and the Little Sisters of the Poor.

At least in one area of welfare, such squabbling was largely avoided, maybe because the Free French were involved at an early stage: the case of some two hundred French schoolchildren. While nearly half of this number had arrived at the time of Dunkirk, the remainder had been attending the French *lycée* in South Kensington.[166] This latter group was initially destined to be rehoused at either Reading or Cambridge Universities, before a country house became available in Bedfordshire; ultimately they were transferred to Cumberland.[167] As to the remaining children, some thirty of these had been farmed out to families in London, but it soon transpired that another seventy-five had been studying at a preparatory school for the prestigious military academy of Saint Cyr, the equivalent of Sandhurst. Most of these boys, or rather young men, had expressed a desire to enlist with de Gaulle and they had been permitted to form a cadet corps. Their example had been seized upon by the Free French, and the British had cooperated in moving them to Rake Manor, near Godalming in Surrey where the headteacher of a neighbouring school allowed access to playing fields and class-rooms. Additionally the British Council provided two teachers, one French and one English, soon to be joined by a British adjutant and two NCOs to act as drill instructors. Such skills appear to have been needed as the discipline of the school was reputedly of a low standard and there was a fear that the Department of Education might be called in. Matters were rectified by the appointment of a new commandant, and the financial upkeep of the boys was assured through the support of the International Commission for War Refugees in Great Britain. Because of the Quaker leanings of this organisation, there was a worry that it might withdraw its assistance when the military purpose of the school became apparent, but this raised no fuss until it actually had contact with representatives of the Free French after which its spokeswoman, a Mrs Crawshay, said 'she would have nothing to do with de Gaulle or the cadet school at Rake'.[168] As the CFR noted, there was no doubt that, 'Mrs Crawshay had been extremely badly treated by Free French Headquarters.' Carlton Gardens was unmoved. Betraying his Bonapartist conception of education, if not his Bonapartist politics, de Gaulle had plans for the 'technicians' to remain at Rake Manor and for the 'intellectuals' to move elsewhere, possibly Lord Desborough's estate, Panshanger. It remains unclear whether this scheme was ever put into operation or whether the International Commission for War Refugees was coaxed back into assisting with the operation.

While much quarrelling went on over the responsibility for welfare, what evidence is there of political infighting among the refugees themselves? This was something that the British government was especially interested in. After all, to whom did they owe their loyalty? Whereas Belgians and Dutch refugees could pledge adherence to their governments-in-exile, governments still at war with Germany, the options for the French were nowhere near as straightforward. It was understood that it was hard for them to indicate a support for Britain. While Britain might have provided a safe haven, it had also failed to recognise their own government of Vichy as the legitimate French regime. Nor were MI5 and the Home Office oblivious to Pétain's appeal as a saviour, a man who was apparently doing his utmost to shelter his people from further suffering, although significantly refugees in Britain were never the direct subject of one of his many radio appeals.[169] By contrast, few refugees, apart from the West Country fishermen, appear to have rallied to de Gaulle. To many, he still appeared an unknown and rebellious quantity who did not even possess the wholehearted support of his British adherents. As a French Welfare report of early 1941 observed, 'A number of the more intellectual had adopted an attitude which, while violently anti-Vichy, approved of the FFL only as a military government, and did not associate themselves with it or with the Français de Grande Bretagne.'[170] Most, it was stressed, kept out of politics, although it was admitted that there were some two hundred who were deemed to be 'dangerous'. These observations are borne out in a wide-ranging report on French subversive activities, prepared by MI5 in January 1941. While the security services had taken an interest in one or two political circles that had formed within London, refugees were not singled out for special attention, and were clearly seen as less of a threat than other groups, including the Free French Navy, which was thought to harbour anti-British opinions.[171]

Because the relevant files have been either withheld or destroyed, it is difficult to say just how much of a threat politically active refugees posed. Three general observations, however, can be made. First, troublemakers among refugees were never regarded with the same degree of seriousness as those exiled soldiers and sailors whose Pétainist sympathies were thought damaging to the overall war effort. Second, politically suspect French refugees largely disappear from the picture after 1941, if French Welfare reports are to be believed, suggesting that they may well have been among the 500 or so civilians that were quickly repatriated (see below). Third, it should be remembered that, in the feverish atmosphere of 1940, fifth columnists were to be spotted every-where, and any eccentric or 'foreign' behaviour invited investigation. Not even government departments were free of exaggeration, the Vansittart Committee alleging that 500 fifth columnists had entered the country along with Dutch refugees in the spring of 1940.[172] It was because of these exaggerated fears that a small number of French refugees with German-sounding names and mixed parentage were interned. For example, the Jewish artist H—de B—R—, who later painted a series of panels for the Air Ministry, spent the first two years of the war in a camp, thanks to the fact that he had been born in Germany to a Dutch father, although his mother was French.[173] A similar case was that of a wine merchant A— M—, who had traded extensively in Britain before the war, and who was held at a camp near to Liverpool because of his German-Jewish mother; his father appears to have been either Swiss or French.[174]

It is in WRVS files, which the Home Office officials grew tired of weeding in the early 1970s, that a handful of other 'doubtful' French cases may be uncovered, testimony to the fact that the Service's tearooms constituted a mine of information for the Home Office and MI5, and proof that government really had little to fear. It is here that we read the sorry tale of one minor aristocrat, a refugee who had sought to supplement his income by going to sea, a move that foundered on the rocks of officialdom.[175] He had subsequently written a letter to the Ministry of War Transport asking that a supposed 'labour ban', forbidding him to take employment at sea, should be removed forthwith as this was his only suitable means of living. On enquiring into his background, the Ministry of War Transport discovered that he was 'an educated young man, of good birth and now penniless, born on 30 March 1912, in possession of a French passport', but clearly 'not the type to be found working as an ordinary seaman on a Merchant ship'. Nonetheless, for several months he had been attempting to sign on to Scandinavian vessels, and had made one trip of eight days, before his vessel was confined to port. In that brief voyage, he had created 'considerable trouble among the crew', although on investigation this mischief proved less serious than originally feared. He then left the ship without authorisation and turned up at the Norwegian consulate in a state of 'nervous tension', 'completely unnerved as a result of the recent bombing raid on Clydeside'. 'In hysterics', 'weeping freely', and speaking of the inevitability of being bombed, he had subsequently been entrusted to the WVS in Glasgow as he was clearly 'unsuited for sea work' and refused to join de Gaulle because news might reach the Germans who were holding his brother, the Duc de F—, as a POW.

Keen to pursue the matter, on 3 June 1941 Captain Alan Williams of French Welfare requested the WVS to provide further information about this man who was now resident in Inverness.[176] A confidential report, dated 26 June 1941, was subsequently obtained from Mrs B—, a canteen organiser.[177] Having invited him to tea on 25 June, she observed that he had work, but no money, and suggested 'he could make some extra cash by teaching French'. 'Being a French man, and by his own account a journalist,' she continued, 'he can talk at any length on any subject, especially politics, with shattering, if superficial logic.' 'If he had disturbed his fellow seamen' this would not have been with 'malicious intent', and she suggested he held his tongue when in the presence of troops or members of the YMCA as, 'not being journalists', they could not be expected to have the same 'detached view'. That he had come under suspicion might be attributed to 'his somewhat misleading voice and bearing', which was to be attributed to his Russian ancestry and ability to speak 'Apache argot' which 'communicated itself to some extent to his manners'! Concluding her report, Mrs B— came to the diplomatic conclusion that here was a man in need of 'a good doctor', especially if he was doing heavy manual work.

If such cases were typical, Britain – or for that matter de Gaulle – had little to fear from Vichy agents. Instead, surviving documentation suggests that the concerns of French refugees were less to do with politics, and more to do with their everyday existence.

Travail, famille, patrie: the everyday life of refugees

As Churchill braced the British people for 'blood, sweat and tears', Marshal Pétain offered his own compatriots a national renovation based on the values of 'travail, famille, patrie'. Such reactionary values were to be inculcated through a wholesale overhaul of French society and institutions: schools were to teach religious values; the Catholic Church was to be restored to a privileged position; peasants were encouraged to return to their farms; women were to give up work to take up their rightful positions as mothers and housewives; industry and agriculture were to be reorganised along corporatist lines; and the administration of France would mirror that of the *ancien régime*. These projects quickly came to naught, undermined by ministerial instability at Vichy, ideological inconsistency, rival projects based on technocratic values, the German presence, and material shortages. People quickly saw through the sham of Vichy propaganda and focused on the harsh reality of their own lives. Nonetheless, in many regards, their lives were still ruled by *travail, famille, patrie*: the need to find work to keep body and soul together; the pressure to keep families as one, especially given the upheaval of the *exode*, the taking of POWs, the introduction of discriminatory legislation and the eventual deportations to Germany; and the decision whether to abandon *attentisme* for resistance. Strikingly, the everyday lives of French refugees in Britain also revolved around the same three core issues of work, family and country, for not dissimilar reasons.

Famille

A primary concern was the family, or more particularly, the reunification of families and friends after the *exode*. The French writer Henri Amouroux has shown how, in 1940–41, the French press and official noticeboards frequently carried such communiqués as the following:

> Clermont Ferrand, 24 février 1941
>
> Le préfet du Puy-de-Dôme à MM. les préfets des départements de zone occupée et libre.
>
> J'ai d'honneur de vous communiquer sous ce pli des listes d'enfants perdus recherchant leurs parents ou recherchés par leurs parents.
>
> AUBE
>
> GRILLOT Françoise, 2 ans et demi (famille de 12 enfants), de Luyères, était avec sa soeur aînée dans un autocar avec des militaires du 173ᵉ R.I. La grande soeur a été très gravement blessée entre les villages de Dôches et Laubressel (Aube), s'est évanouie et, depuis ce moment, aucune nouvelle de la petite Françoise qui a disparu.[178]

Such notices bear an uncanny resemblance to those posted up, courtesy of the Ministry of Information, in refugee reception centres. The following enquiries were made at the King's Canadian School, Bushey Park, Hampton Hill, Middlesex:

> Jacques Le Cavorzin, age 12, probably evacuated from Boulogne by British destroyers. No news since beginning of May.

> Mlle Nicole Guillot, age 15, formerly of 145, rue de Saussure, Pirie. The

enquirer, a Mrs Borrias, is godmother to Mlle Guillot and is willing to take full charge of her if she can be found.

Mme Marie Battez and son Louis Battez, 14 yrs, formerly of 3 Impasse Clément, Le Portel. M. Louis Battez, on board P.95, *Notre Dame de France*, no news of them since May 16th.[179]

It is known that some 90,000 children were separated from their parents at the time of the *exode*, never to be reunited; one wonders how many were separated by the Channel.[180] Government officials were also inundated with a flurry of letters asking after friends and relations. It is in the papers of Noel Baker, a politician deeply concerned for the welfare of internees and refugees, notably Spanish Republicans evacuated at Dunkirk and immediately interned,[181] that may be uncovered several of these examples, notably a request from a South African, long resident in France, who was anxious to trace a Jewish companion who had landed at Falmouth in June 1940.[182]

Alongside discovering relatives, refugees were keen to find new homes. Memorandum WR1 had originally envisaged the requisitioning of empty buildings, which would then be reconnected to power supplies, and the property owners recompensed by central government funds. Yet it soon became obvious this would be a costly business. While the policy was not altogether relinquished, Memorandum WR2 favoured placing refugees with private householders and boarding houses. Whitehall appreciated, however, that this was a risky policy, and that families could not be forced to accept the refugees. Not only had the economic dislocation created by the war made people protective of their jobs, it had also intensified a mistrust of all things foreign, a mistrust that was even deeper following the fall of France. Buck has demonstrated the way unhappy memories of Belgian refugees in the First World War also created apprehensions. He quotes one Cricklewood resident who complained to Mass-Observation: 'They're a dirty lot. I used to be in a hotel as a chambermaid and we had to take them. They ruined all the nice rooms in no time, doing their shoes on the curtains, and all sorts of filthy things.'[183]

French refugees had cause to fear rebuff for other reasons. According to Mass-Observation, before 1939 British public opinion had been more sympathetic to Germans than it was to the French. 'The general stereotype of the French', it observed, 'particularly perpetuated in music halls and cartoons of the popular papers is of a voluble, excessively excitable, often slightly bearded, and somewhat lecherous personality.'[184] As war approached, sympathy for the French state grew, but not necessarily for the French people. As Philip Bell and Ralph White have demonstrated, in 1939 British propaganda made much of the Maginot Line and the solidarity of the Franco-British alliance.[185] The rapid capitulation of the Allied armies, the signing of the Armistice, the bombing of Mers-el-Kébir and the creation of the Pétain government, had thus dumbfounded public opinion. In West London, Mass-Observation observed that people were so 'thunderstruck by the magnitude of the catastrophe that they are as yet unable to express any coherent attitude to it'.[186] It was an attitude also observed by the American diarist and writer Mollie Panter-Downes: 'The people seemed to respond to the staggering news [French capitulation] like people in a dream, who go through the most fantastic actions without a sound. There was little discussion of events, because they were too bad for that'; she added that,'what the average simple Englishman believes about the average simple French man has only made recent events more difficult to understand'.[187] In this situation, it is not surprising that Mass-Observation occasionally overheard such comments as 'Bleeding French'.[188] The depth of such feelings was no doubt hardened by the fact that the Belgian, Czech and Polish exiles in Britain had quickly, and very visibly, thrown themselves back into the fight. There was thus a real anxiety among French nationals in Britain that they would become targets of hostility, a fear shared by Jean Monnet and his close associates who were initially scared to travel on the top deck of a London bus for fear of being recognised as French.[189]

It was, then, an uphill struggle for the local War Refugee Committees, local boroughs and relief agencies to seek out willing landlords, and it is to the credit of these agencies that they succeeded in housing 80 per cent of all London-based refugees with private householders. It is also to the credit of householders that most said 'yes' when asked to take in refugees, testimony to the fact that the British public was genuinely moved by the plight of these unfortunate civilians, and was able to put aside its considerable doubts about unreliable foreigners. Nonetheless, every now and again strings were attached to offers of accommodation. One letter from a nurse in Birmingham to the LCC asked for a refugee who could look after her two small children: 'We would prefer a woman about 35 or so. Good with children, and must be very clean. A person with nice habits, as I want the children to be brought up nicely. Dutch preferably.'[190] Another lady from Crystal Palace, on the advice of her worried daughter, offered places to two refugees in order that they could keep her company during the bombing.[191] Others were much more blunt in their requests, and were clearly out to benefit from the fact that billeting allowances were to be paid direct to landlords, thus creating a guaranteed income. One enterprising proprietor from Harrow Weald wrote to the LCC: 'Should you be requiring flats for refugees, I can offer you three ...'.[192]

It will be recalled that it had originally been the intention to house refugees outside London, but, in the event, most were dispatched to and housed in the capital, as the following WVS/Home Office statistics for August 1940 reveal. Of 23,431 War Refugee cards, the distribution was as follows:

In 16 London boroughs	8,256
In 4 Local Authorities in Essex	733
In 5 Local Authorities in Kent	1,014
In 15 Local Authorities in Middlesex	3,653
In 15 Local Authorities in Surrey	2,206
In 1 Local Authority in Herts	2
Total	15,864

(The remainder were housed in: two London and Middlesex boroughs, which had not sent in returns; five local authorities in Lancashire; three in South Wales; and two in Yorkshire.)[193]

Living in the capital, however, brought with it exactly the problems that had been foretold, especially when the Blitz started in earnest. After the initial bustle of the reception centres, refugees had been impressed by the calm summer skies that hung over London. As Mass-Observation discovered, within France refugees had been deeply disconcerted not so much by the fires that accompanied the *exode* as the Stukas passed ahead, but by the noise and sight of people panicking.[194] The tranquillity of London also struck other prominent exiles, including de Gaulle, and is frequently commented upon in the memoirs of the period. In the words of Robert Mengin, walking through London's parks on 19 June, 'The sky was of a purest blue. The lawns were still green. That silence, that purity, that freshness overwhelmed you with a sense of transience and fragility.'[195]

With the fall of autumn leaves came the fall of enemy bombs. The anxieties of refugees were eloquently put by Bastin, the representative of the Belgium government-in-exile, to Ministry of Health officials, in a meeting that November: 'A great many refugees had the terrible experience of German bombing in their country and it is not surprising therefore to hear most of them say that "they have left a hole to fall into another.'"[196] The question was next raised at the dreary sounding Fourth Meeting of the Welfare Sub-Committee for War Refugees held on 25 November 1940.[197] Here Bastin, in the stodgy language of the minute-taker, 'pointed out how difficult it is for War Refugees restricted as to their movements and not possessing the language, to find for themselves suitable rooms in safer areas. Those desirous of leaving bombed areas are being encouraged to make their own arrangements and for this reason, he raised with the Sub-Committee the question of setting up suitable machinery which would enable the refugees to be transferred in groups to selected areas.' The issue was handed over to the Central Committee for War Refugees, meeting on 20 November, which recommended to the Ministry of Health that certain classes of war refugee, 'women with children and generally family groups, including the men, when the latter had no employment in the London area', could indeed be moved to districts where there were no security objections and in which billets were likely to be found. Rather disingenuously C. F. Roundell, of the Ministry of Health, replied on 2 December 1940 stating that careful consideration had been given for the initial reception of refugees in the London region.[198] Billets elsewhere were so scarce, and general demands on accommodation 'so acute', that the minister 'has found it necessary to make a rule that foreign war refugees as such may only be billeted in those areas specifically set aside for their reception'. He feebly concluded that refugees could take advantage of evacuation schemes available for residents; alternatively, subject to police permission, they could move to any part of the country save those prohibited under the Defence Regulations. He carefully sidestepped Bastin's argument that refugees lacked both the language and the freedom of movement to seek out other homes, although those hurdles clearly did not deter those independent-minded French who were eager to shake off the unwanted attentions of the Vichy consulate.

The Blitz aside, life within refugee homes appears to have been bleak with many chores falling to the women, at least if WVS reports are to be believed. The following is an account of a large house in St John's Wood, just behind Regent's Park in London, which provided shelter to 11 families (7 Belgian, 3 French, 1 Portuguese) 42 people in all (26 adults, 16 children): 'Each family has one bedroom, children curtained off, plus one large sitting room.'[199] There was also a large sitting room shared by all:

> The women are divided in groups to do the house work, the cooking and the general tidying up in the house. The cooking is done by 3 women for

3 days running at the end of which they leave that department spotless for the next group to take on. The three women, who have had their turn at cooking, do their own small laundry and the turning out of their rooms. Once a week, all the women and bigger children knit and mend clothes sent from the Clothing Centre. We hope to get material soon for the people to make their own winter clothes. On Saturday morning, the hot water installation is turned on and everyone takes baths and does the heavier laundry. The catering is possible on a cheap basis because of numbers and allows us to be well in the grant.

As the report implies, refugees were desperately poor. Not only were they destitute when they arrived, they received little financial assistance from their British hosts who devised a fiendishly complex system of welfare support, worthy of the Victorian values of thrift and self-reliance. Whereas those in requisitioned properties (the minority) drew financial aid through the pre-war Prevention and Relief from Distress (PRD) apparatus, administered through central government's Unemployment Assistance Board (UAB), those in billets (the majority) were supported by the Public Assistance Committees (PAC) which fell under the control of the Ministry of Health. As already mentioned, PAC aid was paid direct to the householder who would then decide how to use this money. This had several consequences. First, it denied refugees any real independence of their landlord. Second, it kept them in a state of impoverishment. This was, in part, deliberate. The government had no wish that public monies should favour foreigners over the destitute of this country,[200] and there was clearly some public resentment that, at a time of national crisis, taxpayers' money was being spent on 'outsiders'. Nonetheless, as early as June 1940, Whitehall recognised that refugees needed some measure of financial independence, if only to pay for a cup of tea, and it was thus decided to issue 'pocket money'; it was exactly that.

Given that government paid so little, and given that the complicated welfare machinery it had set in place often failed to function smoothly, it is small wonder that refugees abused the system. On 6 May 1941, the St Marylebone War Refugee Committee, based at 128/134 Baker Street, reported to WVS that there were 107 refugees in the borough.[201] On investigating some 35 cases, 14 were guilty of 'systematic misrepresentation with the purpose of drawing full billeting allowances, Public Assistance, or evading a proportionate rental'. The cases investigated appear mainly to have been Polish, Belgian and Czech. There is no mention of the French maybe because, unlike their Continental counterparts, they could not defraud the system by drawing on benefits from their own government, subsidies that they then did not declare to the British authorities.[202] On several occasions, Colonel Tissier reminded French Welfare that the Free/Fighting French possessed insufficient funds to assist their destitute compatriots living in the British Isles although, as we have seen, this did not stop the Assistance Sociale from attempting to monopolise refugee relief, a project that was doomed from the start.

Ultimately, Vichy stepped in to assist impoverished French nationals, whether refugees or otherwise. In October 1941, the Consulate-General in Bedford Square suggested that the Reciprocal Advances Account, which had been set up to deal with the liquidation of the French government's assets and obligations in Britain, could be used to assist the needy, a gesture that was warmly welcomed by the Foreign Office as Vichy was doing something similar for British nationals in unoccupied France.[203] While wary that this money might be used to promote pro-Pétainist sentiments, reassurance was drawn from the fact that, in the case of refugees, it would be distributed through the auspices of the CEAF, a move which must surely have angered the FGB and Free French. Whatever the case, there was no denying the enthusiasm of the CEAF which, on the death of its Lady Warwick in 1943, chose to bring its good works to the attention of the Foreign Office.[204] By that stage, it was spending approximately £125 a month on refugees and the destitute of the French colony, the following list outlining certain of its costs:

Distributed cash	£22 7s 10d
Oculists bills	£5 5s 0d
Dentists	£5 4s 6d
Milk bills (children)	£6 9s 9d
Patent food	£6 15 s 0d
Clothes distributed (approx value)	£135 7s 2d
Visitors dealt with	75
Employment found for	11
Billeting troubles	7
General info (lodgings)	22
Red Cross messages sent	4
POW parcels sent	6[205]

Such voluntary work was no mean achievement, given that the CEAF no longer relied principally on subscriptions, but on private sources; it remains unclear whether it still benefited from the Reciprocal

Advances Account. In 1943, it boasted that it already possessed the cash to carry on for at least another 18 months,[206] something that could not have pleased the Assistance Sociale.

Travail

Despite the efforts of the CEAF, it was manifest that the only way in which French refugees could escape the poverty trap was to find employment. For its part, the government was also eager to draft as many able-bodied people as possible into the war effort. In February 1941, French Welfare reported on twenty men and women who were employed at the Burtonwood Aircraft Repair Depot in Lancashire and a similar number, over military age, who were attached to demolition squads.[207] Yet the government was far less keen on French refugees taking up their pre-war professions lest this created resentment on the part of British workers fearful for their own livelihoods. So it was that, in July 1941, the case of four Trouville boat workers arrived on Bessborough's desk; it was suggested that they had been sacked from a British shipyard because of trade-union pressure. On investigation, it transpired that they had been dismissed simply because their work had been 'poor'.[208]

This concern about the protection of British jobs might explain why the government made the employment bureaucracy for refugees so daunting, although we should never overlook the Victorian values of thrift and self-help that underscored the whole welfare apparatus. On arriving in Britain, refugees had been issued with a notice in their native language that explained the processing, housing and food arrangements.[209] Within 48 hours of arriving at their billets, all foreigners were to register at a police station where they would be issued with Registration Certificates. If refugees were able to work, it was their responsibility to report next at the local Employment or Labour Exchange. Explaining that there was a 'present need for skilled and unskilled agricultural workers, forestry workers and workers in saw mills', hardly the type of job to be found in London where most refugees were located, a warning ensued that refugees could not take on a job without a permit from the Labour Exchange and notification to the Ministry of Labour. All of this, even if explained in French, must have been terribly confusing to a refugee already disorientated by the experiences of the *exode* and arrival in a strange country.

Confusion naturally ensued. The WVS was especially concerned, and cited the case of a certain De P—, whom its volunteers discovered at CEAF headquarters: 'De P— said that he had first to apply to the police – then to the Labour Exchange – who referred the matter to the Home Office – who held it up indefinitely.'[210] Although De P— was unflatteringly referred to as 'just the sort of person for whom no one would bother to do anything', the WVS concluded, 'There is a great deal of dissatisfaction among the refugees due mostly to their not having anything to do except to make complaints. The effect is to demoralise them and the people among whom they are living.' On occasion, when jobs were found, they were not to the refugees' liking. In October 1940, Lady Warwick complained to the Foreign Office about the behaviour of one Mr O'C— from Denmark Hill, presumably an official at the local Labour Exchange, who had been pressurising French women to take jobs in a munitions factory.[211] He had been 'very rude and rigorous in his methods', continued Lady Warwick, explaining that these women were reluctant to accept such employment as they feared they might end up assembling bombs that would be dropped on France. The jobsworth at Denmark Hill was not alone in his uncaring attitude. In suburban Teddington, one French male, too ill to fight and suited only to a 'light sheltered job', had been told that he had to take up demolition work or forfeit his money. According to Margaret Green, an expert on African matters who had been lecturing the Free French on colonial administration, he had been so dispirited that he had sought repatriation, believing this was the only option left to him.[212]

Perhaps the most contented of the refugees were those fishermen and their families who had landed in the West Country. Some of these had been immediately shipped off to London for registration. There, they had been billeted at empty houses in Pembury Road in Tottenham, only a stone's throw from White Hart Lane, the home of Tottenham Hotspur, whose towering and ramshackle East Stand was being used as a mortuary.[213] Most had registered through the proper channels, several aligning with de Gaulle. In addition, the families were given a fortnightly 75s allowance, yet their great desire was to be allowed to return to Penzance to fish, and to join up with crews they had left behind; only, in 1941, after much pressure from French Welfare, was their request granted. When they eventually resettled in Penzance, they found homes waiting for them, but no furniture. In Newlyn, French fisherwomen reputedly announced that they could not sleep on straw mattresses: 'nous sommes pour de Gaulle, et de Gaulle ne couche pas sur la paille'.[214]

In the meantime, their compatriots in Devon and Cornwall had already begun to adapt to life in exile, although this process had not been without teething problems. Having spoken with the many London-based agencies concerned with the French fishermen, in October 1940 Henry Astor of French Welfare set off on a tour of the West Country to see what was happening with his own eyes.[215] Arriving first at Plymouth, he discovered no French fishermen as such, but only 'Frenchmen serving with the Royal Navy'. According to a Miss Waveney Lloyd, of the Ministry of Information, these men felt they were 'merely tolerated' and were not appreciated as an 'asset'. There was disquiet that English lessons, initially provided by the local authorities, had now stopped, and that the French were kept apart from British ratings, although one Frenchman had complained that he was being forced to work on a vessel manned by his own countrymen! In conversation with Captain Lush of the Admiralty, Astor learned that there were five French fishing boats still lying in the mud at Plymouth; these were, however, in a poor state, and needed considerable amounts of 'time and money' spent on them. In far better shape was a French sand dredger, the *Ingénieur de Jolie*, said to be in 'perfect condition', together with a complete crew, which Lush was keen to have transferred to Liverpool, lest the men set sail for France. For his part, Lush had faith only in those fishermen whose families were based in England, thus deterring them from flight. This point was echoed by Miss Lloyd who was keen to do everything in her powers to reunite the fishermen with their wives. As Lush grumbled, there had already been two cases of boats 'escaping and returning to France'.

Travelling next to Falmouth, Astor discovered a healthier situation with no 'idle boats' and fishermen 'perfectly contented living ashore with their families', occasionally deploying their boats for secret work on behalf of the Royal Navy. Brixham also presented an encouraging picture, with twelve men and four trawlers, earning a good living, happy that their families were ashore. At Newlyn, Astor was unable to meet any of the authorities dealing with the refugees, but was fortunate to speak to the fishermen themselves who belonged to some five boats. Once again, the fact that families had been reunited was a key factor in the contentment of the men, yet given the disadvantage that their boats were only suitable for long-line fishing, there was concern as to what would happen over the winter. Here, no arrangements had been made to support the men, via PAC, should bad weather prevent them fishing, as was the case in Brixham. Over in Salcombe, where many boats had first landed, only four fishermen remained, together with two vessels, the *Pourquoi Pas*, in need of repair, and the unfortunate *Sainte Isabelle*, which had recently sunk. Not surprisingly, the concern of the four remaining Frenchmen was with their material welfare. Unable to fish, they had turned their hands to salvage work, earning paltry wages for the Southern Salvage Company; with the arrival of winter all salvaging had ceased. Lonely and dispirited, with their families in France, these men did not hide their desire to return to their homeland.

Nearby, in Dartmouth, no fishermen remained, two abandoned boats the only sign of their visit. In better shape were the nine boats that Astor discovered in Southampton. These boasted semi-diesel engines and had been refitted shortly before the war by the French government on the condition that the vessels would be put to government disposal at a time of crisis; four had been fitted with mine-sweeping gear, which the Admiralty was now contemplating removing. Probably because of the importance of the port at Southampton and its place in the front line, considerable thought had been given to relocating these particular fishermen, and it was proposed that the boats and their crews be transferred to the west coast of Scotland for the purposes of herring fishing, although it should not be forgotten that the Admiralty also used such boats for spying purposes.[216]

All in all, the French fishermen appear to have been more contented than their Belgian counterparts where quarrels between French and Flemish speakers were rife. As Buck relates, these arguments did not merely reflect national differences but the fact that the Belgians owned numerous well-equipped vessels.[217] Such a catch proved too tempting for the Belgian government-in-exile, yet its ham-fisted attempts to assert authority over the fleet only succeeded in precipitating an almighty quarrel with the fishermen themselves, who were supported by Bryan Stevenson, a local fish wholesaler who doubled up as the Belgian consul. The Belgian government's insistence that the fishermen paid insurance premiums direct to itself only created further discontent.

For once, the French were models of good citizens.[218] The West Country fishermen rarely figure in the CFR minutes and, in 1942, French Welfare reported that the welfare of the remaining *pêcheurs* had passed from the CEAF to the Free French, although problems clearly remained.[219] While the Free French provided free medical attention, children under school age were catered for by the Child Welfare

Department; those of school age came under the aegis of the Ministry of Education. Perhaps typical of a male-dominated profession, it was the women's welfare that was being neglected, leaving the CEAF anxious to establish some kind of health insurance benefit.

One of the reasons why the Free French were happy to take on board the welfare of the fishermen was that most had rallied to de Gaulle and, in 1940, had readily manned his fledgeling navy. Nor did it go unnoticed that the coastlines of Devon and Cornwall were ideal landing grounds for those French men and women escaping metropolitan soil. Whereas in 1940–41 there had been a constant worry that the fishermen would abscond, in 1942 it was more likely that they would be welcoming and assisting boats escaping France. In September 1942 two such vessels, the *Marie Henriette* and *Muse des Mers*, carrying thirteen men, arrived in Newlyn where they were welcomed by representatives of the Admiralty, French Welfare and the Fighting French.[220] In 1940, these boats would have been confined to harbour, this time the welcome was far better coordinated, the police being 'very kind' and the immigration officers 'restrained'. A half-tin of tobacco was drawn from Customs for each man; the local WVS and PACs provided parcels of food and gifts; and French Welfare laid its hands on sizeable quantities of cider and beer. Entertainment was arranged on the quayside and, on 20 September, a party lasted from 6.00 to 9.00 p.m., to which local French fishermen and Free French soldiers were invited. Even the Gaullists could not grumble about the arrangements and, on 26 September, the newly arrived refugees were transferred to London for registration and security purposes, presumably for a stay at the Patriotic School, before being allowed to return to Cornwall.

Patrie

There were those who wished to travel in the other direction, and be repatriated to France. Such a sentiment was, in many senses, perfectly understandable. It will also be recalled that this was an extremely delicate subject, especially with the Free French. When Chartier of the Consulate-General asked that information about repatriation be broadcast on the BBC, his request was flatly turned down; the news was instead to be relayed through French charitable agencies, no doubt pinned on an obscure part of their noticeboards.[221] Moreover, repatriation involved making complicated shipping arrangements, always a hazardous business since the Germans refused to grant a safe passage even to boats flying a neutral ensign. Nonetheless, this prospect of being torpedoed by a U-boat did not prevent some 500 refugees from returning to their homeland in the immediate six months after the Battle of France. Quite who volunteered for repatriation is unclear. While it is likely that this number included troublemakers identified by the British, it also comprised those who simply could not adapt to a new way of life. As we have seen, Britain was a strange land with strange customs, the welcome of officialdom had not exactly been overflowing with charity, few refugees appear to have known the English language, the Blitz was a stark reminder that the war was not over, and there remained the prospect of a German invasion. Yet maybe the greatest attraction of repatriation was the prospect of being reunited with families. Such was the case of a handful of male refugees from Brest and Dunkirk, in the words of Chartier 'travailleurs sérieux', who had taken work in British factories and who were contemptuous of their fellow refugees who preferred to live 'dans l'oisiveté aux frais da la charité publique'.[222] More than anything, he continued, these men were worried about their families.

As the full extent of German oppression and of Vichy impotence became transparent, the prospect of repatriation must have become less than appealing, yet at least the rallying of large parts of the French empire to the Allied cause offered one possibility of returning to lands that were 'forever French'. Until the conquest of North Africa in late 1942, when a large segment of the Free French established itself in Algiers, this process appears to have happened in dribs and drabs and involved military, rather than civilian, personnel. However, in January 1943, French Welfare arranged for two parties of such people to travel to Madagascar via Fleetwood.[223] The local WVS, unaware of the nature of the parties, was accordingly instructed to meet these groups as they arrived from London in the North West, and to arrange for temporary billeting, food and necessary clothing.[224] As handwritten telephone messages in the archives attest, arrangements did not go as planned. Although WVS representatives were instructed not to meet the train, and thereby bring attention to themselves, news of the arrival appears to have been leaked, compromising the safety of the mission, although ultimately the party did manage to set sail without mishap.[225]

By this date, thought was already turning to the Liberation of Europe and the eventual repatriation of all French refugees.[226] De l'Hôpital records how:

in the tense weeks before D Day 1944, top secret plans were put in hand for the reception of persons who it was expected might escape from the coasts of Normandy and Brittany to seek refuge in England soon after the invasion. A large camp was set up in Sussex at Shoreham to be a Reception Centre, staffed by the military assisted by Ministry of Health officials, with WVS responsible for welfare and clothing. This camp was to be the first stop and after a stay of twenty-four hours each batch of refugees would be moved to London where a large centre had been opened comprising several houses in Onslow Square, in which WVS would again be responsible for welfare and clothing.[227]

While WVS officials set out for Sussex, these arrangements never went to plan; and, in the event, the process of receiving refugees bore an uncanny resemblance to circumstances in May–June 1940. To begin with, refugees did not arrive at designated ports.[228] Second, the numbers were fewer than predicted. In a letter to Lady Reading of 20 June 1944, Grace Peel of the Amis des Volontaires Français (AVF) remarked, 'I have heard from the French Consul General that so far the numbers of French refugees are very small and that at the request of the British authorities the work in connection with them is to be undertaken with as little publicity as possible.'[229] Third, there was squabbling among French agencies as to who should cater for the refugees. French Welfare soon found that it was having to act yet again as an arbiter between the AVF, CEAF, FGB and WVS. Fourth, given the launch of the dreaded V1 and V2 rockets, there were considerable doubts about London as a suitable depot. Lady Peel wondered whether it would be better to send refugees down to the West Country where the fishermen were settled: 'Little French colonies exist in Devon and Cornwall, our French Friends would therefore not feel so *depaysés*. The Free French Committee with the help of the British Council have established 4 or 5 little French schools where, after attending English schools, French children continue their French lessons and can qualify for their *Certificat d'Etudes*.'[230] As Peel continued, there were several offers of accommodation:

> I also heard when lecturing at Ilfracombe last week that schools were being circularised asking them to take two or more refugees. Miss Warrell Bowring of the Adelaide Girls' College was willing to take two girls if they were French ... Mr and Mrs Johnstone who have over a period of years collected a large family of about 25 French orphans and brought them over here in 1940 are willing to take 12 more. Mrs Johnstone would like some quite young babies amongst them. I can assure you the children would be wonderfully looked after. There are 12 children of all ages at

Silverton so the newcomers would feel at home. The Johnstones make
only two conditions: the children should be French and above all they
don't want to take any Mothers.'

In a final echo of the situation of 1940, public charity and goodwill
contrasted markedly with the parsimony and obduracy of government.
When, in August 1944, Lady Reading suggested to the Ministry of
Health the possibility of flying over two or three hundred 'delicate
French children', she received a lukewarm response.[231] Having sought
the opinions of the Ministry of Education, Board of Trade and Foreign
Office, a Health representative replied:

> Although, as a general proposition, the value of a successful international
> gesture of this sort can be very great, our feeling is that unless it could be
> extraordinarily well done, it might be as likely to result in complaint or
> misunderstanding as gratitude. Not only would the risks of bringing deli-
> cate or rickety children from the warmer climate of France to the rigours
> of an English winter be serious, but we have lost a great deal of the perma-
> nent accommodation which existed before the war in this country for
> such children and would have to find special ad hoc premises and staff.
> An even greater difficulty perhaps is that if we made such a gesture to
> France we could hardly resist pressure to do so successively for Belgium,
> Holland, Norway and, perhaps, even Poland, Czechoslovakia, Greece and
> Yugoslavia.[232]

In the event, some French children did arrive, but numbers were small.
Often they had been orphaned, and were being sent to these shores
principally for a break, rather than long-term settlement.[233] Many of
their parents appear to have died in concentration camps or had been
killed fighting in the Resistance.[234] Having rested in the Lucy Cohen
Convalescent Home in Hove, they spent two months among English
families before returning to France.

Brighton was, with Shoreham, one of the dispatch points from where
long-term French refugees were returned home. This was a task overseen by the usual bodies – French Welfare, CEAF and WVS – alongside
the newly established delegations of the French government. On 4
April 1946, the WVS regional officer for Brighton and Hove recalled
the scenes in late 1944/early 1945: 'They came through in 50–100 at a
time. I believe the WVS there did a grand job, and on occasions had to
house them for twenty-four hours if the boat failed to sail.'[235] Indeed,
the activities of the Sussex WVS drew warm thanks from Henri Frenay,
the famous resister, recently appointed *Ministre des prisonniers de*

guerre, déportés et refugiés.[236] So it was that the French refugees, unexpected and unwanted in 1940, slipped out of England, unnoticed and unlamented, in 1944.

Conclusions

It remains unknown how many refugees chose to stay in these isles at the end of the war. Surmise suggests it could only have been a few: possibly women who had married British men, and maybe some of those fisherfolk and their families who put down roots in the West Country. Of all the groups making up the French community in exile, the lot of the refugees was the most uncomfortable. In the first place, their arrival had not been foreseen. In the strategic planning for the war, both France and Britain looked on refugees of any nationality as an irritant that might upset carefully laid military plans. During the ensuing discussions, Paris largely triumphed. Keen not to upset its chief ally, and recognising the logic of the French position, Britain reluctantly agreed to accept the majority numbers of Belgian and Dutch civilians, and drew up contingency plans accordingly. Reading these documents some sixty years after the event, they possess a convincing, albeit cynical, logic. Whether they were ever practical remains dubious. Goodness knows how Britain would have coped with the 500,000 Dutch and Belgian refugees it had initially anticipated receiving. If such numbers had ever entered, it is tempting to believe that Britain would have experienced the same confusion witnessed in the *exode*, leaving the country vulnerable to a German invasion. In the event, the small numbers – Dutch, Belgian, French – that eventually arrived could be managed without too much bother. They never posed a security threat and cost little to the taxpayer, however much Ministry of Health officials might have grumbled. The refugees did, however, constitute a political target for Gaullist agencies, yet a majority of them were deeply reluctant to abandon their *attentiste* position. This reluctance was never truly appreciated by the FGB and Free French, which indulged in a constant struggle with the CEAF, a conflict that often degenerated into parish-pump politics. Disorientated, distressed and desolate, the principal concerns of the refugees were, above all, practical ones: housing; clothes; food; and employment. Accordingly, they kept themselves to themselves and made little attempt to mix with the British public. Undoubtedly, their 'foreignness' and their impoverishment set them apart, yet the overriding impression is that, after the fifth-column scare of May–June 1940, they elicited sympathy and support at least among the public, unlike their compatriots in the French army and navy who decided on early repatriation rather than serve with de Gaulle.

Notes

1 I am indebted to R. Ashton, *Little Germany. German Refugees in Victorian Britain* (Oxford, Oxford University Press, 1989) p. 25 for this observation about French refugees.

2 G. Orwell, *The Collected Essays. Journalism and Letters of George Orwell*, vol. 2, *My Country. Right or Left, 1940–1943* (London, Secker & Warburg, 1968), pp. 342–3.

3 J. W. Wheeler-Bennett, *John Anderson, Viscount Waverley* (London, Macmillan, 1962), p. 239. See too R. Tree, *When the Moon was High. Memories of War and Peace, 1897–1942* (London, Macmillan, 1975), p. 119.

4 CCC SPRS 1/182, letter from the Council of Austrians in Great Britain to Spears, 8 April 1940.

5 M. Kochan, *Britain's Internees in the Second World War* (London, Macmillan, 1983), p. 41.

6 G. Ciano, *Ciano's Diaries, 1939–1943* (London, Willian Heinemann, 1947) pp. 289–90.

7 Women's Royal Voluntary Service (hereafter WVRS) Box 198, Mme de l'Hôpital, 'The Story of the War Refugees in Great Britain, 1940–1947'.

8 On the WVS, see C. Graves, *Women in Green. The Story of the WVS* (London, Heinemann, 1948).

9 On the administrative confusion that accompanied the *exode* in France, see especially J. Vidalenc, *L'Exode de mai–juin 1940* (Paris, Presses Universitaires de France, 1957) and N. Dombrowski, 'Beyond the Battlefield. The French Civilian Exodus of May–June 1940', unpublished New York University Ph.D. thesis, 1995.

10 R. Titmuss, *Problems of Social Policy* (London, HMSO, 1950) and F. M. Wilson, *They Came as Strangers. The Story of Refugees to Great Britain* (London, Hamish Hamilton, 1959).

11 V. Caron, *Uneasy Asylum. France and the Jewish Refugee Crisis, 1933–1942* (Stanford, Stanford University Press, 1999).

12 B. Wasserstein, *Britain and the Jews of Europe, 1939–1945* (Oxford, Oxford University Press, 1979), L. London, *Whitehall and the Jews, 1933–1948. British Immigration Policy and the Holocaust* (Cambridge, Cambridge University Press, 2000) and C. Holmes, *A Tolerant Country. Immigrants, Refugees and Minorities in Britain* (London, Faber & Faber, 1991).

13 M. Buck, 'Feeding a Pauper Army. War Refugees and Welfare in Britain, 1939–1942', in *Twentieth Century British History*, 10 (3) 1999, 310–44.

14 P. Cahalan, *Belgian Refugee Relief in England during the Great War* (New York/London, Garland, 1982), pp. 501–2.

15 PRO HO 213 464 203/2/1, letter of Sir Russell Scott, Home Office, to George Chrystal, Ministry of Health, 17 March 1937.

16 PRO HO 213 464 203/2/8, untitled report of 18 January 1940.

17 PRO HO 213 1739 203/2/5, letter of Castellane, French Embassy, London, to I. A. Kirkpatrick, Foreign Office, 15 January 1940.

18 Cahalan, *Belgian Refugee Relief, passim.*

19 PRO HO 213 1739 203/2/7, letter of J. S. Stephenson, Dominions Office, to A. Maxwell, Home Office, 30 January 1940, containing a note on a conversation between the Duke of Devonshire and the High Commissioner for Eire.

20 WRVS Box 31, RFG 25/1, Part 1, Ministry of Health Memorandum WR1, and Circular 1983, both undated, plus Memorandum WR2, and Circular 1984, again both undated.

21 WRVS Box 198, Mme de l'Hôpital, 'The Story of the War Refugees in Great Britain, 1940–1947'.

22 WRVS Box 12, FC42, 'Report on the French Evacuation Schemes, 1939–1940', by Agnes Crosthwaite, Delegate of the British Federation of Social Workers to the Journées d'Etudes de Service Social, held at 6 rue de Berri, Paris, February 1940.

23 On such arrivals on the south coast, see T. Kushner and K. Knox, *Refugees in the Age of Genocide. Global, National and Local Perspectives during the Twentieth Century* (London, Frank Cass, 1999), p. 178, and E. G. Bennett, *In Search of Freedom. The Story of Some Refugees and Exiles who found a Haven in Bournemouth and District* (Bournemouth, Bournemouth Local Studies Publications, 1988).

24 Buck, 'Feeding a Pauper Army'.

25 Reading University Library (hereafter RUL) Box 605, 'The War and Us', the unpublished diary of J. W. Dodgson, vol. 4, 13 May 1940, p. 290.

26 London County Council (hereafter LCC), 'Report of the Civil Defence and General Purposes Committee, 10 June 1940', London County Council, *Minutes of Proceedings, 1940–1942.*

27 *Ibid.*

28 London Metropolitan Archives (hereafter LMA) MCC/WE/PA/2/41, address to refugees, undated.

29 LMA MCC/WE/PA/2/40, letter of E. Ridley, Director of Public Assistance, MCC, to town clerks, 14 May 1940.

30 WRVS Box 31, RFG 25/1, Part 1, 'Report on Meeting of War Refugee Train, from Mrs N—, 23rd May 1940'.

31 See J.-P. Sartre, *Iron in the Soul* (London, Hamish Hamilton, 1950), and René Clément's 1954 film, *Jeux Interdits.*

32 IWM 97/7/1, Diary of Monsieur Vila, 14 June 1940. Vila was eventually demobilised in the southern zone, joined the Resistance and ultimately made the dangerous passage across the border to Spain to join de Gaulle in London in 1942.

33 LMA MCC/WE/PA/2/40, anonymous press report, undated, probably May 1940.

34 I. Hay, *Peaceful Invasion* (London, Hodder & Stoughton, 1946), p. 25.

35 WRVS Box 198, 'Refugees interviewed in one morning, May 17th before regulations re Clearing Houses became strict', 22 May 1940.

36 PRO FO 371 24355 C7860/7559/17, letters of G— R—, 14 July and 4 August 1940.

37 LMA LCC We/M (1) Box 12, letter of A. L—, to Commanding Officer, Crystal Palace, 9 June 1940.

38 LMA LCC We/M (1) Box 10, letter of Mlle Le—, Crystal Palace, to Officer in Charge, King's Canadian Residential Open Air School, Hampton Hill, 9 July 1940.

39 Orwell, *My Country*, p. 343

40 MO 262, 'Third and Main Report on the Refugees', 11 July 1940. See too the earlier reports in MO 238 and MO 245.

41 *Ibid.*

42 *Ibid.*

43 WRVS Box 31, RFG 25/1, Part 1, letter of the Chair, WVS, to Brigadier-General H. L. Ismay, Committee of Imperial Defence, 25 May 1940.

44 LMA LCC We/M (1) Box 10, notes from the King's Canadian Open Air School, Hampton, Middlesex, no date (summer 1940?).

45 Interview with the author, London, 22 March 2002.

46 M-O TC25 Box 1 25/1/G, Report of 19 June 1940.

47 WRVS Box 198, 'On the Squads', 29 May 1940.

48 WRVS Box 198, 'Refugees interviewed in one morning, May 17th before regulations re Clearing Houses became strict', 22 May 1940.

49 CCC SPRS 1/136, Vansittart Committee, second meeting, 21 June 1940.

50 A. Gillois, *Histoire secrète des français à Londres de 1940 à 1943* (Paris, Hachette, 1972), p. 110.

51 A. Koestler, *Scum of the Earth* (London, Eland, 1991 edn), p. 10.

52 *Ibid.*

53 Gillois, *Histoire secrète*, p. 115.

54 J.-L. Crémieux-Brilhac, *La France Libre de l'appel du 18 juin à la libération* (Paris, Flammarion, 1995), p. 83.

55 Gillois, *Histoire secrète*, pp. 115–16.

56 PRO HO 213 1978 203/2/107, draft of a letter of Lord Swinton to the War Office, 12 December 1940. Life at the Oratory School is recounted in Kochan, *Britain's Internees*, pp. 7–8.

57 PRO HO 213 1756 212/1/39, letter of Spears to Newsam, Home Office, 9 March 1941.

58 PRO HO 213 1756 212/1/39, letter of Newsam to Spears, 13 March 1941.
59 *L'Accompagnatrice*, directed by Claude Miller, 1991.
60 PRO HO 213 1756 212/1/39, letter of Newsam to Spears, 13 March 1941.
61 PRO HO 213 451 201/18/10, various correspondence of May–June 1941.
62 PRO HO 213 1981 203/2/141, circular of 5 June 1941.
63 PRO HO 213 1756 212/1/39, letter of Immigration Officer to Home Office, 7 April 1941.
64 *Ibid.*
65 PRO HO 213 1756 212/1/39, letter of Immigration Officer of 29 March 1941.
66 PRO HO 213 1756 212/1/39, letter of 26 March 1941.
67 PRO HO 213 1756 212/1/39, letter of 19 March 1941.
68 PRO HO 213 1981 203 1981 293/2/141, document of summer 1941, Committee on the RVPS.
69 PRO HO 213 1756/212/1/39, letter of Liverpool Immigration Office to Home Office, 29 April 1941.
70 PRO HO 213 1756/212/1/39, draft letter of May 1941.
71 PRO HO 213 1756/212/1/39, undated minutes of the RVPS.
72 PRO HO 213 1980 203/2/137, Agenda for the Committee on the RVPS, 9 September 1941.
73 PRO FO 1055 9, letter of Bessborough to Morton, 7 July 1941.
74 PRO FO 1055 9, letter of Morton to Bessborough, 19 June 1941, to which is attached a letter from de Malglaive to Bessborough, 16 June 1941, plus a copy of the projected FGB letter, dated 16 June 1941.
75 Gillois, *Histoire secrète*, pp. 111–12.
76 PRO HO 213 1980 203/2/137, letter of MI5 to Miss Davis, Home Office, 9 September 1941.
77 PRO HO 215 505, Security Executive Committee on RVPS, 20 November 1941.
78 PRO HO 215 486, letter to Home Office, 22 January 1942, signature illegible.
79 PRO HO 213 1980 203/2/137, Committee on the RVPS, Minutes of Meeting, 12 September 1941.
80 PRO HO 213 1934 35/35/20, Note of meeting at the Home Office on 15 January 1942 to consider various questions regarding volunteers for Free French Forces. It should also be noted that there was a particular concern over the number of Gaullist volunteers from South America, principally Spaniards, who were motivated not by a desire to fight the Germans, but by a wish to escape poverty.
81 Gillois, *Histoire secrète*, pp. 112–14.
82 *Ibid.*
83 PRO HO 215 487, Report of Welfare Officer, RVPS, 25 August 1943.
84 *Ibid.*

85 Letter to the author, 2 March 2002.

86 J. Pierre-Bloch, *De Gaulle ou le temps des méprises* (Paris, La Table Ronde, 1969), p. 97. See too F.-L. Closon, *Le Temps des passions* (Paris, Presses de la Cité, 1974), p. 22.

87 Letter to the author, 2 March 2002.

88 See Crémieux-Brilhac, *La France Libre*, pp. 730–3 who recounts the infamous Dufour case, albeit in sympathetic terms. It is worth looking at the many cases of alleged Free French injustice in PRO FO 371 41908.

89 F. H. Hinsley, *British Intelligence in the Second World War* (London, HMSO, 1981, vol. 2, pp. 32–3, 192.

90 Letter to the author, 2 March 2002.

91 BBC Written Archives, Caversham. See M. Cornick, 'Fighting Myth with Reality. The Fall of France, Anglophobia and the BBC', in V. Holman and D. Kelly (eds), *France at War in the Twentieth Century. Propaganda, Myth and Metaphor* (Oxford, Berghahn, 2000), pp. 65–87.

92 C. de Gaulle, *The Call to Honour, 1940–1942* (London, Collins, 1955), p. 157.

93 WRVS Box 198, Mme de l'Hôpital, 'The Story of the War Refugees in Great Britain, 1940–1947'.

94 See M. J. Proudfoot, *European Refugees, 1939–1952* (London, Faber & Faber, 1957) and Wilson, *They Came as Strangers*, p. 238.

95 WRVS Box 31, RFG 25/1, Part 2, 'Examples of Difficulties or Failure in Tracing Refugees Known to be in this Country', no date (May 1941?).

96 *Ibid.*

97 WRVS Box 31, RFG 25/1, Part 2, Home Office circular of 9 May 1941.

98 *Ibid.*

99 It should be stressed that for the period 1933–39, most refugees came from Germany and Austria, some 60,000–70,000 in total. See A. J. Sherman, *Island Refuge. Britain and the Refugees from the Third Reich, 1933–1945* (London, Frank Cass, 1994, 2nd edn), pp. 269–72.

100 PRO FO 1055 8, War Cabinet, Committee on Foreign (Allied) Resistance, 10 August 1940.

101 WRVS Box 31, RFG 25/1, Part 1, Memorandum for Mr McCoy, signed by Mme de l'Hôpital, Refugee Department, 22 October 1940.

102 LMA LCC We/M (1) Box 9, 'Reception Centres for War Refugees. Nationalities and Admissions to 29th October 1940'.

103 PRO FO 1055 7, Comité d'Entr'Aide, no date (1941?).

104 See N. Atkin, 'France in Exile. The French Community in Britain, 1940–1944', in M. Conway and J. Gotovich (eds), *Europe in Exile. European Exile Communities in Britain, 1940–1945* (New York/Oxford, Berghahn Books, 2001), pp. 213–18 for much of the material in this paragraph.

105 M-O FR 262, Third and Main Report on the Refugees, 11 July 1940.

106 J. Sweets, *Choices in Vichy France* (New York, Oxford University Press, 1985).

107 H. R. Kedward, *Resistance in Vichy France. A Study of Ideas and Motivation in the Southern Zone, 1940–1942* (Oxford, Oxford University Press, 1978), p. 7.

108 H. R. Kedward, 'Patriots and Patriotism in Vichy France', *Transactions of the Royal Historical Society*, 5th series, 32, 1982, 175–92.

109 Bennett, *In Search of Freedom*, p. 9.

110 PRO HO 213 556 217/13/4, 'Daily Statement of Arrivals for June/July 1940'.

111 See H. R. Kedward, *Occupied France. Collaboration and Resistance, 1940–1944* (Oxford, Basil Blackwell, 1985).

112 WRVS Box 31 RFG 25/1, Part 2, 'Statistics of Foreign War Refugees in WVS Index up to June 1st'.

113 PRO FO 1055 7, Comité d'Entr'Aide, no date (1941?).

114 M-O FR 238, 'Refugees: questioning refugees about their reasons for leaving their country', June 1940.

115 PRO FO 371 28366 Z3936/123/17, 'Note' by Hankey, 11 June 1941.

116 LMA LCC We/M (1) Box 12, LCC Public Assistance Department, 'Supplementary List of Refugees for Whom Enquiries Have Been Made', no date (1940?).

117 WRVS Box 12, FC42, 'Lord Bessborough's French Welfare. Savoy Hotel (Under Foreign Office)', 19 August 1940, by Mme de l'Hôpital.

118 M-O FR 262, 'Third and Main Report on the Refugees', 11 July 1940.

119 N. Lytton, *Life in Occupied France* (London, Macmillan, 1942), p. 13.

120 Orwell, *My Country*, p. 342.

121 Crémieux-Brilhac, *La France Libre*, pp. 85–6.

122 PRO FO 1055 7, Comité d'Entr'Aide, no date, 1941.

123 LMA LCC We/M (1) Box 12, letter of A. L—, to Commanding Officer, Crystal Palace, 9 June 1940.

124 See W. D. Halls, 'Catholicism under Vichy. A Study in Ambiguity', in H. R. Kedward and R. Austin (eds), *Vichy France and the Resistance. Culture and Ideology* (London, Croom Helm, 1985), pp. 133–46.

125 M-O FR 238, 'Refugees: questioning refugees about their reasons for leaving their country', June 1940.

126 Wasserstein, *Britain and the Jews*, pp. 112–15.

127 De Gaulle, *Call to Honour*, pp. 95–6. E. Chaline and P. Santarelli, *Historique des forces navales françaises libres* (Vincennes, Service Historique de la Marine, 1989), p. 27, record that these men, 127 total, were aged from 14 to 54.

128 Crémieux-Brilhac, *La France Libre*, p. 86.

129 D. Thomson, *Two Frenchmen. Pierre Laval and Charles de Gaulle* (London, The Cresset Press, 1957), p. 163.

130 PRO FO 1055 4, 'Report on Visit of Mr H. Astor to West Country, Re Breton Seamen, October 18th–26th, 1940, Inclusive'.

131 PRO FO 371 24359 C7736/7736/17, note of 9 July 1940.

132 Hay, *Peaceful Invasion*, p. 11.

133 PRO FO 1055 4, 'Report on Visit of Mr H. Astor to West Country, Re Breton Seamen, October 18th–26th, 1940, Inclusive'.

134 PRO FO 1055 4, letter of E. Ashley Dodd, 6 August 1940.

135 Hay, *Peaceful Invasion*, p. 11.

136 PRO FO 1055 4, Extract from Report by Lieutenant Morrell on his visit to Torquay and Newlyn, no date (late 1940?).

137 Publication forthcoming under the aegis of the Wiener-Anspach Foundation, Brussels.

138 *Ibid.*

139 PRO FO 1055 8, Comité d'Entr'Aide.

140 PRO FO 1055 7, letter of Eric Chetwood Aiken, Secretary of CEAF, to Captain Williams, French Welfare, 10 November 1944.

141 PRO FO 1055 8, 'Report by the Sub-Committee on Welfare and Security of the French Community in the United Kingdom', February 1941.

142 WRVS Box 12, FC42, 'Les Français en Grande Bretagne', 11 September 1940. H. Goiran, *Les Français à Londres. Etude historique, 1544–1933* (Pornic, Editions de la Vague, 1933) records that the Société donated 500,000 francs to the needy in the course of the 1930s.

143 WRVS Box 12, FC42, 'Comité d'Entr'Aide aux Français en Grande Bretagne. Report on Visit by Mrs Pryce Jones and Miss Rae, 19 August 1940'.

144 PRO FO 1055 8, Memorandum on Lord Bessborough's French Welfare, no date (early August 1940?).

145 PRO FO 1055 8, letter of Duff Cooper to Lord Bessborough, 1 August 1940.

146 Lord Bessborough and C. Aslet, *Enchanted Forest. The Story of Stanstead in Sussex* (London, Weidenfeld & Nicolson, 1984), pp. 97–9.

147 Private information, Lord Williams of Elvel.

148 PRO FO 1055 8, Memorandum on Lord Bessborough's French Welfare, no date, early August 1940?

149 PRO FO 1055 8, letter of Bessborough to Sir Desmond Morton, 20 August 1940.

150 PRO FO 1055 8, letter of Morton to Bessborough, no date (late August 1940?).

151 PRO FO 1055 8, French Welfare. 'Report for 1941'.

152 Quoted in P. M. H. Bell, *A Certain Eventuality. Britain and the Fall of France* (London, Saxon House, 1974), p. 240.

153 To be found in PRO FO 371 24360.

154 PRO FO 1055 8, French Welfare. 'Report for 1941'.

155 PRO FO 371 24360 C135565/7736/17, CFR minutes, 3 October 1940.

156 PRO FO 371 24359 C12666/7736/17, note of 15 November 1940.

157 *Ibid.*
158 PRO FO 1055 8, French Welfare, 'Report for 1942'.
159 PRO FO 371 31990 Z897/231/17, note of 27 January 1942.
160 PRO FO 371 31990 Z2045/231/17, letter of Captain Williams, March 1942.
161 PRO FO 371 31990 Z2045/231/17, undated CEAF note on Mme I—.
162 PRO FO 371 31990 Z2045/231/17, note of Lady Warwick, January 1942.
163 PRO FO 371 31990 Z2045/231/17, note of 7 January 1942.
164 PRO FO 371 31990 Z2045/231/17, note of 6 December 1941.
165 PRO FO 371 31990 Z3172/231/13, Memorandum by Lady Warwick, April 1942.
166 The fate of the schoolchildren may be followed in CFR minutes in PRO FO 371 24360.
167 The life of the *lycée* in exile is recalled in Hay, *Peaceful Invasion*, pp. 158–64.
168 PRO FO 371 24360 Z13565/7736/17, CFR minutes, 5 December 1940.
169 See J.-C. Barbas, *Philippe Pétain. Discours aux français, 17 juin 1940–20 août 1944* (Paris, Albin Michel, 1989).
170 PRO FO 371 28365 Z629/123/17, 'Report on the Work of French Welfare' for the Committee on Foreign (Allied) Resistance, 29 January 1941.
171 PRO FO 371 28460 Z 792/792/17, Memorandum discussed by the CFR, 29 January 1941.
172 CCC SPRS 1/136, Vansittart Committee, second meeting, 21 June 1940.
173 CCC SPRS 1/182, letter to Spears, 16 May 1945.
174 CCC SPRS 1/182, letter of Spears to Newsam, 22 August 1940.
175 WRVS Box 12, FC42, 'Note' on A— de M—, Prince de L— and Duc de L—, initialled 12 May 1941.
176 WRVS Box 12, FC42, letter of Capt. Williams, French Welfare, to Lady Reading, 3 June 1941.
177 WRVS Box 12, FC42, Chief Regional Administrator, WVS to Captain Alan Williams, French Welfare, 12 August 1941, to which the handwritten report of Mrs B— is attached.
178 H. Amouroux, *La Grande Histoire des français sous l'occupation*, Vol. 1, *Le peuple du désastre, 1939–1940* (Paris, Robert Laffont, 1976), p. 400.
179 LMA LCC We/M (1) Box 10, letter of Dame Rachel Crowdy, Ministry of Information, to Superintendent, King's Canadian School, 16 July 1940.
180 W. D. Halls, *The Youth of Vichy France* (Oxford, Clarendon, 1981), p. 3.
181 CCC NBKR 4/590, contains the relevant correspondence.
182 CCC NBKR 4/579, letter to Noel Baker, 26 June 1940.
183 Buck, 'Feeding a Pauper Army'.
184 M-O FR 566, 'Public opinion about the French: Opinion trends, 1939–41'.
185 Bell, *A Certain Eventuality*, and R. White and P. M. H. Bell, *Our Gallant Ally* (London, Longman, 1994).

186 M-O FR 201, 'French Surrender', 17 June 1940.

187 M. Panter-Downes, *London War Notes, 1939–1945* (London, Longman, 1971), p. 75.

188 M-O TC25 Box 1 25/1/G, 'Aliens and the East End', 1 August 1940.

189 J. Monnet, *Mémoires* (Paris, Fayard, 1976), p. 169.

190 LMA LCC We/M (1) Box 12, letter, no date (summer 1940?).

191 LMA LCC We/M (1) Box 12, letter, no date (summer 1940?).

192 LMA LCC We/M (1) Box 12, letter of 26 May 1940.

193 WRVS Box 31, RFG 25/1 Part 1, Women's Voluntary Service, Memorandum on Refugees. Appendix VIII, Statistics, Enquiries and Nationalities, August 1940.

194 M-O FR 245, 'Refugees: questions about leaving the country', 'Second report on refugees, 4 July 1940'. Questions were put to 152 people: 103 men and 49 women. Asked what they found most alarming, the replies were as follows: Fire: 20 per cent men and 0 per cent women; noise, 25 per cent men, 92 per cent women; and people panicking 74 per cent men, 8 per cent women.

195 R. Mengin, *No Laurels for de Gaulle* (London, Michael Joseph, 1967), p. 69.

196 WRVS Box 31, RFG 25/1, Part 1, letter of C. F. Roundell, Min. of Health to G. C. Kullmann, Central Com. for War Refugees, no date (late November 1940?). Fortunate were those twenty French orphans, initially rescued by an English couple, found trembling in a cellar in Chelsea and transferred to the countryside. See Wilson, *They Came as Stangers*, p. 231.

197 WRVS Box 31, RFG 25/1, Part 1, 'Evacuation of War Refugees from Bombed Areas, 3 December 1940', signed Mme de l'Hôpital.

198 WRVS Box 31, RFG 25/1, Part 1, letter of C. F. Roundell, Ministry of Health to Chairman, Central Committee for War Refugees, 2 December 1940.

199 WRVS Box 31, RFG 25/1, Part 1, 29 St John's Wood Park House, no date (late July/Aug. 1940?). See, too, F. Raes, 'Female Belgian Refugees in Britain during the Second World War. An Oral History', in M. Conway and J. Gotovitch, *Europe in Exile. European Exile Communities in Britain, 1940–1945* (New York/Oxford, Berghahn Books, 2001), pp. 67–80. The smaller number of French refugees to Belgian makes it impossible to pose the same kind of questions as in this article.

200 WRVS Box 31, RFG 25/1, Part 1, Ministry of Health Memorandum WR1, and Circular 1983, both undated, plus Memorandum WR2, and Circular 1984, again both undated, give the details of all these arrangements.

201 WRVS Box 31, RFG 25/1, Part 2, letter of St Marylebone War Refugee Committee to Lady Gowers, WVS, 6 May 1941.

202 WRVS Box 31, RFG 25/1, Part 2, letter of Mme de l'Hôpital, WVS, to Dr Kullmann, Central Committee for War Refugees, 13 May 1941.

203 PRO FO 371 28368 Z9147/123/17, Minute of 27 October 1941.

204 PRO FO 1055 7, 'Monthly statement for May', dated 24 June 1943.

205 *Ibid.*

206 PRO FO 1055 7, letter from Georges Clerk to Bessborough, 16 March 1943, and 'Points for the Foreign Office', no date (1944?).

207 PRO FO 371 28365, Report of French Welfare to the CFR on 'The French Community in the UK' , 5 February 1941.

208 PRO FO 371 22367 Z6310/123/17, letter of Mack to Bessborough, 20 July 1941, and Bessborough's reply, 22 July 1941.

209 WRVS Box 31, RFG 25/1, Part 1, 'Notice to Refugees'.

210 WRVS Box 12, FC42, 'Comité d'Entr'Aide aux Français en Grande Bretagne. Report on visit by Mrs Pryce Jones and Miss Rae, 19 August 1940'.

211 PRO FO 371 28368 Z9132/123/17, Minute of 11 October 1940.

212 CCC NBKR 4/261, letter of Margaret Green to Noel Baker, 24 January 1941, in which she cites another case where the man in question had been better treated only when he produced his *carnet militaire* to show he had been demobilised from the Free French.

213 PRO FO 1055 4, letter from Lady Warwick, CEAF, to Captain Williams, French Welfare, 11 October 1940.

214 Wilson, *They Came as Strangers*, pp. 230–1.

215 PRO FO 1055 4, 'Report on Visit of Mr H. Astor to West Country, Re Breton Seamen, October 18th–26th, 1940, Inclusive'.

216 See S. Brooks Richards, *Secret Flotillas. Clandestine Sea Lines to France and French North Africa, 1940–1944* (London, HMSO, 1996).

217 M. Buck, unpublished paper.

218 See Wilson, *They Came as Strangers*, pp. 230–1.

219 PRO FO 1055 8, notes for 'Report on French Welfare for the Year 1942'.

220 PRO FO 1055 12, Report by Captain C. Peebles-Chaplin, September 1942.

221 PRO FO 371 24358 C13210/7559/17, letter of Brennan to Chartier, 30 November 1940.

222 PRO FO 371 24358 C13966/7559/17, note of 26 December 1940.

223 WRVS Box 12, FC42, letter of Capt. Williams, French Welfare, to Mme de l'Hôpital, WVS for Civil Defence, 14 January 1943.

224 WRVS Box 12, FC42, letter of Assistant Regional Administrator, Region 10, to Miss Foster Jeffrey, 12 January 1943, 'Reference the impending job at F. Centre, with corresponding arrangements to be made at the L. Centre'.

225 WRVS Box 12, FC42, letter of Regional Administrator to Mrs Goldney, WVS, 19 January 1943.

226 PRO MH 76 519, contains details of this initiative.

227 WRVS Box 198, Mme de l'Hôpital, 'The Story of the War Refugees in Great Britain, 1940–1947'.

228 WRVS Box 31, RFG 25/1, Part 2, letter of Deputy Vice-Chairman, WVS, to Miss Florence Horsbrugh, Ministry of Health, 28 July 1944.
229 WRVS Box 31, RFG 25/1, Part 2, letter of Lady Peel, AVF, to Lady Reading, WVS, 20 June 1944.
230 *Ibid.*
231 WRVS Box 31, RFG 25/1, Part 2, letter of Ministry of Health official, signature illegible, to Lady Reading, 29 August 1944.
232 WRVS Box 31, RFG 25/1, Part 2, letter of Ministry of Health official, signature illegible, to Lady Reading, 13 September 1940.
233 WRVS Box 12, FC42, letter of F. R. Hoyer Millar, Foreign Office, to Lady Hillingdon, WVS, 19 January 1946.
234 WRVS Box 12, FC42, letter of Commandant Boury, representative of the Comité d'Entr'Aide aux Français to Lady Reading, 1 March 1946.
235 WRVS Box 12, FC42, note from Miss Hornby, Region 12, 4 April 1946.
236 WRVS Box 12, FC42, letter of Frenay to Mr J. Poyser, General Inspector, Minister of Health, 20 November 1944.

3

The conflict of exile: servicemen

Qui se pourrait d'elle laisser
Toujours sa beauté renouvelle.
Dieu! Qu'il la fait bon regarder,
La gracieuse, bonne et belle!

Charles, Duke of Orléans (1391–1465)[1]

In late January 1941, French Welfare concluded that the most urgent problem it had confronted during the first six months of its existence was not the handling of refugees, but what to do 'with the considerable number of French soldiers, sailors and merchant seaman in this country who had not immediately expressed their willingness to join General de Gaulle'.[2] These men were, of course, the majority. When, on 18 June 1940, de Gaulle emitted his 'call to honour', the response was feeble, a fact acknowledged by even the most unreconstructed of the general's hagiographers. It has been calculated that, in mid-August 1940, the numbers of Free French, 'volunteers of the first hour', in both Britain and across the world, numbered approximately 8,000.[3] It is, though, these initial *ralliés* whose stories have been told over and over again, both by historians and by themselves.[4] History remembers the winners, and there is little desire to recall the pitiful history of the remainder of the French armed forces during the war years, except to recount how those soldiers, sailors and airmen, principally in the colonies, eventually rediscovered a dignity and retrospective glory by rallying to de Gaulle. Unquestionably, it was these colonials that transformed the Forces Françaises Libres (FFL) into a truly formidable force, enabling it to play an important role in the ultimate defeat of Nazism. By contrast, the rump of the French forces in metropolitan France had an undistinguished war. According to the terms of the Armistice, Vichy was left with an army of 100,000, men whose job was primarily the maintenance of order, and whose every action was closely watched by the Germans. Determined to maintain the principle of conscription, Vichy was compelled to create a series of youth movements, principally the Chantiers de la Jeunesse and the Compagnons de France, which espoused the values of both Baden-Powell and the National Revolution, ideals that are not as dissimilar as might be imagined. The air arm was a shadow of its former self, while the navy, the most advanced section of the French military, had an ignominious campaign: sunk by the British at Mers-el-Kébir in July 1940, and scuttled by the French themselves at Toulon in November 1942.

To read the many histories of the French armed forces during the Second World War is, then, all too often to read the history of the Free French.[5] Little mention is ever made of the sizeable numbers of French sailors and soldiers, over 10,000 in total, stranded in camps in Britain at the time of the defeat, and who largely chose repatriation over enlistment in the Free French or action with the British services.[6] They are alluded to briefly in de Gaulle's memoirs, as one might refer to an embarrassing relative at the dinner table, before they are passed over in favour of another subject.[7] As noted in Chapter 1, de Gaulle conveniently blamed their unwillingness to join him on Mers-el-Kébir, and suggests that the British were not as supportive as they could have been in his recruitment drive. There is a measure of truth in these claims, in particular the accusations against London. The British government had serious doubts about the reliability of French servicemen and their worth in battle. Yet, as will be seen, the reasons behind the failure to rally were far more complicated; and it is significant that the attitudes of many exiled servicemen reflected those of their comrades-in-arms in metropolitan France.[8]

Arriving: Narvik, Dunkirk, Compiègne and Oran

In explaining why large numbers of French servicemen were to be found in Britain during the summer of 1940, it is necessary to read the roll call of Narvik, Dunkirk, Compiègne (where the Franco-German Armistice was signed) and Mers-el-Kébir, hardly the most illustrious episodes in French military history. In Norway, on 8–9 April 1940, a joint Franco-British naval force battled with a German expeditionary mission in an attempt to disrupt the flow of Swedish iron ore that passed through the port of Narvik on its way to Hitler's factories. Although this episode prompted the Norwegians to abandon their neutrality in favour of the Allies, the operation was a disaster for the French and British, because of woeful military preparations and, most importantly, because of insufficient air cover.[9]

As French ships slipped into British harbours, transporting seriously wounded troops from the abortive Norwegian campaign, far greater numbers of retreating servicemen were gathering on the beaches of Dunkirk.[10] Initially, on 27–29 May, it was principally the BEF that was being ferried across the Channel, prompting Darlan to remark acerbically, 'The British Lion seems to grow wings when it's a matter of getting back to the sea,' a sentiment that was shared by several of his countryfolk at the time, and one that has not altogether disappeared since.[11] In truth, the French had been kept fully informed of the Royal Navy's evacuation plans, but had anticipated Dunkirk holding out for longer, and were disadvantaged in that the bulk of their own ships were in the Mediterranean.[12] Aware that British troops were withdrawing in an orderly fashion, whereas their French counterparts were being left to flounder in the waves, and conscious that an overstretched RAF could not provide the air cover demanded by Reynaud, Churchill attempted to save the Anglo-French alliance by agreeing that French and British troops should be evacuated in equal numbers.[13] This decision had a dramatic impact. Whereas, by 31 May, some 150,000 British soldiers had been removed in comparison to a paltry 15,000 French, at the close of so-called Operation Dynamo, on 4 June, the total stood at 224,320 British and 141,842 others, principally French.[14] Such statistics were cold comfort to those 30,000–40,000 French soldiers who remained behind to protect the bridgehead, and who spent the next five years in German prisoner-of-war camps.

The overwhelming impression is that Dunkirk evacuees, of all nationalities, were given a hero's welcome on their arrival in Britain, this to the astonishment of some French soldiers who feared that they would be accused of letting Britain down. Such was the anxiety of a Lieutenant 'B', later killed while fighting with the Free French, who was overwhelmed by the kindness shown to him by the British public.[15] Indeed, the cheering crowds that Orwell witnessed at Victoria and Warterloo were replicated elsewhere. In a wide-ranging thesis on Franco-British relations during 1940, Joan Delin recalls several similar incidents in Southampton where schools were given over to housing the men.[16] Some sixty miles north in Reading, chemistry lecturer Dodgson was so impressed by the manner in which the veterans were received that his diary quotes extensively from one eye-witness account, published in *Home and Country*, on the scenes in southern England during late May/early June:

> Upon arrival I found that trains were pulling up at our little station laden with tired and hungry men and it was our job to cut up sandwiches for them so tables were erected and preparations made for catering on a very large scale. Never have I seen at one place so many loaves, tins of corned beef, eggs, sausages, fruit, etc. Trains were sometimes arriving every ten to fifteen minutes so that we had to work hard to ensure every man having a cup of tea and something to eat. As time went on, helpers came from neighbouring villages and we worked in shifts sometimes 40 at a time. The food was packed in large boxes and taken to the station in lorries. At times, we were held up for bread and butter but in no time such consignments arrived and we carried on. At Headcorn alone, 3,600 loaves, 8,000 eggs and 100,000 cups of tea issued between Wednesday and Friday.[17]

Such morale-stirring accounts were commonplace in the British press that summer. One of the more unusual stories was that included in *The Times Educational Supplement* of 15 June 1940. It reported how the playing fields of a London secondary school adjoined the main line from the south coast to Victoria. For nearly a whole day, trains carrying French troops rescued at Dunkirk were held up outside the school.[18] It was not long before the boys had made contact, scampering down 'the slippery embankment' to offer gifts of sweets, chocolates and biscuits to 'these bearded, tired-eyed and dusty men'. By the afternoon, 'convoys had been organised, bringing water and cakes and fruit'. 'Nous n'oublierons jamais cet accueil chaleureux. Merci!', scribbled one soldier on the back of a packet of cigarettes. Once disembarked in London, there were further gestures of kindness. Helen Long, who later acted as an interpreter among other duties for de Gaulle and his wife, recalls how her Paris-born father was so 'devastated' by the collapse of France that he set off to Olympia, where many of the Dunkirk veterans and early Free French supporters were gathering, his car overflowing with *vin ordinaire*.[19] He later arranged for such troops to receive loaves of bread in the shape of baguettes, a gesture that deeply touched de Gaulle himself, who described it as 'gentil'.[20] In another show of solidarity, the Palladium Theatre, then showing the play *Garrison Theatre*, reinserted the scene in which French soldiers marched through the Arc de Triomphe, to the sound of the 'Marseillaise', the display having been dropped at the time of Dunkirk.[21]

As with the *exode*, it is the eye-witness accounts that convey the horror that was an integral part of the Dunkirk evacuations. The following is an extract from the unpublished diary of Mlle Toutain, a nurse attached to the 68th French Infantry Division, who later became one of the founding members of the Corps Féminin of the FFL:

> As we got nearer the North, refugees and cars were coming in an endless stream. French army lorries were abandoned, no more petrol! ... Wounded French and English soldiers sitting on the side of the road begged us for a lift. But we had no room, we were stocked with supplies. Suddenly a terrific roar and screaming of a plane overhead made us stop. I was just about to get down, when machine-gun fire started. A German Stuka dive-bomber was behind us. We decided to move on. The screaming of the plane was heard again, and at the same time we saw it disappear in front of us, then a terrific explosion shook the ambulance, almost lifting it up. Jacqueline (my friend and driver, to die at Dunkirk) stopped, we got out and looked around. We then saw that two bombs fell in the road just missing us, I made the sign of the cross but my driver, her hands on her hips said: Not very good aim. I could have choked her! ... We then resumed our route.[22]

Despite such bravery, there was no disguising the fact that the morale of French troops was extremely poor on arrival in England. As Robert Mengin observed, 'For us, the French, ... Dunkirk was the collapse of France. For the English, it was a battlefield like any other.'[23] Nor was it likely British propaganda would play well with the French. As Philip Bell observes, broadcasts such as that of J. B. Priestly's in which he urged the steamers *Brighton Bell* and *Gracie Fields* to leave 'that innocent foolish world of theirs to sail into the inferno' merely caused offence.[24] Helen Long remembers how the mood among the French, even at the improvised Gaullist barracks at Olympia, was downcast.[25] For her part, Gwen Rennie, a nurse stationed at a hospital in 'the south of England' recalls how, after Dunkirk, her ward was inundated with French soldiers and Moroccans, 108 men altogether, only a few of whom were injured.[26] Clutching German propaganda leaflets, they 'pelted' the nurses with bread and butter at teatime, and it was not long before a fight broke out between the Moroccans and a French soldier. Rennie was appalled to learn that these men had looted on their way from Dunkirk, and she thus refused a gift of a pair of gloves. When the day came to be repatriated, she records that only two elected to join de Gaulle. To be fair, the overwhelming majority of French troops were never given that choice as, on arriving in Britain in early June, they were immediately ferried back to France, via Normandy or Morocco, to carry on the battle, the intention being 'to stabilise the fighting front on the Seine, Lower Normandy and the Marne, thus repeating the September 1914 miracle'.[27] Not all were keen to return to the fray, recognising the battle lost. One such was Pierre Veydert, but for very different reasons to his comrades.[28] An ardent Anglophile and a truly exceptional figure, he was keen to stay on British soil where he believed he could be of most use in the fight against Germany. Ordered back to France, he later became part of the same Parisian resistance network as Samuel Beckett, and was deported to Mauthausen, where he lived out the war, perfecting his command of the German language.[29]

The soldiers remaining in Britain were soon to be joined by sailors and merchant seamen. At the time of the Armistice, several French ships had taken refuge in British harbours. As with the Dunkirk evacuees, the mood among these men was not good. In a telephone call with his son David, who was serving with the marines in Portsmouth, Lord Astor learned that 'discord' and 'fighting' on the ships was commonplace.[30] The younger sailors, worried about their families and economic prospects, were already keen to go back to France. Troubled by this state of affairs, on 30 June Astor addressed a letter to Dr Alexander, a minister at the Admiralty, in which he recalled how, in the West Country, there were several thousand sailors, some of whom had been there weeks, others a matter of days.[31] On the whole, the 'men and petty officers are sounder in their views about the future than the officers'. The officers' sense of discipline had made them more likely to follow the orders of the Bordeaux government. To win over the ratings, Astor continued, there was a vital need to settle any terms of enlistment in the British armed forces. Overtures also needed to be done through indirect propaganda, difficult as the officers forbade any 'direct approach' to the men; a promise of good pay; and generous hospitality on the part of the local community, especially French-speakers, if possible 'intelligent French ladies'.

Such advice fell on deaf ears. In the aftermath of the Armistice, the British government was deeply concerned about the future of the French fleet and was utterly unconvinced by French reassurances over its future. Nor did it set much store by recruiting among the French sailors who were viewed as highly unreliable, even though rumours quickly grew among an agitated public that they would enlist in large numbers with de Gaulle.[32] So it was that Churchill ordered the shelling of those vessels anchored at Mers-el-Kébir to prevent them falling into German hands, an episode that cost the lives of some 1,200 sailors.

After the decision to attack was taken, Spears recalls how he drove his car through Hyde Park, where he saw French sailors with red pompons on their caps playing games with some English girls, prompting him to think of those other French sailors wearing the same uniform in their ships off the coast of Africa, 'What would happen to them tomorrow?'[33] As de Gaulle himself recalls, the British coordinated this operation with an occupation of 'French warships which had taken refuge in British ports'; their officers and crew were 'taken ashore and interned – not without some bloodshed'.[34] All in all, some 130 French ships were seized in this manner, among them 2 battleships, 2 light cruisers, 8 destroyers and 5 submarines.[35]

Hardly the most natural of Anglophiles at the best of times, these seamen bitterly resented the manner in which they had been rounded up. In September 1940, French Welfare officials, visiting camps in the Liverpool area, reported that a recurring complaint 'was the way in which these officers and men were removed from their boats', often early in the morning 'at the point of bayonet' and, virtually 'frog marched', perhaps an unfortunate turn of phrase, 'down the streets to be locked up in some jail or other'.[36] Much controversy centred on whether the officers had been bundled into Black Marias. Such officers further alleged that they had 'been looted by the British soldiery'. Subsequent investigations, however, had 'proven that a considerable amount of loot has been found in the possession of the French themselves'. When, earlier in 1940, the sailors' camp at Aintree was inspected, a 'good deal of mess plate' was uncovered along with 'the personal belongings of officers'.[37] Apart from seizing the ships themselves, another thing that the British claimed was a sizeable quantity of red wine, some 7,000 barrels in total discovered on board the vessels, and which was subsequently distributed among Gaullist forces.[38] Perhaps most important, Britain seized vital French naval codes, which created intelligence problems at Vichy.[39]

There is little doubt, however, that the French sailors were treated in a rough fashion. Whereas at Dundee, the commander of the submarine *Rubis* was approached in a polite manner, possibly because his men had already opted for de Gaulle, matters were different elsewhere. Warren Tute records how, on 3 July, the two French submarines *Ondine* and *Orion* were docked at Portsmouth to undergo repairs.[40] Their crews resting on shore, the two sentries were easily overpowered and the boats seized. The captains, Vichot of the *Orion* and Bourgine of the *Ondine*, were not informed beforehand of British intentions and were brusquely summoned to Fort Blockhouse, the British submarine head-quarters, where, as Tute writes, they were presented with an ultimatum:

> The Franco-German Armistice terms require the French fleet to be disarmed under the German-Italian control. The British government is aware that the Germans have already broken their word. Under these circumstances therefore we very much regret – but you will realise that we have been so ordered – to require you to choose either to continue to fight loyally and wholeheartedly on the side of Great Britain and its Empire or to return to France.[41]

Not allowed to contact their senior officer, the two captains put the above choices to their men, Vichot opting for repatriation, and his junior colleague Bourgine siding with de Gaulle, together with a majority of the ratings. Further along the coast at Plymouth, the crew of the gigantic submarine, *Surcoeuf*, reputed to be the largest vessel of its type in the world, had no time for Gaullist overtures and actively resisted the British boarding party. Two Royal Navy officers, Lieutenant-Commander Sprague and Lieutenant Griffith, were killed, along with a French engine-room officer.[42] Three other Frenchmen were wounded. Apparently, the man responsible for the deaths of the British seamen was, at the last minute, hauled off the SS *Djenne*, as she prepared to set sail from Liverpool in autumn 1940 with a cargo of repatriated French sailors on board.[43]

Although this was the only act of bloodshed in the takeover of French ships, it created great resentment both at Vichy and among the French in Britain. In May 1941, Admiral Darlan delivered a speech in which he proclaimed, 'Au mépris de toutes les lois de la mer l'amirauté britannique a pris l'habitude en ce que concerne la France, de transformer le droit de visite en droit de prise, même quand les bâteaux sont vides.'[44] Within Britain itself, naval servicemen were always going to be prickly customers. Under the military discipline and Pétainist influence of their officers, the soldiers and sailors had been deeply dismayed by the events of May–June 1940, and were quick to blame London for their misfortune. The demoralising speed of the German advance had reactivated suspicions, present during the phoney war, that the British had not contributed enough to the war effort; the British then had the temerity to rescue the bulk of the BEF on the back of the French army. In these circumstances, an armistice, concluded by the most patriotic and celebrated of French soldiers, had been the only solution; yet perfidious Albion had once again behaved in an ungallant fashion, shelling the fleet at Mers-el-Kébir and interning French sailors in British ports in the most heavy-handed of operations. The manner in which the British subsequently looked after those servicemen exiled from France only exacerbated their discontent.

Counting heads: *les effectifs*

Counting the heads of the servicemen who discovered themselves in Britain during the summer of 1940 is fraught with the same kinds of difficulties as assessing the numbers of refugees. Official figures often contradict one another, and are frequently at variance with those cited in such authoritative works as Crémieux-Brilhac's *La France Libre*. There are several reasons for this. As we have seen, the majority of men rescued at Dunkirk were quickly returned to France. Of the 141,000 rescued at the start of June, 45,000 remained towards the end of that month.[45] Despite the efficiency with which the evacuations had been conducted, it was difficult keeping tabs on soldiers as they were transported across the country to rejoin the battle. Some degree of repatriation also appears to have been conducted immediately after the Armistice, although this proved increasingly difficult especially when, on 24 July, an E-boat sank the *Meknès*, transferring some 1,200 men to France, at the cost of 400 lives.[46] It is further apparent that those who rallied to de Gaulle did not do so in one mad rush; they came in dribs and drabs. To compound matters, it appears that the majority of servicemen were not 'interned' in the strict sense of the word, as was often alleged, but were held in makeshift camps from which it was not difficult to abscond; at White City, Léon Wilson recalls being able to move out of the camp almost at will, on one occasion walking as far as Charing Cross Road; there he went to a dance at the Astoria Theatre where he met his future wife.[47] He later walked as far as Shoreditch, to his fiancée's house, to continue the courtship. Elsewhere, local police authorities reported on French soldiers wandering around the countryside, without any papers, and with far less purpose than Monsieur Wilson. The final complication in counting heads is the question of desertion. To judge from Home Office files, this was commonplace in both the Free French and the Vichyite forces in Britain, although the full scale of the problem is never disclosed.[48]

A memorandum in the files of French Welfare, on the size of the Gaullist forces, reveals both the difficulty in drawing up precise statistics in general and the precariousness of the general's situation in particular. In August 1940, between 2,000 to 3,000 men were believed to belong to de Gaulle's army at Aldershot; and another 300 were thought to be under the command of Admiral Muselier in the Free French Air Force, although several of the officers were flying with the RAF. Figures for the navy were unobtainable as many men were still deciding whether to sail with the British or with Muselier,[49] described as a 'cad and a blister' by Rear-Admiral Watkins following a cocktail party in which the Frenchman accused the Royal Navy of stealing his officers.[50] Crémieux-Brilhac suggests that, at this point, the marine counted 3,200 men.[51] In November 1941, we know that the Free French Navy comprised 287 officers and 3,839 ratings; 20 officers were sailing with the Royal Navy, along with 408 men.[52] By any reckoning, it was a pitiful number. When, on 14 July 1940, de Gaulle marched his troops past the Cenotaph and the statue of General Foch in Grosvenor Gardens, provoking such headlines as 'France Celebrates Liberty. In London Only', the British public had witnessed almost the entire strength of the general's fighting men.[53] As Crémieux-Brilhac reminds us, the Czechs, Polish and Norwegian exiled forces were almost as impressive in numbers as the French.[54] As Mollie Panter-Downes observed, the fact that de Gaulle's men were housed at Olympia, a building associated in most Londoners' minds with Christmas circuses and the Ideal Home Exhibition, did not help the cause.[55]

Outside de Gaulle's forces, it is possible to identify four other categories of French servicemen in Britain. First, there were some 1,000 wounded, housed in four major London hospitals and three large hospitals in the Liverpool and Manchester districts, presumably casualties from both Narvik and Dunkirk.[56] By August 1940, 100 of these men were still too ill to be moved. They had initially been cared for by the Centre Medical Français, based at 14 Grosvenor Gardens, London SW1. This official organisation had been set up in early June 1940 with the specific purpose of looking after French wounded from Dunkirk. At the time of the Armistice, however, 'its personnel turned out to be entirely pro-Pétain' and 'left this country for France with the French Chargé d'Affaires'.[57] The Centre had subsequently lost its financial support and was in the hands of just one French representative, a Mlle Herinex, who was struggling to raise enough volunteers. Nor did it receive much support from the French Red Cross Society, which was under the control of Vicomtesse de la Panousse. In the words of Bessborough, this was no match for the British Red Cross and had displayed a 'rather low standard of efficiency'.[58] The situation was so serious that the United Associations of Great Britain and France Solidarity Committee (UAGBF), founded at the outbreak of the war, had donated £100 to the Centre, and the British Red Cross was looking at how it could assist the situation.

The second group of French servicemen were convalescents. While some of these had been sent to the Victoria Hospital at Westbury (Wiltshire), the overwhelming majority, 1,650 men and 70 officers, were housed at White City in West London. As a matter of prudence, it was deemed necessary to place the officers at the York Hotel in Berners Street where their Pétainist sentiments would be less contagious.[59] Significantly, few of these soldiers had been interned.

The third category comprised 1,000 officers and ratings of the French merchant navy 'who had said they did not wish to continue serving on their ships, but wish to return to France'.[60] They were housed at Crystal Palace, alongside French refugees, and were catered for, in part, by the LCC. Before long, the inadequacies of Crystal Palace, in particular the shortage of blankets and the fact that the men lived under glass with no nearby air-raid shelters,[61] became so obvious that 380 of the officers were moved to the Bedford, Imperial and Royal Hotels in Bloomsbury.[62] Subsequently, 240 of the men, plus 10 officers, were transferred north to the Wavertree Blind School and placed in the care of Ministry of Health Officials and Liverpool Corporation.

Their numbers, however, were dwarfed by the final contingent of servicemen: the large quantities of sailors from the French navy, 341 officers and 6,206 sailors of other ranks.[63] These men fell under the aegis of Western Command, which appointed Rear-Admiral Watkins as its naval liaison officer. Initially rounded up at Plymouth and Portsmouth, they lived in a series of makeshift settlements in the North and Midlands, which also housed 269 colonial troops.[64] There were seven camps in all: Aintree, near Liverpool, and the site of the Grand National (13 officers and 380 sailors); Haydock, also in the Liverpool area (52 officers and 1,305 men); Arrowe Park (55 officers and 140 men); Trentham Park, close to Newcastle-under-Lyme (49 officers and 1,829 men); Doddington, bordering Nantwich (51 officers, 307 petty officers and 880 men); Oulton Park, in the vicinity of Winsford, Cheshire (33 officers and 959 men); and Barmouth, West Wales (6 officers and 500 men).[65] Strictly speaking, Barmouth and Arrowe Park were not 'camps'. At Barmouth, the men were housed in billets in the town. Arrowe Park was more of a detention centre, housing unruly elements. According to Lady Peel of the UAGBF Solidarity Committee

Map 2   The sailors' camps in the North and Midlands

there was a further camp at Towyn in Wales, which housed 500 men and 6 officers.[66] However, French Welfare denied that there had ever been a base at Towyn; the site had been proposed, but had been quickly ruled out.[67] What is known is that, on 3 August, the camps at Aintree and Arrowe Park were scaled down, and the men placed into smaller units, with some of the officers rehoused in Blackpool,[68] described by Georges Blond, the writer and naval engineer held by the British since July, as a 'Jewish town' thanks to its seaside amusements and because of its boast that it had not yet been bombed![69]

At the races: life in the camps

In July and August 1940, the British press, in a morale-boosting effort orchestrated by Churchill, printed photographs of de Gaulle visiting Free French troops at camps 'somewhere in the south of England'.[70] It is almost certain that these barracks were those at Aldershot and Camberley, where Gaullist troops gathered, having enlisted first at Olympia. By contrast, no photographs appeared of the general visiting the large numbers of sailors in the north-west of the country, with good reason, as these men proved almost impossible to enlist. Several reasons combined to undermine his efforts, yet a key factor was unquestionably conditions within the camps themselves, especially those sited in the Liverpool area. Even the government recognised that this sort of bivouac, while adequate for soldiers on active service, could not be accepted by 'neutral sailors awaiting repatriation ... without demur'.[71] Little, however, was done to improve matters, creating a host of resentments.

Although conditions in the sailors' camps varied widely, the camps shared similar problems, suggesting that the problems that had been associated with internment camps in the First World War had not been overcome.[72] The overriding issue was that of the accommodation itself. The best housed appear to have been those men at Barmouth who were billeted in the town, rooms incidentally 'that were urgently required by evacuees from heavily bombed districts'.[73] Elsewhere, the majority of men were under canvas, including a handful of officers. When, on 13 September, 29 officers were transferred from Arrowe Park to Trentham, they were shocked to find only tents awaiting them. This provoked a vigorous letter of complaint from Captain Albertas who, on his arrival, had initially been offered a corner in a building occupied by British troops and officers: 'J'estime qu'il n'est pas digne d'un grand pays de traiter de cette manière des officiers qui ont combattu deux fois à côté de ses marins et dont quelques-uns ne sont plus de la première jeunesse.'[74] In the event, Albertas chose to sleep in the open air. Despite the fact the night was a fine one, his dignity had suffered and his anti-British attitude was later credited to this 'studied insult'.[75] For the most part, however, officers were under more secure cover. At Oulton, they slept in tin huts, and at Arrowe Park they were housed in a cricket pavilion.[76]

The shortcomings of tented accommodation were clearly recognised by the British authorities. Visiting Aintree, Haydock Park and Arrowe Park in late July 1940, Dame Rachel Crowdy, Regions' Adviser to the Ministry of Information, reported, 'Tents are many of them badly pitched [sic], in some cases having subsided owing to the sailors having removed the tent poles in order to saw them up for firewood.'[77] The fact that many shelters were erected on unsuitable ground was also a problem. In autumn 1940, the playwright Edward Knoblock, once described by John Gielgud as 'the most boring man in London', and an author whose name gave rise to adolescent giggles among London's literati,[78] wrote a report on the camps for his new employers, French Welfare. Of Haydock Park, he observed, 'The camp itself is on heavy clay soil, which even with the little rain till now is quite churned up ... In the rainy season this place will become a swamp.'[79] At Doddington, the tents were at the edge of a windswept lake 'very pleasant, no doubt in summer, but already very damp and chilly on the day we called – October 1st'. With winter pressing and repatriation seemingly no nearer, the pressure was on to find alternative accommodation. At Aintree, the men were placed in riding stables. This provoked a storm of protest on the part of their commanding officer, Captain de Vulliez.[80] However, on inspecting the area, the captain discovered that the stables were dry, lighted by electricity and, in some cases, heated, although extra stoves were thought necessary. At Trentham Park there were also proposals to move the men into the stables, this time the disused stalls owned by the Duke of Sutherland.

Facilities in the camps varied widely. Not all had hot and cold running water. While Arrowe Park and Oulton both had 'excellent' showers, at Doddington there was only cold water for washing and cold douches.[81] When visiting the Liverpool camps in late July, Spears remarked that the washing arrangements were 'deplorable' although he admitted that the sanitary arrangements were not too poor 'considering how deplorably bad the French are in this respect'.[82] Kitchens were also primitive. At Haydock, the men cooked in field kitchens surrounded by turf walls, a situation replicated at Arrowe Park where the men prepared meals in 'gypsy' fashion. Matters were relieved by the intervention of various charitable agencies. At Trentham, the YMCA and the Catholic Women's League intervened to set up a series of canteens, and were rewarded with a grant of £200 by the Bishop of Birmingham. Aware of the general shortages, Lady Moncrieffe, based at the International Sportman's Club, was busy getting hold of red wine and *Petit Caporal* cigarettes.[83] Spears thought Woodbines, that thin acrid cigarette favoured by Irish navvies, was more appropriate.[84] Yet, despite these efforts, food apparently remained in short supply and the men were offered an unchanging diet.[85] Matters were made worse by the fact that cooking utensils were scarce, a point of great concern to the senior French personnel; at Arrowe Park, the senior French officer claimed that it was beneath his dignity to eat off tin plates and to drink from mugs rather than glasses, a complaint echoed by his counterpart at Trentham. It was further believed that such officers might be destroying food to exacerbate anti-British sentiments.[86] Blond's

comment that men at Trentham killed the deer because they faced starvation should be treated as the comment of a petty propagandist.[87]

Far more worrying were the shortages of hospital supplies, especially
serious given the number of convalescents. Medical supervision of the
camps was left in the hands of French doctors who were grossly overworked. Whereas Knoblock was generally happy with this level of
provision, especially at Aintree where some of the colonial troops were
suffering from malaria, Beryl Fitzgerald of the UAGBF painted a less
healthy picture.[88] In her mind, the infirmary at Trentham was a
'scandal': 'I feel ashamed of being a British woman every time I go to
the camp and face Dr Laglotte (the camp's doctor) in that awful infirmary.' To be fair, Rear-Admiral Watkins, who it will be recalled was in
overall charge of the camps, recognised that the French doctors worked
hard and 'recommended that they should be paid for their duties'.[89] It
is unknown whether this recommendation was put into effect. It is
further known that the doctors were struggling against widespread
venereal disease, but that their officers had prevented them from
reporting this.[90]

Although the doctors might have been busy, the men were bored. As
a government note observed, 'Nothing demoralises Frenchmen as
much as idleness.'[91] On his trip to the camps, Spears noted, 'What was
deplorable was the lack of employment for the men. Lack of work and
nothing to think about has combined to cause moral deterioration and
exasperation.'[92] While men at Haydock were drafted in to help with the
harvest, elsewhere the sailors whiled away the hours smoking, playing
board games and listening in to the radio, usually to broadcasts from
Paris, hardly a source of pro-British feeling. Aware of the dangers of
such idleness, in early August 1940 Lord Astor suggested to Aneurin
Bevan, at the Ministry of Labour, that the sailors be enrolled into a
French Pioneer Corps, to be involved in agricultural and forestry work,
as were other exiled Europeans.[93] Such a move would engender pro-
British sentiment, reward the men with a better rate of pay than that
they were used to in the French navy, and would not contravene the
Armistice terms, as they would be involved in a non-combatant role.
'Young and healthy men', concluded Astor, 'tend to deteriorate if kept
in enforced idleness without discipline.' Replying on behalf of Bevan, a
ministry official replied that his department was merely a technical
body and, as such, could hardly begin to place 'these men in civil
employment for the duration of the war until the policy has been
decided by some competent authority'.[94] Preliminary enquiries had

been made as to the possible deployment of French exiled labour but, as will be seen in Chapter 5, these became bogged down with technical difficulties.

Unable to work, French sailors became increasingly anxious about money. By early August, the ratings had exhausted their pay. They had been anticipating another instalment from the *mission militaire*, but this was not forthcoming. In this situation, camp commandants had authorised the payment of 6*d* a day as a supplementary mess allowance.[95] By contrast, the officers appear to have been relatively well off receiving, depending on rank, either 4 shillings a day or 2*s* 6*d*, paid through the Vichy consulate in Bedford Square, although occasionally deductions were made to pay for damage perpetrated by the ratings.[96] When the officers came to leave White City, British officials were surprised that they possessed 'very considerable sums of English money to exchange for French';[97] as to the ratings, they had hardly a penny to their name. One explanation for this might lie in an MI5 report of September 1940, which uncovered that officers had seized a large quantity of banknotes, both English and French, at Dunkirk.[98]

Letters from France were a further problem. With the eagerness for news about relatives at home, this lack of information created anxiety and deterred recruits for de Gaulle, although Free French volunteers also experienced difficulties in communicating with friends and relatives. As Stewart Savill of the French in England Fund, remarked: 'Far from being able to send an occasional gift from home, these relations are unable to send even a message to say they are alive, and their fate is a matter of constant anxiety to the men who are carrying on the fight in exile.'[99] He perhaps did not realise that such families might also have been afraid of posting such messages for fear of reprisals by the Vichy authorities, which, through the *contrôle technique*, closely monitored all mail coming in and out of the country.

Although the communications breakdown within the camps was blamed on the British, something repeated in history books,[100] it was in fact the Free French who were to blame, something Blond was quick to point out.[101] In his extensive report of (probably) October 1940, Knoblock discovered that some 200,000 letters, nine-tenths dated June and July, had been held up at Carlton Gardens, which acted as a clearing house. The correspondence had at last been handed over to Rear-Admiral Watkins who employed eight people for five days to sort through the backlog.[102] Problems persisted, thanks again to the Free French who acted as censors on behalf of the British government. In

September 1940, Captain Moret of the Forces Navales Françaises Libres (FNFL) handed over to the commandant of the Crystal Palace camp a list of stipulations that had to be observed by men when writing home.[103] All letters had to contain correspondence only; the content had to be 'rigoureusement personnel'; no mention was to be made of place names, individuals and affairs in England; and nothing was to be said that might endanger families still in France. Although these were, in many regards, prudent guidelines, Chartier of the Vichy consulate bemoaned the complex bureaucracy of the system.[104] He suggested that sailors' letters be collected by a French *vaguemaitre* – a term that baffled the English, until it was discovered it meant a type of naval orderly or baggage handler – who would put them into mail bags to be handed over to the French legation at Lisbon after censorship. The proposal was thought a sensible one, but it remains unclear whether it was ever implemented. In any case, not long after, most of the sailors had been repatriated.

Given these grumbles, it is no surprise that discipline was a problem. Haydock was the exception where morale was described as 'good' and the men 'neat'.[105] Maybe this was to be expected when penalties were severe: seven days in the guardhouse for hunting rabbits.[106] Elsewhere, matters were less impressive. On visiting the camps near Liverpool, Dame Rachel Crowdy observed, 'Waste material and rubbish is thrown all over the camping ground.'[107] In a later report of 16 August 1940, she remarked on the deaths among deer and ornamental geese over at Trentham, deaths, it will be recalled, that Blond had ascribed to hunger.[108] The trustees for the late Duke of Sutherland, who owned Trentham, were quick to present a bill for the cutting down of trees, the killing of deer and the breaking of locks, as well as letters of complaint about the use of the dairy house as a latrine.[109] Blond's claim that the repair costs demanded of the men ran in to millions of pounds sterling was a nonsense.[110] At Arrowe Park, it was rumoured that the men had threatened mutiny, although on inspection this claim proved much exaggerated. A salutary respect for authority had settled in after guards had fired at a Frenchman who had walked too close to the wire.[111] Nor was it just the British authorities who were appalled at events in the camps. The Free French recruiting officer based at Stoke-on-Trent was aghast at the general lack of discipline, especially 'their carryings on with the girls'.[112] Interestingly, locals in the Camberley area made exactly the same complaints about the Free French troops stationed nearby. In his account of exile, Blond was quick to complain of the seductive techniques of British women who had allegedly targeted married French sailors.[113] Clearly sexual politics, and accusations of *collaboration horizontale*, were a means by which officials on all sides could assert moral superiority when fighting out their battles.

Poor discipline among the sailors cannot be attributed solely to poor living conditions. Part of the problem lay with inadequate British supervision where barbed wire compensated for the lack of patrols. In a letter to Desmond Morton, Spears complained that 'the chief difficulty in administering the French camps is the ineffectiveness and inadequacy of the assistance from the army'.[114] The extent of this 'inadequacy' was revealed in a report for Lord Bessborough: 'Rear Admiral Watkins a short while ago asked that at least one company should be stationed at each camp as well as the 15 military police, but none of the camps have anything like this number of soldiers, and the few military police that were stationed there previously have been withdrawn. At one camp the military contingent consists of one officer and 8 men.'[115] Nor were the British commandants necessarily of a high quality. Admittedly some passed muster. Major Orchard at Haydock Park drew particular praise, as did Captain Macbeth at Trentham Park.[116] In the words of Blond 'un rat à moustache', Macbeth was a temporary officer who, according to Dame Rachel Crowdy, had 'lived in France thirty years and understands the French as well as they understand him'.[117] Having taught at the Ecole d'Hydrographie at Marseille, he was a genuine Francophile and had done much to improve living conditions and mutual respect, in particular by organising a football match between French and British officers, which the French had won 4–3. Macbeth even elicited praise from the notoriously disaffected captain of the *Albertas*: 'Je rends hommage à l'activité du commandement anglais le capitaine Macbeth qui s'est employé avec les faibles moyens dont il dispose d'améliorer notre situation matérielle.'[118] Elsewhere, however, the English commandants drew criticism. While it was acknowledged that Major Anderson at Aintree displayed a genuine concern for his men, he was thought to perform his job in a perfunctory fashion. In the words of Knoblock, he had 'grown a bit stale over his work', and was principally concerned with the British troops who were also stationed at the camp.[119] The 'lack of discipline' and deficiencies in the 'sense of trimness in the Frenchmen's appearance' was, in turn, attributed to this lacklustre leadership. At Arrowe Park, Knoblock uncovered two senior British officers, one excellent but the other far less suited: 'rather the old blustering type of major, I gather'.[120] It is not hard to believe that this type of job invited that genre of officer.

Given the dispiriting conditions in many of the camps and the half-hearted leadership of certain camp commanders, it is small wonder that resentment towards the British was widespread. As Beryl Fitzgerald complained to Sir Aidan Baillie, 'Had we a decent camp it might have turned potential bitterness into pro-British feeling amongst those who have been and who I hope will still be our allies in the future.'[121] Yet other factors also played their part, many of which we have encountered already. To begin with, there was a residue of anti-British sentiment, only to be expected among French sailors, and hardened by events at Dunkirk and Mels-el-Kébir. Reporting on sailors in Liverpool, Noble Hall of French Welfare was informed by one medical officer that 'although he hoped Germany would ultimately be beaten, France would never forget that after she had been crushed by the enemy, her former friend and ally destroyed her fleet when it was unable to defend itself and killed more than 1,250 French sailors in cold blood'.[122] When Sir Evelyn Wrench of the Royal Empire Society invited sixty French sailors to an evening's entertainment at the Empire Rendezvous at Liverpool, English members of the audience were aston-ished at the hostility expressed by the ratings, together with their failure to appreciate 'the true facts of the sinking of the French fleet at Oran'.[123] The manner in which the officers had been rounded up also left bitter memories. The Bishop of Liverpool reported how his wife and other French-speaking women had tended to the men at Aintree. There, the episode at Oran clearly rankled, 'but what sticks in their gizzards is the way they were taken off their ships – at 4 am – with very little notice, and by an armed guard. Somebody blundered over this.'[124] In the eyes of many sailors, the treachery of Britain had been further revealed in the abortive attack on the submarine base on Dakar in September 1940 and the blockade of French ports. Noble Hall was brusquely informed that the embargo 'was unfair to France'.[125] 'The unoccupied portion', the interviewee continued, 'had neither wheat nor cattle, and the blockade which could not stop Germany getting food from South-Eastern Europe would be very hard on what was left of France. It was a most unfriendly act.'

Such Anglophobic attitudes caused anxiety in several quarters. For his part, Lord Astor believed that the huddling of men in large camps would contribute to the spread of disorder. In a letter to Oliver Harvey at the Ministry of Information, he urged, 'Do all you can to keep the sailors in relatively small units so that they do not go Red, or even Pink. Remember that Bolshevism is apt to spread like wildfire.'[126] In a further letter to the Bishop of Liverpool, Astor elaborated on his fears and claimed that, if the men at Aintree continued to be treated like animals they would eventually return to France as 'potential Communists with a strong anti-British bias'.[127] There is, however, little evidence to justify these fears. While discipline and morale among the ratings was undoubtedly poor, and while they often disobeyed their British guards, the overwhelming impression is that French officers still retained a measure of respect and military control.

Among the officers, the real danger was not Bolshevism, but Pétainism. Reporting for French Welfare, Noble Hall remarked that nearly all the senior personnel he interviewed 'were in favour of the Pétain government as *honnête et seul capable de remettre de l'ordre en France*'.[128] Although he uncovered a high-ranking medical officer who had been a former member of the Grand Orient, the largest of the masonic lodges, most were Catholic with strong Action Française leanings:

> They said it was not only in military matters that the world had had a lesson from Hitler. They praised the German youth movement and hoped it would be adopted in France. They talked exactly like Sir Neville Henderson did to me in Berlin. He said Pétain, Weygand, Beaudoin [sic], Prouvoust [sic], were blinded by social prejudice, that at heart they hated democracy and were intolerant of everything that had sprung from the French revolution.[129]

Such sentiments were also commented upon by de Gaulle's agents. Returning home after visiting Trentham Park, Sylvia Fletcher-Moulton stumbled across a young French officer in charge of the France Libre recruiting bureau: 'He was in despair and I don't think enough Stoke/Trentites speak French for him to have got it off his chest before!'[130] He denounced those wanting to return to France as 'mauvais garnements' with 'some obvious Nazis in their number, responsible for some violently anti-de Gaulle propaganda'.

From where did this Pétainism spring? It was, in part, ideological: a faith in traditional right-wing values, commonplace among the officer class. It also stemmed from the attitudes of the Catholic priests who visited the camps, as we shall see in Chapter 5. Social status further determined outlook. Accustomed to greater privileges and better pay than their British counterparts, French officers had greatly resented the conditions within the camps, which they saw as an affront to their dignity.[131] Most importantly, their *maréchalisme* originated from the conviction that the old soldier was motivated by the most patriotic of motives. As Blond claimed, his very name was a sufficient safeguard of national honour.[132] To go against his authority was thus to fly in the face of reason. The war was lost, and there was little point in dragging out the suffering. In this respect, de Gaulle, together with his close associate Admiral Muselier, one of the first high-ranking recruits for the Free French and perhaps the originator of the emblem of the Cross of Lorraine, fared badly. Already known to naval men, Muselier was thought 'unapproachable' and lacking in charisma, a view also expressed by Blond.[133] De Gaulle himself was an 'unknown', but was associated with the army, which was blamed for losing the Battle of France.[134] He had also disobeyed his superiors. Several considered that his position might initiate a civil war.[135] This anxiety was noted by Lord Astor who spoke widely with the survivors of the *Meknès*. 'The argument which appears to have carried most weight', he remarked, 'was the suggestion that France must above all remain united so as to prevent the risk of civil war or Bolshevism. Hitler made Pétain and his colleagues believe (just as earlier he convinced Hindenburg and his friends) that civil war is the worst catastrophe a nation can endure.'[136] Through the defeat of the General Strike, concluded Astor, England had maintained its unity, and it was now desirable to 'make the French realise that even civil war with its bitterness is preferable to the imposition of permanent fascism'. Just as Pétain had dismissed the possibility of a guerrilla or civil war when put to him by Churchill at the French Cabinet meeting on 11 June 1940,[137] so too was it rejected by the French officers.[138] Order, stability, discipline: these were the values to be preserved, and it was precisely these qualities that the officers expected of their men, even though they themselves hardly set an example. Indeed, the only area in which the officers appeared anxious to impose some sort of discipline was in threatening the lower ranks with punitive action should they opt for de Gaulle. In July 1940, the registrar at Alder Hey hospital in Liverpool complained that officers from nearby Aintree had visited the wards claiming that any man who volunteered for the Free French would be under 'penalty of death'.[139] It was frequently noted that recruitment picked up when the men were separated from their officers.[140] As we shall see, officers went to great lengths to stymy British propaganda.

The Randolph Hotel, Oxford: a polite exile

The neo-Gothic hotel, the Randolph, built in 1864 and facing the Ashmolean Museuem in Oxford's Beaumont Street, has been the scene of many dramas: political and donnish intrigues; illicit love affairs; and literary whodunnits. In 1940, it was the home to a handful of the most prominent French naval personnel stranded in Britain at the time of Mers-el-Kébir, the hotels's interior splendour thought fitting for such high-ranking officers, described by Spears as 'a polite exile'.[141] There were six men in all.[142] The first, and most important, was Rear-Admiral Gaudin de Vilaine. A First World War veteran, who had seen distinguished service, on the battleship *Courbet*, he had been the commanding officer of all those ships that had taken refuge in Portsmouth at the time of the Armistice.[143] Angered at the manner in which his ships had been seized, he was quickly dismissive of de Gaulle. When Thierry d'Argenlieu spoke to him of rebuilding the French navy, he quipped, 'On what will you build?', adding for good measure that Muselier was nothing more than a womaniser.[144] Less is known about Rear-Admiral Cayol who had exercised similar functions to de Vilaine over French ships at Plymouth, except that he was already struggling to maintain control among both his men and officers, who were angered to see British civilians enjoying their summer holidays.[145] Additionally, there were two captains, Le Chuiton and Guillaume, as well as two other captains whose names are not disclosed in the surviving records. Indeed, there is little on these men in surviving official Foreign Office and French Welfare files, except a letter of protest from Chartier of the Vichy consulate who believed their incarceration would play into the hands of German propaganda, a charge that caused some amusement in Downing Street, which wondered which side of the war Chartier was really on.[146] It is thanks to the private papers of the Astor family that we can glean something of the lives and opinions of these senior personnel. While it should be stressed that these six men were held separately precisely so their opinions did not infect their juniors, there can be little doubt these views were shared by a majority of their officers.

It was while on business, visiting Chatham House transplanted to Oxford during the early stages of the war, that Lord Astor learned of the presence of Admiral Cayol, a man whom he had first known at Plymouth.[147] Anticipating that this wounded sea lord would be 'sulky and unapproachable', Astor was surprised at his attitude. Meeting at the Randolph, they 'reestablished friendly relations, good chat, some

laughs'. To get the 'French sailors in a friendly state of mind',[148] Astor
made arrangements for people in Oxford to show these senior officers
'some of the colleges and buildings, plus tea'.[149] He further wrote to
London requesting that he invite Cayol and his colleagues to the family
house of Cliveden, but recognised that this would require a special
dispensation as his stately pile lay outside the twenty mile restriction
zone imposed on the officers in Oxford.[150] London was apprehensive
remarking that 'Admiral Cayol ... is a very difficult person and has
been a disturbing influence almost from the beginning.'[151]
Nonetheless, permission was granted and the chief constable of Oxford
informed, along with strict orders that the admirals should, at no point
in their journey, come into contact with their ratings.

The two admirals took lunch and tea at Cliveden on the first Sunday
in August, before returning to Oxford for dinner at All Souls. The trip
provoked a warm letter of thanks from Cayol, who deemed it kind in
these 'moments pénibles'.[152] Astor also drew up a lengthy memorandum on his impressions of the two men. He began with an assessment
of de Vilaine.[153] On the 'defensive', the rear-admiral was convinced
that 'Pétain, Weygand and Darlan must have been influenced by inside
information unknown to us outside'. It was 'further essential to keep
France united' as ultimately it would rise again 'just as Germany rose
after 1918 and in Napoleon's time'. On the question of de Gaulle, de
Vilaine was dismissive, calling him an 'unknown':

> Has he any known respected men with him? Who are on his so-called
> Committee? Does it include Blum or Cot or other such discredited politi-
> cians?

Turning to the British, de Vilaine claimed that London merely wanted
French ships, not sailors, an observation not far from the truth. Those
men who went with de Gaulle would be 'sold' and turned into soldiers.
Bemoaning the British blockade, the admiral asked 'What is America?
Always late.' Warming to his themes, although 'mellowing' by the close
of the evening, de Vilaine dismissed Laval as a 'politician', condemned
parliament as 'out of date', and suggested what might be needed was
'some sort of military dictatorship', although Astor observed he had no
liking for Hitler.

As to Cayol, he was 'admiring' of Churchill, but still resented the
seizing of French ships.[154] He considered that he himself would have
ordered the scuttling of the boats rather than let them fall into German
hands. Like his colleague, he was dismissive of de Gaulle, believing his

force 'too small to be of much use'. Only later, when the tide had turned against Hitler, might it serve as a 'rallying cry'. In Astor's mind, he was a 'likeable man', with his 'heart still in the fight', but he was clearly worried about his wife and young children, as well as his son who was with French sailors at Liverpool. When out of de Vilaine's earshot, the officer was more candid, describing the events at Mers-el-Kébir as a 'shame', and bemoaning the pro-Bordeaux and anti-British sentiments of some of his colleagues.

Astor's impressions of the two admirals were borne out by a further report drafted by a L. J. Beck, an official at the Ministry of Information's offices at Chatham House, who had invited all six officers to his house in Oxford.[155] Of the two admirals, de Vilaine was 'the most striking and leading figure'. He seemed 'to dominate the others in every way'. He was an 'authoritarian', frequently speaking of 'the need for discipline'. Although not a practising Catholic, he expressed a strong resentment for 'politicians and Jews', bearing a particular grudge against the Jewish mayor of Le Havre, together with a more general hatred of Communists and Russians. Cayol was not such 'a strong character'. He was 'rather talkative and a bit of a bore', with less definite opinions than his superior and generally less well informed about political matters, although neither of the two admirals knew much about current affairs. Taken as a whole, Beck concluded that all six officers at the Randolph were in want of news from France, and reported that they felt they were being 'deliberately kept from seeing French papers'. While there were occasional flashes of Anglophobia, the men restrained their anti-British sentiments and spoke highly of the English people, although de Vilaine found it hard to keep his tongue, a trait put down to his Normandy ancestry. They were, at least, unanimous in their hatred of 'les Boches', but pessimistic about Britain's chances in the coming air war. In de Vilaine's mind, the Germans were 'invincible'. Oran was a subject best avoided, yet de Gaulle cropped up regularly in conversation, albeit as a *persona non grata*. In their eyes, he had committed the unpardonable offence of having disobeyed orders. In France itself, 'il y a travail à faire', and much praise was heaped on Pétain. The admirals were especially pleased he was appointing naval men to colonial posts, although it was pointed out to them that they were unlikely to benefit as they had probably been put on to the 'retired list'. Whatever the case, their social standing and rank weighed heavily with them. In a separate letter of 19 August 1940, Heather Harvey told Astor that she had recently had Captain Le Chuiton to dinner, where he had been terribly embarrassed by the fact that he had only one suit; his dress wear had been seized with his ship.[156] He was clearly bored at the Randolph, and annoyed that he could not go to the cinema because he did not possess a gas mask.

Despite Astor's good intentions, on 6 September 1940 Duff Cooper wrote to the proprietor of the *Observer* to let it be known that his Ministry considered 'de Vilaine a hopeless case and that Cayol is completely influenced by him and would not disobey his superior'.[157] Morale among the six officers was undoubtedly on the wane. On 9 September the admirals were described as 'increasingly reserved'.[158] Their ordeal was, at least, near a close. On 18 September, they quit Oxford to be repatriated. On departing, their mood was characterised as 'anxious and resigned rather than happy; but all longing to see their families again'.[159]

Clearly, it would be hazardous to generalise about the overall sentiments of French naval officers held in Britain on the basis of British-prepared reports on six unusual and high-ranking personnel. Nonetheless, so many of their attitudes seem to reflect those of their fellow officers elsewhere in England: a respect for military discipline; an admiration for Pétain; a belief that France was somehow in need for renewal; a dislike of the Germans; a seething resentment over Mers-el-Kébir; a strong suspicion of de Gaulle; a sense that their dignity and status had been undermined, especially by the manner in which they were initially arrested; a wish to return to their families; a fear for economic security; and a mistrust of the British and their intentions. Small wonder that in August–September 1940 further efforts were made to segregate the officers from their ratings, especially in the troublesome Liverpool area.[160]

Recruiting and proselytising

Although officers and ratings were separated, the concerns of the two bodies of men were not dissimilar, explaining why ultimately recruitment for both the British and the Free French forces was disappointing. Charles Ingold, a fighter pilot and a early recruit for the Free French, noted in his diary how, at Arrowe Park, all the men were in a hurry to return home as they considered the war lost.[161] Even de Gaulle himself could not hide his frustration. In his memoirs, he recalls how, on 29 June 1940, he visited Trentham Park where he rallied:

a large part of the two battalions of the 13th Half Brigade of the Foreign Legion, with their leader, Lieut-Col. Magrin-Veneret, known as Monclar, and his number two, Captain Koenig, two hundred Chausseurs Alpins, two-thirds of a tank company, some elements of gunners, engineers and signals, and several staff and administrative officers, including Commandant de Conchard and Captains Dewarin and Tissier.[162]

The next day at Aintree and Haydock Park, he had less luck, being turned away by the British authorities in Liverpool, lest he provoked disorder. Arrowe Park, visited a few days later, proved more rewarding, yet indifference and hostility were still the overwhelming responses. White City proved a particular disappointment, given the proximity of de Gaulle's recruiting bureau at nearby Olympia. Of the 1,600 or so troops that passed through there in the first two months of the camp's existence, only 152 signed up with de Gaulle, a further 34 with the British army, and another 35 with the Royal Navy.[163] Within the sailors' camps recruiting moved at a snail's pace. Although men at Haydock were relatively enthusiastic, by mid-September a mere 100 men a week were volunteering to serve with either de Gaulle or the British, the latter option being the more popular, largely because the pay was better,[164] although those who did choose thus soon became objects of derision on the part of their comrades.[165] It is also worth noting that in the case of those few eager to enlist, enrolment with the British Army offered a much quicker return to action than would be had by joining the Free French.[166] Whatever the reasons, recruitment soon tailed off. When it was learned that a majority of the soldiers at White City, and men in other camps, had plumped for repatriation, and that some vessels had already sailed for France, 'recruiting dropped badly, as the predominant desire of all these men is to return to their families in France'.[167]

For the British, at least, these results were not overly disappointing. Although there were those Francophiles like General Spears and Lord Astor willing to lend initial support to de Gaulle's recruitment drive, elsewhere there were reservations about supporting this campaign. The Admiralty, War Office and Foreign Office all had sizeable doubts about allowing large numbers of French servicemen to remain in England. Whereas the last of these departments was apprehensive of de Gaulle himself, neither the War Office nor the Admiralty wanted to enlist large numbers of French servicemen. Dill, the CIGS, summed up such sentiments when he quipped that all French troops should be told, 'any man who wants to stay and fight here can do; and then I hope they will all go back'.[168] Not only was the loyalty of the French in doubt, given the advent of the Vichy regime; they would also need to be trained – difficult in view of the language difficulties and general shortage of weapons. As Knoblock commented: 'The difference of language makes it difficult for the them to follow commands. Their habits and their ideas of food are different from ours. Besides the innate French characteristics of questioning and doubting orders might at times lead to serious misunderstandings.'[169] With an invasion pending, it was thus preferable to concentrate efforts on British and Imperial forces. As de Gaulle himself complained, the result was that the British only lent half-hearted support to his recruitment campaign. In his biography of Major-General Spears, Max Egremont recalls how, on 22 July at one London hospital, wounded French soldiers were asked whether they wished to stay in England.[170] None of the nurses involved could speak French, and the invalids were given a 10-minute period to make up their minds. Anxious for news, the men were not impressed and resented being treated like prisoners, a complaint echoed elsewhere.[171] As one wounded soldier remarked, 'Si les Anglais nous traitent comme des prisonniers ici, vaut mieux rentrer et être des prisonniers chez nous.'[172] Not that the Free French themselves were any more agile in presenting their case. One official at Saint James's Hospital in Leeds was dumbfounded at the cack-handed recruitment methods of one Gaullist officer who reminded any potential recruits that, should they enlist, they would be immediately under sentence of death; later, he was unable to field any questions about rates of pay, the position of the British and the prospect of returning to France.[173] So it seems that the example of aloofness set by de Gaulle himself was emulated by several of his officers!

While the government was not inclined to help any real recruitment drive, either for the Gaullist or the British side, it was keen to promote better Anglo-French understanding. In the short term, this would ease discipline problems among the servicemen. In the longer term, it would promote goodwill towards London when repatriation eventually took place. Such a campaign might also distract from criticism in the press. *The Times* followed the fortunes of the soldiers at White City with a feverish interest.[174] Far more critical of the government was the left-leaning *New Statesman and Nation*. In an article for its 'London Diary' of 10 August 1940, it rehearsed several familiar complaints about the treatment of French sailors:

I am constantly hearing fresh instances of our total failure even to try and win the support of French soldiers and sailors. A French merchant ship, for instance, arrived at Glasgow: its crew of 40 was immediately thrown into jail. Then it was transferred to an internment camp near London where they are living under canvas, idle and embittered. No effort was made to enlist the support of the men nor were British seamen from the Seaman's Union encouraged to get on friendly terms with them.[175]

The article went on to contrast the situation with the Norwegians. Here, contact had immediately been forged between the Seaman's Union and its Norwegian equivalent. The WEA had also done its bit to encourage good relations among fellow sailors with the result that 40,000 Norwegians were helping in the war effort. The article concluded with a further criticism of government and its failure to create comradeship. It did, though, provoke a riposte from one French colonist André Clast, living in Exeter. On 17 August, the *New Statesman and Nation* published his letter in which he congratulated the WEA and the Ministry of Information for organising talks to French sailors in the Plymouth area, efforts no doubt aided by Lord Astor.[176] In a rejoinder to this correspondence, the editor said how pleased he was that such good work was being done in Plymouth, but still drew a contrast between the Norwegian navy and the French sailors.[177]

Ultimately, this attempt to build bridges proved a fruitless campaign. To begin with, the British had to get to the men themselves; they might have been in British-run camps, but they were overseen by their superiors who were especially bloody-minded and threatened their underlings with retaliation.[178] At Liverpool, the Anglican bishop reported how the commanding officers had declined to hand out 1,000 copies of a Ministry of Information tract on the Armistice on the grounds that it was 'propaganda'.[179] At Haydock and Aintree, Edward Shiel, a company director with strong ties to France, was dismayed at the way in which the officers thwarted all attempts to promote propaganda,[180] a situation replicated at Crystal Palace and White City. Major-General Spears had a particularly torrid time when attempting to combat such actions. Visiting Aintree, where French sailors had recently been pelting their British guards with stones, he discovered that the loudspeaker wires had been cut when he attempted to address the officer body.[181] On mentioning Vichy, hecklers called out 'the government of France'. Discovering that officers were deploying *gardes mobiles* to prevent the circulation of Gaullist propaganda, he was fearful for his own safety and, at one point, thought he might be assaulted.[182] Shortly afterwards, the Earl of Derby, who hosted a reception for French officers at the Adelphi Hotel in Liverpool, advised Spears and others not to deploy the words 'Vichy government' as it simply backed the argument that the Pétain regime was the true government of France.[183]

On a day-to-day basis, the lack of good interpreters also hindered attempts to promote Anglo-French goodwill. Few of the servicemen, even among the officers, knew English, and few British troops spoke French. It appears that most interpreters were Royal Army Service Corps drivers and held non-commissioned ranks. In a letter to Western Command, Rear-Admiral Watkins stressed that several of these men had 'carried out excellent work, which has proved invaluable in providing information unobtainable and also in furthering recruiting'.[184] Especially commended were the six corporals and lance-corporals at Doddington and Oulton Park, who were also acclaimed by Knoblock.[185] 'It is regrettable', continued Watkins, 'that these men had been obliged to draw on their private means in order to entertain French sailors.'[186] It was thus recommended that these 'ambassadors' should be given special allowances and promotion. Further praise was heaped on the interpreters at Barmouth and Haydock, although one private at the latter camp was deemed 'incompetent and lazy'. At Trentham a lance-corporal and two privates were said to possess 'insufficient knowledge of French', while one man was to be retained because of his standing among the sailors. Worryingly, at Arrowe Park and Aintree, there were no interpreters whatsoever. Curiously, however, French Welfare and Western Command were reluctant to accept outside help. When the Manchester businessman, Edward Shiel, a fluent French speaker, offered his services, aware that men at Haydock and Aintreee were willing to sign up for either harvest or fishing work until the wider situation of the war became clearer, his proposal was turned down.[187] At least, his *démarche* brought the situation to the attention of both the Ministry of Information and the British Council, although it remains unclear exactly what was done.[188]

To compensate for the lack of interpreters, lectures in French were arranged. In the West Country, Lord Astor arranged for a Dr Chaput, a French Canadian and professor at the University of Exeter, to give talks to seamen at Devonport.[189] How successful such lectures were is open to doubt. On 14 October 1940, John Christie, 'a teacher of English', filed a report on life at Trentham Park, in which he had

No. 1
Mercredi,
24 Juillet,
1940

J O U R N A L   du   C A M P

Ce journal sera édité quotidiennement pour vous
renseigner et vous distraire. Les dernières nouvelles
vous seront données d'une façon tout a fait objective

NOUVELLES RETROSPECTIVES.

LA GRANDE-BRETAGNE RECONNAIT LE GENERAL DE GAULLE.
Le Ministère de l'Information britannique annonce officielle-
ment que le gouvernement de Sa Majesté a décidé de reconnaître le
Général de Gaulle, ancien sous-secretaire d'Etat à la guerre dans le
Cabinet Paul Reynaud et président du Comité National Français de
Londres, comme "chef de tous les Français libres qui se joindront à
l'Empire britannique pour défendre la cause commune des Alliés".

A ce sujet, nous sommes en mesure de démentir les bruits qui
ont circulé ces jours derniers, selon lesquels des hommes politiques
français entreraient dans ce Comité. Le général de Gaulle a
formellement affirmé que seuls feraient partie de ce Comité des
militaires et des techniciens en petit nombre.

PLEINS POUVOIRS POUR LE GOUVERNEMENT PETAIN (11 Juillet, 1940).

Au cours d'une séance secrète, heir soir, la Chambre et le Sénat
ont donné au Gouvernement Pétain pleins pouvoirs pour l'élabora-
tion d'une nouvelle Constitution suivant un programme fasciste.
Le scrutin était de 569 voix pour, 80 contre, et 15 abstentions.

Le vice-président, Pierre Laval, agissant au nom du
Maréchal Pétain, communiqua à l'Assemblée un message de Maréchal
qui s'excusait de ne pouvoir assister à la réunion. La Constitution
sera, paraît-il, présentée au peuple sous forme de référendum.
M. Laval ne précisa pas si ce référendum serait appliqué dans toute
la France, ou seulement dans la partie de la France non-occupée.
De nombreux télégrammes émanant de députés s'excusant de ne pouvoir
être présents furent communiqués à l'Assemblée. Il paraît que
certains députés de droite raillèrent le nom de Daladier lorsque
celui-ci fut prononcé. En plein brouhaha, M. Herriot se leva contre
cette manifestation et prit la défense de M. Daladier.

D'après le "PETIT DAUPHINOIS", le préambule de la Constitution
annonce: "A travers l'un des plus cruels moments de son histoire,
la France doit accepter la nécessité d'une Révolution Nationale. Le
Gouvernement doit avoir tous pouvoirs pour sauver ce qui peut encore
être sauvé, comme pour détruire tout ce que doit être détruit. La
Nation doit prendre une oreintation nouvelle et doit faire partie
intégrante du système continental de production et d'échange. La
France doit, avant tout, revenir à la vie des champs et developper
son agriculture. Il est par conséquent indispensable de mettre fin
aux désordres économiques par l'organisation rationnelle de la
production et de ses institutions corporatives.

Les allemands prétendent qu'il y eut de nombreuses dissensions
parmi les Parlementaires français. Certains auraient demandé que
les notes sténographiques soient publiées pour que leur opposition
au mouvement constitutionnel soit portée à la connaissance du public.

Figure 4   The first edition of the *Journal du Camp*, a newsletter hastily
improvised by the government to promote better understanding of the
British war effort. This was distributed among French servicemen held in
camps across the UK

spoken on English life and customs, addresses he had first delivered at the University of Lyon.[190] The welcome he received was not the same as that he had experienced in peacetime.

Alongside lectures, the British prepared printed material. To begin with, this took the form of amateurish roneoed newsletters, entitled *Journal du Camp*, rapidly produced by the Ministry of Information. From these, it is clear that the British favoured a 'softly-softly' approach, reporting on British successes in the war and highlighting German cruelties. Issue 7 of 31 August 1940 spoke of political developments in France, in particular the emergence of the out-and-out collaborators at Paris:

> Il est évident que Paris est aujourd'hui en rivalité avec Vichy – exactement comme la Commune était en rivalité avec le gouvernement légal de Versailles en 1871. Seulement, aujourd'hui, quels sont les maîtres de Paris?[191]

The answer was Doriot and Bergerey [sic], the editors and ideologues of such papers as *La France au Travail* [sic] and *L'Oeuvre*. Issue number 8 of the *Journal du Camp*, 1 August 1940, spoke of how Vichy's efforts to mollify the invader 'ne racontrent que le sarcasme, cynisme et menaces de repression futures'.[192] After announcing that leading members of the Third Republic were going to be put on trial, the journal referred to a 'mécontentement général de la population'. In a further comment on life in occupied France, the paper reported on high unemployment in the unoccupied zone, angry crowds gathering at factories, food shortages and demonstrations, especially at Marseille, Lyon and Clermont-Ferrand. Ominously, the report concluded by remarking that many firearms had not been handed in to the authorities.

In preparing such propaganda, the Ministry of Information was not short of advice from interested parties. Having spoken to the French admirals at Oxford, Lord Astor urged that the following points be borne in mind:

- That de Gaulle is unknown and a young man. Reply: Among other things, when Napoleon started his career his contemporaries probably said exactly the same thing.
- The French navy would never have yielded a ship to Germany even if they had been allowed to return to France. Reply: If we were able to seize the ships Germany could have done so, especially if the ships had been laid up temporarily and the crews demobilised.

- Continue emphasising the treachery of Hitler. The French don't half understand that. Remind them that Hitler has murdered the young Nazi colleagues when he thought this necessary, has deceived his own general public, has bumped off his own German generals, etc. It is most important to keep rubbing this in: also to explain how Hitler took in the aged Hindenburg.
- Need to prepare the French for the starvation which is coming this winter – this due to Hitler, not to Great Britain.[193]

Whether this advice was heeded remains unclear, but it is known that the *Journal du Camp* gave way to a far more impressive publication, entitled *France*, which had the look and feel of a proper newspaper, being produced on Fleet Street presses. Something of the controversy over this newspaper, its left-wing stance and occasional criticism of de Gaulle, will be tackled in Chapter 5; what should be noted here is its impact on the morale of French troops. French Welfare was upbeat, remarking that this fledgeling paper was 'quite a success and is being freely distributed in all of the camps although the news items are read with some scepticism'.[194] That scepticism was perhaps more deep-rooted than French Welfare cared to acknowledge. In the words of John Christie, the lecturer seconded to the Liverpool camps, the paper was regarded as nothing more than 'English propaganda' and was widely ignored.[195] It is in the Spears papers that a copy of *France*, recovered from one of the camps, may be found with the handwritten injunction, 'Lire entre les lignes.'[196] Beside the phrase 'Paroles d'un chef', the word 'chef' crossed out, is added 'acheté par l'Angleterre'; 'L'ex' is placed before 'Général de Gaulle'. On the reporting of the blockade, there is appended the following, 'Voilà comment les anglais traitent nos femmes et nos enfants en France. C'est vrai que M. de Gaulle lui ne risque rien. Les lieux sont bien au chaud en Angleterre.' Blond reports that when at Blackpool, officers read collaborationist papers such as *Gringoire* and *Candide*, which had been smuggled off French ships in Liverpool port.[197]

Repatriation

With such a lacklustre response, Whitehall focused less on promoting Franco-British understanding and more on repatriation, despite the episode of the *Meknès*. Several other factors concentrated minds on this possibility. An unsigned report of 5 September 1940, for the CFR, remarked that the War Office, Admiralty and French Welfare all agreed 'that repatriation is as urgent as ever, more so in view of air raids'.[198] There was also the problem of morale. While a good number of the sailors were out of the public eye in Liverpool, in London it was learned that the French wounded from White City were threatening to demonstrate in front of the American embassy in Grosvenor Square to win over US public opinion and so bring pressure to bear on London to facilitate their speedy resettlement.[199] Moves were quickly put into place to ensure that large numbers of the internees at White City did not abscond. Conditions in that particular camp were recognised to be reasonable; the same was not true elsewhere. In view of the coming winter, which was likely to prove especially cold, the British agreed that it would no longer do to have large numbers of men sleeping in their tents 'under the stars'. Should the sailors outstay their welcome into the new year, they would have to be found new homes and would become an even costlier burden with still no prospect of them joining de Gaulle.

A further impetus to repatriation sprang from the wish to clamp down on the behaviour of the Vichy consuls, especially in Liverpool. Here, the Naval Liaison complained that 300 ratings, who had disappeared from Aintree and elsewhere, had been demobilised by the French consulate.[200] The consulate apparently had ready the necessary English documentation for the men to travel on Portuguese and Japanese steamers, and thus back to France.[201] French officers were also assisting illegal repatriation. Léon Wilson recalls that when recuperating in a hospital outside London, after being rescued at Dunkirk, senior ranks mentioned to him that they could assist him in returning home.[202] What is astonishing is that the British should have allowed such behaviour to go unchecked although, as will be seen in Chapter 4, eventually the Liverpool consulate, along with those at Glasgow and Cardiff, was relocated out of harm's way.

While the Vichy consuls might have done their bit to ease repatriation, their government took retaliatory action. In addition to a feeble bombing of Gibraltar in revenge for Mers-el-Kébir, on 3 July the French seized six British-registered ships on the West African coast. On 1 August, the steamships *Hermes* and *Temple Pier* were held at Algiers, and their crews detained at Camp Carnot. While the *Hermes* had 12 British seamen on board and 57 from Calcutta, the *Temple Pier*'s crew comprised 40 British ratings, including some Lascars. Through the American Consul General in Algiers, it was learned that 'the official reason for detention of crews of the two vessels is given as alleged ill treatment of French officers and sailors in a detention camp at Liverpool. The Consul General states that such allegations are contributing to a growing animosity against British subjects in French naval circles, even among persons who have hitherto been favourably inclined.'[203] US representatives had thus been asked to look after the crews and help arrange their repatriation. Meanwhile, in Beirut, the French had seized the crews of the *Brodwal*, *Pegasus* and *Lesbian*. Whereas the ratings had been interned, the officers had succeeded in obtaining parole and were living in a hotel. By early October, much to the dismay of the Ministry of Shipping, there had been little success in obtaining the release of British sailors in either Algeria or the Lebanon, and it urged that a full enquiry be made into the conditions at the Liverpool camp to refute the French allegations.[204]

Although events in Africa called for an early release of the French sailors in Britain, this was no easy matter. To begin with, the men had to be rounded up. Theoretically, this should have been an easy task, yet the lack of discipline in the camps meant that several men had gone AWOL. Blond recalls that he travelled to London, and went to see Stoke City play football.[205] Watkins was alarmed to learn that some 500 sailors had returned late one evening after their passes had expired.[206] At Haydock, it was reported that 4 officers and 75 men were 'adrift', even though provisions had been allocated to these individuals for some time. It was thought possible that they had already been demobilised by the French Consulate-General in Liverpool or that they had joined either the Free French or the British armed forces without Watkins knowing. Blame, it was agreed, could not be attached to the British commandant as he had only one officer and 10 men to run the whole settlement. At Arrowe Park, a further four French officers were reported missing; another two had gone for two weeks, and it was supposed they had been repatriated by the French consul. For his part, Knoblock claimed some 300 men were at large in the Manchester area, many of whom were no longer wearing uniform.[207] He had no doubt where blame lay: 'French commandants are very lax about keeping a proper list of the men in their camps.' Roll-calls were perfunctory and rare. 'It will give the police a lot of work to round these men up', he moaned. 'If they are not caught they will ultimately become a charge to the community, or, what is worse still, will fall into bad habits and end by being imprisoned.' This was also the concern of MI5 whose officers periodically dressed up as refugees and took to the streets of Soho where they mingled with French sailors, eventually asking them to produce identity papers to prove that they were with de Gaulle, netting both Free French deserters and escapees from White City and elsewhere.[208]

The other problem holding back repatriation was the fact that the Germans would give no guarantees for a safe passage.[209] It will be recalled that on 24 July, the *Meknès*, carrying French repatriates, was sunk by an E-boat. Rather than send the men back to the camps from which they came, they were billeted in Plymouth, Portsmouth and Skegness.[210] Guy Millard, a former Foreign Office official conscripted into the navy, witnessed the survivors arrive at Skegness.[211] The men were in an 'appalling condition', many without shoes, some half naked, others in women's clothes; the officers, however, were still in uniform, having taken to the lifeboats first. The mood at Skegness was downcast except for the behaviour of one homosexual British guardsman who organised concert parties, and delighted in saying, '500 sailors in this camp and every one of them normal except me'.[212]

Repatriation was not helped by the fact that Vichy subsequently impounded two British boats that had been earmarked for the task. As a leaflet for the men in the Crystal Palace camp explained, London and Vichy now intended to use French boats, presently in US waters, for repatriation purposes.[213] Given the ensuing difficulties over the suitability of the boats to be deployed, the suspicion arises that Vichy itself wanted to prolong the repatriation process as long as possible so as to create good anti-British propaganda. It also appears that, at one point, the Pétain regime hoped to break the British blockade by loading the boats with supplies from Canada and the USA, a move that was scuppered with the assistance of the Americans themselves.[214] Such delaying tactics naturally played badly with the British, one high-ranking official suggesting that the men should simply be dumped on a Moroccan beach.[215]

The first men to be successfully repatriated were those invalided soldiers at White City, who left, via Liverpool, on 16–18 September. Watching the scenes by the quayside, Knoblock, Noble Hall and Hugh Astor, all of French Welfare, were not impressed: 'too many official fingers in the pie'.[216] First to arrive, on the morning of 16 September, were the *grands blessés* on stretchers. Rather than being embarked as quickly as possible they 'were kept waiting for some time on the floor of the outer shed where it was cold and drafty'. The French medical officer and the MI5 officer soon fell out with one another, the latter making matters worse by his 'tactlessness'. In Knoblock's eyes, he was clearly not up to the job and went off in a 'huff', eventually turning up late in the afternoon 'and then did nothing but strut around'. While the examination of the men's luggage passed off without incident, it soon became clear that the Vichy consul did not have enough French currency to distribute. So it was that Western Command in Chester provided some 3 million francs to bail out the situation. The next day, 17 September, was the 'most strenuous' as it was then that the bulk of the troops from White City appeared. Arriving by train early in the afternoon, they had a five-and-a-half hour wait before embarking. They were remarkably patient despite the fact there was 'no food, no drink, no way to get it to them'. Apparently the Salvation Army had been asked to provide a mobile canteen, but had refused on learning the men were not joining de Gaulle. 'A strange attitude', observed Knoblock, 'for an institution that prides itself on following the Good Samaritan's example.' Customs and the censoring of papers followed, both procedures proving farcical, although one man was caught in possession of a bag of diamonds. The next day further special cases boarded the ships, the *Sphinx* and the *Canada*, which were ready to set sail. When they did, 'Nazi planes appeared, and amused themselves by trying to bomb us – an effort which, luckily for our French friends as well as for ourselves, was not successful.' For future embarkations, Knoblock recommended the changing of money at the original camps whence the men came, the provision of mobile canteens (at least two, providing coffee as 'they don't like tea'), and the distribution of gifts such as cigarettes and playing cards at the London stations.

Whether these recommendations were implemented remains unclear. It is known that from November onwards the steamers *Canada*, *Djenne*, *Winnipeg* and *Massilia*, the famous vessel that had carried a small number of parliamentarians from Bordeaux to North Africa, were kept busy ferrying men back to France. By Christmas 1940, 6,574 officers and men had been repatriated, and the French camps were closed down.[217]

One unexpected upshot of their departure was that the British made a determined effort to improve the lot of Gaullist troops at Aldershot and Camberley. When attempts had initially been made to encourage families to show hospitality to these men, it quickly became clear that the public did not distinguish between Free French volunteers and those servicemen desirous to get home, admittedly a difficult task as their uniforms were more or less identical bar the Cross of Lorraine, a point of detail also picked up by the reporters for Mass-Observation.[218]

As Bessborough remarked of the aid given to sailors in northern England, 'helping the French came wrongly to be regarded in the minds of some as service to a body of people who preferred to endeavour to return to their homes than to continue to fight against Germany',[219] a sentiment no doubt reinforced by reporting in the *Daily Express* which had labelled the sailors 'fifth columnists'.[220] Similar sentiments were expressed by an outraged vicar from Chester who noted how French sailors near to his parish freely moved around and were housed in 'first-class army bell tents' on which were inscribed the signs 'Nous voulons rentrer en France'.[221] Further worrying news came from a Ministry of Information poll of January 1941, which displayed that the public, while overwhelmingly against Vichy, were 40 per cent pro-de Gaulle, 30 per cent anti-de Gaulle and 30 per cent uninterested. Nearly everyone canvassed believed that Anglo-French friendship in the future was either unlikely or undesirable.[222] In this regard, it is not difficult to believe that the role of other nationalities in Britain damaged the Gaullist cause. At the height of the Battle of Britain, though the heroics of Pierre Clostermann were always accepted, it seemed in government newsreels that only Czech and Polish airmen were flying alongside the RAF.[223] This courage contrasted badly with the lack of organisation displayed at Dakar, which, according to Mass-Observation, had given rise to a general feeling that de Gaulle's men were 'ineffectual'.[224]

To promote better relations between the Free French and the British, in early 1941 commanding officers of units near Aldershot and Camberley were instructed to invite their French counterparts to 'regimental dances, concerts and other functions'. In addition, families in the neighbourhood, especially those who understood French, were encouraged to take the men 'to their homes for meals and friendly visits'.[225] This proved highly successful. In February 1941, the whole of the Free French army in England was given seven days' leave, and virtually all the men were placed with families where they were surprised by the levels of 'generosity, hospitality and kindness shown to them by the average English person'. Such temporary billeting continued throughout the war. Georges Le Poittevin remembers how he stayed for a week at Wembley among a family who treated him as though their own son.[226] To encourage further fraternisation, trips were organised to the local countryside, including picnics on the Thames between Reading and Shillingford.[227] Within the camps themselves, the AVF, a Franco-British initiative, which we shall meet later in Chapter 5, was especially active in improving facilities: better sleeping arrangements; more frequent post; and greater entertainments. In July 1943, Lieutenant-Colonel Black could say of Camberley, 'The camp is in good order and calls for no remarks; the messing of both officers and men is better than I have known in any camp.'[228] In December that year, he once again remarked on the 'very good order' of Old Dean Camp, 'a very different state of affairs to formerly', and commented on how the 1,000 or so men were rapidly dispersing to elsewhere in the country, presumably in readiness for the invasion of Europe, thus necessitating the running down of the site.[229]

Conclusions

Ironically, the poor behaviour of service personnel awaiting repatriation had favoured the Free French, although it is certain de Gaulle would have preferred more recruits. These were never forthcoming. The overwhelming majority of French servicemen stranded in Britain at the time of the Armistice and Mers-el-Kébir always wanted to return home, regardless of the discomforts that awaited them on their arrival, and it is not difficult to ascertain why. Gaullist and British propaganda had been inept; the influence of the Pétainist officers had been disconcerting; conditions in the camps had been demoralising; boredom had set in; there was a desire to reunite with lost families; the war was considered lost; money was in short supply; de Gaulle himself seemed a dangerous element; Britain appeared untrustworthy, especially after Oran; there was peer pressure to avoid enlisting with 'perfidious Albion'; and the manner of their original round-up still rankled. Yet whatever the rights and wrongs of these matters, it is hard not to feel a certain smidgen of pity for the exiled servicemen. They had not chosen to be in Britain, they endured a hard life in the camps, and knew little of the wider events of the war. If they had been able to forecast events, it is possible that more would have remained. For their part, the British had little wish that they should stay for any longer than was necessary and, to a point, sympathised with their plight, although little was done to improve matters within the camps themselves. When, in early August 1940, unfavourable reports of life in the Liverpool region reached Downing Street, they did not concern Cabinet long; this instead was a matter for French Welfare.[230] Although de Gaulle thought differently, during that autumn Britain had more pressing worries than the concerns of stranded French sailors and seamen.

As a postscript, it is worth noting here the insubstantiality of the claims, peddled by *Je Suis Partout*, that Britain was behind the assassination of Darlan in December 1942 in an act of revenge for the failure to recruit among French personnel in 1940.[231] Such allegations say more about the desperate and fabulous nature of collaborationist propaganda. Nonetheless, this Anglophobia was very real and was to be replicated among the French consulates still present in London and elsewhere in the period 1940–42.

Notes

1 (Who of her sight could ever tire? Her beauty springs each day anew. Across the straits – and O Great sire, She's gracious, kind, fair and true), translated in R. Mengin, *No Laurels for De Gaulle* (London, Michael Joseph, 1967), p. 9. Charles was held captive by the British for several years after Agincourt and came to be known as the 'caged songster'.

2 PRO FO 371 28365 Z629/123/17, 'Report on the Work of French Welfare' for the Committee on Foreign (Allied) Resistance, 29 January 1941.

3 J.-L. Crémieux-Brilhac, *La France Libre de l'appel du 18 juin à la libération* (Paris, Flammarion, 1995), p. 95.

4 Among the many memoirs of Free French volunteers, see Général de Boisseau, *Pour combattre avec de Gaulle* (Paris, Plon, 1981), R. Dronne, *Carnets de route d'un croisé de la France Libre* (Paris, Editions France-Empire, 1984), C. Robet, *Souvenirs d'un médecin de la France Libre* (Paris, SIDES, 1994), P. Sonneville, *Les Combattants de la liberté. Ils n'étaient pas 10,000* (Paris, La Table Ronde, 1968), and the interviews collated by F. Moore, 'Les Engagés de 1940. Des hommes qui, en 1940, se sont engagés à vingt ans dans les FFL, se souviennent', in *Espoir*, no. 71, juin 1990, 14–26. On the history of the Free French Forces, see ENSTA, *Les Armées françaises pendant la deuxième guerre mondiale, 1939–1945* (Paris, Institut Charles de Gaulle, 1986), E. Chaline and P. Santarelli, *Historique des Forces Navales Françaises Libres* (Vincennes, Service Historique de la Marine, 1989), and C. Christienne and P. Lissarague, *Histoire de l'aviation militaire. L'Armée de l'air, 1928–1981* (Paris, Charles Lavanzelle, 1981).

5 A. Martel, 'De Gaulle et la France Libre. L'Appel du soldat', in A. Martel (ed), *Histoire militaire de la France* (Paris, Presses Universitaires de France, 1994), vol. 4, pp. 77–130.

6 See C. d'Abac-Epezy, *L'Armée de l'air des années noires* (Paris, Economical, 1997) and P. Masson, *La Marine française et la guerre, 1939–1945* (Paris, Tallandier, 1991).

7 C. de Gaulle, *The Call to Honour, 1940–1942* (London, Collins, 1955), p. 92.

8   R. O. Paxton, *Parades and Politics at Vichy. The French Officer Corps under Marshal Pétain* (Princeton, Princeton University Press, 1966).

9   F. Kersaudy, *Norway 1940* (London, Collins, 1990).·

10 Among the many books on the evacuation, see B. Bond, *France and Belgium, 1939–1940* (London, Brassey's, 1990); E. Dejonghe and Y. Le Maner, *Le Nord-Pas-de-Calais dans la main allemande, 1940–1944* (Lille, Presses Universitaires de Lille, 1999); D. Divine, *The Nine Days of Dunkirk* (London, Faber & Faber, 1959); R. Collier, *The Sands of Dunkirk* (London, Collins, 1961); H. Cras, *Dunkerque* (Paris, Editions France-Empire, 1960); G. Blaxland, *Destination Dunkirk* (London, Military Book Society, 1973); N. Gelb, *Dunkirk. The Incredible Escape* (London, Joseph, 1990); N. Harman, *Dunkirk. The Necessary Myth* (London, Hodder & Stoughton, 1980); and P. Oddone, *Dunkirk 1940. French Ashes, British Deliverance. The Story of Operation Dynamo* (Stroud, Tempus, 2000).

11 Darlan quoted in Bond, *France and Belgium*, p. 168.

12 Oddone, *Dunkirk 1940*, p. 85.

13 A brilliant account of this meeting is provided in E. Spears, *Assignment to Catastrophe* (London, William Heinemann, 1954), vol. 2, pp. 263–96.

14 Figures from P. M. H. Bell, 'The Breakdown of the Alliance in 1940', in N. Waites (ed), *Troubled Neighbours. Franco-British Relations in the Twentieth Century* (London, Weidenfeld & Nicolson, 1971), p. 203. See also P. M. H. Bell, *A Certain Eventuality. Britain and the Fall of France* (London, Saxon House, 1974), p. 17 for a much more detailed breakdown of figures, together with times of embarkation.

15 F. Christol, *Comme au temps de nos pères. Ceux de la France Libre* (London, Hamish Hamilton, 1946), p. 69.

16 J. Delin, 'L'Opinion britannique et les français en Grande-Bretagne pendant l'année 1940', *doctorat*, Université de Lille III, 1993.

17 RUL Box 605, Dodgson Diary, vol. 6, September 1940, p. 310.

18 *Times Educational Supplement*, 15 June 1940, p. 225.

19 H. Long, *Change into Uniform. An Autobiography, 1939–1946* (Lavenham, T. Dalton, 1978), p. 24.

20 Interview with the author, London, 19 April 1994.

21 CCC SPRS 1/134, letter of Brendan Bracken MP, to Colin Coote, WO, 27 June 1940. Apparently the audience cheered when the episode was restituted.

22 IWM, Diary of C. E. Toutain.

23 Mengin, *No Laurels*, p. 38.

24 Bell, *Certain Eventuality*, p. 18.

25 Interview with the author, London, 19 April 1994.

26 G. Rennie, unpublished war diary, kindly shown to the author by Dr Tom Buchanan of the University of Oxford. The same diary is available in the IWM.

27 Letter to author by Professor Martin Alexander, 21 January 2002.

28 Interview with the author, Mauthausen, Austria, March 1995.

29 J. Knowlson, *Damned to Fame. The Life of Samuel Beckett* (London, Bloomsbury, 1996).

30 RUL MS 1066/1 Box 38 702, letter of Lord Astor to Dame Rachel Crowdy, Ministry of Information, 30 June 1940.

31 RUL MS 1066/1 Box 38 702, letter of Astor to Dr A. V. Alexander, also sent to Ernest Bevan and Arthur Greenwood, 30 June 1940.

32 M. Panter-Downes, *London War Notes, 1939–1945* (London, Longman, 1971), p.75.

33 Quoted in M. Ophuls, *The Sorrow and the Pity* (London, Paladin, 1971), p. 36.

34 De Gaulle, *Call to Honour*, p. 96.

35 W. Tute, *The Reluctant Enemies. The Story of the Last War between Britain and France, 1940–1942* (London, Collins, 1990), p. 70. Darlan puts the total at 143. See *Le Figaro*, 1 June 1941, in CCC NBKR 4X/10/3, 'Dossier Darlan'.

36 PRO FO 1055 1, 'Memorandum of Visits Paid to French Camps in the Neighbourhood of Liverpool', 5 September 1940.

37 RUL MS 1066/1 Box 38 702, letter to Lord Astor, 30 August 1940.

38 PRO FO 371 24360 C13565/7736/17, CFR minutes, 30 August 1940.

39 Ministère des Affaires Etrangères (hereafter MAE) ZV 291, carton 95, dossier 1, telegram of 22 July 1940 to Peyrouton.

40 Tute, *Reluctant Enemies*, p. 66.

41 *Ibid.*

42 CCC SPRS 1/182, letter to Spears from Ernest Alterskye, 7 March 1949, who had served with Spears in the camps.

43 *Ibid.*

44 CCC NBKR 4X/10/3, 'Dossier Darlan', press cutting from *Le Figaro*, 1 June 1941.

45 CCC NBKR 4/261, letter of Noel Baker to Atlee, 28 June 1940, in which he mentions that morale was 'rapidly falling'.

46 C. Williams, *The Last Great Frenchman. A Life of General de Gaulle* (London, Little, Brown, 1993), p. 114.

47 Interview with the author, London, 22 March 2002.

48 PRO HO 213 1739 203/2/111, 'Demobilisation of Members of HM and Allied Forces. Synopsis of Information on General Files 204/13/ – Series up to 31st December 1941', by Cann.

49 PRO FO 1055 8, 'Memorandum on the French Armed Forces in Britain', no date (summer 1940?).

50 CCC SPRS 1/135, letter of Watkins to Spears, 23 August 1940.

51 Crémieux-Brilhac, *La France Libre*, p. 95.

52 PRO FO 371 28368 Z10127/123/17, Memorandum of the Security Executive, 24 November 1941.

53   *Daily Mirror*, 15 July 1940.

54   Crémieux-Brilhac, *La France Libre*, p. 95.

55   Panter-Downes, *London War Notes*, p. 75.

56   PRO FO 1055 8, 'Memorandum on the French Armed Forces in Britain', no date (summer 1940?).

57   *Ibid.*

58   RUL MS 1066/1 Box 38 702, letter of Lord Bessborough to Sir Horace Wilson, 8 August 1940.

59   PRO FO 371 28365 Z629/123/17, 'Report on the Work of French Welfare' for the Committee on Foreign (Allied) Resistance, 29 January 1941.

60   PRO FO 1055 8, 'Memorandum on the French Armed Forces in Britain', no date (summer 1940?).

61   PRO FO 371 24357 C10102/7559/17, CFR minutes, 13 September 1940.

62   PRO FO 371 28365 Z629/123/17, 'Report on the Work of French Welfare' for the Committee on Foreign (Allied) Resistance, 29 January 1941.

63   *Ibid.* See too D. Thomson, *Two Frenchmen. Pierre Laval and Charles de Gaulle* (London, The Cresset Press, 1951), p. 162 and Chaline and Santarelli, *Forces Navales*, p. 22.

64   PRO FO 371 28365 Z629/123/17, 'Report on the Work of French Welfare' for the Committee of Foreign (Allied) Resistance, 29 January 1941.

65   PRO FO 1055 1, 'Report on French Camps', Edward Knoblock, no date (October? 1940). M. Kochan, *Britain's Internees in the Second World War* (London, Macmillan, 1983), pp. 37–40, recalls how the racecourse at Kempton Park was used as a processing centre for internees.

66   PRO FO 1055 1, letter of Lady Peel to Oliver Hardy, 9 August 1940.

67   PRO FO 1055 1, 'Report on French Camps', Edward Knoblock, no date (October? 1940).

68   PRO 1055 1, 'Report on Visit to French Camps in the Liverpool Area by Dame Rachel Crowdy, 29–31 July 1940'.

69   G. Blond, *L'Angleterre en guerre. Récit d'un marin français* (Paris, Grasset, 1941), p. 185.

70   See the photograph reproduced in Bell, *Certain Eventuality*. It is well known that de Gaulle disliked being promoted in this fashion and refused photographs of himself and his family, largely to shield his handicapped daughter, Anne. One of the rare photographs of the general and his wife appeared in the *Daily Herald*, 24 June 1940. See M.-L. Clausard, 'De Gaulle et la presse anglaise en 1940. Du ministre inconnu au célèbre homme d'Etat', *Mémoire de maîtrise*, University of Paris X–Nanterre, 1997, p. 149.

71   PRO FO 371 28365 Z629/123/17, 'Report on the Work of French Welfare' for the Committee on Foreign (Allied) Resistance, 29 January 1941.

72 R. Graves, *Goodbye to all that* (London, Penguin, 1960 edn), p. 73.
73 PRO FO 1055 1, letter of Lord Bessborough to R. J. B. Anderson, Ministry of Shipping, 2 October 1940.
74 PRO FO 1055 1, letter of capitaine Albertas to Rear-Admiral Watkins, 21 September 1940.
75 PRO FO 1055 1, 'Report on French Camps', Edward Knoblock, no date (October? 1940).
76 *Ibid.*
77 PRO FO 1055 1, 'Report on Visit to French Camps in the Liverpool Area by Dame Rachel Crowdy, 29–31 July 1940'.
78 J. Mortimer, *Summer of a Dormouse* (London, Penguin, 2000), p. 175.
79 PRO FO 1055 1, 'Report on French Camps', Edward Knoblock, no date (October? 1940).
80 *Ibid.*
81 *Ibid.*
82 PRO FO 1055 1, 'Major General Spears' Report on the Situation in the Camps Occupied by French Sailors in the Neighbourhood of Liverpool, 31 July 1940'.
83 RUL MS 1066/1 Box 38 702, letter of Lady Moncrieffe to Lord Astor, 19 November 1940.
84 CCC SPRS 1/134, note of 3 July 1940, and a cigarette once favoured by the author in different days!
85 G. Thierry d'Argenlieu, *Souvenirs de guerre, juin 1940–janvier 1941* (Paris, Plon, 1973), p. 107.
86 PRO FO 1055 1, 'Report on Visit to French Camps in the Liverpool Area by Dame Rachel Crowdy, 29–31 July 1940'.
87 Blond, *L'Angleterre*, p. 150.
88 PRO FO 1055 1, letter of Beryl Fitzgerald to Sir Aidan Baillie, French Welfare, 10 September 1940.
89 PRO FO 1055 8, 'Report by Admiral Dickens on the French Camps, 6 September 1940'.
90 CCC SPRS 1/135, Report of Watkins to Dickens, 13 August 1940.
91 CCC NBKR 4/261, 'Employment and Morale of French Troops in Great Britain', 15 July 1940.
92 PRO FO 1055 1, 'Major General Spears' Report on the Situation in the Camps Occupied by French Sailors in the Neighbourhood of Liverpool, 31 July 1940'.
93 RUL MS 1066/1 Box 38 702, letter of Lord Astor to Aneurin Bevan, 2 August 1940.
94 RUL MS 1066/1 Box 38 702, letter of Scott, Ministry of Labour, 7 September 1940.
95 PRO FO 1055 1, 'Report on Visit to French Camps in the Liverpool Area by Dame Rachel Crowdy, 29–31 July 1940'.

96   PRO FO 371 24353 C10337/7407/17, intercepted letter out of Haydock.

97   PRO FO 1055 1, 'Report on French Camps', Edward Knoblock, no date, (October? 1940).

98   CCC SPRS 1/135, note of MI5 to Spears, 6 September 1940.

99   RUL MS 1066/1 Box 38 702, letter of Stewart Savill to Lord Astor, 12 November 1940.

100 Martel, 'De Gaulle et la France Libre', and Masson, *La Marine*, p. 193.

101 Blond, *L'Angleterre*, p. 101.

102 PRO FO 1055 1, 'Report on French Camps', Edward Knoblock, no date (October? 1940).

103 LMA LCC We/M (1) Box 12, letter of Moret to Commandant of the Crystal Palace Camp, September 1940.

104 PRO FO 1055 1, letter of Speaight, Foreign Office, to Brennan, French Welfare, 4 October 1940.

105 PRO FO 1055 1, 'Report on French Camps', Edward Knoblock, no date (October? 1940).

106 PRO FO 371 24353 C10337/7407/17, intercepted letter.

107 PRO FO 1055 1, 'Report on Visit to French Camps in the Liverpool Area by Dame Rachel Crowdy, 29–31 July 1940'.

108 PRO FO 1055 1, letter of Crowdy to Bessborough, 16 August 1940.

109 CCC SPRS 1/134, letter of 26 June 1940.

110 Blond, *L'Angleterre*, p. 150.

111 PRO FO 1055 1, 'Major General Spears' Report on the Situation in the Camps Occupied by French Sailors in the Neighbourhood of Liverpool, 31 July 1940'.

112 PRO FO 1055 1, letter of Hon. Sylvia Fletcher-Moulton to Lady Reading, 13 October 1940.

113 Blond, *L'Angleterre*, p. 112.

114 PRO FO 1055 1, letter of Spears to Morton, 28 August 1940.

115 PRO FO 1055 8, 'Report by Admiral Dickens on the French Camps, 6 September 1940'.

116 PRO FO 1055 1, 'Report on French Camps', Edward Knoblock, no date (October? 1940).

117 PRO FO 1055 1, letter of Dame Rachel Crowdy to Bessborough, French Welfare, 16 August 1940. See, too, Blond, *L'Angleterre*, p. 148.

118 PRO 1055 1, letter from le Capitaine de Frégate *Albertas* to contre-amiral Watkins, 21 September 1940.

119 PRO FO 1055 1, 'Report on French Camps', Edward Knoblock, no date (October? 1940).

120 *Ibid.*

121 PRO FO 1055 1, letter of Fitzgerald to Sir Aidan Baillie, MP, 10 September 1940.

122   PRO FO 1055 1, 'Note for Lord Bessborough', 21 September 1940, by H. Noble Hall.

123   PRO FO 1055 1, letter of Sir Evelyn Wrench, to Duff Cooper, Ministry of Information, 16 August 1940.

124   RUL MS 1066/1 Box 38 702, letter of the Bishop of Liverpool to Lord Astor, 14 August 1940.

125   PRO FO 1055 1, 'Note for Lord Bessborough', 21 September 1940, by H. Noble Hall.

126   RUL MS 1066/1 Box 38 702, letter of Lord Astor to Oliver Harvey, 8 August 1940.

127   RUL MS 1066/1 Box 38 702, letter of Lord Astor to the Bishop of Liverpool, 12 August 1940.

128   PRO FO 1055 1, 'Note for Lord Bessborough', 21 September 1940, by H. Noble Hall.

129   *Ibid.*

130   PRO FO 1055 1, letter from Sylvia Fletcher-Moulton to Lady Reading, 13 October 1940.

131   PRO FO 1055 1, 'Report on French Camps', Edward Knoblock, no date (October? 1940).

132   Blond, *L'Angleterre*, p. 92.

133   Masson, *La Marine*, p. 131. See, too, E. Muselier, *De Gaulle contre le gaullisme* (Paris, Editions du Chêne, 1946).

134   PRO FO 1055 1, 'Major General Spears' Report of the Situation in the Camps Occupied by French Sailors in the Neighbourhood of Liverpool, 31 July 1940'.

135   PRO FO 1055 1, 'Memorandum of Visits Paid to French Camps in the Neighbourhood of Liverpool, 5 September 1940'.

136   RUL MS 1066/1 Box 38 702, letter of Lord Astor to Oliver Harvey, 8 August 1940.

137   On this meeting, see Spears, *Assignment*, pp. 133–59.

138   PRO FO 1055 1, 'Memorandum of Visits Paid to French Camps in the Neighbourhood of Liverpool, 5 September 1940'.

139   PRO FO 371 24339 C7797/7328/17, letter of Registrar to Major Allen, 22 July 1940.

140   CCC SPRS 1/135, Memorandum by Watkins, 27 August 1940.

141   CCC SPRS 1/135, letter of Spears to Sir Ronald Tree, MP, 1 August 1940, who had invited the French entourage to his house, Ditchley Park, north of Oxford.

142   RUL MS 1066/1 Box 38 702, letter of Lord Astor to AV, 9 September 1940.

143   Tute, *Reluctant Enemies*, p. 67.

144   Thierry d'Argenlieu, *Souvenirs*, pp. 75–6.

145   Sonneville, *Les Combattants*, p. 13.

146 PRO FO 371 24358 C7920/7559/17, letter of Chartier to Morton, 31 July 1941.

147 RUL MS 1066/1 Box 38 702, letter of Lord Astor to AV, 31 July 1940.

148 *Ibid.*

149 RUL MS 1066/1 Box 38 702, letter of Lord Astor to Oliver Harvey, Ministry of Information, 1 August 1940.

150 RUL MS 1066/1 Box 38 702, letter of Lord Astor to AV, 31 July 1940.

151 RUL MS 1066/1 Box 38 702, letter of AV to Lord Astor, 1 August 1940.

152 RUL MS 1066/1 Box 38 702, letter of Cayol to Lord Astor, no date (early August 1940).

153 RUL MS 1066/1 Box 38 702, unsigned and undated document.

154 *Ibid.*

155 RUL MS 1066/1 Box 38 702, letter of L. J. Beck to Lord Astor, 23 August 1940.

156 RUL MS 1066/1 Box 38 702, letter of Heather Harvey to Lord Astor, 19 August 1940.

157 RUL MS 1066/1 Box 38 702, letter of Duff Cooper to Lord Astor, 6 September 1940.

158 RUL MS 1066/1 Box 38 702, letter of Lord Astor to AV, 9 September 1940.

159 RUL MS 1066/1 Box 38 702, letter of Heather Harvey to Lord Astor, 19 September 1940.

160 RUL MS 1066/1 Box 38 702, letter of Heather Harvey to Lord Astor, 5 August 1940.

161 G. Ingold, *Un matin bien rempli ou la vie d'un pilote de chasse de la France Libre, 1921–1941* (Paris, Charles Lavauzelle, 1969), p. 106.

162 De Gaulle, *Call to Honour*, p. 94.

163 PRO FO 371 28365 Z629/123/17, 'Report on the Work of French Welfare' for the Committee on Foreign (Allied) Resistance, 29 January 1941.

164 PRO FO 1055 1, 'Report on French Camps', Edward Knoblock, no date (October? 1940).

165 Letter to the author by Georges Le Poittevin, 8 February 2002.

166 Interview with Léon Wilson, 22 March 2002.

167 PRO FO 1055 1, 'Report on French Camps', Edward Knoblock, no date (October? 1940).

168 Quoted in Bell, *Certain Eventuality*, p. 197.

169 PRO FO 1055 1, 'Report on French Camps', Edward Knoblock, no date (October? 1940).

170 M. Egremont, *Under Two Flags. The Life of Major General Sir Edward Spears* (London, Weidenfeld & Nicolson, 1997), p. 199.

171 CCC SPRS 1/134, letter of Virginia Cloe to Spears, 22 July 1940.

172 CCC SPRS 1/134, letter to Spears from C. Coote, War Office, 11 July 1940.

173 PRO FO 371 24355 C8460/7559/17, letter from Miss Ruth Newling to Halifax, 1 August 1940.

174 Various editions for July and August 1940.

175 *New Statesman and Nation* (hereafter *NS & N*), 10 August 1940, vol. XX, no. 494, p. 130.

176 *NS & N*, 17 August 1940, vol. XX, no. 495, p. 160 and PRO FO 1055 8, 'Memorandum on the French Armed Forces in Britain', no date (Summer 1940?).

177 *NS & N*, 17 August 1940, vol. XX, no. 495, p. 160.

178 RUL MS 1066/1 Box 38 702, letter of Lord Astor to Dame Rachel Crowdy, Ministry of Information, 4 July 1940, in which he mentioned that on board French battleships in Cornwall notices announcing the Armistice terms had gone up stating that anyone who disobeyed these would be treated as *francs-tireurs* and retaliation would be taken against their families in France.

179 RUL MS 1066/1 Box 38 702, letter of the Bishop of Liverpool to Lord Astor, 14 August 1940.

180 PRO FO 1055 1, letter of Edward Shiel, to French Welfare, 20 July 1940.

181 Egremont, *Under Two Flags*, p. 200.

182 PRO FO 1055 1, 'Major General Spears' Report of the Situation in the Camps Occupied by French sailors in the Neighbourhood of Liverpool, 31 July 1940'.

183 CCC SPRS 1/135, letter of the Earl of Derby to Spears, 23 August 1940.

184 PRO FO 1055 1, Report from Rear-Admiral Watkins to HQ, Western Command, 9 September 1940.

185 PRO FO 1055 1, 'Report on French camps', Edward Knoblock, no date (October? 1940).

186 PRO FO 1055 1, Report from Rear-Admiral Watkins to HQ, Western Command, 9 September 1940.

187 PRO FO 1055 1, letter of Edward Shiel, to French Welfare, 20 July 1940.

188 PRO FO 1055 1, letter of H. B. Brennan to T. P. Tunnard-Moore, acting secretary of Advisory Committee on British Teachers Abroad, British Council, 17 August 1940.

189 RUL MS 1066/1 Box 38 702, letter of Lord Astor to Oliver Harvey, 26 July 1940.

190 PRO FO 1055 1, letter of John Christie, 14 October 1940.

191 LMA LCC We/M (1) Box 12, *Journal du Camp*, no. 7, 31 August 1940. Issues are also to be found in RUL MS 1066/1 Box 38 702.

192 LMA LCC We/M (1) Box 12, *Journal du Camp*, no. 8, 1 August 1940.

193 RUL MS 1066/1 Box 38 702, letter of Lord Astor to Oliver Harvey, 5 August 1940.

194 PRO FO 1055 1, 'Memorandum of Visits Paid to French camps in the Neighbourhood of Liverpool, 5 September 1940'.

195 PRO FO 1055 1, letter of John Christie, 14 October 1940.

196 CCC SPRS 1/135, contains the document.

197 Blond, *L'Angleterre*, p. 139.

198 PRO FO 1055 3, Memorandum of 5 September 1940.

199 PRO FO 371 24355 C8461/7559/17, Foreign Office Minute 13 August 1940. In an interview with the author (22 March 2002), Léon Wilson had no recollection of this episode.

200 PRO FO 371 24356 C9280/7559/17, note of 28 August 1940.

201 PRO FO 371 24353 C10337/7407/17, intercepted letter from Haydock.

202 Interview with the author, London, 22 March 2002.

203 PRO FO 1055 1, letter of Theodore C. Achilles, American Embassy to Sir George R. Warner, Foreign Office, 19 September 1940.

204 PRO FO 1055 1, letter of R. J. B. Anderson, Ministry of Shipping, to Lord Bessborough, 2 October 1940.

205 Blond, *L'Angleterre*, pp. 44–8, 169.

206 PRO FO 1055 1, Communication Sheet, from Watkins to General Officer Commanding HQ Western Command, 30 September 1940.

207 PRO FO 1055 1, 'Report on French Camps', Edward Knoblock, no date (October? 1940).

208 PRO FO 371 24360 C13565/7736/17, CFR minutes, 28 November 1940.

209 Blond, *L'Angleterre*, p. 68 naturally claims the contrary.

210 PRO FO 1055 8, 'Memorandum on the French Armed Forces in Britain', no date (summer 1940?). See M. Gilbert, *The Second World War* (London, Collins, 1991), p. 111. Blond was also on the *Meknès*. See Blond, *L'Angleterre*, pp. 71–2.

211 PRO FO 371 24355 C8323/7559/17, letter received in the Foreign Office, 12 August 1940.

212 *Ibid.*

213 LMA LCC We/M (1) Box 12, leaflet 'Le Repatriement des marins français'.

214 PRO FO 371 24357 C11430/7559/17, telegram to Washington embassy, 28 October 1940.

215 CCC SPRS 1/135, Memorandum of 27 August 1940 by General Finlayson.

216 PRO FO 1055 6, 'The Embarkation of French Wounded at Liverpool', by Knoblock, 23 September 1940.

217 PRO FO 371 28365 Z629/123/17, 'Report on the Work of French Welfare' for the Committee on Foreign (Allied) Resistance, 29 January 1941.

218 M-O FR 566, 'Public opinion about the French: opinion trends, 1939–1941', report dated 1 February 1941.

219 PRO FO 371 24347 C13466/7328/17, letter of Bessborough to de Gaulle, 2 December 1940. This led Bessborough to ask de Gaulle to speak at the

Savoy to broadcast his cause. When he failed to reply, the Foreign Office mischievously toyed with the idea of forwarding this particular example of the general's rudeness to the Royal Thames Yacht Club, which wished to put him up as an honorary member.

220 Blond, *L'Angleterre*, p. 124.

221 CCC SPRS 1/135, letter from Rev. H. E. B—, 22 August 1940, destined for *The Times*, yet not published.

222 PRO FO 371 28419 Z150/150/17, CFR minutes, 30 January 1941.

223 Letter to the author from Professor Martin Alexander, 21 January 2002.

224 M-O FR 566, 'Public opinion about the French: opinion trends, 1939–1941', report dated 1 February 1941.

225 PRO FO 1055 10, 'Report of visit by Lt.-Col. C. Black DSO, on Friday, 14th February, 1941'.

226 Letter to the author, 2 March 2002. Such kindness, he continues, was probably the reason why he stayed in England, marrying a British girl from a family with whom he stayed while convalescing from illness.

227 PRO FO 1055 10, 'Rapport sur une visite à Old Dean Camp en compagnie du Sous Chef de l'Etat Major Français', by Lt.-Col. Black, 4 June 1941.

228 PRO FO 1055 10, Memorandum, 5 July 1943, by Claud Black.

229 PRO FO 1055 10, 'Report on a Visit to the French Centre of Military Instruction, Old Dean Camp, Camberley, by Lt.-Col. Claud Black, WO, 1.12.43'.

230 J. Colville, *The Fringes of Power. Downing Street Diaries* (London, Hodder & Stoughton, 1985, vol. 1, p. 243, although in his own memoirs Churchill expresses concern over the camps. See *The Second World War* (London, Collins, 1949), vol. 2, p. 150.

231 *Je Suis Partout*, 7 January 1943. I am grateful to David Smith for this reference.

4

The surveillance of exile: the Vichy consulates

Whom have you come here to insult? England in her people or France in her exile? Leave freedom in peace!
(Victor Hugo on Napoleon III's visit to England)[1]

The history of Vichy at London is usually told as the secretive and mysterious negotiations conducted in late 1940 between Churchill and Pétain, a line of communication manned by such self-appointed intermediaries as the Canadian diplomat Jean Dupuy and the enigmatic Professor Louis Rougier. This is the so-called 'double game' strategy, the notion that Pétain hoodwinked the Germans by professing his genuine interest in collaboration while persuading Britain to ease its blockade on France and so allow General de Gaulle to carry the torch of resistance overseas. Contrary to what is sometimes thought, the double-game theory was not an invention unveiled at the marshal's trial in 1945 by his defence lawyer Jacques Isorni; instead it originated in the minds of those Pétainists of the first hour who refused to believe that their hero was consorting with the Germans unless he possessed some ulterior motive, especially when he met Hitler at the hitherto unknown railway station of Montoire-sur-Loir on 24 October 1940, their railway carriage parked conveniently near a tunnel so it could be shunted to safety should the RAF appear on the horizon. Jules Roy remembers being informed, 'trust the old fox, he's going to con Adolf'.[2] While chastising Pétain for his government's anti-Semitism, as late as 1942 the right-wing Resistance journal *Défense de la France*, founded in the cellars of the Sorbonne, acknowledged that in his foreign policy the marshal was 'resisting' and that this was 'too shrewd a game to be played in public'.[3] It was, though, those unreconstructed Pétainists such as Isorni, Rougier and Louis-Dominique Girard who, in the aftermath of the marshal's disgrace of 1945, resuscitated the mythology of a double game. Girard, a former member of Pétain's entourage and later the author of a sensationalist biography of his hero, disclosing details of the marshal's many mistresses,[4] encapsulated the sense of this supposed diplomacy in the title of his 1947 publication, *Montoire. Verdun diplomatique?*[5] a work that so scandalised the Ministry of the Interior that it was classified alongside works of pornography and thus banned from being displayed in shop windows.[6] It is tempting to believe that had it really contained erotica rather than dreary, and forged, annexes about Franco-British relations then the senile old man, held prisoner on the Île d'Yeu, and suffering from visions of naked women, would have bothered to read it. When presented with a copy by his wife, he put it to one side complaining that it was far too long; only later did he enthuse about its contents, and even then it is unclear whether he had actually read the thing. After all, reading had never been his forte, unless it was the romantic tales of Sir Walter Scott.

The sterling endeavours of diplomatic historians, notably R. T. Thomas, Jean-Baptiste Duroselle and Robert Frank, have since exposed the double-game theory as pure fantasy, something dreamt up in the febrile minds of purblind *maréchalistes*.[7] While it is certain that London maintained a dialogue with Vichy during 1940, this was in the forlorn hope, entertained most especially by the Foreign Office, which despaired of de Gaulle, that the marshal's regime might reconstitute itself in Algeria, taking the sizeable French navy with it. Pétain would have none of this. In unconscious imitation of Lord Nelson, another warrior keen to thwart Anglo-French understanding who placed his blind eye to the telescope and declared 'I see no ships', in December 1940 the Vichy leader immediately denied having received proposals from Churchill stating that Britain would assist France militarily so long as it re-entered the fight from North Africa.[8]

There remains an underside to this London–Vichy dialogue, a story that has never been told and which has been previously dismissed as unimportant, namely the life of those Vichy consuls, both in London and other major cities, who remained in Britain after the severing of diplomatic relations in July 1940. Certainly de Gaulle was wary of their presence. While the soot-stained brick frontage of the Vichy consulate in Bedford Square could not compare with the Regency grandeur of the white-marbled Carlton Gardens, the very presence of these officials was a source of discomfort and a reminder of his own parlous position. That few volunteers, whether expatriates or the marooned sailors of

Narvik and Dunkirk, enlisted in the Free French was frequently blamed on these consuls, notably those at London, Liverpool and Newcastle, who were believed to be illegally assisting refugees and service personnel with repatriation. With hindsight, it is easy to scoff at such paranoia, but it was perfectly understandable, given the general's precarious footing, and was to some extent justified. It should be further stressed that the British, too, kept a close watch on the consular staff, fearful lest they constituted a fifth column and instigated discontent among the many French communities.

This is the history of that potential fifth column. Rather than being the story of secretive, double-talk conversations between London and Vichy conducted by shady emissaries, it is an illustration of how the remorseless wheels of petty bureaucracy – form-filling, passport applications and personal references – kept turning despite the breakdown of diplomatic relations. The history of the consuls is also that of uninspiring men, caught up in bewildering circumstances, who had to please two masters, Vichy and the British, and who inevitably ended up satisfying neither. It is, moreover, a tale of subterfuge, a deliberate attempt to promote Pétainist sentiment among the French in Britain and, indeed, on occasion, to assist with repatriation. Whether the Vichy consuls were engaged in more nefarious activities – the compiling of lists of Gaullist and Allied sympathisers in order that retaliatory action could be taken against their families in France, and the passing on of military and political intelligence – remains a moot point.

The diplomatic community in London: adieu

On 26 June 1940, a day after the terms of the Franco-German Armistice had been broadcast, a po-faced Charles Corbin, French ambassador to Britain and a veteran advocate of Anglo-French friendship, made his way to the Foreign Office. There he was received by the Foreign Secretary Lord Halifax, to whom he made known both his resignation, a 'sad decision', and the urgent need for 'new representation in London'.[9] The embassy, he continued, would for the time being be placed in the capable hands of Roger Cambon, the descendant of a long line of Cambons who had worked for the *entente cordiale*, although it was not long before he too had resigned.[10] Both men had quickly understood what the new Pétain administration augured. For his part, Cambon remained in London throughout the war, never missing an air raid even at the height of the Blitz.[11] Corbin persevered in Britain until

July 1940, when he made his 'tender farewell' to diplomatic friends and colleagues.[12] Believing it undiplomatic to remain in a nation that had repeatedly attacked his own country – both on the airwaves and on the sea where the Royal Navy imposed a strict blockade – he eventually resurfaced in Rio de Janeiro in mid-August 1940. It is sometimes claimed, notably by de Gaulle's biographer Jean Lacouture, that he remained in South America for the duration of the war.[13] This was not the case.[14] Increasingly despondent at the situation in France, in late 1940 he published a statement from Brazil, which in private he denied, claiming that he was awaiting instructions from Pétain to serve in some capacity at Vichy.[15] February 1941 found Corbin in Lisbon en route to France, a journey that dismayed Daniel Roché, the Anglophile second secretary of the French legation in Dublin, who feared the former ambassador would be arrested by the Germans on trumped-up charges pounded out of his one-time London colleagues.[16] In a meeting with Sir Ronald Campbell, British ambassador at Lisbon, Corbin constituted a sorrowful picture: 'he struck me as rather bitter and distinctly flabby ... There is no fight in him and he gives the impression of a broken man.'[17] Haunted by Mers-el-Kébir and Dakar, he harped on about 'the ghastly spectacle of starving children', their condition a direct result of Britain's blockade. A month later, in Madrid, he likewise struck Sir Samuel Hoare, ambassador to Spain, as 'defeatist', arguing that while Britain might not be beaten, Germany was 'invincible'.[18] Once in France, it was believed his 'black mood' lifted and in 1942 it was rumoured that he had the good sense to turn down an offer from Pétain to become Vichy's representative in Washington, preferring retirement in the south of France where in his private correspondence, which seems to have been read by the British, he readily criticised the marshal's policies.[19]

With Corbin, an open admirer of British tradition and culture, unwilling to make a categorical stand against Vichy, what hope was there for the other French representatives in London, the several hundred or so staff of the embassy (typists, clerks as well as professional diplomats), and the predominantly military contingent, some seven to eight hundred strong, who belonged to the naval, air and military missions that had arrived with the outbreak of war, and who had often mobilised members of the existing French colony 'en place'?[20] Disturbing reports of anti-British behaviour, especially on the part of the military missions, many of whom were not full-fledged diplomats but still enjoyed diplomatic immunity, arrived on the desks of government officials thick and fast in June/July 1940. In the lull between the creation of the Pétain government and the declaration of the Armistice, Sir Desmond Morton was visited by John Miller, a chartered accountant attached to the French Military Purchasing Commission, who reported how two members of that body, a Colonel M— and A—W—, had been making 'the most bitter remarks about this country' and were looking to leave as quickly and 'as unobtrusively as possible'.[21] Together, these men had asked Miller to draw cheques to the value of 4,200 sterling, all in one-pound notes, valuable foreign currency for the French government, and had requested lists of all purchases made by the French Armaments Commission in this country, sensitive information that disclosed the whereabouts of war industries. The prime minister himself had been alarmed by these developments, and was personally convinced that members of the missions 'were actively working against our interests'.[22] Further evidence was soon at hand. On 6 July, the French chargé d'affaires complained about the treatment of one diplomat who, on the initiative of MI5, had been stopped while embarking for France and questioned at length about the materials he was carrying in his diplomatic bag, and at Vichy there were complaints that personnel of the naval mission had been arrested for speaking in Breton to sailors.[23] While cases of potential spies were relatively few, the possibility of French representatives distributing anti-de Gaulle propaganda remained ever present. In late July 1940, the Foreign Office flatly turned down a request from the French consul for five non-commissioned officers from the missions to visit troops at White City to handle the distribution of wages lest they peddled anti-Allied sentiments.[24]

At least on this occasion, the proper diplomatic channels had been deployed. On 4 July, a day after Mers-el-Kébir, Corporal Boyle of the Field Security Police filed a report on a recent incident at Olympia where de Gaulle was recruiting.[25] Three suspects had been held after breaking into the barracks. They claimed to belong to the French naval mission, but it transpired they were clerks attached to the French naval attaché, living at the nearby Maison of the Institut Français. While none of the men had national registration cards, they were all carrying diplomatic passes issued by the embassy. The ringleader, a thirty-four year old, who claimed to have been living in England for seven years, said their task had simply been to contact a particular officer, whose name he refused to surrender. It soon transpired, however, that their real job was to discover the number of ratings there and to distribute 'seditious propaganda'. Witnesses reported how the men had claimed that it was unpatriotic to fight for de Gaulle; he was not their leader; the English had let them down. One even had the temerity to quiz an English sergeant on the whereabouts of British regiments. The three men also possessed considerable quantities of cash for purposes they would not disclose. They were detained overnight, apparently in the lavatories. When police called on one of the men's wives, she was quite unsurprised that her husband had been arrested. His release, and that of the others, was secured by two senior officers of the naval attaché, although this did not prevent a furious exchange of words with a Free French colonel who questioned the diplomatic immunity of the naval mission.

It is highly possible the above men were in the employ of Capitaine de Vaisseau de Rivoyre, former naval attaché to the French embassy, who quickly decided against joining de Gaulle, placing his trust instead in French civilisation, which he hoped would ultimately defeat the barbarian.[26] It is more likely that such talk hid a defeatist attitude, which was revealed in a leaflet he designed for Olympia.[27] In this, he claimed that men were being persuaded to support the Allied cause by 'false representation', that de Gaulle was under warrant of arrest, and that war would shortly commence between Britain and France; so it was that Frenchmen who had enlisted in de Gaulle's forces, despite their ships having been seized by the British, would soon be fighting their brothers. As Maurice Hankey wryly observed, 'Olympia seems to have been fairly lively.'[28] In a similar vein, another high-ranking member of the naval mission was belatedly discovered to have been distributing a letter among sailors at Southampton warning that they would be treated as *francs-tireurs* if they joined de Gaulle.[29] None of these propagandists quite managed to live up to the sinister image of one 'little fellow with a bandage on his head', originally a native of Jersey, perhaps a member of the naval mission, working as interpreter among French sailors at Euston station where he also dished out defeatist opinions to anyone who would listen.[30]

Given these anecdotes, it is little surprise that few among the diplomatic staff and the missions volunteered for either de Gaulle or the British. On 10 July 1940, an ad hoc meeting of the Vansittart Committee noted that a mere 'eight members of the French Armaments Mission had placed their services unconditionally at the disposal of His Majesty's Government'.[31] A similar number had requested permission to leave for the USA. Nor is it any surprise that their numbers should have been so low. The example of Corbin was hardly inspiring. As François Coulet observed, there was also a strong sense of collective discipline among the diplomatic staff: it was their professional responsibility to obey their government's orders, even if they were uncomfortable with them.[32] Walking along the corridors of the French embassy on 17 June 1940, shortly after the broadcast of Pétain's speech, Robert Mengin overheard one military attaché remark, 'In wartime, a man can't just resign. Resignation equals desertion. One receives an order, one carries it out, and no nonsense.'[33] Mengin himself sought a return to France in order to be reunited with his baby in Brittany, but on arriving at Plymouth in early July 1940 he could not find a single French sailor in sight as 'they were all behind bars – prison bars'.[34] More British-based diplomats might have broken ranks and put aside family worries had their colleagues within France come to Britain. This was not to be. Lacouture cites the example of Roland de Margerie, a professional civil servant, an associate of Reynaud and an early admirer of de Gaulle, who ultimately considered it his duty to serve his country in France not in London, much the same decision that was reached by the famous resister Jean Moulin who stayed at his prefectoral post at Chartres only to be ousted by Vichy in October 1940.[35] Nor did de Gaulle – the 'rebel', the 'dissident', the 'unknown quantity' – cut much ice with a body of men accustomed to following orders, and who had not figured explicitly in his appeal of 18 June when he called on 'soldiers, engineers and skilled workers of the armaments industries' to join his cause.[36] Lacouture suggests that it was unfortunate that the general cancelled a dinner party with leading diplomats in early July.[37] Yet given de Gaulle's failure to recruit when he visited the servicemen's camps, this remains a dubious argument. His autocratic and high-minded attitude might further have damaged his cause. It was partially this that alienated Aléxis de Léger, secretary-general of the Quai d'Orsay, who met with de Gaulle on 22 June, and who quickly decided his destiny lay in the USA. Léger was courageous in his decision. Other diplomats were fearful for their families in France. Miller, the accountant who spoke with Morton, mentioned that those officials with relatives in southern and central France were keen to be reunited as soon as possible so as to safeguard their collective futures.[38] Those with kin in occupied France apparently believed they could ensure their families' safety by trading information about Britain to the Gestapo. Such anxieties were also noted by other British observers, Noel Baker wondering whether the missions should be outwardly 'interned', yet privately allowed to go about their business and help the Allied cause, so as to give these men and their families the necessary 'cover'.[39]

There remains a further reason why a majority of the diplomatic and mission staff were unwilling to rally to the Allied cause, that is a latent anti-British sentiment. This might seem strange emanating from a body of men led by such eminent Anglophiles as Corbin and Cambon, and which included such characters as Paul Morand, a member of the Economic Mission, and a man fascinated by the Anglo-Saxon world, having written eloquently about London and his travels in the USA.[40] Mengin recalls how none of the senior embassy staff wanted to be the one who had to hand over the papers breaking off relations with the UK.[41] Moreover, several of these officials had been selected precisely because of their command of the English language and knowledge of English customs. Perhaps the answer to this question is again supplied by Mengin, who stayed in London throughout the war, without joining de Gaulle.[42] When, in September 1939, he travelled to Britain from France he was struck by the contrast between the mournful atmosphere he had observed in Paris and the gaiety in London. His diplomatic colleagues had an answer: 'The English did not have 6 million men mobilized; and anyway they are insensitive, a stolid lot.'[43] Such views were replicated in a document authored by Morand in July 1940 and intended for his Pétainist masters, but which was known to the British. Set in the context of the explosive events of that summer, this painted 'a most disparaging report about the French embassy in London'.[44]

If members of the diplomatic staff and the missions were eager to leave, the British were only too glad to assist them in this whenever possible. Vichy was also anxious to help with resettlement, at least in the case of the diplomatic personnel, contrasting with the lethargic manner in which the regime approached the question of repatriating servicemen, suggesting that those stranded soldiers and sailors made good anti-British propaganda. So it was in later July that the diplomatic staff, accompanied by their families, congregated at Addison Road station in North London, significantly not one of the main termini where they might have become the target for public hostility, to catch a train for Liverpool docks.[45] All in all, some 600 or so embassy personnel quit in total, sailing on the *Orduna* on 19 July and arriving at Lisbon four days later.[46] The missions were, however, another matter, largely because many of them were in possession of sensitive military intelligence.[47] Thanks to this, in early July 1940 the War Cabinet discussed the possibility of segregating elements of the missions, some to be accommodated in Cheltenham Ladies' College where they could cause no mischief; the girls, it should be added, had already been evacuated preventing mischief of another nature.[48] It was appreciated, however, that the numbers to be isolated should stay small so as not to alienate any French who might wish to join the Allied cause.[49] When news of possible segregation reached the French chargé d'affaires, he vigorously protested, pointing out that these individuals could 'hardly swim across the Channel'.[50] It may well have unsettled members of the missions themselves. Spears drew a graph of the mood of these men for the period 27 June to 19 July plotting how their morale passed through 'unshakeable resolve', 'determination', 'prudent mood', 'dolce', 'procrastination', 'flaccid', and 'complete negation of all action'; appended is a handwritten cartoon of two particularly fortunate members of the mission, granted permission to leave in July, sailing away from Angleterre cocking a snook at their former home.[51] News of segregation also seemed to have caused consternation among 'well-disposed elements' of the London-based colony, giving rise to unfounded fears about general internment.[52] In the event, British action was not draconian. A small number, ten altogether, who had been engaged in subversive activities, such as Capitaine de Vaisseau de Rivoyre, were to be detained for the duration of the war,[53] although it seems that most of these were repatriated at the close of the year. Those pertaining to 'the Food, Textiles, Oil, Timber, Coal, Economic Warfare and Sea Transport Missions, together with the French Representatives of the Air and Shipping Executive Committees' were free to leave immediately if they so desired.[54] Non-commissioned officers, other ranks and civilian personnel of the military, naval, air and armaments missions were also given grace to depart. Officers and senior personnel belonging to these bodies were, however, to be detained, at least for the time being. It was proposed to repatriate these officials after a three-month time lag by when the information they possessed would be out of date.

Interestingly, Vichy happily colluded in British plans. In 1940, the regime was not prepared to surrender everything to the Germans, and appreciated that knowledge about Anglo-French military capabilities best remained out of harm's way across the Channel. So it was that several months elapsed before these individuals pertaining to the missions were repatriated, via a boat to Marseilles, although by this stage, December 1940, some had clearly developed cold feet about returning, opting instead to stay in London.[55] Those kept indefinitely belonged to the air mission, and included technical experts such as Professor D— who deployed argument after argument to be allowed to go home: to look after his 'ophaned nephews', to cater for his students,[56] and to tend for his wife.[57] It was understood his real reason was to take up a prestigious post at the Sorbonne, proving that the unpropitious circumstances of enemy occupation are no bar to academic ambition. All these complaints cut little ice with the Foreign Office, and D—stayed. It should also be pointed out that the British were eager to hold a small number of French back to trade them off for the repatriation of British officials held in France.

With the departure of the embassy staff and the subsequent withdrawal of the missions, Vichy no longer possessed any diplomatic representation in London.[58] This partially explains why those curious London–Vichy dialogues were conducted through semi-official emissaries and the Spanish government. There remained, however, the UK French consulates, which were designated to look after 'various non-political matters on behalf of Vichy'.[59] Thought had been given to expelling these straightaway given that British consular staff had been ousted from French colonies in North and West Africa, as well as in the unoccupied zone. Their stay of execution rested on the needs of those large numbers of French who were based in the British Isles. In 1941, the Foreign Office recorded that consulates were open in London, Liverpool, Newcastle-on-Tyne, Cardiff, Swansea and Edinburgh, together with representation in other large towns, some 15 consular offices in total.[60] The numbers of consular officials and their staff are hard to assess, but may have amounted to over 200, most concentrated in London. Some of the representatives were merely consular agents who doubled up their day jobs with looking after immigration enquiries and trading arrangements; the remainder were professional diplomats, often well travelled around the globe. Additionally, a small number of staff were retained in the liquidation missions appointed to tidy up the financial aftermath of the Franco-British war effort: the financial mission (8 people); the armaments mission (2); the sea transport mission (7); the textiles mission (7); the food purchasing mission (1); the petroleum mission (3); the coal and minerals mission (4); the Liquidation des Services de l'Attaché Naval (2); and the Services de l'Attaché de l'Air (1).[61] What is extraordinary is that such a paltry number of men and women were to cause so much trouble, and so greatly agitate both the British and Free French.

Map 3   The principal Vichy consular offices in 1940

Agents consulaires or agents provocateurs?

With the breaking off of diplomatic relations, the British had anticipated that the consular staff would be headed by Paul Morand who
possessed the cumbersome title of *Agent pour la liquidation des affaires
économiques et commerciales du gouvernement français en Grande
Bretagne*.[62] He, though, left for France on 19 July 1940 with the other
embassy staff.[63] This was to the relief of the Germans who viewed him
as a 'propagandiste anglophile'.[64] It was also to the relief of the British
who had been perturbed by rumours that he was thinking of joining de
Gaulle.[65] In British eyes, he was a defeatist, a 'weak character', who had
never concealed his pessimism from his staff.[66] His leaving was ultimately credited to the fact that he was a friend of Pierre Laval and was
in possession of property in both the German and Italian occupied
areas of France. Paradoxically for a man who, in 1940, had been
deemed self-interested and weak willed, a year later he would publish
Chroniques de l'homme maigre, a eulogy to self-discipline and a critique
of the indolence and lack of spirit among his fellow countrymen.

Morand's place was taken by Jacques Chartier, a career civil servant,
and a *conseiller* in the French Diplomatic Service. He introduced
himself to the Foreign Office on 19 July 1940 where he cut a poor
impression, his initial concerns largely revolving around himself.
While he possessed a diplomatic passport and his British identification
papers were in order, he had lost his valued yellow pass as secretary-
general to Morand's economic mission. Having purchased the car of
the ill-fated Captain de Rivoyre, who before his detention had taken to
inviting officers 'of very good standing and family' to his house where
he had put pressure on them to return to France,[67] he was also anxious
for petrol coupons. He further wished his official title to be the same as
Morand's, so that technically he was only acting head of the liquidation
missions, rather than acting head consul and thus Vichy's chief diplomatic representative in Britain. Knowing what we do about the
pusillanimous nature of his character, which will become increasingly
clear in the ensuing pages, this might well have been because he wanted
an ambiguity to surround his position, enabling him to wriggle out of
any embarrassing situations. This was not easy to do. It was through
Chartier that Vichy quickly made known it would not accept the
accreditation of Neville Bland and W. H. B. Mack as consuls to Vichy,
unless mission staff were released immediately and the British desisted
from dropping propaganda leaflets on Morocco.[68] To Vichy itself,

Chartier feebly reported that London would not allow him to treat current issues, and he later complained bitterly about his material lot.[69] As we shall see, it was events in September 1940 that forced him to acknowledge his wider responsibilities, although these never extended to facilitating high-level Anglo-French dialogue as is sometimes claimed in older histories.[70]

Initial reports about Chartier's political attitude were not encouraging. Like Morand, he was described as a defeatist, and the fact that he had not brought his wife and children to England, despite their being resident in the Normandy resort town of Trouville, only a short boat trip across the Channel, counted against him. When asked about their safety, he replied that the Germans would not harm them.[71] It was further known that he had not assisted those of his staff who wished to stay in London, leaving them without money, and threatening them with the prospect of a concentration camp should they ever wish to return to their homeland. De Gaulle was also quizzed about Chartier. While he admitted he did not know him, his men had quickly formed the opinion that he 'was more than pro-Vichy'.[72]

Although supposedly only acting head of the liquidation missions, Chartier quickly conducted his own *épuration* of diplomatic staff in Bedford Square. Through Roché in Dublin, who broke with Vichy in October, it was learned that the new consul was trying to 'get all the old regime' out of the Consulate-General, attention focusing especially on Bougnet, a *consul de carrière*, who acted as an archivist.[73] According to Roché, a regular conduit of information about the goings-on among Vichy consular staff, Bougnet was 'a sound fellow', anxious to stay in London and facilitate Anglo-French relations, whereas Chartier wanted him off his turf to take up the far-flung consular post in Newcastle that had recently become vacant. When the Foreign Office spoke to Chartier about this, he launched into a highly personal attack on Bougnet, describing him as 'lazy, obstinate, only intent on keeping his post, where he drew a disproportionately high salary for doing nothing'.[74] Bougnet, he continued, exercised a destabilising effect on his staff and refused to take orders. That Roger Cambon was asked to vouch for the unpopular archivist was perhaps evidence of his pro-British views, the real reason why Chartier wanted him out of London.

With such a man at the helm, it was inevitable that anti-British and anti-Free French activities, practised by some of the mission staff, should have continued. Nonetheless, it should be stressed that not all consuls were so-minded, maybe because some were well integrated into British life; indeed, one or two were, in fact, British and immediately resigned their posts at the time of the Armistice, for instance a W. B. D. Shackleton of Bradford who also worked as a solicitor.[75] For those who remained in position, autumn 1940 brought with it frequent visits by local police officers, acting on the behalf of the Foreign Office. The officers were encouraged, in general conversation while pretending to be carrying out other duties, to press their interviewees on political matters, a task that must have taxed the investigative capabilities of the ordinary constables involved. Alternatively, intelligence had been gathered by speaking to the consul's associates and drinking partners.

Through such ham-fisted techniques, and through the tough leather prose of police reports, it is subsequently possible to identify three groups of consular officials. The first were those, notably at Manchester, Birmingham, Swansea, Blyth and Brighton, who had clearly flagged their pro-Allied sentiments, and who remained in post merely for financial reasons or out of the belief that this was the best way of harming Pétain's cause. A good example is that of the Brighton official, born in Saint-Sauvant in 1873 and a resident in Britain since 1916, who coupled his consular duties with acting as a minister in the local French Protestant Church. For many years he had held extreme Germanophobe views and regularly insulted Germans in the street. At the time of Dunkirk, he had visited men in hospital and advised them not to return to France. Although he had not resigned his office, he had admitted this was only because he could not afford to lose his income, and readily broadcast his admiration for de Gaulle.[76]

A second group of consuls were more ambiguous in their allegiance, although it was clear the British had collated no hard evidence against them. In North and South Shields, there were no grounds to 'doubt' the consul's pro-Allied views, maybe to be expected of a man with a Jewish wife, but it was noted that he was generally uncommunicative and unpopular with the locals; across in Sunderland, the consul, down on his luck thanks to the war terminating his business activities and now to be found working as a chauffeur, had grumbled that 'England had not given France all the help it might have done', but that was it; and in Bristol, the consul, who doubled up as teacher of French in a nearby secondary school, had denounced the Pétain regime as a 'puppet government', unrepresentative of the real France, while on other occasions he had been far less willing to speak in such a manner, something that the police thought in itself suspicious.[77] In Folkestone, the consul himself was thought to have definite 'pro-British tendencies', yet his son, a 'brave' boy who worked part-time as a messenger for the local air warden, had been reported for defeatist talk, albeit only on one occasion. He was alleged to have said that the 'war was costing 6 millions a day and to save this it would be better if we gave up and came under Germany as we should probably be better ruled'.[78] The air warden-cum-informant had subsequently been pressed to talk to the consul himself, but had been unwilling to sharpen his investigative abilities further.

The third group of consuls were those known to be openly 'working actively against us', assisting in the repatriation of servicemen and the distribution of propaganda.[79] Significantly, these were all professional, career diplomats based in Swansea, Liverpool, Newcastle and Glasgow, port towns and key strategic areas, where sizeable numbers of French troops were stationed, both Free French and servicemen awaiting their voyage home. From Newcastle emanated the report that the French consul, one Jacques Le Serre, was refusing any assistance to sailors anxious to get in touch with de Gaulle, and that such men were having to be processed through Customs and Immigration.[80] Over in Swansea, the Consul Guy René Brun, who had been prevented from leaving the country on account of the technical intelligence in his possession, had quickly got himself 'into trouble with the police by working against General de Gaulle among French sailors at Falmouth'.[81] MI5 had also taken an interest in his case, discovering that he had occupied a consular position in Saarbrucken, which he had been forced to vacate because of currency irregularities.[82] It was further uncovered that he spoke good German, was in regular contact with three German women, frequently spread anti-British views, and had devised pro-Vichy propaganda for French merchant seamen.

Further north in Liverpool, the behaviour of the consul, Jacques Dufort, was even more brazen. In early September 1940, Lieutenant-Colonel Macbeth, in charge of Trentham Park, was amazed to be visited by one of his internees who naively confessed that he had been given permission by the consul to travel to Liverpool where a berth awaited him on a steamer of the Yeoward Line along with his papers, which were all in order.[83] Even more naively, the man wanted to leave immediately for the port in a lorry being used by de Gaulle's recruiting agents! Dufort also intervened in the case of one soldier in Carlisle who had been required to attend the local police station on a weekly basis where he had allegedly been pressurised into joining de Gaulle's men. This behaviour was 'all the more regrettable', continued the consul, as the man in question had no intention of following these suggestions and had been declared 'unfit' for service.[84] Such an intervention was only one case among several.

The fullest report on consular misdeeds was filed by Glasgow police in the case of Camille Henry Alfred Parent de Curzon.[85] This minor aristocrat had been in trouble with the authorities before. In 1937, the police had received a report from the Italian tutor whom he employed to coach his son. Fearful for his job and personal security should he later go abroad, the hapless teacher complained that the consul was making his life unbearable because of his republican and liberal views, which conflicted with the monarchist politics of de Curzon himself and his White Russian assistant, who worked as a caretaker in the consular office. In 1940, the consul had interfered in the activities of the Glasgow branch of the Franco-Scottish Society, which had organised a campaign to raise money for French families whose menfolk were fighting in the army. De Curzon had taken charge of this venture, appointing a board of trustees, which was described as 'very ill selected'. On 10 September, the Executive Committee of the Franco-Scottish Society, on which the consul sat ex officio, had assembled for a meeting at which one of the members had suggested to de Curzon that he should resign on ground of ill health and take a holiday. He had replied that he was 'too busy'. 'Busy doing what?', he was quizzed. 'Writing reports', he replied. 'Writing reports about what and to whom? You cannot have any communication with your government at present.' 'I just file my reports for future reference', adding he could not afford a holiday. When the meeting got properly under way, it was suggested that the Society should organise a series of lectures on 'The Spirit of France', maybe inviting the former Popular Front minister, Pierre Cot, to which the consul objected saying that this would be an 'insult' to his government, as would any lecture about the defeat of France. To cool tempers, de Curzon had been asked to leave the room temporarily while the Committee could take stock, but he had misinterpreted this request as one to depart permanently and had gone off in a huff, only to reappear at a further meeting where he disputed a recommendation that the Society should recognise only 'de Gaulle's party' as the true representation of France. Refusing to assist at further sessions, he had nonetheless attended a lecture by Denis Saurat, held at the Royal Philosophical Society, in which he sat silently at the back of the hall making notes. A devout Catholic, a staunch monarchist and rather 'German in appearance and outlook', de Curzon was generally unpopular with the French community in the city, the police concluded, but was too 'stupid' to involve himself in espionage, merely contenting himself with the diffusion of Pétainist sentiments

Whether Chartier personally involved himself in such skulduggery remains unclear. It was believed that if he did exercise any influence it was when interviewing servicemen and other nationals over passport applications in the privacy of his own office, and it appears that he was concerned chiefly with men of status.[86] When, in late 1940, the journalist Bret visited the consulate to obtain a visa for North Africa, where he felt he could be of more value to the war effort, he kept a close watch on what he said on interrogation by Chartier; in Bret's own words, this was the first time in his life when he knew to keep his mouth shut.[87] Others, too, were wary of Vichy's man in London. On bumping into Chartier at the Foreign Office, Palewski, one of de Gaulle's closest associates, timidly asked, 'Am I condemned to death?'[88]

That Chartier's immediate officials were involved in subterfuge seems less contentious. From Crystal Palace, where a contingent of French sailors was housed, came complaints from the Ministry of Shipping that one of the London French consular staff had been distributing unfavourable propaganda about de Gaulle although, to be fair, the Foreign Office noted that this complaint might have emanated from Admiral Muselier who had been bitterly disappointed because of his own failure to recruit.[89] Meanwhile, the attention of Special Branch had centred on two officials belonging to Bedford Square who were known to be carrying large amounts of money and circulating among members of de Gaulle's forces, where they readily spread disturbing rumours.[90] The two individuals had yet to be identified, probably because they kept their associations with the consulate from view, but clearly a sojourn at Pentonville awaited them when they were apprehended.

At this point, the question must be asked whether Chartier and his cronies were involved in more sinister practices, notably in collecting military intelligence and in collating lists of de Gaulle's volunteers to be relayed to Vichy for subsequent action to be taken against the men's families in France. After all, consulate offices had been used for spying purposes in the past. Robert Graves recalls how, before 1914, the German consulate had been a regular conduit of information for Berlin.[91] The prudence of Bret when interviewed by Chartier will also be recalled, as will the behaviour of the French missions. Nevertheless, evidence of the consuls as spies is not convincing. There is nothing in the German Foreign Ministry Archives to suggest that the consulate at

Bedford Square was relaying intelligence to Berlin via Vichy or Paris.[92] Admittedly, it is unlikely that Vichy, anxious to cling on to whatever authority it possessed, would have shared such information with Berlin in the first place; whatever the case, surmise suggests that little of value came out of Pétain's London base. As we have seen, Vichy provincial consuls were clumsy and under constant surveillance. They also lacked the necessary equipment to communicate with their government. This was even true of Chartier, the only consul who had regular contact with his government. In August 1940, he requested use of the cypher facilities within Bedford Square.[93] The head of MI6, known merely as 'C', who undoubtedly possessed a mole inside the Consulate-General, was keen that this wish be granted so that any communication with Vichy could be monitored, although it was admitted that Chartier was unlikely to send out any sensitive information as his cypher was so primitive it was probable the Germans had already decoded it, as indeed the British appear to have done. The Foreign Office, however, was opposed as reciprocal arrangements had not been granted to British consuls who had recently been allowed to return to Lyon and Pau. Clearly British secret dispatches out of France were of a superior sort. So it was that Chartier was forced to telegramme *en clair*, meaning that his contacts with Vichy were open for all to read and were thus largely confined to run-of-the-mill information. As he himself acknowledged to his Vichy masters, in a telegram of 22 August, the cypher had been denied him for fear that he would report on the activities of French political refugees in the United Kingdom.[94] In a later telegram of 12 September, Baudouin, Vichy's Anglophobe Foreign Minister, expressed his sympathy to Chartier, acknowledging that he had a difficult job on his hands having to deal with the British.[95]

While it remains almost certain that Chartier secreted intelligence through diplomatic bags, these took an eternity to arrive in France, going first through the Spanish embassy in London and then via Madrid; the material must have been long in the tooth when it reached the hotels of Vichy. Suggestions, probably made by Spears, that Chartier was responsible for spreading news of the Dakar expedition, and was thus responsible for its failure, are risible given what we know about the lack of security cover in the preparations for this ill-fated adventure.[96] Similar allegations that Chartier was writing to the Germans, via the Dublin legation, using secret ink should also be treated with a pinch of salt, especially as the Dublin officials had mostly defected from Vichy;[97] nor is there anything in the German archives to verify such stories.[98] As we shall see, the value of Chartier's reports was questionable in other respects, often echoing what he believed his government wanted to hear. In this situation, it is probable that the consuls, and then only some, restricted themselves to assisting in repatriation, the diffusion of propaganda and the distribution of monies, intended as bribes to dissuade servicemen from enlisting with either de Gaulle or the British.

Such activity was damaging and destabilising enough, and Chartier only avoided expulsion thanks to the inability of the British to pin anything definite on him and because of his worth to 'C'. This did not stop British Intelligence making life difficult for him by conveying to Vichy rumours about his duplicitous behaviour.[99] Indulgence was not, however, accorded to the consuls at Liverpool, Swansea and Newcastle. On 29 September Chartier was invited to an interview at the Foreign Office where he was informed that the government was withdrawing the 'exequaturs' (effectively an expulsion order) for consuls involved in 'anti-allied activities'.[100] At this, Chartier's face apparently 'grew longer', perhaps because he feared his name was in the frame, or that some of his London agents had been rumbled. When told the identities of Brun, Dufort and Le Serre, he 'almost clapped his hands in glee'. He said Brun was 'a ridiculous creature', and he 'was very glad that he had got into trouble'. Le Serre was 'a lunatic', and was already to be recalled by Vichy. As to Dufort, he had retired, but had then obstinately stuck to his post. Once Chartier had lunch with him and his Jewish wife along with her two sisters, and 'he had felt that he was sitting in the Warsaw ghetto'. If only the British had forewarned him, he continued, arrangements would have been made through Vichy for their withdrawal. Yet as he was only in charge of the liquidation missions, a reference to the title he had assumed in July, he disingenuously added that he could have done little. Maybe he later regretted this remark, as soon after the Foreign Office pressed him to clarify his position, thus forcing Chartier to acknowledge the wider remit he had always possessed as Vichy's chief representative in Britain.

There ensued negotiations as to who should fill the vacancies at Liverpool, Newcastle and Swansea, Chartier putting his own names forward, no doubt again to increase the scope of his patronage and cement his own position (the case of Bougnet will be recalled), and the British eagerly weighing up the probity of the suggestions. Meanwhile, the chief consul behaved disloyally to his dismissed colleagues, particularly Dufort and his family who, on their withdrawal from Liverpool, had taken up residence in suburban Wembley, expressing a strong wish to stay in England, unlike all those sailors the consul had helped resettle in France. Maybe in a misguided attempt to please the British, or more probably in an attempt to assert his own command, Chartier would have none of this, refusing to give the family money and divesting himself of any responsibility in their regard, something that they interpreted as a threat.[101] In the event, they were repatriated at the close of the year. Chartier 'has gone from bad to worse', noted one Foreign Office official at the close of 1940.[102] Little did he know what 1941 was to bring.

La conduite consulaire: conduct unbecoming

Through his pro-Vichy views, his sanctioning of anti-Gaullist propaganda and his ready willingness to abandon his colleagues when it suited him, Chartier had made few friends among his British hosts who saw through his double-talk, yet the Foreign Office was prepared to tolerate him because of the help he gave to refugees, and his willingness to help out with the passports of Free French volunteers who were arriving in large numbers at the start of 1941. No doubt his indirect value to MI6 also played a part in their calculations. Yet Chartier had made dangerous enemies in the shape of Carlton Gardens and the Spears Mission which, at this point, was often willing to act as the *porte-parole* of de Gaulle's organisation, often parroting the same complaints, usually about supposed snubs to the general himself, and adopting similar causes. So it was that, in February 1941, their line of fire centred on Bedford Square, and Chartier in particular, who was said to be 'aiding and abetting deserters from the Free French forces'.[103] While it will be recalled that the French soldiers and sailors belonging to the camps in northern England had by then been sent home, some stragglers were still at large in Liverpool and Manchester. Ultimately, however, it was the outside developments of the war, notably in Syria, that brought about Chartier's forced withdrawal.

Suggestions that Bedford Square was facilitating the repatriation of Free French deserters were to lead to an almighty row within British circles. When, on 25 February 1941, the Spears Mission made these allegations, it did not mince its words: 'Under our very noses the Vichy Consulate is doing deadly harm to the FFF.'[104] Our own army, continued the general, would not accept a situation where a soldier could visit the offices of the ILP (Independent Labour Party) and obtain money, demobilisation papers and a railway ticket. So it was that 'the French Consulate constitutes fifth-column activities of a most dangerous sort since they tend to undermine the moral and efficiency of an allied force'. Berating the MI5 for adopting a theological attitude to Bedford Square's responsibilities, Spears suggested the intelligence agency should adopt as a motto, 'See no evil, hear no evil, speak no evil'. The general also warned French Welfare not to have any further dealings with Bedford Square, and urged Bessborough's organisation to launch an enquiry into how such repatriations could be stopped in future. Behind this complaint undoubtedly lay an attempt to spike the guns of the CEAF whose dealings with French refugees, often through the consulate, caused continued outrage in Carlton Gardens. Reading between the lines, it may also be that Spears and the Free French had deliberately attempted to set up the consulate by sending two rather dubious individuals as agents provocateurs to Bedford Square to ask delicate questions.[105]

This somewhat maladroit piece of diplomacy, worthy of de Gaulle himself in its brusqueness, went down badly in Whitehall where it caused 'alarm and despondency'.[106] Copies were quickly withdrawn except from one or two people. Bessborough was clearly still a recipient as he denounced the memorandum as 'tantamount to an accusation against us of treason'.[107] He then went on to explain why French Welfare, and for that matter Chartier, could not possibly help with any desertions, men who were apparently dressing up as refugees and obtaining forged papers. Betraying a somewhat naive faith in bureaucratic procedures, Bessborough explained that this would be impossible as 'by arrangement with the Home Office and MI5 any civilian refugee who wishes to be repatriated must fill in an Exit Permit form supplied to him by the French Consulate General'.[108] This document, together with the refugee's registration card, was then forwarded to Passport Office, which processed the necessary paperwork under the vigilant eye of MI5. The upshot, claimed Bessborough, was that the emigration authorities at the quayside were armed with a list of all refugees granted authority to quit the British Isles, and only those on the list were given permission to embark. Meanwhile, Carlton Gardens supplied to MI5 and local police forces the names of all deserters. Bessborough drew further reassurance from the fact that Chartier supplied to his own office the names of French sailors and soldiers who had approached the consulate requesting repatriation. Should any man have once belonged to de Gaulle, his case was given extra special attention. In this way, all possible loopholes had been closed.

To disprove the watertight nature of these procedures, Muselier brought to the attention of the Foreign Office the case of one F—B—, an Alsatian sailor, who had recently been discharged from the Free French Navy on the grounds of ill health.[109] While in the waiting room of the CEAF, there to collect charitable handouts, B— had been joined by another man, a former member of the crew of the *Courbet*, who had refused to enlist in the Free French. While in conversation, they had been approached by a third man from the same ship who confessed 'that he was a deserter'. This individual then 'volunteered the information' that the CEAF regularly helped fugitives such as him by supplying them with the identity papers and false documents of refugees who had already left the country. Thanks to these papers, the deserters had then been able to avoid the attentions of the police, although quite how they circumvented the system described above by Bessborough remains unclear. Failing to address this point, Muselier claimed the leadership of the CEAF was behind this scheme, especially the Baron de P—, formerly secretary-general of French Teachers in Great Britain. While there was no direct evidence linking Chartier to the scam, this was attributed to his 'cunning' rather than his 'innocence in the matter'.

Whether the CEAF was truly behind this particular bolt-hole remains doubtful. As already implied, this appears to have been yet another attempt to smear a rival, and non-Gaullist, organisation. As to whether Chartier and his associates were more generally facilitating repatriation, the answer is probably yes, but not in the numbers the Free French alleged. 'What sort of proof will be required to convince you that Chartier's activities are dangerous?', thundered Spears in a letter to Bessborough of 4 March 1941.[110] While it cannot be discounted that this proof might have since disappeared, little further evidence was forthcoming, other than vague allegations, notably that an Italian waiter with fascist sympathies overheard officers' conversations at the Savoy, subsequently passing on his information to Chartier.[111] As to Muselier, his complaint may well have been a reflection of the precarious footing of Free French Forces at the start of 1941. Many of the volunteers for de Gaulle had signed six-month engagement forms in June/July 1940, contracts that were now coming to a close. It was widely known that morale and overall discipline within the general's forces was not good, especially after the fiasco that was the

Dakar expedition and the return of those stranded sailors at the close of the year. Reports about the poor organisation within the general's forces were legion, and caused the Foreign Office some concern. Among many disturbing tales was that of a young Frenchman, an escaped POW, who had smuggled himself out of France to enlist with de Gaulle.[112] When he arrived at the recruiting depot, he found this 'dirty' and 'generally unattractive'. Nor was life in the garrisons at Camberley and Aldershot especially appealing. While the military discipline of these sites was judged to have improved, the social life and amenities were virtually non-existent, partially thanks to the attitude of the British themselves who, it will be recalled, had failed to distinguish between Free French and servicemen awaiting repatriation. As Lieutenant-Colonel Claud Black of the War Office reported to French Welfare, 'the local population, both military and civil, tend to be very preoccupied with the various problems which the war brings in its train, and the question of entertaining the French does not occur to most people'.[113] Spears made similar observations, and was especially struck by an interview with a Breton boy who said he was 'quite all right in London, but in Camberley, Aldershot etc, the reception he and his companions get from the British troops and civilians in restaurants and especially "dancings" is anything but cordial'.[114] Acknowledging that the Bretons 'are not the most adaptable of people', Spears considered it a pity not more could be done to improve levels of hospitality, if only to stop the 'bagarres' that frequently broke out with the locals. For his part, Black knew of only one scuffle, an unseemly argument in a Reading canteen.[115] It will be recalled from the previous chapter that it was only in 1941, when most non-Free French servicemen had been repatriated, that real efforts were made to improve life in these barracks.

Thus it may well have been that, in his complaints about Chartier, Muselier was exercising a more general frustration about recruitment. This did not stop yet another round of enquiries into the activities of the consuls, although once again this produced little incriminating evidence. For instance, in January 1941 the Cardiff police filed a report on Pierre Chesnais, the local attaché in the city.[116] A professional diplomat, he had first served in Wales in 1931–32, before being transferred to Montréal, Philadelphia and Vienna. At the outbreak of war, he was stationed at Warsaw; he had subsequently escaped to France, via the Balkans, and was posted to Amsterdam, only for the German invasion to necessitate another transfer, first to London and then to Cardiff. A known Anglophile, Chesnais had, on several occasions, made known his fervent desire for a British victory and had not been caught up in any murky business; his pro-Allied views were even noted in Vichy where they were brought to the attention of Laval.[117] As before, Liverpool was the real trouble spot, despite the appointment of a new consul. The Home Office and Admiralty complained of 'constant interference' and thundered that it was 'a scandal that the French Consular Officials should be allowed to exercise anything like the powers they have got'.[118] Meanwhile, in Glasgow, de Curzon continued to aggravate the natives. Having been invited to the board of the Allied Seaman's Reception Centre, he had proved a real nuisance and had to be 'frozen out',[119] proof that the city's elders had not taken stock of his earlier comportment.

To cauterise an open wound, in early 1941 the Foreign Office took long overdue action against the troublesome consular offices. Complex negotiations were conducted with Chartier for the removal of the Liverpool consulate to nearby Newcastle-under-Lyme and the Glasgow office to Edinburgh, where they would be less troublesome. Aware that these moves amounted to a loss of face, in a telegram to his masters, Chartier attempted to put the best possible gloss on the situation, a gloss that was applauded by the Foreign Office, which was fearful that any action might provoke retaliation against the remaining British consuls in France.[120] So it was that Chartier explained to Vichy that Liverpool was in a 'forbidden zone', denied to aliens; the move mattered little, however, as Newcastle-under-Lyme was only 50 kilometres away.[121] The French representative, a Monsieur Delessart, could still visit the Liverpool area, although Chartier made no mention of the fact that he would need the permission of the local police, and a special permit should he ever wish to visit the docks themselves. Turning to Glasgow, Chartier again pointed out that this city lay in a 'forbidden zone', and remarked that the consul there had often spoken of the advantages of being based in Edinburgh. At Swansea, Chartier concluded, another consulate had moved, this time to the city outskirts, because the consular buildings had recently been destroyed (presumably by bombing).

Time was also running out for Chartier himself. What appears to have been the cause of his downfall was not the complaints of the Spears Mission or the Free French, nor the alleged repatriation of Gaullist deserters. Instead, it was matters abroad. Under the command of the Anglophobe Admiral Darlan, Vichy had become ever more unreliable in the eyes of the Foreign Office, which now saw little point in trying to appease the regime. Within domestic affairs, Darlan had taken Vichy down an authoritarian, technocratic route, presiding over the persecution of Jews, Communists and others. More importantly, in his foreign policy Darlan had sidled up to Germany in a way Laval would never have done, hoping that a tough anti-British position would persuade Germany into making concessions to France, in particular by granting it a colonial and naval role in the New Order that Hitler was building. So it was that Darlan ordered British consuls out of France and warned Chartier's colleagues in London to have as little to do with the British as possible.[122] When, in May 1941, Darlan met Hitler at Berchtesgaden to do a deal over the supply of Rommel's Afrika Korps through Syria, Britain and France were, in the words of Robert Paxton, virtually engaged in an undeclared 'naval war'.[123] Significantly, such developments deeply troubled British public opinion, which was more anti-Vichy than ever before.[124] 'They're beyond words', remarked one respondent to Mass-Observation about the marshal's men, 'I can't say anything bad enough to describe them.'[125] 'There's only one word for them – traitors. They're worse than Hitler', was the reply of another.

It was in this context that, on 21 April 1941, the consul was warned that his position was tenuous;[126] on 6 May he was requested to quit London, arriving at Lisbon three days later. Once in Portugal, Vichy immediately requested information as to what he was doing there, the regime's ignorance of his fate further evidence of the consul's difficulties in communicating with his masters.[127] Nonetheless, before his departure, he had apparently agreed to present to Vichy 'a faithful account of his position in this country',[128] in effect a bland statement of protocol authored by the Foreign Office. He chose instead to write his own document, which was intercepted by the British. If this was the type of intelligence that Chartier had been returning to France on a regular basis, then it was of dubious value. Even allowing for the natural indignation of the Foreign Office, it was described as 'grossly biassed [*sic*]' and 'highly inaccurate'. Speaight was under no illusions; 'This is just what one would have expected of M. Chartier.'[129] 'It is what he thinks Darlan would like to hear', he continued, '... the intention is evidently to give the impression that we are rotten with the same lack of public spirit, industrial discontent and disorganisation, and abuse of privilege as wrecked the Third Republic.' It was 'the work of a clumsy and pedestrian propagandist', but was not something to be forgotten. 'We must remember this against Chartier', concluded Speaight, 'when he comes fawning up to us again at the Peace Conference.'

What had Chartier said to cause such offence?[130] Clearly written with the technocratic Cabinet of Darlan in mind, the document comprised a damning indictment of the British war effort. The events of June 1940, began Chartier, had brought the English face to face with reality, and the recognition that it would require 'un effort colossal' to overcome German power. Convinced that the Franco-British alliance, together with the contribution of its air force and navy, would suffice to ensure naval supplies and effect a blockade of enemy ports, the English had dangerously neglected their military preparations. Chartier recalled how the Labour government had foreseen how disarmament would give an example to the rest of the world and how the City, recognising the advantages of this, immediately gave its approval. Everything the British had done in the military arena, up to the day war was declared, was 'futile', designed to fool the French who demanded serious preparations. Hore-Belisha might have introduced work conscription, but this had been riddled with exemptions so as to render it useless. Everything relating to equipment, arms, munitions, war factories, was still to be created and organised. Amazingly, as soon as the French signed the Armistice, these factories doubled and tripled their efforts, food supplies were overhauled and put on a different footing. Warming to his theme, Chartier claimed conscription had been 'un faux'; the British had preferred to rely instead on the French army. Moving on to politics, he spoke of how the replacement of Chamberlain by Churchill had been well received, but how an important opposition was now brewing among intellectuals, parliamentary circles and elements of the middle classes. It was important not to underestimate this opposition, claimed Chartier, as elections gave little indication as to popular feelings. The three main political parties had come to an agreement not to contest seats that became vacant. Churchill could thus count on the support of parliament and effect ministerial reshuffles without worry. Decrying the prime minister for his autocratic tendencies, Chartier claimed that the Cabinet was not of the quality of yesteryear, lacking a Lloyd George, although praise was heaped on Lord Beaverbrook for his efforts in promoting war production.

Praise was also extended to the working classes for their goodwill and hard work. This Churchill had achieved by bringing socialists into his government such as Attlee, Alexander, Morrison and Dalton. Secret deals between capital and labour had further reduced the possibility of strikes and industrial unrest. Even so, among socialists there was an unease about the way in which industrial relations were being managed: organisation was still slipshod; hours were far too long; specialists were not well distributed among factories; and frequently the workforce was left idle because important machine tools had been torpedoed en route from the USA. As in 1914–19, women had been drafted in to replace those men conscripted to fight.

The final paragraphs of Chartier's letter concerned everyday life in wartime: censorship; rationing; the black market. It concluded with another swipe at government and the manner in which it kept news of all dissent quiet. Recently, claimed Chartier, prominent politicians had been overtaken by a scandal concerning Czech bonds. A commission of enquiry had been set up, comprising MPs, and one member had been found guilty of behaving 'indiscrètement', although this had not prevented him from occupying an administrative post in the air force. So it was that this growing number of scandals was hushed up, ended Chartier.

Small wonder that the Foreign Office was outraged. 'The perniciously hostile flavour which colours every sentence of this horrible document', remarked Hankey, 'confirms more fully than it was possible to expect the duplicity of M. Chartier.'[131] Indeed, Chartier's wish to have it all ways became evident in his subsequent actions. On quitting Britain, he expressed a wish to be sent to Australia 'since he professed to be anxious to keep up his connections with the Empire,' although it is more likely he knew the uninviting state of affairs in occupied and unoccupied France.[132] Should there be any possibility of Canberra agreeing to this, both the Foreign Office and Downing Street decided that the Commonwealth authorities should know about the 'unpleasant document' found among his papers at the time of his expulsion. As Downing Street remarked, 'it was typical of Chartier that he should produce such stuff to please his masters at Vichy while at the same time assuring us of his devotion to the allied cause. We now hear through the United States Embassy that he has been speaking well of us at Vichy, but it is quite consistent that he should do so in conversation with persons known to be anglophile while taking a very different line with the others.'[133] Chartier, it was announced, will always say 'what he thinks will please his listener, especially if the listener is in a position to help his career'. Although evidence is fragmentary, it seems that the Foreign Office line was correct. At the end 1941, Chartier was making trouble for Jalenques, his successor at Bedford Square.[134]

Further dirt on Chartier was subsequently produced by the Trading with the Enemy Branch.[135] Before his expulsion, he had apparently been 'collecting patent fees in this country due to Frenchmen': 'He had no authority from this branch to do so and thus became, at any rate technically, liable to proceedings under the Trading with the Enemy Act.' More significantly, it transpired that the liquidation missions had been collating information 'to which they were not entitled', but which had then been communicated across the Channel by none other than Chartier himself. How valuable such information really was remains questionable. Overall, Vichy's senior representative in Britain had been more of a nuisance, an obsequious Uriah Heep figure rather than an accomplished spy or, indeed, diplomat.

Endgame

Chartier's replacement was Jalenques, another career diplomat in Bedford Square. When he introduced himself to the Foreign Office, he was courtesy personified, yet he too did not give a favourable impression. In a report of 25 May 1941, he was described as a 'poor creature, completely lacking in character', who lived on patent medicines and suffered from perpetual colds.[136] At the close of the year, it was even speculated whether the developments in Syria had led him to consider switching sides. In a minute of 28 November 1941, Speaight reflected, 'I imagined that his conscience was at last compelling him to break with Vichy on political grounds, but it now appears he is only concerned with his personal position.'[137] Promises of better pay and promotion had apparently bought off any possibility of defection. Nonetheless, the Foreign Office was prepared to be indulgent towards him as 'whatever his shortcomings, he is on the whole as helpful to us as his position allows and his sympathies are, so far as I can judge, genuinely pro-British'. Indeed, he performed his consular duties with panache, happily renewing passports for Frenchmen in Britain, even when he knew they were supporters of de Gaulle. In the eyes of the Foreign Office, far more important was that he granted travel visas for British officials wishing to cross occupied France on their way to Switzerland, not even bothering to inform his Vichy masters. 'He could easily be less obliging', concluded Speaight, 'and it seems worth while to keep him sweet by allowing him occasional favours which cost us nothing.'

While permitting such indulgence, in the aftermath of Chartier, a close check was kept on Jalenques to ensure that he was not abusing his position. Still allowed to telegram merely *en clair*, he was quickly told in no uncertain terms that he could report matters only in an objective, as opposed to an interpretative, sense.[138] This inevitably led to conflict. When in 1942 Britain accepted refugees from the newly liberated colony of Madagascar, Jalenques intended to send his government several lengthy telegrams, which related 'in immense and redundant detail' the problems encountered by civilian officials and officers on their arrival.[139] These further alleged that there had been a 'breach of faith' on the part of the British in the interpretation of the Protocol of Surrender, and it was feared that they might amount to a propaganda gift to the Germans. Jalenques was thus forced to rewrite his communiqués which were read by the British before being deposited in the diplomatic bags for Lisbon.

By that stage, however, Jalenques could do little damage as most of his officials had already been returned to France, leaving him to preside over a skeleton staff at Bedford Square. With Britain and Vichy at daggers drawn in Syria, a Foreign Office memorandum of 10 June 1941 had asked 'whether the time has come to expel the remaining French consuls in the United Kingdom and the members of the various liquidation missions'.[140] It also appears that the transfer of the consuls at Liverpool and Glasgow had not done the trick. In a letter to Jock McEwen MP, the Foreign Office confessed that the regional consuls, especially in the ports, could still report 'on important aspects of our war effort'.[141]

Preparations for expulsion were accordingly put in place. Before this, however, various government departments were asked whether they still considered the liquidation missions fulfilled a useful function. The Treasury replied that it was

> anxious to retain the Financial Mission since, without it, it would be difficult, if not impossible to work the Reciprocal Advances account whereby Vichy provides *francs* for payments to British subjects in unoccupied France (we are spending over a million pounds a year under this head which would otherwise have to be found by converting dollars into francs), while any British creditors of the French government whose claims are being met through this account would have to go unpaid.[142]

For its part, the Ministry of Supply considered that the armaments and textiles missions were performing a useful service; some contractors might be adversely affected if these liquidation offices were thus shut down.[143] As to the Mines Department, it felt that the coal and minerals mission could carry on, but that its staff should be cut from four to two. The Ministry of Food also wanted the food purchasing mission to remain.[144] In its reply, the Ministry of War Transport still regarded the sea transport mission as helpful, although it was not thought essential for it to stay.[145] The Admiralty, likewise, no longer thought there a need for the Liquidation des Services de l'Attaché Naval while the Ministry of Air reached the same conclusion about the Liquidation des Services de l'Attaché de l'Air, although it was hoped that its one member, with whom it had established cordial relations, would not be expelled.

Having canvassed the opinions of the above departments, the Foreign Office outlined three possible courses of action:

(a) to expel all the consuls and members of the liquidation missions;
(b) to expel all the consuls but leave the missions;
(c) to expel the provincial consuls leaving only the Consulate-General in London with its staff and the missions that are normally attached to it.[146]

Point 'a', continued Speaight, had 'little to recommend it' since there was little point in initiating action against the missions, some of which still served a useful function. Point 'b', he continued, was 'the course recommended by MI5'. While the security services acknowledged that most of the consuls were individually harmless, their offices inevitably provided a focal point for disaffected Frenchmen who might otherwise join de Gaulle. If the consuls were not by now assisting with repatriation, they were certainly distributing money to French refugees whose financial insecurity might otherwise have led them to sign up with either the British or the Free French. The drawback of option 'b' was that Vichy might, in any case, withdraw the liquidation missions, and retaliate 'by expelling our Consuls in Indo-China'. This would make the whole business of passport procedures a real nightmare. Considering point 'c', Speaight argued that this would avoid the pitfalls of point 'b', but reiterated the fact that the London consulate was the 'most dangerous from a security point of view' and the one most likely to do harm to de Gaulle's cause.

Given the complicated pros and cons of these arguments, it was wondered whether a decision should be postponed, pending the conclusion of events in Syria.[147] Ultimately, however, in mid-to-late June an announcement was made that largely followed the course of action outlined in point 'c'. This declared 'all the French Consulates, including Honorary Consulates, in the United Kingdom and in

Northern Ireland, apart from the French Consulate General in London, are to be closed forthwith'.[148] The liquidation missions would stay.

When Jalenques was informed of the decision, he manifested a greater loyalty to his colleagues than had Chartier and looked for ways and means by which he could hang on to at least some of his staff. Now that the provincial consulates were to be closed down, he pointed out, not unreasonably, that his office in London would have expanded functions. It was thus necessary that he should be allowed to employ more administrators, perhaps members of the London colony, or maybe some of the provincial consuls.[149] In the event, he plumped for this latter option, employing the services of Chesnais, the ex-French consul at Swansea, and the ex-consular agent at Folkestone.[150] Although the Foreign Office had no wish that Bedford Square should become a rest home for redundant consuls, in the eyes of the police and MI5 Jalenques's two recommendations were acceptable: both wanted to remain in England and both had strong ties with the British, the latter being married to an Englishwoman. It will be recalled that earlier police enquiries had found nothing amiss about the two men. At one point in these negotiations, Jalenques appears to have been fearful how Vichy would react to the expulsions, fearing personal retribution. When he sought advice from the Foreign Office as to how he should present the British actions,[151] he discovered officials less than sympathetic. 'I told him', wrote Mack, 'that from our point of view we had no objection to the Post Master, or anyone else at Vichy, knowing what we thought of the Vichy Government's collaboration with Germany.'

With such exchanges out of the way, the Home Office and MI5 got on with the task of counting how many French consular officials were on British soil, in readiness for expulsion. Given the brouhaha that had surrounded their actions, it might have been expected that this would have been an easy task. Yet, as is the case of nearly all the 'forgotten French', their numbers were elusive. Being diplomatic staff, they were often exempted from the requirement to register with police.[152] The ensuing enquiries thus produced numerous anomalies, discrepancies in the spelling of names, and discoveries that officials had come and gone without proper authorisation.[153] By mid-July 1941, the Foreign Office still lacked 'confidence in the accuracy of the list' of consular officials, despite several updates and revisions.[154] As soon as one list appeared, it was supplanted with another, replete with spelling corrections and pencilled additions.[155]

Just as it had proved difficult to repatriate French soldiers and sailors in the autumn of 1940, so too was it difficult to relocate the consular officials. On 14 July 1941, the Foreign Office wrote to Jalenques to inform him that it was intending to ferry the consular party across to New York; Vichy could then arrange the subsequent return crossing to France.[156] As no neutral ship would be available for some time, it was suggested the group might wish to sail on board an English boat leaving in August. There was, however, no hurry in getting the various parties away and, if they so wished, they could remain in London, where accommodation would be arranged for them, until a neutral ship was eventually found.

Vichy had other ideas. Whether desirous to assert its autonomy, whether genuinely concerned for the safety of French officials sailing under the British ensign in U-boat-infested waters, or whether just bloody-minded, the Pétain government made known to Jalenques that it was seeking its own solution to the problem.[157] Ever eager to save on hotel bills, the British were happy to listen to these proposals, although they soon articulated objections to the two suggestions that emerged. The first, favoured by Jalenques, was for the consular party to be trans-ferred by air, from Britain to Lisbon, and then to France. As the Foreign Office objected to British aircraft being used for this purpose, the possi-bility arose of Vichy planes coming over, and the views of Air Ministry officials were sought.[158] Unsurprisingly, they were intensely hostile to the idea. As a Foreign Office note records, 'The Air Ministry has strong objections, both because the Vichy pilots could not be prevented from seeing things, and because it is undesirable that the party should reach enemy-controlled territory a few hours after leaving the UK, possibly bringing scraps of red-hot info about targets with them.'[159]

The other proposal was for Vichy to send a ship over. This sugges-tion was far more to the liking of the Foreign Office. Such a ship might even carry on board UK citizens stranded in the south of France. Arrangements had been made for the return of these unfortunates the previous winter, but the Armistice Commission at Wiesbaden had not been able to guarantee a safe passage.[160]

With so many possibilities being canvassed, deadlock ensued. Because there was no guarantee of a safe transfer, Vichy was unhappy at the shipping of the consular party to New York on board a British ship, and again demanded a neutral vessel.[161] In response, the Foreign Office told Jalenques flatly that 'as the Germans torpedoed ships of all nationalities indiscriminately, the party would be no less safe under a British than under a neutral flag'. Perhaps betraying his Pétainist colours, the Consul-General disagreed, insisting once again on a neutral passage to New York or an airlift to Lisbon. This latter option was given some thought. As places did occasionally become available on the Lisbon air service, run by BOAC, it was speculated whether the consuls could be repatriated in dribs and drabs, although it was admitted that those with children could not be expected to travel in this manner as it was important to keep the families together.

So it was that repatriation became dependent on standby air tickets to Lisbon becoming available through the travel agents, Thomas Cook. This hare-brained scheme soon ran into difficulties. While the Foreign Office insisted that it was 'most unsatisfactory' that these people should be 'hanging about indefinitely',[162] the Ministry of Air responded that Vichy staff came low on its list of priorities:[163] 'we simply cannot have these people occupying precious seats on the UK–Lisbon Service in the place of priority passengers who are advancing the war effort. We also are reluctant to take these people at the expense of our own people on our compassionate standby list.'[164]

As the search for a neutral ship continued, the frustrations of the French diplomatic staff awaiting repatriation can only be guessed at. It seems likely that they shared the sentiments of their colleagues belonging to the missions who had experienced lengthy delays following their expulsion in July 1940. As one of this party had lamented at the time, 'I am in a foreign country in a false situation, unable to work or to move from where I am, and almost without friends.'[165]

For this individual, both the British and the French were to blame for the hold-up, yet then, as in late 1941, the real problem was Germany. In October, there emerged a further possibility that the stranded French diplomats could sail on a British ship to Lisbon, alongside a Finnish diplomatic party, safe conduct arrangement having being secured from the Germans through Swedish channels, even though the Germans had not been told that French personnel would be on board;[166] indeed, the Germans were under the impression that all consular staff had left immediately after the Syria affair in June.[167] It was hoped that Jalenques would leap at this chance as he was now known to be the unhappy recipient of numerous letters of complaint from his colleagues demanding an explanation for the delay. It transpired, however, that the safe passage assured by the Germans was not as watertight as previously imagined; they had merely agreed to take 'certain precautions', demanding in turn a welter of information about the vessel, to be supplied 'in good time' to Berlin.[168] Because of the delay, the Ministry of War Transport declared that the vessel could no longer be kept waiting, and deployed her for other work 'from which she cannot be released in less than a month'.[169]

Repatriation was further held up as various of the consular staff asked to remain in Britain. Some did so for principled reasons. One such was Saffroy. Employed at the French Consulate General in London before the Armistice, he had then been 'loaned out on a temporary basis to the French Legation at Dublin about the time when Vichy broke off diplomatic relations'.[170] While he was strongly opposed to Vichy, he thought he could still do a useful service by remaining in post and relaying information to the Foreign Office 'where he has many friends'. He had eventually decided Vichy was 'beyond hope' and resigned, ensuring that his letter of resignation to Darlan reached the British press. He now wished to cooperate with the Free French, but wanted to do so on his own terms and was not anxious 'to give immediate and unconditional allegiance to General de Gaulle'. The Foreign Office fully sympathised with this attitude and agreed he could 'fill a useful role'. It was thus thought helpful that Saffroy should not be subject to the full rigours of the Aliens Restrictions Act, and he was allowed to move freely between his house in London and country cottage in Essex. Similar leniency was also extended to Roché, second secretary to the Dublin legation, who had resigned in similar circumstances, and who had since returned to England after his temporary spell in Ireland.

Others appear to have got cold feet at the last minute. Such was C— A—.[171] Born in 1913 at Moulins, he was a vet in civil life, but at the outbreak of war had become a second-lieutenant in the French army attached to the Direction de la cavalerie et du train.[172] In this capacity, he had assisted in the conveyance of horses from Canada to France. When France fell, he was en route home from Canada on board the SS *Nevada*. The ship docked instead at Glasgow and, along with members of the crew, he was sent to White City to await repatriation. He had subsequently been released and had taken up residence in the Royal Hotel, alongside other French officers. He had only stayed there a matter of days before he was employed by the French consulate, although he still maintained he was an officer in the French army and was not a diplomatic official. Working with Lieutenant Vacher, tidying up the financial affairs of those soldiers who were leaving for France, he had initially demanded to be repatriated among their number, but had a last-minute change of heart. Without informing his Vichy superiors, in early December 1940, he applied to join the Free French and demanded that his name be taken off the repatriation list.

While A— may have been genuinely attracted to de Gaulle, in other cases it appears that family and job interests came before politics. This was the case of M— who had replaced Chesnais as the vice-consul in Cardiff. He had initially been suspected of anti-British feeling, but subsequent police enquiries had revealed that he had close contact with a French family in the city who testified to his trustworthiness: 'The members of this family are all very pro-British and enthusiastic supporters of the Free French movement. It is thought that if this family had the slightest reason to suspect M— of having any feeling hostile to this country the existing friendship would at once end.'[173] Nonetheless, such feelings did not stop M— from wanting to return to France: 'As he depends upon his post in the French Consular Service for his livelihood … he feels that his early return to France may be the means of his obtaining any vacant post existing in the service.' He was thus fearful that a 'delay in return' might mean any vacancy in the French Diplomatic Service being filled by someone else. Ultimately, however, he decided that his professional interests would be best looked after by Carlton Gardens. As a Foreign Office note of 10 September 1941 reads: 'With a wife and family to support M. M— has evidently felt bound to hedge before committing himself finally to the Free French.'[174] Hedging his bets he clearly was. He said nothing of his intentions to Jalenques, who was doing his utmost to help his family, and it remains unclear whether ultimately he stayed or was repatriated.[175]

Far more blatant in the protecting of his own interests was de Curzon, French consul in Edinburgh, who it will be recalled had been an object of intense suspicion in 1940. In a letter to the Foreign Office of June 1941, he requested that he should be allowed to stay, at least until August. Having lived in Britain since 1919, with only a four-year break when he was attached to the French embassy in Brussels, he protested his pro-British views. Moreover, he made known that all of his children had been born here: 'It is very hard for me to be told to go by my friends – particularly at a time when two of my children are to pass examinations in July and risk losing a full year of studies and preparation if they are not here to sit for these examinations.'[176] Such plaintive letters were treated with scorn by the British. As one official remarked, 'It is clear from this that M. de Curzon is a rather stupid individual who was not doing much harm even when he was Consul at

Glasgow.'[177] Nonetheless, de Curzon's case was not treated unsympathetically. As he was no longer considered to be a security threat, and as it was not easy to find safe passages for repatriation, he was permitted to stay in the capacity of a private individual, expressly forbidden to engage in any further consular duties. As a postscript, 1942 found de Curzon back in France where he filed a report on the French community in Scotland to Darlan, although in truth this was more a report of consular responsibilities in Glasgow and Edinburgh interlarded with attacks on particular individuals.[178]

As the archival trail goes cold in late 1941, it is difficult to know how exactly the repatriation of personnel was conducted. It seems likely, despite the protests of the Air Ministry, that individuals were found seats on flights to Lisbon, or were transported by boat to the USA and then back to France. The eventual fate of the consular staff in Bedford Square, however, is known. Betraying their lack of political prescience to the very end, in November 1942 they all opted to rally to the ill-fated General Giraud, whom the Americans hoped they could use to win over French forces in North Africa.[179] Maybe this was not a surprising decision. Having refused to side with de Gaulle, and recognising the hopelessness of the Vichy position in late 1942, this at least offered some prospect of saving face, although it seems unlikely that it guaranteed them a future in the French diplomatic service. From November 1942, therefore, Vichy had no representation whatsoever in London. Although in the following year it requested that the Swiss government should act as a protecting power for those French nationals in the British isles, this request was flatly turned down.

Conclusions

As with so many of the groups making up the 'forgotten French', the Vichy consuls did not have a particularly happy time in Britain. They were under suspicion from the outset, and were always *personae non gratae* in the eyes of the Free French, the Spears Mission and MI5 who worked tirelessly for their expulsion. Whether they truly constituted a threat to national security remains doubtful, otherwise they would surely have been expelled sooner. The greatest danger was posed in the summer of 1940 when there were numerous mission staff who had the financial wherewithal and propaganda facilities to undermine the morale of Gaullist volunteers. Such activities were abruptly halted, however, and only a limited number of individuals were involved.

Thereafter, some consuls, especially in Liverpool, Newcastle, Cardiff and London, clearly assisted with the repatriation of soldiers, forging papers and circumventing immigration procedures. They may also have collated intelligence, but it must have been difficult to have communicated this to their government. The figure of de Curzon writing his reports and making notes of a lecture springs to mind. Only the Consulate-General in Bedford Square had the ability to speak directly to Vichy, but even its potential was seriously limited, forced to telegram *en clair* and make use of diplomatic bags. Given the contents of Chartier's letter on his expulsion, the value of his intelligence must also be doubted. Yet whatever the case, there was certainly no intention, on the part of either Chartier or his government, to pass on any information to the Germans. The fact that Vichy still had some diplomatic presence in London was always a source of unease in Berlin lest this became a channel of communication for high-level Anglo-French dialogue, especially after Syria.

Whether Chartier and his cronies could ever have coped with such dialogue must be doubted. These were not, by and large, thoughtful, intelligent or far-sighted men. The cream of the diplomatic staff had gone in July 1940, leaving those whose ambitions were clearly of a different level. They were not cut out for spying, for complex diplomatic exchanges or for political decision-making. They were at their best when form-filling and stamping passports. Ultimately, it was what they represented that caused so much offence. Whether Bedford Square possessed a portrait of Marshal Pétain on its walls is not known, and on many occasions it resorted to using notepaper with the masthead 'République française', either to curry favour or simply because it was short of stationery.[180] But the very fact that Vichy possessed some symbol of its authority on British soil was always going to create difficulties; and when, in 1941, the spinelessness and immoral character of the marshal's regime became transparent, the fate of the consulates was sealed.

Notes

1   Hugo quoted in F. M. Wilson, *They Came as Strangers. The Story of Refugees to Great Britain* (London, Hamish Hamilton, 1959), p. 139.

2   R. Vinen, *France, 1934–1970* (Basingstoke, Macmillan, 1996), p. 37.

3   *Défense de la France*, no. 9, 25 January 1942, reproduced in D. Veillon, *La Collaboration. Textes et débats* (Paris, Livre du Poche, 1984), pp. 128–9.

4 L.-D. Girard, *Mazinghem ou la vie secrète de Philippe Pétain* (Paris, privately published, 1971).

5 L.-D. Girard, *Montoire. Verdun diplomatique?* (Paris, André Bonne, 1947). See, too, L. Rougier, *Mission secrète à Londres. Les Accords Pétain-Churchill* (Paris, La Diffusion du Livre, 1948).

6 J. Simon, *Pétain, mon prisonnier* (Paris, Plon, 1978), p. 141.

7 R. T. Thomas, *Britain and Vichy, 1940–1942* (London, Macmillan, 1979), J.-B. Duroselle, *L'Abîme. Politique étrangère de la France, 1939–1944* (Paris, Imprimerie Nationale, 1982) and R. Frank, 'Vichy et les britanniques, 1940–1941. Double Jeu ou double langage?', in J.-P. Azéma and F. Bédarida (eds), *Vichy et les français* (Paris, Fayard, 1992), pp. 144–63.

8 Thomas, *Britain and Vichy*, p. 80.

9 PRO FO 371 24352 C7463/7407/17, letter of Lord Halifax to Sir Ronald Campbell, 26 June 1940.

10 H. Nicolson, 'Les deux Cambon et mon père', *FL*, vol. 3, no. 16, 16 February 1942, pp. 285–90.

11 R. Mengin, *No Laurels for de Gaulle* (London, Michael Joseph, 1967), p. 23.

12 A. Cadogan, *Diaries* (London, Cassell, 1971), entry for 17 July 1940, p. 314.

13 J. Lacouture, *The Rebel* (London, Harper Collins, 1986), p. 239.

14 MAE ZV 291, Jules Henry to Vichy, 13 August 1940. See too A. Werth, *De Gaulle* (London, Penguin, 1965), p. 109–10.

15 PRO FO 371 42115 Z7345/7345/17, note of October 1944.

16 PRO FO 371 28336 Z1777/82, letter of Roché to Ralph Stevenson, Private Secretary to the Foreign Secretary, 4 January 1941.

17 PRO FO 371 28337 Z1432/82/17, letter of Sir Ronald Campbell to Sir A. Cadogan, 13 February 1941.

18 PRO FO 371 28337 Z1808/82/17, letter of Samuel Hoare, 4 March 1941.

19 PRO FO 371 42115 Z7345/7345/17, note of October 1944.

20 PRO FO 371 24352 C7407/7407/17, Minute of 9 July 1940.

21 PRO FO 371 24352 C7407/7407/17, letter of Sir Desmond Morton to Gladwyn Jebb, 20 June 1940.

22 PRO FO 371 24352 C7407/7407/17, War Cabinet Conclusions, 1 July 1940.

23 PRO FO 371 24352 C7407/7407/17, Minute by R. M. Makins, 6 July 1940, and MAE 2V 291, 'Note pour le Ministre. Relation Sommaire de la Situation à Londres de 17 juin au 20 juillet', 20 July 1940.

24 PRO FO 371 24355 C8132/7559/19, Minute of 1 August 1940.

25 PRO FO 371 24339 C7797/7328/17, Report of 4 July 1940.

26 Amiral Thierry d'Argenlieu, *Souvenirs de guerre, juin 1940–janvier 1941* (Paris, Plon, 1973), p. 61.

27 PRO FO 371 24339 C7797/7328/17, leaflet of 15 July 1940. The same leaflet can be found in CCC SPRS 1/135.

28 PRO FO 371 24339 C7797/7328/17, note by Hankey, 18 July 1940.

29 PRO FO 371 24354 C12579/7407/17, undated report of 1940.

30 PRO FO 371 24339 C7797/7328/17, Report of 4 July 1940.

31 PRO FO 371 24352 C7407/7407/17, Record of meeting, 10 July 1940.

32 F. Coulet, *Vertu des temps difficiles* (Paris, Plon, 1967), pp. 74–5.

33 Mengin, *No Laurels*, p. 58.

34 *Ibid.*, p. 85.

35 Lacouture, *The Rebel*, p. 239.

36 D. Schoenbrun, *The Three Lives of Charles de Gaulle. A Biography* (London, Hamish Hamilton, 1966), p. 100.

37 Lacouture, *The Rebel*, p. 239.

38 PRO FO 371 24352 C7407/7407/17, letter of Sir Desmond Morton to Gladwyn Jebb, 20 June 1940.

39 CCC NBKR 4/261, 'French Armament and Service Missions to London', 15 July 1940.

40 See especially P. Morand, *Londres* (Paris, Plon, 1933) and the many commentaries on his literary endeavours: M. Burrus, *Paul Morand, voyageur du Xxe siècle* (Paris, Séguier, 1987), G. Guitard-Auviste, *Morand (1888–1976). Légendes et vérités* (Paris, Hachette, 1981) and P. Thibault, *L'Allure de Morand. Du modernisme au Pétainisme* (Birmingham, AL, University of Birmingham, 1992).

41 Mengin, *No Laurels*, p. 93.

42 This move guaranteed that he was a suspicious personality in the eyes of the British who, unbeknown to him, regularly read his correspondence, albeit without discovering any incriminating evidence. Private information.

43 Mengin, *No Laurels*, p. 23.

44 PRO FO 371 28336 Z1777/82/17, letter of Roché to Ralph Stevenson, 4 January 1941.

45 P.-L. Bret, *Au feu des évènements. Mémoires d'un journaliste. Londres-Alger, 1929–1944* (Paris, Plon, 1959), p. 193.

46 MAE ZV 292, telegram of 15 July 1940.

47 MAE ZV 292, telegram of Bressy to Vichy, 4 July 1940.

48 PRO FO 371 24352 C7407/7407/17, War Cabinet Conclusions, 2 July 1940.

49 PRO FO 371 24352 C7407/7407/17, War Cabinet Conclusions, 3 July 1940.

50 PRO FO 371 24352 C7407/7407/17, Minute of 9 July 1940.

51 CCC SPRS 1/136, 'Chart of morale, 12 June–19 July 1940'.

52 PRO FO 371 24352 C7407/7407/17, Minute by Makins, 9 July 1940.

53 PRO FO 371 24352 C7407/7407/17, Record of meeting, 10 July 1940.

54 *Ibid.*

55 PRO FO 371 24358 C13252/7559/17, Repatriation of French military missions, 9 December 1940.

56 PRO FO 371 24354 C13132/7407/17, letter of Mack to Morton, 23 December 1940.

57 PRO FO 371 24352 C8319/7407/17, letter of Lord Cadogan to Cadman, Foreign Office, 12 August 1940, to which D—'s letter is attached.

58 PRO FO 371 42031 Z4476/4184/17, note of 14 July 1940.

59 *Ibid.*

60 PRO FO 371 28424 Z6364/179/17, letter of Michael Law, Foreign Office, to Captain Jock McEwen MP, 28 July 1941.

61 PRO FO 371 28367 Z5986/123/17, personnel of the liquidation missions, 14 July 1941.

62 PRO FO 371 24352 C8131/7407/17, Minute of 19 July 1940.

63 MAE ZV 291, telegram of Chartier to Vichy, 22 July 1940.

64 MAE ZV 291, Memorandum of Arnal, Directeur politique adjoint, for minister, 26 July 1940.

65 E. de Miribel, *La Liberté souffre violence* (Paris, Plon, 1981), p. 38.

66 PRO FO 24355 C7854/7559/17, Report of 22 July 1940 by the Director of Naval Intelligence.

67 M. Egremont, *Under Two Flags. The Life of Major-General Sir Edward Spears* (London, Weidenfeld & Nicolson, 1997), p. 199.

68 MAE ZV 291, telegram of Chartier, 23 July 1940.

69 MAE ZV 291, Chartier to Vichy, 22 July 1940, and 4 January 1941.

70 See A. Hytier, *Two Years of French Foreign Policy, 1940–1942* (Westport, Greenwood Press, 1974).

71 PRO FO 371 24355 C7854/7559/17, Report of 22 July 1940 by the Director of Naval Intelligence.

72 PRO FO 371 24353 C8821/7407/17, letter of Morton to Strang, 18 August 1940, in which Morton remarks that he had known Chartier at the Ministry of Economic Warfare and did not trust him then.

73 PRO FO 371 24353 C9977/7407/17, Foreign Office note, 17 October 1940.

74 PRO FO 371 24353 C9977/7407/17, Foreign Office note, 26 October 1940.

75 PRO FO 371 41990 Z5811/3375/17, letter to Foreign Office 5 September 1944, saying he was ready to take up the job he had resigned in June 1940.

76 PRO FO 371 24353 C9977/7407/17, Report of Brighton CID, 11 October 1940.

77 Reports to be found in PRO 371 24354 C12690/7407/17.

78 *Ibid.*

79 PRO FO 371 24353 C9977/7407/17, Foreign Office Minute, 21 August 1940.

80 PRO FO 371 24353 C9230/7407/17, letter from Flag Officer in Charge, Tyne area, to Admiralty, 19 August 1940.

81 PRO FO 371 24353 C9977/7407/17, Committee on Foreign (Allied) Resistance, 18 September 1940.

82 PRO FO 371 24353 C10440/7407/17, MI5 letter to Foreign Office, 22 September 1940.

83 PRO FO 371 24353 C10440/7407/17, letter of Macbeth to Watkins, 7 September 1940.

84 PRO FO 371 24353 C10440/7407/17, letter of Consul-General, Liverpool, to Carlisle Police, 29 July 1940.

85 PRO FO 371 24353 C10440/7407/17, Report of Glasgow police, 11 October 1940.

86 Interview with Léon Wilson, London, 22 March 2002.

87 Bret, *Au feu des événements*, p. 209.

88 G. Palewski, *Mémoires d'Action, 1924–1974* (Paris, Plon, 1988), p. 146.

89 PRO FO 371 24353 C10105/7407/17, letter of the Ministry of Shipping to Steel, Foreign Office, 17 September 1940, to which a note of 24 September 1940 is attached.

90 PRO FO 371 24353 C9977/7407/17, note of 22 August 1940.

91 R. Graves, *Goodbye to all that* (London, Penguin, 1960 edn), p. 50.

92 PA-AA R29585–R29606, PA-AA R29570–4 and PA-AA 1106, 1120b, 1158b, 1158c, 1228–31, 1295–6, 1361, 2483.

93 PRO FO 371 24353 C9080/7407/17, contains the lengthy correspondence tackling this issue.

94 MAE ZV 291, telegram of Chartier to Vichy, 22 August 1940.

95 MAE ZV 291, telegram of Baudouin to Chartier, 12 September 1940.

96 CCC NBKE 4/259, 'Memorandum on the Activities of Undesirables Still at Large in England', no date.

97 CCC SPRS 1/137, Memorandum by Spears of 25 February 1941.

98 PA-AA R29585–R29606, PA-AA R29570–4 and PA-AA 1106, 1120b, 1158b, 1158c, 1228–31, 1295–6, 1361, 2483.

99 PRO FO 371 24353 C9977/7407/17, note of 26 October 1940.

100 PRO FO 371 24353 C10562/7407/17, note by Mack, 29 September 1940.

101 PRO FO 371 24354 C13903/7407/17, Foreign Office Minutes of 6 November 1940 and 26 November 1940. An attached MI5 report of 11 December 1940 makes it clear the security services wanted them out.

102 PRO FO 371 24354 C13903/7407/17, note of 26 November 1940.

103 PRO FO 1055 8, letter from Lord Bessborough to Spears, 27 February 1941.

104 CCC SPRS 1/137, 'Activities of M. Chartier', 25 February 1941.

105 CCC SPRS 1/137, letter of Captain Knox to MI5, 20 February 1941.

106 CCC SPRS 1/134, note by Sommerville-Smith, 1 March 1941.

107 PRO FO 1055 8, letter from Lord Bessborough to Spears, 27 February 1941, also in CCC SPRS 1/134.

108 *Ibid.*

109 PRO FO 371 28365 Z1456/123/17, 'Undesirable Activities of French Men in the UK', 26 February 1941.

110 CCC SPRS 1/134, letter of 4 March 1941.

111 CCC NBKR 4/259, 'Memorandum on the Activities of Undesirables Still at Large in England', no date.

112 PRO FO 371 24344 C11509/7328/17, letter of 24 October 1940.

113 PRO FO 1055 10, Report of 14 February 1941.

114 PRO FO 1055 3, Minute of the CFR, 6 February 1941.

115 PRO FO 1055 10, Report of 14 February 1941.

116 PRO FO 371 28421 Z801/179/17, letter of T. Holdsworth, Cardiff police, 14 January 1941.

117 MAE ZV 291, note of général de division aérienne to Laval, 3 June 1942.

118 PRO FO 1055 8, letter of Dickens to Spears, 27 February 1941.

119 PRO FO 371 28422 Z1996/179/17, letter of Norman, Ministry of Shipping, to Mack, 14 March 1941.

120 PRO FO 371 28422 Z2551/179/17, Minutes by R. L. Speaight, 1 April 1941.

121 PRO FO 371 28422 Z2551/179/17, telegram by Chartier, April 1941. See, too, MAE ZV 291, telegram of Chartier to Vichy, 9 May 1941, in which he makes clear the archives of the Liverpool consulate had been destroyed.

122 MAE ZV 292, Darlan circular, June 1941.

123 R. O. Paxton, Vichy France. Old Guard and New Order, 1940–1944 (New York, Alfred A. Knopf, 1972), p. 116.

124 M-O FR 523B, 'Attitudes to other Nationalities, 10 December 1940'. Of 101 people questioned, 71 were 'unfavourable' in their assessment of Vichy, 7 'favourable', 14 'half and half', and 9 'vague'.

125 M-O FR 713, 'Feelings about Vichy France', 26 May 1941.

126 MAE ZV 292, Chartier telegram to Vichy, 11 May 1941.

127 MAE ZV 291, Vichy telegram to Chartier, 9 May 1941.

128 PRO FO 371 28422 Z2551/179/17, handwritten note by Speaight, 11 June 1941. Charter's statement, authored by the British, is contained in MAE ZV 292.

129 PRO FO 371 28422 Z2551/179/17, handwritten note by Speaight, 11 June 1941.

130 PRO FO 371 28422 Z2551/179/17, letter of Chartier, impounded on 7 June 1941.

131 PRO FO 371 28422 Z2551/179/17, handwritten note by Hankey, 9 June 1941.

132 PRO FO 371 28422 Z2551/179/17, letter of Speaight to G. Kimber, Prime Minister's Office, 13 June 1941.

133 PRO FO 371 28424 Z6007/179/17, letter of G. Kimber, Downing Street, to R. R. Sedgwick, 14 July 1941.

134 PRO FO 371 28426 Z10235/179/17, Minute by Speaight, 28 November 1941.

135 PRO FO 371 28424 Z5941/179/17, letter of R. H. Landman, Trading with the Enemy Branch, to A. B. Hutcheon, Consulate Department, Foreign Office, 9 July 1941.

136 PRO FO 371 28423 Z4343/179/17, Report of Mack, 25 May 1941.

137 PRO FO 371 28426 Z10235/179/17, Minute by Speaight, 28 November 1941.

138 MAE ZV 291, note du directeur politique adjoint at Vichy, 30 December 1942.

139 PRO FO 371 32114 Z6061/6061/17, Minute of 24 July 1942. On the wider issue of refugees from French colonies, see T. P. Maga, *America, France and the European Refugee Problem, 1933–1947* (New York/London, Garland, 1985).

140 PRO FO 371 28423 Z5154/179/17, 'Action Against French Officials in the United Kingdom'.

141 PRO FO 371 28424 Z6364/179/17, letter of Michael Law, Foreign Office, to Captain Jock McEwen MP, 28 July 1941.

142 PRO FO 371 28423 Z5154/179/17, 'Action Against French Officials in the United Kingdom', 19 June 1941.

143 PRO FO 371 28367 Z4966/123/17, letter of D. W. Barrington, Ministry of Supply, to Speaight, Foreign Office, 6 June 1941.

144 PRO FO 371 28423 Z5154/179/17, 'Action Against French Officials in the United Kingdom', 19 June 1941.

145 See too PRO FO 371 28366 Z4921/123/17, letter from Sir Cecil Kisch, Petroleum Department, to Speaight, 10 June 1941.

146 PRO FO 371 28423 Z5154/179/17, 'Action Against French Officials in the United Kingdom', 10 June 1941.

147 PRO FO 371 28423 Z5154/179/17, note by W. H. B. Mack, 12 June 1941.

148 PRO FO 371 28423 Z5154/179/17, note of 16 June 1941.

149 PRO FO 371 28423 Z5154/179/17, Minute by W. H. B. Mack, 18 June 1941.

150 PRO FO 371 28424 Z5795/179/17, letter of Harry Hohler, Foreign Office, to MI5, 11 July 1941. This letter refers to a meeting between Jalenques and Speaight on 7 July 1941 where numbers at the London consulate had been discussed.

151 PRO FO 371 28423 Z5237/179/17, Minute by W. H. B. Mack, 20 June 1941.

152 PRO FO 371 28423 Z5701/179/17, letter of MI5, to Miss Davies, Home Office, 20 May 1941.

153 PRO FO 371 28423 Z5701/179/17, letter of Harry Hohler, Foreign Office, to Miss Davies, Home Office, 16 July 1941.

154 PRO FO 371 28423 Z5701/179/17, Minute by Hankey, 11 July 1941.

155 See the lists in PRO FO 371 28426.

156 PRO FO 371 28424 Z6006/179/17, letter of Speaight to Jalenques, 14 July 1941.

157 PRO FO 371 28424 Z6298/179/17, Minute of Speaight, 21 July 1941.

158 PRO FO 371 28424 Z6298/179/17, letter of Speaight to Mackenzie, 23 July 1941.

159 PRO FO 371 28424 Z6298/179/17, note by Speaight, 24 July 1941.

160 PRO FO 371 28424 Z6298/179/17, Minute of Speaight, 21 July 1941.

161 PRO FO 371 28424 Z 6535/179/17, note of Speaight, 1 August 1941.

162 PRO FO 371 28425 Z7449/179/17, Minute of Hankey, 3 September 1941.

163 PRO FO 371 28425 Z7449/179/17, letter of Captain J. J. Hebertson, Ministry of Air, to W. L. Dunlop, Foreign Office, 29 August 1941.

164 PRO FO 371 28425 Z8021/179/17, letter from Air Ministry to H. Jones, Foreign Office, 18 September, 1941.

165 PRO FO 371 28366 Z2283/123/17, letter of J— R—, 26 February 1941, intercepted by MI5.

166 PRO FO 371 28425 Z8021/179/17, Minutes of Hankey, 26 September 1941.

167 MAE ZV 292, telegram of French representative to the Armistice Commission to Darlan, 22 February 1942.

168 PRO FO 371 28425 Z8021/179/17, note of 27 September 1941.

169 PRO FO 371 28425 Z8021/179/17, note by Hankey, 14 October 1941.

170 PRO FO 371 28341 Z9774/82/17, letter of Speaight to E. N. Cooper, Home Office (Aliens Department), 18 November 1941.

171 PRO FO 371 28426 Z10402/179/17, letter of F. W. Turness, Home Office (Aliens Department) to under-secretary of state, Foreign Office, 8 December 1941.

172 PRO FO 371 28424 Z6060/179/17, Police report of 27 June 1941.

173 PRO FO 371 28425 Z7722/179/17, letter of Clayton, Home Office, to Mack, Foreign Office, 8 September 1941, which gives details of a letter from Cardiff City Police to Clayton, 4 September 1941.

174 PRO FO 371 28425 Z7722/179/17, note by Hankey, 10 September 1941.

175 PRO FO 371 28425, Z7294/179/17, note of Mack, 10 September 1940.

176 PR0 FO 371 28423 Z5282/179/17, letter of de Curzon to Speaight, 20 June 1941.

177 PRO FO 371 28423 Z5282/179/17, Minute of 20 June 1941.

178 MAE ZV 291, de Curzon to Darlan, 28 March 1942.

179 PRO FO 371 42031 Z4476/4184/17, note of 14 July 1944.

180 It is interesting to note that at the close of the war, officials at Vichy started to use notepaper headed 'République française'. Examples may be found in AN F^{17} 13390.

5

The tradition of exile:
la colonie Française

I recall an astonishing description of the sounds and smell of a Parisian working day, the first faint rumblings of the Métro, and the unique odour of that surrealist underground railway, in the monthly review *La France Libre*. (Richard Cobb, *Promenades*)[1]

In a three-volume conspectus of London life, published in 1901, several chapters were devoted to those immigrant communities, Greeks, Germans and Italians among others, that had made London their home. In the pages devoted to the French, the following observation was drawn:

> The French in London form a sober, well-behaved, industrious and law-abiding community. They give very little trouble to the police and law courts, and it is seldom that the name of a French resident obtains an unbelievable notoriety in the newspapers. There are about 21,000 French sojourners in England, and about 11,000 of them in the metropolis.[2]

Clearly, what appealed to the Victorian values of the English authors was that the French community largely kept itself to itself yet, at the same time, integrated well into London life. Colonists were 'not to be found loafing in the neighbourhood of Leicester Square and Piccadilly Circus', it was observed, 'They are to be found in City offices and warehouses, in workshops and studios, in West End establishments and shops, in schools and in private families.'[3] Another comforting aspect was their lack of political activity, testimony to the fact that most Communards had retreated to their homeland after the Amnesty of 1878.

What is remarkable is that this piece could have been written shortly after the colonial dispute of Fashoda in 1898 when Britain and France nearly went to war, and when the French in Britain were under intense suspicion. What is even more remarkable is that the French are described as 'passive' precisely when their country was engulfed in the Dreyfus Affair. We know that Zola, in exile in Weybridge, was able to follow developments in the *Standard* and the *Daily Telegraph*, with an English grammar by his side, as well as a set of Nelson's *Royal Readers* for children, to assist with his English.[4] London press headlines had featured little other than the goings-on of the Paris courts, and inveighed against the miscarriage of justice, just as French newspapers had earlier attacked Britain over Fashoda.[5] It is inevitable, then, that Dreyfus was discussed among French exiles but the overriding impression is that this remained a private quarrel that never spilled out into the public arena, maybe because such men and women had no wish to draw attention to themselves. Perhaps the only tangible way in which the British public was aware of the ways in which this scandal had split French opinion was the arrival of religious orders – for instance the Benedictines of the Abbey of Solesmes, who resettled on the Isle of Wight until 1922,[6] and the Jesuits who made a temporary home in Jersey. These had been expelled after the formation of Radical anti-clerical Cabinets, which were determined to protect the Republic from the perceived clerico-military threat, incidentally the same governments that sealed the Anglo-French entente of 1904, which soothed recent colonial resentments.

Remarkably much the same observations about the anonymity of the French *colons* could be made on the eve of war in 1939. They remained a silent and unassuming community, doing little to attract outside publicity, even though they had witnessed yet another dramatic phase in their country's history. In the same way that the Dreyfus Affair split families, so too the election of the Popular Front had polarised opinion. Yet these divisions were once again kept out of the public view, an internal matter; it was only during the war years that they came fleetingly to the surface, prosperous elements of the community blaming defeat on Blum and being suspicious of de Gaulle lest he harboured left-wing elements.

This silence might explain why so little has been written about French expatriates. It is astonishing that the volume of 1901 cited above was one of the few studies published in the entire twentieth century that focuses specifically on the French, this despite the fact that, in 1931, they comprised 9.2 per cent of all foreign nationals living in England and Wales.[7] After the Polish and Russian communities, the French constituted the third largest European group of émigrés, their numbers even greater than those from Italy, a land whose overcrowded southern territories had witnessed a steady drip of European emigration.[8] For the first half of the twentieth century, the French continued to number around 30,000 inhabitants, yet the outbreak of war in 1939 reduced this figure to just over 10,000.[9] The irony was that, at this moment of contraction, it became increasingly difficult for them to retain their anonymity. Not only did the new arrivals from France seek out their countrymen and women as a point of reference in a foreign land, but Gaullists and others were eager to recruit among their ranks while, in the background, the British government kept a close watch on their activities, ensuring that any pro-Vichy sympathies did not get out of hand. Wartime was thus an uncomfortable experience for those who had long settled in Britain for whatever reason: economic, political, religious or otherwise. No longer would they be able to play out their quarrels in private.

The pre-war French community: a statistical overview

It was, of course, Britain's proximity to France, together with its tradition as a haven, that attracted French exiles over the centuries. In this sense, de Gaulle's flight on 17 June was little different to that of earlier émigrés, although it might be objected that the scale of the violence and repression that Hitler and Vichy were to visit upon France was much greater than that inflicted on the Huguenots, *ancien régime* nobility and Communards, however barbaric their own particular experiences of persecution. De Gaulle was also similar to other exiles in that his stay in Britain was intended to be temporary; in 1943, he left for Algiers in the belief that the North African capital was closer to his homeland than was London. With the exception of the seventeenth-century Huguenots and those regular orders expelled in the early 1900s, significantly both the subject of religious discrimination, other groups of predominantly political refugees, most notably the Communards, had returned to their homeland as soon as it was thought safe to do so.

In the course of the late nineteenth and early twentieth centuries, it appears that most of the French who came to British shores did so for commercial interests, or in search of employment, an indicator of London's pulling power as a hub of enterprise, and maybe a sign of the slowdown in the French economy during the 1880s. It is telling that the French Chamber of Commerce in Britain, a lively supporter of free trade, was founded in 1883;[10] *La Chronique de Londres*, a gazette devoted to French businesses and social gatherings, was established at more or less the same time. Traditionally, French businesses in Britain had been 'merchants, wholesalers or retailers dealing in predominantly fresh food and luxury goods, such as wine, champagne, chocolate, silk, lace, glassware and clothing'.[11] As Fraser Reavell has demonstrated, during the *belle époque* these were joined by several others. Four major commercial banks – Comptoir National d'Escompte de Paris, Crédit Lyonnais, Société Générale du Crédit Industriel et Commercial and Société Générale de Paris – established themselves in London. These were accompanied, adds Reavell, by key industrial concerns such as Saint-Gobain, Duchesne, Michelin and Peugeot, firms that would receive a boost during the First World War. Advertising (Agence Havas), travel accessories (Louis Vuitton), fashion houses (Worth) and news agencies (Pathé) were not far behind, an example of the way in which commercial life was expanding at this time.

It is against this background that the French lived and worked, and thanks to the 1931 census we know a good deal about their social profile, although it must be remembered that such statistical material is open to question: human error; an unwillingness to register; and the fact that the census is only a snapshot taken every ten years. It is fortunate that the trends perceived in 1931 reflect those of the pre-1914 period; the 1921 figures are distorted by the First World War.

This continuity is immediately seen in the numbers of French men and women in England and Wales for 1931: 29,175 in total, of whom 2,062 were classed as 'visitors', for instance sailors in port, travelling salesmen and other itinerant workers.[12] This overall figure was roughly the same as in 1911 and 1901 and, as already noted, ensured that the French were the third largest European group after the Poles (43,912) and the Russians (36,133), both displaced by the tumultuous events in Eastern Europe. Incidentally, the Germans (28,048), counted a group whose size was to increase as Jews and others fled Nazi persecution. Of the French total, there was a clear gender divide: 9,979 men and 19,196 women. Significantly, for a people proud of their national traditions, only 13,547, some 46.4 per cent, possessed British citizenship: 2,889 men and 3,852 women were British subjects by birth; 1,020 men and 5,786 women were British by naturalisation, the latter figure suggesting that many females had found British husbands.

In terms of occupation, five key categories stand out among males. The largest proportion were employed in 'personal services' (classified as 'domestic servants, restaurant keepers, lodging/boarding house keepers, publicans, waiters, hall/hotel porters, laundry workers, and hairdressers/manicurists and chiropodists'): 1,377 in total, 22.7 per cent of all those 6,070 Frenchmen working in England and Wales.[13] The second category comprised those involved in 'commercial, finance and insurance occupations' (proprietors and managers of retail/wholesale businesses, brokers/agents, commercial travellers, salesmen, costermongers/hawkers, bankers and officials): 588 (9.7 per cent). The third group belonged to 'professional occupations' (clergymen, doctors, dentists, teachers, music tutors, engineers, articled pupils, authors and painters): 456 (7.5 per cent). The fourth section were 'in transport and communication' (haulage contractors, drivers, ship owners, ship officers, pursers, stevedores, dock labourers, managers and porters): 333 (5.5 per cent). A final contingent were 'clerks/draughtsmen': 314 (5.2 per cent). After these categories, the remainder were scattered among a variety of trades, notably metal workers 170, 2.8 per cent), textiles (182, 3.0 per cent), wood and furniture businesses (94, 1.5 per cent) and entertainment and sport (62, 1.02 per cent), to name but a few.

Figures for female labour largely reflect those of men, and again point to the underlying economic factors determining French emigration to England and Wales. Strikingly, the same five categories stand out, although it was those involved in 'professional occupations' (nuns, mission workers, nurses, schoolteachers, teachers of music, articled pupils, authors and painters) that dominated: 1,866, 19.5 per cent of the 9,558 total French female workforce (all ages).[14] Those in 'personal services' (domestic servants, waitresses etc.), were the next largest group: 1,428 (14.9 per cent). Third came 'Makers of textile goods/articles of dress': 647 (6.8 per cent). 'Commercial, finance and insurance' constituted the fourth group: 214 (2.2 per cent). As with men, the final principal grouping was 'clerks/draughtsmen' although, in a reflection of the gendered nature of working conditions, typists were also included: 232 (2.4 per cent). The remainder were engaged in a wide variety of occupations, while a sizeable figure, 3,711, were classified as 'unoccupied or retired'. No doubt a good proportion of this latter figure were married women who no longer actively pursued a career. Prostitutes might also have been among their number, especially as Soho retained its reputation as a red-light district. As the writer Thomas Burke remarked in 1915, 'Soho – magic syllables! For when the respectable Londoner wants to feel devilish he goes to Soho, where every street is a song. He walks through Old Compton Street, and, instinctively, he swaggers; he is abroad; he is a dog.'[15]

If the occupational profile of the French could have been anticipated, given the underlying economic nature of their immigration,
their geographical concentration also holds few surprises. In 1931, the
overwhelming proportion were located in London and the surrounding districts. In itself, the South-East region, including the capital and
the Home Counties, counted 7,219 men and 14,165 women, 73.3 per
cent of the entire French population in England and Wales.[16]
Elsewhere, the Northern Region contained 1,023 men, 1,828 women
(9.8 per cent of the total French population); the Midlands, 684 men,
1,466 women (7.4 per cent); the East Region, 193 men, 404 women
(2.05 per cent); the South-West Region, 448 men, 904 women (4.6 per
cent); and Wales, 413 men, 429 women (2.9 per cent). Within the
London Administrative County alone, there were 3,795 men and 6,730
women. Among those metropolitan boroughs making up this unit, the
majority were located in fashionable districts, notably in the west of the
city, and areas of cheap housing, both south of the river and around the
great railway termini of Paddington and King's Cross-Saint Pancras:
Chelsea (86 men, 192 females); Hampstead (162 men, 365 females);
Kensington, a traditional French heartland, being the home of both the
embassy and the cultural centre, the Institut Français (320 men, 769
females); Lambeth (359 men, 432 females); Paddington (220 men, 590
females); Saint Marylebone (191 men, 487 females); Saint Pancras (383
men, 555 females); Wandsworth (283 men, 589 females); and
Westminster (543 men, 745 females), comprising Soho still known as
the 'French quarter'.[17] Although Soho had traditionally been a
favourite residence for exiles of all nationalities thanks to its plentiful
supply of cheap hotels, and although by the interwar years it had come
to be dominated by Italians, in the 1930s it was said that Old Compton
Street, with its array of butchers, greengrocers and patisseries was 'as
French as the rue St Honoré'.[18] Away from central London, figures for
Middlesex Administrative County contained 958 men and 1,769
women, the highest proportion concentrated in suburban Hendon
(131 men, 283 women). At the end of the Underground's Central Line,
Essex was the home to 297 men and 616 females. Among the commuter
belts of Surrey, and its associated boroughs, dwelled 638 men and 1,196
females. Croydon had always housed a small colony of French City
workers,[19] while in Kent, only a short steamboat ride from Calais, lived
405 men and 1,122 women.[20]

Most of the figures for individual boroughs in London, Middlesex and the Home Counties outweighed those of entire towns, cities and administrative districts elsewhere.[21] Here, the biggest groups tended to live in densely populated and built-up areas, no doubt again because of employment opportunities: Lancaster Administrative County with Associated Boroughs, including Manchester and Liverpool (403 men, 722 females); Southampton Administrative County (315 males, 729 females); Stafford Administrative County (112 men, 224 females); Warwick Administrative County with Associated Boroughs, notably Birmingham (171 men, 246 females); York/West Riding Administrative County and Associated County Boroughs (277 men, 438 females); Glamorgan Administrative County with Associated County Boroughs (294 men, 163 females); and Devon Administrative County with Associated County Boroughs (154 men, 300 females). In far-flung parts of the country, French residents were negligible: Carlisle (2 males, 13 females), Cumberland (7 males, 17 females), Barrow-in Furness (7 males, 11 females), to cite but three examples. As will be seen, in 1941 police forces in such districts reacted with some bemusement when asked to comment on the political attitudes of their local French communities, which often numbered no more than a dozen people.

Although the disruption of the war prevented a census from being conducted in 1941, internal Home Office statistics reveal that the onset of fighting involved change and continuity in the lives of French men and women in Britain: change in that their numbers contracted sharply, and continuity in that those who remained were concentrated in London and the Home Counties. On 25 May 1940, French aliens in the United Kingdom registered with the police amounted to 4,910 men and 6,825 women, making a total of 11,735, 5.1 per cent of the 228,072 total of all registered aliens. The French were now the fourth largest European group overtaken, not surprisingly, by Germans (55,023), Italians (18,374) and Russians (44,704).[22] Given the future problems with facilitating repatriation, nor is it any surprise that this figure remained more or less constant for the duration of the war: 12,794 in 1941;[23] 13,639 in 1942;[24] and 13,348 in 1943.[25] It should be stressed, however, that these figures were not foolproof. The Home Office readily acknowledged that the *Central Register of Aliens* did not include children below the age of 16, British-born wives who might have taken French citizenship, temporary visitors and those recently granted certificates of naturalisation.[26] Whereas in the past naturalisations had been officially announced in the *London Gazette*, this practice was stopped on security grounds.

Explaining the sudden drop in the French population is not difficult. It was well known that London would be a target for the *Luftwaffe*, prompting both better-off British and foreign residents to find alternative accommodation in the countryside or overseas. The call-up of reservists for Gamelin's army also cut a swathe among French exiles; all male children born to French couples in Britain were still 'registered in Paris for military service'.[27] Such was the case of Monsieur Vila, whom we encountered in an earlier chapter with his regiment in Montreuil in June 1940, having worked previously at the French Railways Office in Piccadilly.[28] Small wonder, that the number of males in England and Wales dropped from 9,979 in 1931 to 4,910 in 1940. That the number of women also plummeted from a total of 19,126 to 6,825 is perhaps to be explained by the fact that many were engaged in temporary employment, for instance nursing, teaching and waitressing, and may well have been eager to rejoin their families in France.

As already observed, those that did stay remained concentrated in London and surrounding areas. In 1941, 6,476 French (3,252 men and 3,224 women) resided in the Metropolitan Police District; 4,784 (1,697 men and 3,087 women) in provinces of England and Wales; 273 (113 men and 160 women) in Scotland; and 43 (17 men and 26 women) in Northern Ireland.[29] As in the early 1930s, outside London, the French gathered in heavily populated areas, such as Manchester and Birmingham, and the Home Counties: 154 in Berkshire; 141 in Buckinghamshire; 143 in Hertfordshire; 127 in Kent; and 183 for Surrey.[30] Within London itself, the French continued to huddle together in such obvious districts as Soho and Kensington.

Who stayed in Britain? Almost inevitably, we know most about the wealthy and articulate, men and women who had extensive interests in Britain and who were to play a leading role in organising the French community in London.[31] Businessmen feature prominently: Monsieur Petit, ex-president of the French Chamber of Commerce; the elderly Monsieur Guéritte, formerly head of the Society of Engineers, and a leading advocate of a Channel Tunnel;[32] Monsieur de Malglaive, managing director of the Compagnie Générale Transatlantique; Monsieur Boucher, another eminent light of the Chamber of Commerce; Monsieur Espinasse, a member of the United Associations of Great Britain and France; Etienne Bellanger, head of Cartier jewellers, who famously offered his Bentley and services as a chauffeur to de Gaulle; Comte de Sibour, a graduate of Trinity College, Cambridge, who had established himself in the City of London; and

Captain Métadier, director of a large pharmaceutical company, who lent de Gaulle a sum of a thousand pounds to cover initial expenses.[33] Lawyers were another prominent community, including Monsieur Picarda, a member of the Middle Temple, as were journalists: Paul-Louis Bret, an English-based reporter for the Havas agency;[34] Monsieur Massip, the London correspondent of *Le Petit Parisien*; Emile Delavenay, a correspondent for the BBC;[35] Paul Gordeaux, writer for *Paris-Soir*;[36] Pierre Maillaud who, in 1942, authored an elegy to the France he had known before it was distorted by Vichy;[37] and Elie J. Bois, the former editor of Massip's paper who published a scathing account of the defeatism of Laval and those other parliamentary *Munichois*, having spent time observing the goings-on at Bordeaux in June 1940, and who later wrote weekly columns for the *Sunday Times*.[38] Then there were prominent figures in charge of long-established French organisations, notably Mme de Lapanousse, head of the French Red Cross, who commuted from her home in Belgrave Square to Windsor where her husband was in hospital and her son at school.[39] On her death in 1942, her place at the head of the Red Cross was taken up by her daughter, the Comtesse de Salis.[40]

Aside from such prominent figures, three other groups made up the French community. First, there were the less prosperous: governesses, schoolteachers, au pairs, waiters and waitresses, and those the Census would have classified as being involved in 'personal services'. It is likely that several of these people were working in Britain on short-term contracts, only to be cut off in June 1940. This appears to have been the case of Mlle Touchard, whose family was in Le Mans, and who was teaching conversational French at the University of Glasgow.[41] A friend of the Personalist philosopher Emmanuel Mounier, she was so angered by Vichy's foreign policy that she opted to stay in Scotland where she married and raised a family. Second, figures indicate that women still dominated the colony, even though their numbers had dropped sharply, leading to the plausible supposition that many of those who remained were married to British men. Such women frequently offered their services to those French charitable organisations operating in England and Wales, and were commonly pointed by government in the direction of the Corps Féminin. Typical of such volunteers was Marie Antoinette Thompson, from West London, who had been married for twenty-six years to an English doctor. Her son having been killed with the RAF, she was now keen to do welfare work among her compatriots.[42] And, finally, there were a significant number of children, although exactly how many remains unknown as those under sixteen years of age were excluded from government statistics on aliens. Within London, several of these children had attended the Lycée Français in Kensington, which had operated under the aegis of the Institut Français. It will be recalled that to escape the bombing, this prestigious school had been transferred, via either Cambridge or Reading Universities, to the Waterfoot Hotel, near Penrith in Cumberland, where it was assisted by the British Council, and had opened a kindergarten and elementary school.[43] Other boys, as we have seen, went to Rake Manor. It is further known that some 75 boys, aged between 14 and 18, had been pursuing their studies in Britain on an exchange programme, only for their stay to prove longer than antici-pated; their education continued in camps on the Welsh hillside.[44] Astonishingly, educational authorities in both England and France were still organising such exchanges as late as June 1940,[45] just as they were encouraging schools to designate parts of their classrooms a 'coin de la France', full of French maps and things French, an initiative that foundered because of the defeat.[46]

   Although the British government would not have admitted it, Whitehall, or at any rate MI5, would probably have preferred the whole of the French community to have been based in Wales, diligently working for the war effort, distant from security-sensitive areas in London, and hidden from public view. As it was, the attitudes of the French *colons* were a key concern for the first two years of the war; after that point, when it became apparent that Vichy was little more than a malleable tool of Hitler's empire, such anxieties largely disappeared. How, then, did the French colony respond to the events of June-July 1940? And how did the government react to the presence of some 11,000 *colons* on British soil?

The colonist response to defeat: organising, rallying and integrating

On 10 July 1940, the very same day that the deputies were convening in Vichy's Casino to vote full powers to Marshal Pétain, the War Cabinet gathered at Downing Street to consider what action, if any, should be taken against French men and women present in Britain.[47] It was a many-sided question. To whom would these colonists owe their loyalty? Could they still be counted as allies in view of the Armistice and Vichy's early forays into collaboration? Would the marshal's personal charisma and magnetism extend beyond the Channel? Would

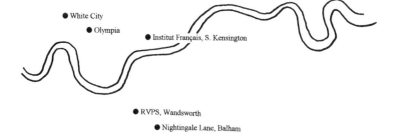

Map 4   The London of the forgotten French: outer areas

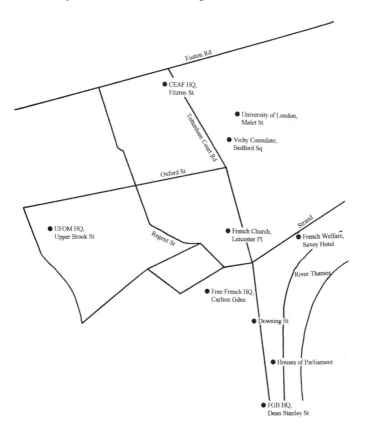

Map 5   The London of the forgotten French: inner areas

the colonists follow the lead of the London consulate, as they were known to have done in the past?[48] Could the colonists be relied upon instead to rally to de Gaulle, a man whom the British themselves did not even trust? What would happen if France declared war on Britain, not such an unlikely prospect after the sinking of the fleet at Mers-el-Kébir and with the presence of such well known Anglophobes as Paul Baudouin, Admiral Darlan, Doctor Ménétrel and Raphäel Alibert in the marshal's personal entourage? Would a general internment of all the French thus become a necessity?

Reading government files, especially surviving Home Office and MI5 reports, it is clear that government anxieties stemmed from the fact that it did not have a clear picture of the colonist response to events across the Channel, only occasional snapshots that did not convey the whole picture. This was hardly surprising. The present study has repeatedly stressed that the French were a self-contained and well integrated community who kept themselves to themselves, doing little to antagonise their British hosts. This ability to keep their heads down was much in evidence in 1940. Indeed, during the widespread fifth-columnist scare of May 1940, when anyone with a foreign accent was distrusted, the French were not singled out in the same fashion as were the Belgians and Dutch. Thereafter, it appears to have been newcomers from abroad, especially Jews, that most agitated commentators, especially within right-wing circles. As late as May 1941, the Tory MP Major Sir Ralph Glyn, in the language of Private Eye's Sir Hufton Tufton, was complaining to government about the large numbers of aliens, 'especially the Jews', who had targeted property and British jobs in Buckinghamshire, Berkshire, Surrey and parts of Oxfordshire, anywhere within 'an easy train journey of London'.[49] It would be better, he concluded, if these people were 'further afield' where they could no longer come down 'by motor car or other hired conveyances'. As Herbert Morrison replied, in the eleven counties surrounding London such foreigners counted less than one-ninth of the entire alien population of the UK.[50]

That the French colonists were largely able to escape such intemperate outbursts is further evidenced in the fact that they are invisible in the English press at the time. Instead, newspapers concentrated their attentions on those exiled communities of soldiers and sailors, people who could immediately assist with the war effort. For much of the summer/early autumn, The Times ran a series of 'Will they?' or 'Won't they?' articles about whether these reluctant exiles would rally to de

Gaulle, in retrospect hardly the type of journalism to bolster public morale.[51] No doubt colonists also benefited from the growing tendency of both the press and public opinion to identify all the French, outside those renegade servicemen, with the general's movement, a trend also picked up in Mass-Observation surveys.[52] Nor did the community possess its own newspaper to make clear its views, *La Gazette de Londres*, the successor of *La Chronique de Londres*, being little more than a diary of social activities, although it is hard to believe that the censors would have permitted the publication of pro-Pétainist opinions. When French journals did begin to appear, notably *France* and *La France Libre*, they were either government-run, or led by exiles of 1940 implacably opposed to the marshal's regime. The same is true of those French broadcasts on the BBC, which, in any case, were directed at metropolitan France, not the French colony.

So it is, that the colony's response to the defeat remains obscure and impressionistic. MI5 agents took to dressing up as refugees and going among French circles in Soho where they eavesdropped on conversations. From such evidence, however piecemeal, one overriding characteristic nonetheless stands out. While there was general dismay at the rapid collapse of their homeland, there was little initial enthusiasm for de Gaulle who was looked upon with either scorn or indifference. As Lady Astor's son David explained in an interview with Jean Lacouture, one of the general's most famous biographers:

> The English people admired de Gaulle, their companion of the darkest days, and they respected his courage. In political circles it was neither his ideas nor his character that was criticized but rather the want of sympathy that he showed for Great Britain ...
>   Yet the most surprising aspect of the relations between de Gaulle and other people was the attitude of the French. We were constantly being surprised by the ill-will of those who could have been called intellectuals, of almost all the politicians and of many soldiers. This distrust that he aroused among the most outstanding members of the French community in London could not fail to strike us. In our country it was not with the British but chiefly with the French that he had trouble. And the reason these quarrels did not become more public is the pressure brought to bear by the British to restore calm.[53]

Whether the British were really successful in keeping these squabbles from public view is open to doubt. The many organisations that quickly sprang up among the French community could only give the impression of a people uncomfortable with one another. In her study of wartime London, Susan Briggs relates how Londoners considered that the French had brought France (including its quarrels) across the Channel with them.[54]

How do we explain this attitude to de Gaulle? The answer is that the *colons* shared the same concerns as many of those other groups making up the 'forgotten French'. To begin with, he was 'an unknown'. What the French community knew about de Gaulle was much the same as what the British public knew, information gleaned from the sporadic newspaper coverage of his early days in London. As much of this publicity was controlled by Whitehall, and given that the general depended largely on Churchill's goodwill, a feeling quickly spread that this soldier was not his own agent. Even to untrained eyes, it was clear that Carlton Gardens did not equate a government-in-exile, something recognised by the prime minister himself when, on 28 June, he acknowledged de Gaulle merely as the head of the Free French, and not the head of the French state. So it was that during his early months, de Gaulle was often slightingly referred to in colonist circles as a 'puppet',[55] an impression strengthened by the abortive Dakar mission, which was severely criticised in the press.

It further appears that de Gaulle's pre-war career, when eventually revealed to the public, had little to distinguish it, particularly when placed alongside the military accomplishments of Marshal Pétain, whose curriculum vitae hardly needed publicising. In this respect, it seems that British and French colonist perceptions of his past were determined by their own particular circumstances. The British, aware that they were on their own and facing imminent invasion, were anxious to nurture any flicker of resistance, however small. So it was that de Gaulle's pre-war views on tank warfare were widely circulated, his victory at Abbeville extensively publicised, and his famous 1934 volume *The Army of the Future* printed in translation.[56] As one feature in the *Listener* of August 1940 declared, 'this is something of a man, this de Gaulle, believe me. He was wounded three times in the last war, the last time at the inferno of Douaumont, where he was captured by the Germans.'[57] Even his misfortunes at Dakar only momentarily dented this enthusiasm.

For the French colonists, however, these factors counted for little. Having already seen their nation fall and their army routed, they believed that de Gaulle had few things to offer. One prominent Frenchwoman, who was actively involved in charitable work for refugees, caught this mood accurately when she described de Gaulle as

a 'chocolate soldier'.[58] According to another source, who frequented a
French circle within London, 'the general and his staff are referred to
in tones of condescension, amounting almost to scorn. A visitor could
not fail to get the impression that the movement is of little account.'[59]
Rumours also grew up that de Gaulle had surrounded himself with
some dubious personalities whose politics reflected his own. The accusations that de Gaulle was a Bonapartist or Boulanger figure are, of
course, well known, and stemmed from those exiled intellectuals such
as the Gombault brothers, André Labarthe and Raymond Aron. The
paradox is that, at the time of his arrival, colonists, especially business
elements who had deeply resented the Popular Front,[60] often perceived
him as a man of the left; it was reported, in particular, that Pierre Cot,
the former minister of air in the Popular Front Cabinet of 1936, was
among his entourage. This might have been because Cot was one of the
few politicians of note to have fled France in 1940, thus avoiding the
farcical Riom trials in which Vichy attempted to lay blame for defeat on
the politicians and soldiers of the Third Republic. For this very reason,
de Gaulle kept his distance from Cot. The general might also have been
conscious of British suspicions. There was a good deal of sniping at Cot
on the part of British politicians, principally Conservative MPs, something that Eden and Noel Baker came to deplore.[61] Such sniping was
also apparent among British-based French circles reflecting the socially
conservative nature of the chief representatives of the French colony in
London who, as we have seen, did not look back on the Blum experi-
ment with any nostalgia. Although de Gaulle's early supporters usually
came from right-wing officer circles, and although Cot himself quickly
left for the USA, the stigma remained. The Comte de Sibour, for
example, described as 'entirely pro-British and anti-Vichy', only joined
the Free French when he reassured himself about the general's supporters.[62]

De Gaulle might have helped his cause if he had made a greater effort
to broaden his appeal. Yet his aversion to publicity was profound, ironical given the way that he would later play the media in the Fifth
Republic. Not only did he want to protect his handicapped daughter
Anne from unwanted attention, he had no wish to be manipulated by
the British. Yet this reluctance also stemmed from his belief that, in
taking his stand, he had adopted the only position possible, and thus
commanded the moral high ground. Because of this, he needed to do
little further to explain his actions. As Crémieux-Brilhac relates, this
was why he behaved as though Rome was no longer in Rome; it was in

London instead.[63] As Julian Jackson adds, de Gaulle's notorious rudeness might further have originated from the belief that he had to show that his movement, however small, possessed teeth.[64] Certainly colonists were witnesses to this sharp behaviour. One recalled to Churchill his experiences of Carlton Gardens, where he discovered that 'many Frenchmen who have offered themselves to the general were received and interviewed in such a way that they came out with their confidence shattered'.[65] After one distinguished gentleman, a veteran of the First World War, emerged from his interview, he quipped, 'I understand now why we have been beaten.'[66] Emile Delavenay relates the story of Jean-Jacques Mayoux, a naval officer attached to the Admiralty, who was so put off by his reception by de Courcel that he rejoined his family in France, eventually becoming a prominent figure in Ceux de la Résistance.[67] All this was ultimately of little concern to Carlton Gardens. If de Gaulle was convinced he was right in his decisions and was indeed the embodiment of France, he was certainly not going to moderate his demeanour for the sake of men who had forsworn their country for long-term exile, a concept he himself could not comprehend.

Above all, de Gaulle appears to have alienated colonist support because he was a 'rebel'. Many colonists, used to obeying the injunction of the consulate, no doubt feared that retaliation might be meted out against their families in France, as did those servicemen stranded after the Armistice, and indeed members of the Free French themselves who adopted pseudonyms. Delavenay cites the case of Pierre Isoré, employed as an interpreter in the navy, who was unfortunate enough to be interned in one of the sailors' camps, and who chose to return to his home in the Corrèze.[68] Fear, however, was not the only factor that led many to see de Gaulle as a rebel. This notion originated from the widely held view that Vichy was the legitimate government of France, whatever the general himself might say. This viewpoint was most vividly expressed in a letter of July 1940, intercepted and read by the British, from a prominent leather merchant to Semet, a leading light of the FGB:

> I consider, and I still consider that it is quite possible for Frenchmen to be devoted to the English cause, obedient to the laws of England, and at the same time loyal to the French government and its representatives. I do not know any French government other than that called the Government of Vichy.[69]

In early 1941, MI5 could report that this view was still prevalent among well placed colonist circles, notably in the CEAF: 'Vichy remains the true government.'[70]

It was appreciated, however, that such opinions did not make such men necessarily 'anti-British or pro-German',[71] although it was likely that they were Pétainist. Delavenay despaired at such *maréchaliste* sympathies among fellow expatriates who were only too glad the Third Republic was gone and that the hated figures of Daladier and Blum would stand accused of its failings.[72] Sensibly, they kept these opinions to themselves; and, to be fair, their Pétainism was generally of a 'passive' kind. Apart from those Vichy consular figures and senior officers we encountered in earlier chapters, few French men and women were what could be best described as 'active' Pétainists, in that they were committed wholeheartedly to the reactionary values of the marshal and his National Revolution.[73] The exception was those *catholiques avant tout*, whom we will meet later, and whose influence was quickly curbed. As in metropolitan France, the admiration that existed for Pétain was of a 'passive' nature, a belief that he constituted a symbol of enduring France, a protector of his people, a bulwark against the decadence that had led to the collapse of the nation. The notion that the marshal was playing a double game with the Germans also did the rounds, and in early 1941 there were rumours that de Gaulle himself was in contact with Vichy, although this gossip might also have been an attempt on the part of the general's many enemies to slur his name.[74] Whether an underlying sympathy for Pétain endured much beyond 1941 is hard to know, testimony again to the ability of French colonists to keep their views to themselves, yet it seems likely; it is not difficult to believe that expatriates convinced themselves that de Gaulle was the sword of France while the marshal acted as its shield.

Organising

If French exiles had carried one national characteristic across the Channel with them, it was an ability to organise, combined with an extraordinary inability to settle mutual concerns. Before 1940, there existed a myriad of such groupings, often representing business interests, which were often at loggerheads with one another. In 1939, in an attempt to patch up outstanding differences, they were assembled together under the aegis of the Comité Central Permanent de la Colonie Française,[75] a committee comprising delegates from sixteen different societies, who worked together in the prosecution of the war effort, the exiles' own attempt to emulate the Union Sacrée of 1914 when competing political and religious factions within metropolitan France had agreed to bury the hatchet for the duration of hostilities with Germany.[76] Among the sixteen were the following: the Association Culinaire Française,[77] the Chambre de Commerce, the Société des Anciens Combattants (founded 1927), the Société de Bienfaisance, the Alliance Française (1907), the British Section of the French Red Cross, the Assistance aux Familles des Soldats Français, and the Hôpital Français (1867). The unity provided by the Comité Permanent proved fragile, however, and in the immediate aftermath of the defeat, a series of new organisations began to emerge, much to the dismay of Bessbrough's French Welfare, which had, of course, been set up to keep the peace.

The most prominent of these new bodies were: the Union des Français d'Outre Mer (UFOM), anti-Vichy but not pro-de Gaulle; the CEAF, which we have encountered already and which retained Pétainist ties; the FGB, the so-called civil wing of the Free French; and the Amis des Volontaires Français, an Anglo-French inspiration, which assisted de Gaulle's troops.

The UFOM was the first new organisation to emerge, having been founded sometime during the phoney war. The brains behind it were Métadier, who had earlier helped de Gaulle, Dr Pierre Picarda, and de Bellaing. The last of these, in the words of French Welfare, was of 'French parentage, but educated in England' and spoke 'perfect English'.[78] More is known about his fellow countryman, Picarda.[79] Born on 7 August 1897, he was the son of a French barrister and was himself a member of the Paris Bar. He also possessed a distinguished service record. He had fought in the First World War with the 25th Battalion of Chasseurs, and had volunteered for the *Corps Francs*. Wounded in 1918, he had been awarded both the Croix de Guerre and the Légion d'honneur. In 1926, he had married an Englishwoman, Winifred Laura Kemp, by whom he had four children, all born and raised in England. In 1937, he had been called to the Middle Temple and established a practice in London; on the eve of war, he was the legal adviser to the French consulate. Interestingly, he had also worked as a lawyer in Germany where he had witnessed first-hand the rise of the Nazi party.

Enjoying the patronage of Sir Thomas Moore, the new head of Hatchard's bookshop in Piccadilly,[80] and the Duke of Westminster, the UFOM had been granted the use of 33 Upper Brook Street at a nominal rent of £2 per annum. It was there that the organisation developed its statutes, which made manifest the organisation's opposition to Pétain and Vichy, but also its distance from de Gaulle, who was already viewed as a Boulanger-in-waiting.[81] With the motto 'Loyauté nous lie', the UFOM's purpose was to coordinate 'on civil lines the efforts of all free Frenchmen in Great Britain as well as the rest of the world'. It thus welcomed all Frenchmen into its ranks so long as they acknowledged 'their attachment to France and their desire to see her freed', 'their continued friendship with Great Britain whose allies they remain', and 'their will to pursue, by all possible means, the struggle against the German and Italian aggression and their confidence in the final victory of the Allies'. The UFOM further set up a fellow movement, Amis de France, to collect together British supporters who were dedicated to the preservation of French culture and the liberation of Europe.[82] This never got off the ground, merely attracting the curiosity of a handful of intellectuals.

Warming to its task, the UFOM established a French club in London with a reading room, a French mutual aid society, a canteen, a legal advice centre and a series of leisure activities (film shows, lending library and lectures). It also formed an Information Department to keep the French people, wherever they might be, up to date with the progress of the war. Detailing its support of the Allied war effort, the UFOM promised to cooperate with the British official services by providing propaganda, especially for the BBC. It even aspired to the use, via the British authorities, 'of a broadcasting station for several hours daily which on a wave-length of our own, would permit us to speak directly to our compatriots as independent Frenchmen and to convince a whole section of French opinion which is at present on guard against all exclusively British information but which is, however, far from accepting enemy propaganda'.

This remained a pipe dream, as did plans to set up a newspaper, a scheme endorsed by Sir Thomas Moore.[83] Nonetheless, the UFOM was active in producing its own propaganda under the direction of Bret, for many years the London correspondent of the Havas agency, who, on the eve of war, was press attaché to the French embassy. Elie J. Bois, formerly of the *Petit Parisien*, also contributed to this propaganda drive. Thanks to the involvement of Bois, the UFOM initially enjoyed a good relationship with Massip, the London correspondent of *Le Petit Parisien*, who had recently become press director under de Gaulle.[84]

Whether this camaraderie survived is open to doubt. It was in the basement of Upper Brook Street that the Ministry of Information newspaper *France*, the successor to the *Journal du Camp*, was edited by the Gombault brothers, Charles and Georges, two socialist exiles from France who became prominent in their denunciations of de Gaulle's dictatorial tendencies, reflecting the left's traditional mistrust of military figures. When Georges Gombault was introduced to de Gaulle on 4 July 1940, he later quipped that he had never expected to meet General Boulanger himself.[85] Although the Gombaults gravitated to the left-wing Groupe Jean-Jaurès, founded in August 1940 by Louis Lévy, himself a severe critic of the general, they still devoted a considerable column space to the Free French in the pages of *France*, and did not openly attack the movement.[86] It was this evenhandedness that contributed to the paper's success, ensuring a circulation of 25,000 per copy, many of its readers being congregated among the colonist community.[87] This success also owed much to the Ministry of Information, which insisted on a high measure of editorial impartiality, pointing out that the initial intention had never been for the newspaper to be edited in UFOM's headquarters. This had become necessary merely because the original building had 'been partially wrecked'.[88] Indeed, on reading the many articles about the conduct of the war and events within occupied Europe, the untrained eye might have difficulty in spotting the left-wing bias of *France*, and the implied criticism of de Gaulle. This is to underestimate the extreme sensitivity of Carlton Gardens, and its allies, to reproach, real or imagined, and their fear of the left. It did not go unnoticed that the Gombaults employed other socialist sympathisers, for instance Gustave Moutet, the son of the Popular Front Minister for Colonies.[89] In November 1940, the Spears Mission denounced the alleged left-wing leanings of *France*, questioning in particular a recent review of the defeat of France, which had been attributed to a misguided sense of 'militarism', something interpreted as a veiled attack on de Gaulle.[90] In the words of Lady Spears, *France* 'speaks with the voice of Blum and the Front Populaire'. Taking heart from these criticisms and upset at recent coverage of King Leopold of the Belgians,[91] the FGB also had its twopenn'orth, Massip making known that he was personally prepared to put up money to expand the newsheet to eight pages so long as the Free French had a hand in editorial policy.[92] Maybe more offensive was an article crafted by Robert Mengin, entitled 'Les Priviligiés' of October 1940, in which he accused French exiles of living it up in high-class restaurants in Soho,[93] a claim vehemently denied by de Gaulle's supporters, and maybe an explanation why so many exiles mention their eating habits in their memoirs,[94] either that or they simply could not get over their first experience of British food.[95]

When none of these grumblings was taken seriously, one Foreign Office official remarking that 'both the French and Belgians should be treated like the schoolboys most of them are',[96] in 1941 Carlton Gardens made a direct approach to the Ministry of Information offering to share in editorial responsibilities, but only on the condition that the Gombaults, Lévy and Pierre Comert were removed.[97] This gesture was declined on the grounds that the paper would then become nothing more than an expression of 'right-wing' opinions fashionable in Free French circles.[98] The quarrel thus rumbled on, even when, in 1942, the Free French were given the go-ahead to print their own paper, *La Marseillaise*, which quickly alienated the Foreign Office because of its 'extreme de Gaullist line'.[99]

Meanwhile, without its own newspaper, in early September 1940 the UFOM, through the intermediaries de Bellaing and a Mlle van de Berg, approached the British Council for an annual grant of 3,200 francs.[100] When French Welfare was subsequently told of the request, its response was lukewarm: 'We should certainly not give our blessing to any proposal to grant a large sum of money to the suggested French centre at 33 Upper Brook Street.'[101] Although Bessborough's organisation did promise to look further into the matter, requesting a 'line' from the French Division of the Ministry of Information, it is clear that its hesitation arose from the problems of already having to deal with the FGB and the CEAF.[102] After all, French Welfare had been set up specifically to promote unity among French exiles, and there was little desire to work with a third organisation that contained members from the FGB and the CEAF. As to a 'line' on the UFOM, the Ministry of Information gave the same response as it did to a telegram from a British diplomatic official in Tokyo where, presumably, Picarda's agents had also been active:

> Union referred to is small organisation which, while not owing allegiance to General de Gaulle, is in favour of resistance. At present, our only criticism of it is that it pretends to be something more than it is.[103]

Internally, however, the Ministry was especially critical of Picarda, who was regarded as 'an ambitious politician'.[104] Suspicion also centred on some of the UFOM's supporters, in particular a certain American businessman who, it was believed, had involved himself in the movement simply to recover investments in France at the end of the war.[105] Without friends in either French Welfare or the Ministry of Information, UFOM was also held in doubt by the Foreign Office, which harboured a particular dislike of Métadier who was described by one official as 'a little mad ... and [someone who] from a kind of megalomania produces schemes' that were impractical.[106] The fact that the UFOM was also opposed to the FGB further irritated the Foreign Office, which, like French Welfare, despaired of the rivalries and factionalism that characterised the French communities in exile.

The Gaullists also did their bit to sabotage their rivals. When a French resident in Putney Hill, probably put up to the task by a UFOM supporter, deluged the Foreign Office with letters asking whether His Majesty's Government supported the movement and whether there was official approval of its aims,[107] the full extent and nature of Free French hostility became apparent. In an internal note, the Foreign Office observed that 'de Gaulle's people regard it with extreme disfavour; it has no connexion with them ... and they disapprove of the people who organise it, not so much because they are not perfectly loyal to the cause of free France, but because they will not join up definitely on the side of de Gaulle'.[108]

The reluctance of the British to lend support, the internal rivalries, the growing magnetism of de Gaulle and the superior organising abilities of the FGB, ensured that, at the close of 1940, the UFOM was on its last legs.[109] As early as September that year, Foreign Office officials noted that it did not enjoy any 'wide support among Frenchmen in this country'.[110] It subsequently became the Union des Français under the direction of André Labarthe, the leading physicist, who, together with the philosopher Raymond Aron, had arrived in London in the summer of 1940. Initially, Labarthe had helped de Gaulle, working at Carlton Gardens, organising supply, but personality differences led him to leave in August. He had further felt alienated in that he was the sole civilian at the headquarters and was 'treated with scant respect' by the military.[111] For their part, de Gaulle's men had seen Labarthe as a hindrance as his presence lent credence to claims that the general was a man of the Popular Front, Labarthe having earlier acted as an adviser to Cot when he was minister in the Popular Front.[112]

A free agent, Labarthe approached the Ministry of Information for support of a publication, described as being of 'a somewhat highbrow and scientific nature', Labarthe himself being characterised as 'a sincere patriot' but 'somewhat of a fanatic, very intolerant and therefore probably intolerable'.[113] Aware that he had been an associate of Cot, the Ministry asked the Foreign Office whether anything was known against Labarthe as it did not wish to be associated with anyone who might be 'shot in the Tower!'[114] Certainly MI5 reports, based on Gaullist black propaganda, were not favourable: Labarthe was accused of surrounding himself with Communists, notably his secretary, a Pole who was alleged to be a Soviet spy, and was held responsible for the leaking of the Dakar mission, a somewhat wild charge given that de Gaulle's men had openly kitted themselves out in colonial outfits at Simpson's in the Strand and had been spotted at Liverpool Street station with maps of West Africa.[115] Wisely, the Ministry of Information recognised that Labarthe was victim of 'an Anglo-French Blimp offensive';[116] and, on 15 November 1940, he founded the journal *La France Libre*.

This soon became the leading intellectual journal of the French community in Britain, the *New Statesman and Nation* describing the editorial skills of Labarthe as nothing short of 'genius'.[117] Devoted to culture as much as to politics and propaganda, it regularly published articles by a wide range of contributors, among them Raymond Mortimer, Alexander Werth, Eve Curie, Camille Husmans and Charles Morgan, and in its first edition drew the support of such heavyweights as G. M. Trevelyan and Somerset Maugham.[118] Thanks to the high quality of its journalism, it was this journal, rather than the rump of the UFOM, that became the more important. Ten thousand copies of the first edition of *La France Libre* quickly sold out, and a further 8,000 had to be published. It proved popular with all sections of the exiled community, and regularly published articles about English customs, yet whether it truly reflected the concerns of the London-based *colons* remains open to doubt. Labarthe, who edited articles by Robert Marjolin on economic planning, bemoaned the fact that he regularly received pieces from French hairdressers, chefs and waiters, about their experiences of London life.[119] The experiences of *la vie quotidienne* were left in the capable hands and artistry of Jean Oberlé.[120]

Whether *La France Libre* met with the approval of de Gaulle's supporters, given their earlier doubts about Labarthe, also remains questionable, although Carlton Gardens was initially an enthusiastic subscriber. By 1942, however, Labarthe had completely lost patience with de Gaulle, and championed the cause of Admiral Muselier who had been dismissed by the general that year.[121] Labarthe later took up the case of Maurice Dufour, training his journalistic sights on the alleged Cagoulard connections of Colonel Passy. For his part, Aron was more restrained in his anti-Gaullism and, on only one occasion, wrote on the subject, an article of August 1943 entitled, 'The Shadow of Bonaparte'.[122] Indeed, spotting the anti-Gaullist stance of *La France Libre* requires a trained eye, and an awareness of the hair-trigger sensibilities of Carlton Gardens. In 1942, an editorial crafted by Labarthe, introducing an article by Camille Rougeron on tank warfare, was seen as a criticism of de Gaulle's military views; the result was that Carlton Gardens refused to take that particular issue, lodging a protest with the Foreign Office for good measure.[123]

While *La France Libre* became an irritant to de Gaulle, it did not incur the same wrath as did the CEAF. We have come across this organisation on several occasions already, and it will be remembered that its function was primarily to assist 'refugees and all necessitous French nationals'.[124] What grated with Carlton Gardens was that this organisation, under the patronage of Lady Warwick, had particular links with the Vichy consulate; indeed, its first president was Bardot, an official of Bedford Square. Its other principal representatives were prominent businessmen who had shown a deep mistrust of de Gaulle, and an early admiration for Pétain: the then president of the Chambre de Commerce; the leather merchant whom we met earlier; and H—, a 'distinguished chef'. It should be stressed, however, that there were limits to their Vichyite sympathies and that, in many ways, they reflected the right-wing tendencies that could be identified among Resistance movements in metropolitan France, especially La Défense de la France, founded in the cellars of the Sorbonne. As French Welfare made clear to the CFR in February 1941, these individuals were not pro-Nazi but 'belong to that category of right-wing Frenchmen, whose hatred of the Germans has been watered down by the perpetual fear that the only alternative to good relations with the Nazis is a Communist revolution in France'.[125] All that mattered to them was that Blum was out and that Pétain was in; and it was in these circles that the rumours of de Gaulle's left-wing leanings freely circled. Moreover, they considered that the marshal had legally attained power, whatever the Free French said to the contrary. Yet, as already noted, this suspicion towards the Free French did not necessarily equate outright hostility. E— had a nephew living with him who was a member of the Free French Air Force, and the CEAF regularly assisted Free French troops. Nor was there any evidence, concluded Bessborough's Committee, that 'these non-supporters of de Gaulle have ever attempted openly to disrupt the movement'.[126] Their quarrel was not with those who wished to continue the struggle but with their compatriots who adopted a 'rebel' attitude to Pétain.

As well as incurring the wrath of the Free French, the CEAF also earned the disapproval of the FGB. Overlooked in virtually every book on the French in London, this had begun life in June 1940, and was not inspired by the general's *appel* of that month. With the decision of the Bordeaux government to cease fighting and request an armistice, prominent members of the French colony in London were frightened that Franco-British relations would deteriorate in such a way that there would be no organisation left to represent their future interests.[127] In a letter of 15 July, Semet, the FGB vice-president, explained to Sir Alexander Maxwell of the Home Office, how 'the catastrophic events' in the first fortnight in July had confirmed these fears leaving the community 'bewildered'. The closure of the embassy had further compounded the issue, and had meant the *colons* were 'in need of a lead'.[128] Thus, on 5 July, Semet and his associates had decided to marshal the French colony in Great Britain into an organisation, the Association des Français de Grande Bretagne (FGB). The chairman was the engineer, M. Guéritte, and, in the words of Semet, 'one of the best known and respected Frenchmen in England'. Its vice-presidents included de Malglaive, managing director of the Cie Générale Transatlantique and A. Boucher, formerly head of the French Chamber of Commerce. Two meetings had already been conducted; and, at the second of these, held on 9 July, a letter was sent to Churchill, assuring him of 'the complete devotion of the French Colony in England to all war efforts until victory and placing our services unreservedly at the disposal of the British authorities'. Thanked by Bevin on behalf of the prime minister, the FGB had also drawn praise from de Gaulle who, related Semet, took 'complete satisfaction' that the FGB should deal with civilian affairs, although, as we shall see, whether this approval was wholehearted remains doubtful. Promising to work in 'complete cooperation with the British authorities', Semet concluded that the FGB would include practically all Frenchmen who were permanent residents in Britain, and requested that it be recognised by the Home Office as the 'liaison' between the British government and those French residing in this country.

Alongside this request, Semet enclosed the statutes of his new organisation.[129] These reiterated the following aims: the desire to act as a liaison between the British government and the French colony; the support for a British victory; and the desire for the liberation of France.

The second statute expressed the FGB's intention to become an association of individual members, not merely a federation of existing French
societies and organisations, an early sign of the movement's ambitions.
After subsequent articles listed its twenty-seven founding members and
the responsibilities of executive posts, there followed a rousing appeal
to the French colony:

> Nous ne nous soumettons pas, parce que nous avons partagé avec
> l'Angleterre, les mauvais et terribles jours de la guerre, parce que, unis à
> elle, nous avons échangé nos secrets les plus intimes, parce que sur les
> champs de bataille nous avons combattu et souffert à côté de nos frères
> anglais et parce que nous sommes engagés, sur l'honneur, à continuer
> ensemble la lutte jusqu'au bout.[130]

While sympathetic to the aims of the FGB, the Home Office was
already on its guard, fearful to entrust any sensitive intelligence to this
embryonic movement, which had yet to prove its bona fides. When, on
15 July, leading lights of the FGB, Guéritte, de Malglaive and Boucher,
visited Newsam at the Home Office, they were reminded 'that any
scheme or proposal for obtaining and placing at the disposal of the
British government the names of French citizens in this country who
were prepared to assist actively in the prosecution of the war would be
a matter for Departments other than the Home Office to consider'.[131]
The function of the Home Office in respect to aliens, continued
Newsam, was 'primarily the preservation of the security of the
country'. The ways in which the FGB could help the Home Office
would be to supply the names of French citizens 'who were engaging in
anti-British propaganda or other activity likely to impede the prosecution of the war'. Although they agreed energetically to this request, the
French visitors were no doubt disappointed that Whitehall had not
readily volunteered information of its own, especially in regard to the
names and addresses of the *colons* in Britain. As would later become
clear, this was the information they treasured above all else.

For the moment, the FGB developed an impetus of its own. On 27
July 1940, over six hundred people assembled for a general meeting
held at the YMCA in Tottenham Court Road.[132] Here, Guéritte quoted
a declaration of support from Churchill, before hinting at the developing relationship with Carlton Gardens:

> Notre Association ne dépend d'aucun gouvernement; elle ne dépend pas,
> non plus, du Général de Gaulle. Mais indépendance n'empêche pas
> collaboration avec ceux qui ont en vue le même but que nous: la victoire

britannique qui amènera la libération de la France. L'Association a donc pris contact avec le Général de Gaulle, pour voir de quelle façon nos deux actions parallèles peuvent se coordonner en ce qui concerne l'élément civil, tout en maintenant notre indépendance.[133]

Not long after, the FGB claimed to have become the civil wing of the Free French. The movement was especially excited when de Gaulle instructed the Technical Department at Carlton Gardens to contact the FGB with a view to launching a recruitment drive, targeting technicians and engineers in particular.[134] After further contact between Passy and Guéritte,[135] on 14 September 1940 Pierre Fontaine of the FFL apparently explained that de Gaulle had studied with care the statutes of the FGB, and was pleased to recognise the organisation as the 'partie civile' of La France Libre.[136] It was further claimed that the general had urged his compatriots in Britain to join the FGB, and had appealed to all existing French organisations to fuse with Guéritte's body. On 26 October 1940, René Cassin delivered a speech at Westminster House in which he described the organisation's mission as 'particulièrement belle'.[137] On 21 February 1941, de Gaulle personally addressed a letter to Semet in which he reiterated his hope that the FGB would recruit for his cause.[138] The FGB took special pride when in November 1941 it helped organise a public meeting for de Gaulle in the Albert Hall, where it was able to display its 4,000 members.[139]

Whether the FGB ever officially became the civil wing of the Free French is debatable. Carlton Gardens never made any public statement to such effect; rather these claims always emanated from inside the FGB itself, maybe explaining why the organisation is usually invisible in histories of the Free French. It is further significant that the Spears Mission, an organisation very much in tune with the Free French, insisted in October 1940 that the FGB change its statutes so as to make its support for de Gaulle unequivocal.[140] Moreover, it will be remembered that the general had little time for the wider question of the colonists, other than to win recruits. Their allegiance he expected as a matter of course, and it is significant that de Gaulle never made approaches to the FGB other than to help him uncover technicians and engineers among the exiled community. The Gaullist line on the FGB was best put in January 1942 by Tissier who, like British officials, clearly saw it as a jumped-up organisation. In conversation with Foreign Office representatives, he alluded to it as essentially 'opportunist and commercial' in nature, and was disconcerted that it took under its wing movements that accepted Vichy money such as the Comité d'Assistance aux Familles des Soldats Français.[141]

While the FGB might never have officially become the civil wing of the Free French, it nonetheless became the most prominent organisation among French colonists, muscling in on the activities of others. On 12 December 1940, the Comité Central Permanent de la Colonie Française voted itself out of existence handing over its functions to the FGB; the Société de Bienfaisance also agreed to affiliate with the FGB,[142] probably because it realised that this was the surest way of guaranteeing its financial survival, having been refused a British grant and with all of its French assets, mainly invested in the railways, rendered worthless by the war.[143] Another long-standing organisation of the French community in Britain shortly followed suit: the Vichy-funded Comité d'Assistance aux Familles des Soldats Français. In January 1941, Lady Warwick complained that the FGB was attempting to take over the French Chamber of Commerce, putting up new conseillers for election.[144] These new people were a 'dangerous lot', she added, and might attempt to oust our own people in important trading centres abroad.

Whether the FGB was successful in this démarche remains unclear, but it certainly had aspirations overseas. Having assembled prominent businessmen into a colonial committee, the FGB dispatched a series of letters to those governors in the empire who had rallied to de Gaulle.[145] The FGB scored a particular hit when the Fédération Britannique de l'Alliance Française (FBAF), the British branch of the French overseas cultural body, decided that Vichy was a government operating under duress, and so gave its support to de Gaulle, and by proxy to the FGB.[146] This was much to the disgust of E— of the CEAF who declined an invitation to become part of the Council of the Alliance as it meant sitting alongside such prominent Gaullists as Guéritte. Requests quickly followed that the FBAF should receive British government subsidies, requests that were sympathetically received in the knowledge that most other branches of this worldwide organisation, especially in South America, were sympathetic to Vichy.[147]

One cultural outpost remained outside of the growing tentacles of the FGB: the Institut Français in South Kensington, originally founded in 1910.[148] In July 1940, the future of this distinguished body was in doubt as its source of funds from the University of Lille had been severed, and its chairman, Lord Askwith, in the words of a British Council representative, suffered from the 'twin infirmities of old age and deafness', and was thus unable to exercise 'those qualities of active and skilful leadership'.[149] Tellingly, it was the Free French, rather than the FGB, that made the first initiatives, another indication that the two bodies were not necessarily hand in glove. In his capacity as *Commissaire National à l'Instruction Publique,* René Cassin explained to the British Council that the Institut, 'could be of the highest usefulness to the Free French movement', both in producing propaganda and in awarding degrees, 'subject to eventual ratification by appropriate universities', especially to engineers and those who had passed their exams in France and were keen to fight alongside de Gaulle.[150] As to the creation of a Maison Française in Trafalgar Square, he continued, this was an FGB proposal, and was intended principally as a social club, not as a rival to the Maison Française that was associated with the Institut Français. For its part, the Foreign Office, increasingly pro-de Gaulle by late 1941, was sympathetic to Cassin's request, but the plans faltered on two rocks of opposition. The first was Professor Saurat, the director, and professor of French Literature at the University of London since 1926. Not only had he fallen out with Cassin and other Free French personalities, he was determined that the Institut should continue its specialised cultural work, and disliked the notion that it should be deployed as a propaganda tool. No doubt his later likening of de Gaulle to Napoleon stemmed from the general's intention to turn his foundation into a finishing school for technicians, a project that smacked of the utilitarianism of Bonapartist educational policy. It is also likely that Saurat garnered support from several residents at the Maison of the Institut: Mengin, Labarthe, Aron and Etienne Dennery.[151] Yet whether Saurat would have been able to stand his ground, given the Foreign Office's desire to see him transferred to Bristol, which acted as the University of London's wartime home,[152] remains doubtful. The latter was fortunate that there emerged a second, far more formidable, rock of opposition, in the shape of Lord Bessborough. He was alarmed to hear that the Free French had interested themselves in the affairs of the Institut. The establishment, he argued, belonged properly to the French government, and was only temporarily in British hands. No doubt in the back of his mind was the fear that if it was entrusted to the Free French, de Gaulle would be able to make yet stronger claims to be the legitimate government of France.

Quite how the arguments played out remains unclear as the archival trail goes cold. In any case, it is likely that the Institut became less of a prize catch for either the FGB or the Free French as, in 1942, the

Maison was the victim of a severe bombing raid. Tellingly, however, Saurat remained the director, and in 1943 was prominent in agitating against the 'Cagoulard' Passy.[153]

Having colonised many of the existing French societies and cultural outposts in London, the FGB sought to boost membership. This was to be achieved by fair means or foul. Among the business community in London, it was learned that Guéritte had spread 'threats that if they do not join de Gaulle the British authorities will throw them into concentration camps',[154] maybe an exaggerated rumour as Guéritte was profoundly deaf. What caused the Foreign Office greater anxiety was the news that the FGB intended to organise a 'manifestation of Allied civilians in Great Britain, and that this manifestation should pass a resolution of gratitude to Great Britain and faith in the future'.[155] Bessborough immediately recognised that this was a 'self-advertising stunt', but in an interview with de Malglaive chose more diplomatic language, pointing out that such an event would do little good and much harm as inter-Allied affairs 'were rather tricky and delicate'. De Malglaive agreed, but claimed he was being strongly pressed by members of the FGB who had been heartened by an earlier meeting of Inter-Allied representatives at St James's Palace and by the fact that the royal family had recently received Allied heads of state. The Foreign Office remained unimpressed and sided with French Welfare. It was understood that such a manifestation would create resentment on the part of other Allied citizens many of whom might refuse to partake in the event. The example of the Norwegians was cited. They were so angered by the self-aggrandising instincts of the FGB that they refused to have anything to do with the organisation. Accordingly, Bessborough thanked the FGB for its endeavours but declined the request, pointing out that 'in the present circumstances' it would 'serve no useful purpose'. Further alarm bells rang in autumn 1941 when it was learned that FGB representatives had been speaking to TUC officials over the possibility of creating a British association, drawn from trade union members.[156] Given the conservative nature of the FGB's leadership, this was truly a remarkable move, yet it does not seem to have originated from any Pauline conversion to collectivism. Rather, the FGB was looking to replace the ailing UAGBF and, 'puffed up' by the success of organising de Gaulle's speech at the Albert Hall in November 1941, approached the unions probably because they had a lengthy membership list that could be easily contacted. Membership lists were everything to the FGB, as we shall see.

Increasingly agitated by the behaviour of the FGB, in autumn 1941 the Foreign Office hoped that it would be able to control the direction of the movement, and contain its many initiatives. With the AGM close at hand, it was naturally expected that Guéritte would stand down as president as he was 'practically stone deaf'.[157] Semet, the vice-president, was thought an unlikely contender as replacement as he was widely perceived to be, in the distinctly non-Gallic phrase, 'not much of a chap'.[158] This, then, was the ideal moment to put forward Roger Cambon, the living embodiment of the *entente cordiale*, as the new leader. At a recent lunch, Cambon had been heard to utter some favourable remarks about de Gaulle, and it was said his dining companion the Vicomtesse de la Panousse, who in December 1940 had backed General Catroux against de Gaulle, now kept photographs of Free French soldiers in her *oeuvroir* [*sic*]. Cambon's appointment would not only make the FGB easier to control, it would also lend prestige to the movement, encouraging the remaining two thousand or so London colonists to sign up. Needless to say, neither Cambon nor the FGB were susceptible to these intrigues, and Guéritte, deaf as a post, remained in post.

Unable to influence the FGB, Whitehall had to field several of its requests. The first of these, presented immediately after the meeting of 27 July 1940, was that its members should enjoy the privileges of allies that they had been enjoying up to 17 June; since the Armistice, they had become the subject of Aliens Restrictions Orders, limiting their freedom of movement and compelling their registration with the police.[159] In July, it was thought far too early to concede this kind of privilege. Later, in October, while the CFR acknowledged that there could be no relaxation of this restrictive provision, it was recommended that FGB members should receive 'lenient treatment'.[160] How far this operated in practice remains uncertain, although it is known that it was not until the closing months of the war that overall restrictions were lifted.

Next, the FGB sought from the Home Office 'a complete list of French residents', something it had been too shy to request explicitly when its representatives met Newsam in July,[161] so that it could mount a recruitment drive. 'We will leave it to the British authorities', remarked the FGB, 'to decide what is best to be done with those of our compatriots who, for whatever reasons, have decided or will decide not to join our Association of Free Frenchmen [*sic*].' Such a move would enable the association to issue a membership card, stamped by both the

Home Office and police, which would then confer on its holder the privileges of an ally, another move designed to get round the Aliens Restrictions Act. The FGB even suggested that MI5 should assist them in the vetting of members, something that was rejected out of hand as a government security agency could not be placed at the disposal of a private organisation.

This quest for the names of French residents never ceased, yet government was naturally cautious about handing over such material as it ran counter to the general policy of not disclosing 'to any third party names of aliens in this country without their consent'.[162] In practice, the Home Office was prepared for police forces to disclose 'for the benefit of the Belgian, Czech, Dutch and Norwegian authorities information regarding respectability of persons offering hospitality to soldiers of these foreign countries'.[163] Such information was not for the French. The government was disturbed that the CEAF had also requested a full list of French residents,[164] and there remained the perennial fear of Vichy reprisals. When, in February 1941, MI5's regional officer in Reading reported that he was certain that police forces were in fact giving information to the Free French, chief constables were warned once again of the dangers of this action.[165]

The final request of the FGB was to receive a similar type of blessing to that that had been granted to de Gaulle's movement on 28 June. This received a sympathetic hearing, especially after Bessborough outlined the situation of the French colony in London. In his view, this comprised two communities, the first in complete support of de Gaulle, the second consisting 'of persons who have been here for years and who proclaimed themselves to be just as loyal to our cause as the first group'. Bessborough further added both groups frequently 'abused one another'. It was thus agreed that there was an urgent need to clear up the existing situation and so encourage all those sitting on the fence to come out openly in support of the Allied cause. If there was a single society that could facilitate this union, then it was deserving of support, suggested Bessborough. Whether he would have made the same recommendation knowing the troubles the FGB would bring him in 1941 is doubtful. In any case, the Foreign and Home Office both held that 'HMG could not give official recognition to a private body.'[166] In this situation, all government was prepared to do was to endorse de Gaulle's support of the movement and inform other departments, notably the Treasury, which could provide financial aid, that the FGB constituted the only grouping 'deserving of our support'.[167]

There remained one organisation that the FGB was less eager to colonise, partly because it was an Anglo-French creation, partly because it was already Gaullist in orientation, partly because it included FGB members on its committee, and partly because its intentions were very different from its own. This was the Amis des Voluntaries Français (AVF) which held its first meeting on 6 September 1940. Here, an executive was formed comprising the following: Earl de la Warr (president); de Malglaive (vice-chairman); Lord Ivor Spencer Churchill and Captain Hesse (honorary secretaries); Bellenger (honorary treasurer); and committee members the Marchioness of Crewe, Lady Peel, the Hon. Crawshay and M. Morhange.[168] The objectives of the organisation were laid out thus:

> The Association, exclusively authorised by General de Gaulle, has been set up in London to coordinate all offers of help and to centralise all gifts emanating from Great Britain and abroad sent to him for the welfare of the volunteers. The aim of the Association is to establish a link between organisations and individuals, whatever their nationality, who wish to extend moral and material help to the French volunteers.[169]

As a later AVF letter to *The Times* of 7 October 1943 pointed out, in its three years of existence, the organisation had managed to establish 57 branch committees throughout the British Isles 'grouping over 30,000 associate members of whom the great majority are British'.[170] As well as raising the impressive sum of £53,542 15s 0d in 1943 compared to £19,239 4s 7d in 1941,[171] the AVF had set up canteens, clubs and foyers for the use of de Gaulle's troops, including a Maison des Ailes at Ditchley Park for personnel of the Armée de l'Air.[172] Enjoying the patronage of the British Council and French Welfare, with which it enjoyed cordial relations,[173] the AVF in 1943, was prompted by the creation of the Committee of National Liberation in Algiers, to assist all French forces fighting for the Allied cause 'irrespective of their past affiliations'.[174] At the close of August 1944, membership of the AVF had swelled to 40,000, but it aimed for 100,000 by the close of the year.[175] Paradoxically, as Allied troops swept across France and, as many French in Britain prepared to return to their homeland, the AVF busily promoted its film *Born in Britain* portraying the lives of those babies that had been delivered in exile.[176] A further paradox was that it was only at the Liberation that squabbling over the AVF became open, although it is apparent that Carlton Gardens had assiduously monitored the attitudes of its committee, alleging in March 1941 that Ivor Churchill had let drop pro-Vichy remarks.[177] In 1944, arguments largely revolved around what honours should be distributed to its leading acolytes, and what should be done with its remaining monies, some £30,000 in total, together with a considerable amount of goods.[178] Exasperated by the continuing struggles within the French community, Bessborough offered simple advice: wind the organisation up.[179]

Les catholiques avant tout

There remained one group of French colonists, bolstered by new arrivals from their homeland, who generally remained outside any organisation but who nevertheless retained a distinct identity in that they were united in their faith and were eager to see the institutionalised secularism of the French state vanquished once and for all: *les catholiques avant tout.*

Religious intolerance had, of course, always been a spur to French emigration to Britain: the Massacre of Saint Bartholomew and Louis XIV's Revocation of the Edict of Nantes had displaced thousands of Huguenots who had since settled in England, especially in London's East End. Over the centuries, however, they had largely assimilated English culture and were no longer *the* prominent religious force among French colonists. This distinction had passed to those religious orders that had been expelled at the start of twentieth century when, in the fall-out of the Dreyfus Affair, the state had denied such men and women the right of association (law of 1901) and had subsequently banned them from teaching altogether (law of 1904). Although many religious defied this legislation, several had settled elsewhere: in Belgium, where de Gaulle himself had attended the school of an exiled order, travelling across the border each day to school, and in Britain. The 1931 Census recorded 133 French priests and monks, along with 765 nuns and Sisters of Charity.

In June 1940, these men and women were joined by several of their co-religionaries. It will be recalled that, among the refugee population, there came some fifty priests and novices, together with nuns displaced from the coastal towns of Dunkirk and Calais. It was further recognised that many of the servicemen trapped in England were extremely devout. This was especially true of the officer class. It was noted that officers held in Blackpool, deliberately segregated from their men, were 'intensely Catholic', and believed Pétain was the only means of restoring 'the spiritual greatness of France'.[180] The same observation could be made about several of the naval ratings, despite the fact that Admiral

Darlan, a non-believer, was at their head. French Welfare officers frequently commented that a majority of the sailors held in the camps of north-west England were 'intensely religious' Bretons.[181] Furthermore, it is well documented that Action Française supporters, their hatred of the *Boche* greater than their admiration of Pétainist principles, were among early recruits for de Gaulle. As one early volunteer complained to Morton, such men were already attempting to resurrect 'la vieille France' within the general's movement, even though this was responsible for the defeat.[182] Tereska Torrès, a Jewish convert to Catholicism, met some of these Action Française adherents on her voyage to Britain, the first time she had ever encountered this political group face to face.[183] Appreciative of their courage, patriotism and enthusiasm, she was nonetheless alienated by their anti-Semitism, snobbish attitude and pretentious airs.

In 1940, fears about these *catholiques avant tout* were essentially threefold. First, how would they respond to the overtly pro-clerical policies that Pétain was pursuing?[184] Within the first six months of his regime, he abolished freemasonry, the scourge of clericals; sacked allegedly secularist schoolteachers; provided minor financial palliatives to Catholic schools; removed the ban stopping religious orders from teaching; and, for a brief moment in January 1941, restored the catechism into the timetable of the state primary school, an institution hitherto strictly neutral in religious matters. Such measures had, in turn, given great delight both to the Vatican, whose newspaper *L'Osservatore Romano* called the creation of Vichy 'the dawn of a new radiant day',[185] and to members of the French episcopacy who fell over themselves to praise Pétain, the 'man of the moment'. It is now known that the French Church was deeply divided in its attitude to Vichy, and that the rank-and-file clergy, youth movements and laity quickly lost their initial enthusiasm for the regime, especially when it began its merciless persecution of Jews and other minorities. Nonetheless, this early enthusiasm gave rise to a second fear. Would the presence of *catholiques avant tout* in Britain disturb other members of the French colony, turning them into fifth columnists? In this regard, the government had at hand regular reports of the High Commissioner in Canada who had spoken of how French Canadians openly admired the marshal whom they cheered whenever he appeared on newsreels. While they did not like Laval, whom they viewed as a traitor, they applauded him as a good Catholic, something he clearly was not, whenever Protestants in the audience hissed him.[186]

From such reports emerged a third fear, reminiscent of the anxieties of British governments in the 1790s when there had been another great influx of devout Catholics.[187] Might *catholiques avant tout* pollute the loyalties of their British co-religionaries? Not only were such men and women traditionally viewed as 'outsiders', in the 1930s it had not gone unremarked that leading Catholic intellectuals, men such as Douglas Jerrold, John Strachey Barnes, Michael de la Bedoyère and Robert Sancourt, had displayed an unhealthy interest in fascism.[188] In the six months immediately after the French defeat, the leading Catholic journal the *Tablet* devoted no fewer than twelve major articles to France, which were bitterly critical of the Third Republic, and even uncovered a connection between the French Revolution of 1789 and the Nazi takeover of 1933.[189] There was also talk of a Latin bloc, comprising France, Italy and Spain, which would act as a deterrent to Bolshevism. As Horsfall Carter bemoaned in the pages of *New Statesman and Nation*, 'A careful scrutiny of the Catholic press in this country since the downfall of France is highly instructive. The "line" may be summed up as a pathetic attempt to reconcile an attitude of faith, hope and charity with regard to the new France – which has broken with the pernicious liberal, rationalist and secularist tenets of the Third Republic – with the patent fact that Marshal Pétain and co are entirely under Nazi domination.'[190] This provocative article sparked off a running correspondence between Catholic and non-Catholic intellectuals in the *New Statesman and Nation* that continued until the end of the year.

The reasons why British Catholics ultimately remained loyal to the Allied cause have since been amply explored.[191] Apart from the influence of the Ministry of Information and BBC, which were keen to rein in any overly pro-Pétain sentiment, historians have stressed the ability of British Catholics to put their own house in order. Particular credit has been attached to Cardinal Hinsley who deftly handled the media, both Catholic and otherwise, and the success of the Sword of the Spirit, a Catholic movement inspired by, among others, Christopher Dawson, A. C. F. Beales and Manya Harari, which campaigned tirelessly for the victory of the Allies. It is also questionable whether the presence of a small number of French *catholiques avant tout* would have had any impact on British Catholics who had their own structures and hierarchies. In this respect, it was perhaps fortunate that their number did not include any significant intellectual figure such as Emmanuel Mounier, the Personalist philosopher, whose early sympathy for the values of the National Revolution led him to establish the leadership school at Uriage. Other leading voices, such as Jacques Maritain and Georges Bernanos, chose exile in the USA and South America respectively, where they quickly made known their distaste for Vichy's authoritarian leanings and compliance with Nazi Germany.[192]

The absence of a domineering intellectual presence also goes some way in explaining why *catholiques avant tout* were not to influence French Catholics in Britain, yet several other reasons also present themselves. To begin with, the Ministry of Information once again had an impact. Having warned such leading publications as the *Catholic Herald* against adopting an overly sympathetic line on Pétain,[193] it also ensured that its own publication *France* included plenty of anti-Vichy ammunition directed by prominent Catholic writers and politicians.[194] This included Cardinal Villeneuve's speech at Quebec in which he praised the Free French, a broadcast from Bernanos, an article by Thierry d'Argenlieu, and Cardinal Hinsley's speech at the Foyles luncheon in honour of de Gaulle. Bernanos himself volunteered to publish propaganda in Britain, approaching the British ambassador in Brazil as early as July 1940, an offer that was taken very seriously.[195] The Ministry also helped with the publication of the monthly Catholic newspaper *La Volontaire pour une Cité Chrétienne*, which in 1943 achieved an annual circulation of 15,500.[196] Edited by the prominent émigré Francis-Louis Closon, ably assisted by Guy Hattu, a commando, René de Nauvois, a priest and another commando, and Andrée Desloyers, a doctor, this publication was largely distributed in the Middle East and African colonies, rather than the London community, but stressed the anti-totalitarian tendencies of the Free French and helped counter the impression that the French Catholic press was entirely pro-Vichy. Closon was especially pleased by the paper's title, which was designed to be a deliberate snub to Vichy which portrayed all overseas resisters as adventurers without faith nor a sense of law.[197] Outside the Ministry's publications, *La France Libre* also did its bit, printing the 'message' from Jacques Maritain,[198] and publishing an extremely perceptive article by Jacques Rochelle highlighting the splintered opinions within the French Church, especially the resistance shown by Mgr Sal*i*ège, archbishop of Toulouse.[199]

Hinsley himself was just as significant in containing the Pétanist sympathies of the French community as he was in controlling British Catholics. In August 1940, following the pronouncements of *L'Osservatore Romano* on Vichy, he announced that these had been 'quoted in this country to create a wrong impression'.[200] 'We must make it clear', he stressed, 'that Catholics are and will remain loyal to their country's cause while they are also trustfully devoted to the Holy See.' Hinsley also took practical measures, interviewing priests destined to tend to the men at White City to ensure that they were suitable.[201] He also reined in the Marist priest at the French Church in Leicester Place, near Leicester Square, recognising the importance of this institution to the expatriate community. Founded in 1865, it had become just as central to expatriate life as was the consulate in Bedford Square,[202] and was often the first port of call for many new arrivals in 1940, including Tereska Torrès.[203] All the more disturbing, then, that in July the priest delivered a series of ambiguous sermons on the fall of France. He was severely rebuked by his superior. In a letter of apology to Hinsley of 28 August, he admitted that he had used the pulpit to make 'veiled' references to politics, and claimed that these must have been 'misunderstood' by the congregation.[204] It is not known exactly what was contained in his addresses, but it appears to have been criticism of the Third Republic. Nonetheless, he promised that there would be no further cause for complaint and agreed with the cardinal's ruling that 'the pulpit should be used only for purely religious matters'. Shortly afterwards, his church was destroyed by a German bomb, and the Ministry of Works and Buildings questioned whether it should be rebuilt, despite its status as 'the official and only church of the French colony in London', as reconstruction meant 'the use of scarce materials and of still scarcer labour'.[205] Both the Foreign Office and Ministry of Information backed the application,[206] despite the fact that the priest remained Vichy in instinct.[207] In the words of one government report, he was a fifth columnist of the 'worst sort'.[208] Yet, like many other French institutions in London, because his church was colonised by a whole range of French – FGB and the Free French members as well as Vichy consular officials – something of the priest's Vichy sympathies were diluted.[209] After the war, the Church became a meeting place for Free French veterans, especially on Armistice Day when they commemorated fallen colleagues.[210]

Apart from Hinsley, other leading members of the Catholic hierarchy did their bit to contain any Vichyite sympathies, both at home and abroad. In September 1940, Postal Censorship intercepted a letter from the Catholic writer Robert Speaight, then in New York distributing pro-British propaganda, to Bishop Mathew at Westminster Cathedral.[211] There in America he had met with Maritain, and together they had agreed that a Pontifical High Mass, attended at Westminister by de Gaulle, members of the British government and the French community, would go some way in countering Pétainist propaganda both in Britain and the USA, particularly the unfounded claims that de Gaulle was anti-clerical; as in the case of his supposed left-wing leanings, it appears that the lack of information about the general gave rise to some wild rumours about his religious position. The scheme for a mass had, however, been frowned upon by a Spanish priest in their company, a representative of the papacy, who remarked that, 'Le Vatican n'entend que des menaces.' While acknowledging Churchill's support for Italian and German missions, the same priest had also denounced the 'indolent and aristocratic manner of the British government'. For its part, the Foreign Office thought such a mass was a good idea, bringing out the 'best in Catholic France',[212] although on approaching Desmond Morton, himself a Catholic, it was learned that Carlton Gardens was more or less empty thanks to the Dakar mission; those who remained were 'super atheists'.[213] Nonetheless, such masses would become a common feature in the life of Westminister Cathedral during the remainder of the war.

Elsewhere within Britain, the Catholic archbishop of Liverpool, Mgr Downey, warned the government from employing, in the sailors' camps, leading officials of the French colony from the city, many of whom were members of the Catholic Women's League, as these ladies were 'suspect' in their political outlook.[214] Such warnings were especially apposite as it was among stranded soldiers and sailors that *catholiques avant tout* were most active. In July 1940, Castellane, the French chargé d'affaires, urged that Abbé P—, attached to the consulate and the French Church in Leicester Square, should be allowed to visit wounded troops at White City where he would 'abstain from any politics'.[215] His earlier failure to hold his tongue had led to his exclusion, and the request was turned down.

'Troublesome priests' were, though, active elsewhere, especially in the North-West. Particular suspicion was levelled at a Father N— M—, an Irish priest, an Italian rather than French-speaker and a member of the Benedictines, who was attached to the camp at Trentham Park, and who was well known to Georges Blond, the right-wing naval engineer whom we met earlier.[216] In a lengthy letter to Lady Peel, he vigorously refuted allegations that he was pro-Pétain.[217] 'Vichy I detest', he declared. 'Pétain and Weygand I disapprove of in the strongest terms. That they are Catholics is none of my business: my disapproval of them is based not on religious grounds, but rather on the fact that they represent a government and country which has broken faith and treaty with ours.' He further condemned their association with Laval, and was deeply troubled by Pétain's private morality: 'I learn on good authority, long before I came here, that Pétain married a divorcee, so I have no great opinion of his Catholicity, though I believe the matter of his marriage has been rectified.' The letter went on to say that he approved of de Gaulle's actions, having listened to him on the radio, something to which his fellow fathers could attest. Condemning those who wanted to return to France, he cited the many occasions on which he had recruited for de Gaulle, and spoke of how he had reported one French officer for helping sailors to escape in civilian clothes to Liverpool, from where they arranged a safe passage home. Concluding this lengthy rebuttal, he suggested that his reputation for being anti-Gaullist stemmed from an early reluctance to distribute pro-British propaganda and an association with a certain Père B— D— from the Doddington camp who had earlier visited Trentham Park. When the two men had called in at the de Gaulle recruiting office in Stoke, a political argument broke out and it had soon become clear where D—'s loyalties lay even though 'he was soundly whacked by all the others on every point under discussion'. The letter certainly did the trick. Rear-Admiral Watkins was said to have considered the continued presence of Father M— at the camp 'a matter of "national importance", as he has had an extremely favourable good influence on the men'.[218]

Ultimately, *les catholiques avant tout* represented a minority grouping within the colony. Despite many of them being members of the clergy, both secular and regular, they lacked organisation and were easily isolated by Hinsley, French Welfare and others. The fact that, in 1941, de Gaulle's own spiritual loyalties became apparent might also have contained their anguish. He might have bemoaned the fact that 'the synagogue sends me more than the cathedral', but several prominent Catholics emerged in his entourage, among them Maurice Schumann, a former editor of *L'Aube*, René Pleven, the jurist and former head of the Asociation Catholique de la Jeunesse Française, and Thierry d'Argenlieu, who along with Muselier is credited with devising the Cross of Lorraine.[219] So it was that *catholiques avant tout* amounted to little more than a nuisance.

The British government and the *colons*: internment and restrictions

In preparation for war, 'the Government had decided that there should be no general internment of aliens in Britain at the outbreak of hostilities'.[220] Nonetheless, restrictions were placed on freedom of movement and, as early as April 1939, it was agreed that general internment would, at some point, be necessary. Preparations were thus put into place and lists of foreigners drawn up. Three categories of enemy aliens (A, B and C), principally Italians, Germans and Austrians, were distinguished: the first group were the most dangerous and were earmarked for internment immediately on the outbreak of hostilities. During the fifth-column scare of May 1940 Category B aliens, initially subject to restrictions on movement, particularly in coastal and other security-sensitive areas, were likewise interned. The final C group, who had not been targeted for either internment or curtailment of their liberties, men and women about whom the British government had no real grounds for suspicion, were rounded up the next month.

Being allies, the French of course had not figured in any of these discussions, but the dramatic events across the Channel quickly focused government attention. In several regards, Whitehall's approach mirrored the general policy it had adopted towards enemy aliens, and it was a close-run thing that the French colony was not eventually subject to the same fate that had befallen Italians, Germans and Austrians.

Early internees

It will be recalled that the question of interning French men and women figured in Cabinet discussions soon after the Armistice. On 10 July ministers gathered at Downing Street to consider what action should be taken against French nationals in the event of France declaring war on Britain, seemingly a real prospect after Mers-el-Kébir and the Vichy retaliatory bombing of Gibraltar.[221] Here, a report of the Aliens Advisory Committee, which recommended no general or immediate internment of Frenchmen, was endorsed. Nonetheless, lists were to be made of those special cases who would need rounding up should the occasion arise. While it was admitted that the numbers were not likely to be large, confusion arose as to who should be included. The Home Office believed it should comprise those who would have to be detained 'on account of their knowledge of British plans and preparations or in view of their technical skill'.[222] Inevitably, this would include members of the French missions, who were returned in

September 1940, leading to discussions as to whether they should be joined by the remainder of cases filed by the government.[223] To clarify matters, the Home Office acknowledged that should Vichy now declare war, 'the whole of the French colony would have to be considered each on his own merits', especially as it was rumoured that 'a fair proportion of the French Colony is by no means pro-British'.[224] It was concluded, however, that there was nothing 'to do before the event, but if Vichy declares war we shall want a Tribunal for the French'.[225]

Who, then, were interned during these early months? We know their numbers were not large. In a letter of February 1941, the Foreign Office explained to Chartier that 64 Frenchmen had been held since July the previous year.[226] Of this figure, 39 had been repatriated; 18 had been released; only 7 remained in detention.

Surviving evidence suggests that the majority of internees were not colonists but awkward members of the missions, such as Captain de Rivoyre who will be remembered from the preceding chapter, and servicemen, guilty not so much of fifth-columnist activities but of a defeatism that threatened to poison their colleagues. Such was the case of F— G— K—, an officer evacuated from Dunkirk and subsequently held at Winchester gaol for having said that troops should not join de Gaulle and that England was on the verge of revolution.[227] Another case was that of commander R—. Before the Armistice, he had been attached to Bomber Command.[228] Because of his strong Pétainist sentiments, Air Chief Marshal Sir Charles Portal had requested he be confined. The conditions of his internment were not hard. Under house arrest at Selsdon Park Hotel, Surrey, he was still at liberty to wander round the surrounding area. MI5 kept a close watch on these movements, but did not uncover any evidence to prove that he was distributing anti-British or anti-Gaullist propaganda, as the Spears Mission alleged. It was known, however, that he was in receipt of funds from Chartier at the Vichy consulate. In view of his predicament, this charity was not unreasonable. In the eyes of the Spears Mission and Carlton Gardens it was a sure sign R— was guilty. René Pleven of the Free French expressed astonishment that he was permitted such license to roam and urged that he be placed under closer surveillance, for instance at the hotel in York, the home of other suspect French officers.[229] There, in the provinces, he would not get up to any mischief, and would not be in contact with the Vichy consulates. In the event, such draconian action appears to have been scuppered by the Air Ministry, which thought it improper to treat one of its former staff in such a manner.[230]

R— 's fate remains uncertain as does that of P— H— C—. On 3 March 1941, Chartier wrote to the Foreign Office requesting that this man be freed from the camp at Lingfield and allowed to go to Brazil; at the very least, he should be placed in 'forced residence' at a hotel.[231] On investigation, it was discovered that C— had been interned on account of 'professional misconduct', most likely defeatism rather than spying, while working as a technician in certain 'war processes' at Hull. He had subsequently been placed in a camp to prevent him coming into contact with others. For this reason, the Foreign Office saw no reason why he should be allowed to go to Brazil or be given 'more comfortable accommodation'.[232] Nevertheless, his case came before the Lindley Committee, dealing with troublesome aliens, where it was recommended that he be released so long as the Free French accepted him for service.[233] C— was subsequently interviewed by de Gaulle's men but was found wanting. The result was that he was moved to Mooragh Camp on the Isle of Man.[234]

Other cases, for instance that of a man held since August 1940, because of his knowledge of technical matters and association with a German agent, and that of a refugee who had spread defeatist views in the factory in which he worked, also came up for periodic review, but they appear to have been among the seven unfortunates held for the duration of the war.[235]

It was not just suspected Pétainists and defeatists who fell foul of the British authorities. In early 1941, the British embassy in Washington forwarded to London a letter that it had received from James Cannon, National Secretary of the Socialist Workers Party in New York. This alleged that Robert Frank, 'a well known French revolutionist' had been sentenced by a London police tribunal at Marylebone to six months hard labour for not having registered properly with the police.[236] At his trial, the defendant protested that this lapse was through fear that he might be turned over to Vichy who had condemned him to an unknown penalty *in absentia*. As we have seen, this was not an uncommon anxiety among French exiles who fretted that reprisals might be taken against their relatives back in France. On hearing the explanation, the judge was unimpressed and denounced Frank as 'a subversive person'; copies of *The Tragic Situation of the Workers and Peasants of France* and *The Imperialist War and the World* had been found among his possessions in College Crescent Hampstead.[237] Cannon was shocked. Having been hounded out of France by 'democrats who preferred Hitler to a resurgence of the

French people', Frank now found himself in the paradoxical position of being imprisoned by a country that was opposed to Vichy. 'Elementary justice', concluded Cannon, demanded that Frank be freed. When the Foreign Office looked into the case, however, it was discovered that Frank had also been engaged in anti-British activities, and was deemed 'a danger to the community'.[238] The prison term had since been extended on account of this, although it was determined that Frank should not be returned to France where he was likely to receive even less favourable treatment. Instead, he was transferred to the internment camp on the Isle of Man where, fittingly for a former secretary of Trotsky, he was quickly mobilising the anti-fascists against others in the compound, organising a hunger strike and popularising his anti-Gaullist views.[239]

How much of a danger Frank truly was remains in doubt. At least he had done something to attract the attention of the authorities, unlike the unfortunate J— B—, an engineer who had lived for some time in the UK dealing in patents for oil-refining machinery.[240] He had been arrested on 16 August 1940 and subsequently held at Pentonville. Despite both he and his family having close contacts with de Gaulle, and despite his plight being championed by the MP Dr Leslie Burgin, B— had been expelled and repatriated in Marseille. The case caused some embarrassment within Whitehall where no one would take responsibility and where it was admitted nothing untoward was known against him. 'Looks like another MI6 muddle', scribbled one Foreign Office official on the file; 'no doubt MI5 are the niggers in the wood pile', wrote another in less diplomatic language.

Justice at least seems to have been served in the case of Mlle Nicole. On 28 July 1941, the Rabat newspaper *La Vigie Marocaine* recorded her story under the headline 'L'odieux traitement infligé par les Britanniques à une infirmière française'.[241] A member of the automobile section of the French Red Cross, Nicole had served in the First World War and, in 1940, had again transported the wounded. With the Armistice, she did not consider her role ended; instead, she travelled to Britain on 17 September to assist those refugees and soldiers stranded across the Channel. Having been furnished with the necessary papers by the British, she was astonished to be arrested eight days after her arrival. No explanation was given as to her internment, and she subsequently spent 279 days in prison, thirteen of which were spent in a 'cachot'. She was eventually released on 11 June 1941, yet still no reason was given for her incarceration, which clearly distressed the nurse. In early July, British censors intercepted a letter she sent from Portugal, where she had been deported, to a Mr Griggs of the American Red Cross in London.[242] In this, she recounted her 279 days in jail and the 'cruel treatment' she had suffered. She was furious that the British Red Cross had taken so long to vouch for her, despite the fact Anthony Eden's sister had been a member of her motor corps and that de Gaulle's own nurses had come to see her. 'A victim of wilful cruelty', she had been sent third class to Liverpool, accompanied by detectives, and then dumped on a cargo vessel for the 20-days' voyage to Lisbon, although 'anything was better than Holloway'.

Perturbed by the story, the British consulate at Tangier requested from the Foreign Office the full facts of this 'exaggerated case' so it could put these to the French authorities and quash the propaganda of the two local French newspapers, which were becoming 'ever more virulent'.[243] Worryingly, the German press was also publicising the case, the *Völkischer Beobachter* claiming that 1,200 women were being tortured in London.[244] So it was that the Foreign Office looked into the matter. As a note of 13 January 1941 revealed, Nicole had come to Britain, alongside a colleague, Mlle Terré, whom we met earlier. Both had been arrested on the suspicion of spying, the distribution of anti-British propaganda and the engineering of a 'clandestine loophole in the blockade'.[245] Her colleague was quickly released when it became apparent that she had travelled across the Channel in good faith; meanwhile, further worrying discoveries were made about Nicole. In a letter of March 1941, the Foreign Office revealed that Nicole, laden with 'defeatism even before the Armistice', had been sent over, with German connivance, to spy on de Gaulle's organisation and to execute a plan whereby supplies would be sent to France, ostensibly for refugees but in truth to break the blockade.[246] It was because of the seriousness of her crimes that the British government remained unmoved in the face of protests from both Chartier and the American Red Cross.[247] As one official later reflected, she was 'an unpleasant personage' and 'far from being an injured innocent',[248] although it was agreed by all that Holloway had not been the place to keep her, especially at the time of the Blitz.[249] Whether this treatment or her latent Anglophobia inspired her later actions can only be guessed at. In August 1941, back in France, she was reported to be in charge of the Section Sanitaire Automobile where she was conducting anti-British propaganda which she proposed to export to West Africa.[250]

With only a few French men and women interned in the first six

months after the Armistice, it may have seemed that colonists had little
to fear for the future. Even if some retained an admiration for Pétain,
they could still point to their anti-German credentials. Yet the issue of
internment did not go away, especially given the turn for the worse in
British-Vichy relations at the start of 1941.

General internment?

With the dismissal of Laval on 13 December 1940, and his eventual
replacement by the Anglophobe Darlan as chief minister and dauphin
to Pétain, the Foreign Office braced itself for the worst. There seemed
to be a real possibility of war breaking out between Britain and France,
thus forcing government to return to those questions that had figured
in the War Cabinet discussions of July 1940. Where would the loyalty
of Frenchmen in Britain lie, and what policy should be adopted in their
regard?

It is testimony to the seriousness of these questions that they regularly figured in government discussions for the first six months of 1941.
Strikingly, the minutes of the CFR reveal that the agency keenest on
some general internment was Carlton Gardens. Even though the Free
French did not have a seat on the CFR, it is significant that the Spears
Mission, still very much the *porte-parole* of de Gaulle, spoke most
emphatically about 'doubtful' French elements in this country. At the
meeting of 28 January 1941, Spears himself presented a memorandum,
which relayed the awful choices that had confronted Frenchmen in
Britain since the Armistice.[251] While he acknowledged the Free French
were not entirely reliable, much praise was lavished on de Gaulle's
men, who had at least chosen sides. 'As long as there are any doubtful
Frenchmen in this country', he continued, 'there is bound to be a great
danger of this information percolating through to pro-Vichy individuals, who may pass it on to Vichy itself, and that is equivalent to its
falling into enemy hands.' That there were 'a great many Vichyites in
this country', was not in doubt, and Spears berated MI5 for not doing
enough about them. The policy of the security services, he surmised,
was to do as little as possible to antagonise the French community,
hoping this would 'prevent them from becoming violently hostile'.
This policy was flawed as no neutrally-minded person would turn into
a 'dangerous pro-Vichyite' simply because MI5 was watching him or
her. The inevitable conclusion was that 'every Frenchman, who is not
enrolled with the Free French (and even these require very careful
watching) or who cannot be vouched for by English friends of long

standing should … be requested to leave the country'. 'There can be only one consideration', concluded Spears, 'and that is security.' If there was an invasion, it was not inconceivable that the enemy would attempt to get in touch with Frenchmen on British soil. Thus whenever a French ship was intercepted in the future it should immediately be put to work repatriating unreliable French nationals.

Calculating that these elements numbered only 'a few hundred', Spears anticipated little opposition to his scheme. Yet the CFR was not ready to rush into any hasty action and commissioned French Welfare to prepare a report on the French community in the UK. This was produced for the meeting of 5 February 1941 and focused principally on the *colons* in London.[252] Little effort, the authors acknowledged, had been made to contact French residents in the provinces, as their numbers were few and it was assumed that those living in Bristol, Glasgow, Birmingham, Manchester and Liverpool, that is areas where there were active Anglo-French societies, shared similar sentiments to their compatriots in London. Within the capital, the report stated, the key question was the attitude to adopt towards the Free French movement. It was recognised, however, that those who were not for de Gaulle were not necessarily for Vichy or anti-British, or that this attitude towards the Free French 'takes any active form beyond refusal to cooperate'.

The above paper, together with that of Spears, was discussed by the CFR Sub-Committee on Welfare and Security at its meeting of 7 February 1941, and at subsequent meetings that month.[253] Here, the participants reiterated their positions. For its part, MI5 declared that it had insufficient evidence to justify taking action against any Frenchman in respect of anti-de Gaulle activities, a position supported by both the Home and Foreign Offices. Against, Captain Knox of the Spears Mission argued that those hostile to the Free French represented a real danger in the event of an invasion. Knox was, however, in a minority. The overwhelming opinion of the meeting was that the French community was not a threat to national security. The most dangerous elements were deemed not to be colonists, but the handful of sailors who had deserted from British camps before repatriation and who were now wandering about the countryside without proper papers. Nonetheless, there was a strong feeling that more should be done to enlist the French community in support of the war effort. There remained particular concern about men of military age who had failed to join either the British armed services or de Gaulle, as we shall see.

That the above conclusions amounted to a fudge was recognised by the War Cabinet, which was becoming ever more jittery given the bellicose noises coming from Darlan. In a furious letter of 25 February 1941, Downing Street made known to the Foreign Office that the Home Office was 'failing altogether' to get a grip on the issue of Frenchmen in the UK.[254] 'They (ie the Home Office) give me the impression', it was declared, 'of proceeding in a governess-cart at a leisurely pace along a quiet Victorian by-road whilst the Germans are minute by minute gaining upon them in a Mercedes, rushing along a motor road.' It was now eight months since the French collapse, yet no machinery was in place to keep track of French servicemen discharged from Ministry of Health hospitals, or for the police to monitor the opinions of the colony. This was even more vital given the changing circumstances of the war. It was not unlikely, suggested the War Cabinet representative, that three French authorities could soon emerge: de Gaulle in London; a Laval regime in Paris; and a Weygand or Pétain government in North Africa, which might well be tempted to re-enter the war on the Allied side. What, then, would be the position of those French nationals in the UK? In this situation, they would have to be confronted with the following statement: 'Either you will support one or other of the French leaders who stand for what we consider to be true France, or if you persist in supporting the traitor Laval and his crew, we shall treat you as an enemy alien and intern you forthwith.'

It is now known that Weygand, High Commissioner in North Africa since September 1940, was doing little more than reorganising French forces there. Despite his hatred of Nazism in general and Laval in particular, whom he compared to a dog 'rolling in the shit' of a German victory, he had no intention of siding with the Allies.[255] Yet there is little doubt that Laval, nursing his wounds in Paris, was talking with Abetz and Déat about the possibility of creating an alternative government to that of Pétain.

To be fair to the CFR, this scenario had already been discussed on 12 February 1941.[256] Outwardly the issue seemed fairly straightforward. The Laval government would duly be deemed hostile and its supporters in Britain interned as enemy aliens. The matter was confused by a series of hypotheses raised by both the Home and Foreign Office. Would the North African government immediately side with the Allies? Would it be recognised by HMG? Would the Germans even bother with a Laval government? Would they not merely place Vichy more directly under their control, and leave the unoccupied zone in place? In any case, by this point would not Frenchmen have already been drafted into labour or military service in Britain?[257] Inevitably, such questions made the phrasing of any legislation to intern Frenchmen nigh impossible. When the Home Office put forward a draft clause providing for the arrest of anyone who 'adhered openly to the Vichy Government', French Welfare queried exactly whom it had in mind. The response was anybody 'who, in the event of France being occupied by the enemy, adhered openly to the French authorities in enemy-occupied territory'.[258] Should this have ever become law, it is not difficult to believe that it would have been the source of endless wrangling.

It took events in Syria in summer 1941 for the Home Office to overcome its scruples. With British forces fighting the troops of General Dentz and Darlan promising air bases to Berlin, the possibility of war with Vichy seemed imminent, bringing the question of security into even greater relief. To meet this situation, a convoluted circular was hurriedly drafted for police authorities throughout the British isles.[259] Should HMG and Vichy find themselves at war, it explained, all French citizens would technically become enemy aliens, at least until a belligerent authority emerged in North Africa and was recognised as such by London. It was understood, however, that a great many French citizens in the UK would not adhere to a Vichy government in these circumstances, so no general internment was being proposed. Rather police authorities were requested to compile information on any French national who was 'unreliable' and likely to pose a security threat.

The replies to this circular, at least those that have survived, suggest that there were few fifth columnists at large among the French community. It is only a pity the London reports have not been preserved. Crudely speaking, the responses fall into three categories.[260] To begin with, there were those areas such as Dewsbury, Walsall, Kilmarnock, Inverness-shire and, maybe not surprisingly, the Orkney islands, where there were no French residents in the first place. Second, there were areas such as East Lothian, Reigate, South Shields, Middlesbrough, Belfast, Southampton and Worcester where there was only a sprinkling of French men and women, none of whom was regarded with suspicion. Typical was the reply of the senior officer at Eastbourne: '9 French residents in district: four males and 5 females. All are elderly and have resided here for many years. I have no reason to regard any of these persons with suspicion.' The final category are cryptic in their reply, acknowledging that the circular had been

received and its contents noted. Significantly, these came from potentially sensitive areas where there was a relatively large French
community, for instance Manchester and Staffordshire, close to where
some of the sailors' camps had been based. Even then, such cryptic
responses do not necessarily mean that colonists were fifth columnists,
merely that the police were being prudent.

In the event, the fighting in the Middle East did not lead to a splintering of French authority, as Vichy experienced cold feet in supporting
the German war effort and only provided half-hearted military assistance to Rommel; ultimately, Syria was conceded to the British. While
the armistice Dentz signed with the British deeply angered the Free
French, and destroyed the relationship between Spears and de Gaulle,
it did not beg any further questions about the loyalty of *colons* in
Britain. Berlin quickly abandoned any further collaborationist dealings
with Vichy to concentrate on prosecuting the invasion of the USSR.
When Hitler resumed his interest in France in April the following year,
bringing Laval back to power, it was obvious to everyone the extent to
which the marshal's government was now subject to German domination. The round-up of Jews and the deportation of French labour to
Germany only confirmed France's status as a milch cow in the Nazi
empire. As such, neither Vichy nor Pétain held any particular appeal to
the *colons*, and the issue of internment faded from the picture.

Conscription

While the question of internment might have faded, there remained
that of conscription. This had been discussed in July 1940, but had
been put to one side, partially because of the position of the Admiralty
and the War Office, which had quickly put a ceiling on the number of
French recruits they were prepared to accept, largely because these men
were difficult to train and integrate into the ranks.[261] It was further
appreciated that the Free French, not being a sovereign government,
could not be given the authority to conscript in the same way that the
Belgian, Norwegian, and Dutch authorities were doing. This would
only play into de Gaulle's campaign to have himself recognised as a
head of state. In any case, as the Home Office pointed out, it was not a
crime for a Frenchman merely to adopt an indifferent attitude towards
de Gaulle, or for that matter, towards the British. How then could such
men be conscripted?

Despite these scruples, the issue dragged on. Those young men who
had not enlisted for de Gaulle were seen as a drain on morale, and it

was asked why they should enjoy 'a more favoured position than either British or Allied subjects of similar age and health'.[262] While it was recognised that deportation was unfeasible in their respect, and there was an awareness that neither the War Office nor the Admiralty wanted any more French recruits, and that de Gaulle was not empowered to conscript, it was still felt that more effort could be made to enlist these men, possibly in the Transport and Supply Services or the Pioneer Corps.[263] It was further recommended that the Minister of Labour should 'make an order under his existing powers requiring the compulsory registration of all male Frenchmen between the ages of 18 and 65 in the same way as it is intended to require the compulsory registration of all Allied nationals in that age group',[264] so that they could be conscripted into employment. Any Frenchman who subsequently refused such employment or service with de Gaulle or the British would be liable to deportation, or at the very least, to internment should he be engaged in subversive activities.

This might have sounded a severe sanction, but was yet again a fudge. Not only did repatriation remain a virtual impossibility in 1941 (witness the problems with the French consular staff later that year), but few Frenchmen were likely to be caught engaging in subversive behaviour, especially given the way in which the colony remained a community apart. Nor was there government consensus over the issue. The Ministry of Labour feared Germany would exploit any gesture towards conscription for propaganda purposes.[265] After all, it was not until 1942 that Germany itself requisitioned French labour. It was also feared that conscription might provoke retaliation against British subjects in France.[266] Taking recourse in international law, the Foreign Office further objected that to conscript French labour forcibly was contrary to Article 11 of the Anglo-French Commercial Treaty of 1882.[267] Finally, doubts were raised about the exact numbers of Frenchmen who were at large, who were not registered and who were not employed in war work; in retrospect, it might be thought the absence of information was even more of a reason to press ahead with registration.[268]

It did not assist government deliberations that the FGB, and Carlton Gardens, thought the occasion of registration an excellent opportunity to press French Welfare and the Home Office yet again for a full list of the names, addresses and occupations of all Frenchmen in the UK.[269] These registrations, wrote Semet, 'sont une source d'informations précieuses'.[270]

Naturally enough, no such material was handed over,[271] yet the order for compulsory registration was eventually issued in May, with an amendment insisted upon by the Free French that stated that the preamble should make clear that the war effort was not purely a 'national' affair, but a 'common' and 'Allied' one. Thanks to the British government's intense desire to keep the registration files secret, or least hidden from Carlton Gardens, it remains unknown how many Frenchmen were subsequently caught in the registration net; the impression is very few. Even fewer appear to have been drafted into war work.

Postscript: nationality and restrictions

Although the questions of internment and conscription pointed to a hard line on the part of Whitehall, it is known that Churchill had favoured granting British citizenship to those men and women who served either among de Gaulle's army or the British forces, in many ways a natural corollary to his earlier plans for an Anglo-French Union in June 1940.[272] To this end, various drafts of the necessary bill were discussed, but these encountered numerous hold-ups, several engineered by the Free French officials who feared they might lose their identity should they adopt citizenship. They further pointed out that the gesture was of little practical use as Vichy had not withdrawn the nationality of their recruits, only in the cases of prominent individuals such as Bois. Moreover, British nationality might well prove to be a danger to those Free French taken as prisoners of war. Given that the Dominions Office also had its reservations, fearing such moves would have to be extended to Commonwealth and imperial troops, it is perhaps no surprise that the matter came to naught. In any case, what was more important to French residents in Britain was not so much the possibility of a British passport, but the chance to be free of the Aliens Restrictions Order. It was this issue over which the FGB and Carlton Gardens would tirelessly campaign throughout 1941.

It was not until July 1942, when matters had quietened down on the French security front, that the Home Office, after some prompting from the Free French, agreed to the relaxation of the restrictions imposed on aliens.[273] These had led to some embarrassing incidents when first implemented in the summer of 1940, for instance a convent of French nuns was forcibly moved out of Norwich, the city being in a 'restricted zone', and had only been allowed back after Cardinal Hinsley vouched for their political impartiality.[274] In another case, a

French family had been removed from St Leonards-on-Sea to Bromley, despite having lived in England for thirty-three years.[275] In 1942, such obvious supporters of the Allied cause no longer had reason to fear such dislocation. Those individual French men and women who were deemed 'trustworthy and loyal supporters of the allied cause' could in future apply to their local police authority for the freedom of movement permitted to Allied nationals. Nevertheless, French residents were still classed in an inferior position to other nationals at war with Germany and could not visit certain coastal areas, especially in southern England, points which irked Carlton Gardens although, to the astonishment of the Foreign Office, they were never raised in negotiations.[276] It was not until after the D-Day landings in June 1944 that the government moved to end this anomaly.[277] Now that France was being liberated and Vichy was in a state of disintegration, there seemed no reason not to allow the French into what had previously been aliens-protected areas.[278] Additionally, the French were exempted from the curfew although, like other foreigners, they still had to record their movements and whereabouts with the police.

Conclusions

The fact that the *colons* largely escaped the punitive restrictions that befell enemy aliens may be put down to a series of factors. While they had retained much of their indigenous culture, they were well integrated into British life and knew how to keep their heads down. As such, they did not become targets for public hostility, even during the fifth columnist scare of May-June 1940, and they no doubt benefited from the growing tendency of the British to associate all French men and women with de Gaulle. That the community was initially suspicious of the general can hardly be disputed. He was a rebel, an unknown, a seemingly dangerous element, who did not even enjoy the wholehearted support of the British. Given the way in which Vichy consular officials still operated in London, there were very genuine fears about relatives in France. Yet antagonism to de Gaulle did not necessarily equate with trust in Vichy. While many business elements in the London-based community initially registered some sympathy with Pétain, they still made plain their loyalty to Britain, and the overriding impression of the colony, despite internal quarrels, is that it was as law-abiding as in the past. The most potentially disloyal group, *les catholiques avant tout*, remained on the fringes, easily controlled both by the British authorities and by Cardinal Hinsley. In any case, it was difficult to maintain much enthusiasm for Vichy after 1941. Just as in France itself, the *colons* began to dismantle Pétain mythology, and saw through Vichy's hypocrisy. Accordingly, they were not to be feared, and were treated leniently by government. While they might have grumbled about restrictions placed on their freedom of movement, unlike their compatriots on metropolitan soil they had no reason to fear a knock on the door in the middle of the night and were never subject to swingeing draconian legislation requiring them to work in a foreign country. While they might also have grumbled at the ways in which the Free French, and its supporters in the FGB, came to colonise London life, taking over independent French institutions in the process, they still retained an abiding faith in the Allied war effort, and gradually overcame their mistrust of the general himself. Anti-Gaullism would find its most articulate spokesmen in the ranks of political exiles and their British sympathisers. These prejudices would be transported back across the Channel in 1944; within London, the community reverted to its normal way of life.

Notes

1   R. Cobb, *Promenades* (Oxford, Oxford University Press, 1980), p. 58.
2   P. Villars, 'The French', in G. R. Sims (ed.), *Living London* (London, Cassell, 1901), vol. 2, p. 133.
3   *Ibid.*, p. 134.
4   A. Schom, *Emile Zola* (London, Queen Anne Press, 1987), p. 202.
5   M. Cornick, 'Distorting Mirrors. Problems of Anglo-French Perceptions in the *fin de siècle*', in C. Crossley and M. Cornick (eds), *Problems in French History. Essays in Honour of Douglas Johnson* (London, Palgrave, 2000), pp. 125–48.
6   See R. Graves, *Goodbye to all that* (London, Penguin, 1960 edn), pp. 26–62, for a commentary on their life.
7   *Census of England and Wales, 1931*, vol. 1, *Preliminary Report Including Tables of Population* (London, HMSO, 1931), p. 222. Also see H. Goiran, *Les Français à Londres. Etude Historique, 1544–1933* (Pornic, Edition de la Vague, 1933).
8   *Census of England and Wales, 1931*, vol. 1, p. 222.
9   These figures may be found principally in PRO HO 213 314, 828–30 and 2046–7.
10 Information supplied by Fraser Reavell who is in the process of writing a University of Reading Ph.D. thesis on 'French Exiles in Britain, 1870–1914'.

11 F. Reavell, 'The French Chamber. A Bit of History', *Info*, vol. 24, Jan–Feb 2002, 28–9.

12 *Census of England and Wales, 1931*, vol. 1, p. 179.

13 *Ibid.*, pp. 222–8.

14 *Ibid.*, p. 158.

15 Quoted in J. White, *London in the Twentieth Century. A City and its People* (London, Viking, 2001), p. 105.

16 *Census of England and Wales, 1931*, vol. 1, pp. 179–221.

17 See K. Carpenter, 'London. Capital of the Emigration', in K. Carpenter and P. Mansel (eds), *The French Emigrés in Europe and the Struggle against Revolution, 1789–1814* (Basingstoke, Macmillan, 1999), pp. 43–67, and her *Refugees of the French Revolution. Emigrés in London, 1789–1802* (Basingstoke, Macmillan, 1999), pp. 49–61.

18 Cited in White, *London*, pp. 104–5. See, too, M. Henery, *An Exile in Soho* (London, Dent, 1952).

19 White, *London*, p. 105.

20 Goiran, *Les Français à Londres*, p. 221, stresses the importance of railways and steamboats in facilitating French emigration to south-east England.

21 *Census of England and Wales, 1931*, vol. 1, pp. 179–221.

22 PRO HO 213 314 42/1/58, 'Number of Aliens Registered with the Police on 25 May 1940.'

23 PRO HO 213 314 42/1/58, 'Number of Aliens Registered in UK on 31 March 1941'. Figures exclude refugees.

24 PRO HO 213 2046 300/70/3, 'Census of Aliens in the United Kingdom on 31 March 1942'. Figures exclude refugees.

25 PRO HO 213 2046 300/70/5, 'Census of Aliens Registered in the United Kingdom on 31st March 1943'. Refugees again excluded.

26 PRO HO 213 315 42/1/61, 'Tabular Statement for Period 1932–1941'.

27 White, *London*, p. 105.

28 IWM 97/7/1, Diary of Monsieur Vila.

29 PRO FO 371 28365 Z1753/123/17, 'Census of French Subjects over the Age of 16 Registered in the UK and NI on 6th February 1941'.

30 PRO FO 371 28365 Z1753/123/17, 'Detailed Figures of French Residents in Districts having 50 or more Residents'.

31 PRO HO 213 474 204/15/21, letter from Semet to Alexander Maxwell, Home Office, 15 July 1940, gives some background information on these figures.

32 CCC SPRS 1/154, letter of Guéritte to Spears, 10 April 1940.

33 PRO FO 371 24340 C8235/7328/17, Minute by F. A. Gwatkin, Ministry of Economic Warfare, 2 August 1940, and J.-L. Crémieux-Brilhac, *La France Libre de l'appel du 18 juin à la libération* (Paris, Flammarion, 1995), p. 77.

34 See P.-L. Bret, *Au feu des événements. Mémoires d'un journaliste Londres-Alger, 1929–1944* (Paris, Plon, 1959).

35 E. Delavenay, *Témoignage d'un village savoyard au village mondial, 1905–1991* (Aix-en-Provence, Diffusion Edisud, 1992).
36 G. Gombault, *Un journal, une aventure* (Paris, Gallimard, 1982).
37 P. Maillaud, *France* (London, Oxford University Press, 1942).
38 E. J. Bois, *Truth on the Tragedy of France* (London, Hodder & Stoughton, 1941).
39 PRO FO 371 28366 Z3263/123/17, letter of Roger Cambon to Strang, 31 March 1941.
40 PRO FO 1055 8, French Welfare, 'Report for 1942'.
41 IWM Touchard 63/34/1.
42 PRO FO 1055 11, note by Captain Williams, 10 January 1942.
43 PRO FO 1055 8, French Welfare, 'Report for 1941'.
44 PRO FO 1055 8, 'Paper A', 29 August 1940 prepared for the Welfare and Security Sub-Committee of French Welfare.
45 *Times Educational Supplement*, 15 June 1940.
46 CCC SPRS 1/140.
47 PRO HO 213 1724 200/271/1, letter of Newsam, HO, to W. R. D. Robertson, WO, 1 August 1940 gives details of this meeting.
48 Bret, *Au feu*, p. 172.
49 PRO HO 213 314 42/1/58, letter of Major Sir Ralph Glyn MP to Herbert Morrison, 20 May 1941.
50 PRO HO 213 314 42/1/58, letter of Herbert Morrison to Major Sir Ralph Glyn, 20 June 1941.
51 *The Times*, various editions of July/August 1940.
52 M-O FR Reports 523B, 541, 566, 1669Q and 2023.
53 Quoted in J. Lacouture, *The Rebel* (London, Harper Collins, 1986), p. 253.
54 S. Briggs, *The Home Front. War Years in Britain, 1939–1945* (London, Weidenfeld & Nicolson, 1975), p. 130.
55 PRO FO 371 28460 Z792/792/17, Memorandum of MI5 presented to CFR, 29 January 1941.
56 C. de Gaulle, *The Army of the Future* (London, Hutchinson, 1940).
57 *Listener*, 15 August, no. 605, p. 237.
58 PRO FO 371 28460 Z792/792/17, Memorandum of MI5 presented to CFR, 29 January 1941.
59 *Ibid.*
60 Delavenay, *Témoignage*, p. 181.
61 CCC NBKR 4/261, letter of Eden to Noel Baker, 1 October 1943.
62 PRO FO 371 24340 C8235/7328/17, Minute by F. A. Gwatkin, Ministry of Economic Warfare, 2 August 1940, accompanied by letter of the Spears Mission to Foreign Office, 17 August 1940, giving details of Sibour's enlistment.
63 Crémieux-Brilhac, *La France Libre*, p. 47. Léon Wilson remarks that de Gaulle was 'too French'. Interview with the author, London, 22 March 2002.

64 J. Jackson, *Charles de Gaulle* (London, Cardinal, 1990), p. 13.
65 CCC SPRS 1/134, letter of A. Oswald Hotz to Churchill, late July 1940.
66 *Ibid.*
67 Delavenay, *Témoignage*, p. 183.
68 *Ibid.*
69 PRO FO 371 28365, Report of French Welfare, 'The French Community in the United Kingdom', to the CFR, 5 February 1941.
70 PRO FO 371 28460 Z792/792/17, Memorandum of MI5 presented to CFR, 29 January 1941.
71 *Ibid.*
72 Delavenay, *Témoignage*, p. 181.
73 Y. Durand, *Vichy 1940–44* (Paris, Bordas Poche, 1972).
74 PRO FO 371 28460 Z792/792/17, Memorandum of MI5 presented to CFR, 29 January 1941.
75 Goiran, *Les Français à Londres*, p. 240, observes that this committee was originally set up on 4 December 1913 to bring some order to the many French societies in London.
76 PRO FO 371 28365, CFR, 'The French Community in the United Kingdom', 5 February 1941.
77 Formed out of the Club Culinaire Français and the Société Culinaire in 1932 to demonstrate the 'superiority' of French cooking. Goiran, *Les Français à Londres*, p. 229.
78 PRO FO 1055 2, 'Note of an interview with M de Bellaing, 15 August 1940, by Brennan'.
79 PRO FO 1055 2, 'Note of an interview with Dr Picarda on the 9th October 1940'.
80 PRO FO 371 24340 C8236/7328/17, note of French Department, Foreign Office, 5 August 1940.
81 PRO FO 1055 2, 'Note of an interview with Dr Picarda on the 9th October 1940'.
82 PRO FO 371 24340 C8236/7328/17, note of French Department, Foreign Office, 5 August 1940.
83 PRO FO 371 24341 C8756/7328/17, internal minute of Mack to Harvey, Foreign Office, 6 August 1940.
84 See the obituary of Bois in *FL*, vol. 2, no. 7, 24 May 1941, p. 85.
85 Quoted in A. Gillois, *Histoire secrète des français à Londres de 1940 à 1944* (Paris, Hachette, 1972), p. 52. See too Gombault, *Un journal, passim.*
86 Crémieux-Brilhac, *La France Libre*, pp. 192–5.
87 Gombault, *Un journal*, p. 37, who recalls that some families wrote to the editorial offices on a daily basis.
88 PRO FO 1055 2, Sandford, Ministry of Information, to Brennan, 17 October 1940.
89 LSE DALTON 7/3, Memorandum of 28 January 1942.

90   PRO FO 371 24345, 'The Daily Newspaper *France*, 13 November 1940'.

91   PRO FO 371 24345 C12846/7328/17, letter of Baron Albert de Dorlodot, Belgium Embassy, to Lt. Manuel, Carlton Gardens, 15 November 1940.

92   PRO FO 371 24345 C12846/7328/17, letter of Law to Morton, 10 December 1940.

93   R. Mengin, *No Laurels for de Gaulle* (London, Michael Joseph, 1967), p. 144.

94   See Delevaney, *Témoignage* p. 195, and R. Cassin, *Les Hommes partis de rien* (Paris, Plon, 1975).

95   It was in the aeroplane to Britain on 18 June 1940 that de Gaulle himself was introduced to English food when he tasted that liquid 'the British call both tea and coffee'. E. Spears, *Assignment to Catastrophe* (London, William Heinemann, 1954), vol. 2, p. 323.

96   PRO FO 371 24345 C12846/7328/17, Minute of 9 December 1940.

97   According to Charles Gombault, de Gaulle was keen that André Rabache, *Le Matin*'s Rome correspondent, should join the editorial staff. See Gombault, *Un journal*, p. 31.

98   PRO FO 371 31924 Z34/34/17, note by Nigel Law, Ministry of Information, 31 December 1941.

99   PRO FO 371 36056 Z4476/371/17, Memorandum of 6 April 1943.

100 PRO FO 1055 2, letter from Miss Parkinson, Secretary to the Resident Foreigners Committee, British Council, to Brennan, French Welfare, 2 September 1940.

101 PRO FO 1055 2, letter of Brennan to Parkinson, 3 September 1940.

102 PRO 1055 2, letter of Brennan to Nigel Law, French Division, Ministry of Information, 17 October 1940.

103 PRO FO 1055 2, Sandford, Ministry of Information, to Brennan, 17 October 1940.

104 PRO FO 1055 2, 'Note of an interview with Dr Picarda on the 9th October 1940'.

105 PRO FO 371 24340 C8236/7328/17, note by Hankey, 9 October 1940.

106 PRO FO 371 24340 C8236/7328/17, Minute of Mack to Harvey, Foreign Office, 6 August 1940.

107 PRO FO 371 24341 C8867/7328/17, letter of D. F—, to Foreign Office, 20 August 1940, one letter among many.

108 PRO FO 371 24341 C8867/7328/17, note by Hankey, 9 October 1940.

109 PRO FO 28365, Report of French Welfare, 'The French Community in the United Kingdom', to the CFR, 5 February 1941.

110 PRO FO 371 24341 C8756/7328/17, letter of R. A. Butler, Foreign Office, to Sir Thomas Moore, 5 September 1940.

111 CCC SPRS 1/136, Memorandum, 15 August 1940.

112 CCC SPRS 1/136, Memorandum, 21 July 1940.

113 PRO FO 371 24343 C10514/7328/17, letter of Nigel Law, Ministry of Information, to W. H. B. Mack, Foreign Office, 3 October 1940.

114 *Ibid.*
115 PRO FO 371 24343 C10514/7328/17, note of Mack, 29 September 1940.
116 PRO FO 371 24343 C10514/7328/17, letter of Law to Mack, 3 October 1940.
117 *NS & N*, 26 July 1941, no. 544, p. 94.
118 Crémieux-Brilhac, *La France Libre*, p. 191, and *FL*, vol. 1, no. 1, 15 November 1940, pp. 93–5.
119 IWM Touchard 63/34/1.
120 Many are collected together as J. Oberlé, *Images anglaises ou 'L'Angleterre occupée'* (London, Hachette, 1943). See, too, *FL*, vol. 2, no. 10, 15 August 1941, pp. 355–8.
121 J. Jackson, 'General de Gaulle and his Enemies. Anti-Gaullism in France since 1940', in *Transactions of the Royal Historical Society*, 6th series, vol. IX, 1999, p. 47.
122 All of Aron's contributions are reprinted in R. Aron, *Chroniques de guerre. La France Libre, 1940–1945* (Paris, Gallimard, 1990).
123 PRO FO 371 32001 Z2971/2971/17, contains the copy, plus relevant correspondence.
124 PRO FO 371 28365, Report of French Welfare, 'The French Community in the United Kingdom', to the CFR, 5 February 1941.
125 *Ibid.*
126 *Ibid.*
127 PRO HO 213 1744 204/15/6, Les Français de Grande Bretagne, 'Historique de l'Association, 19 September 1940'.
128 PRO HO 213 474 204/15/1, letter of Semet to Sir Alexander Maxwell, 15 July 1940.
129 PRO HO 213 474 204/15/1, *Projet des statuts*.
130 *Ibid.*
131 PRO HO 213 474 204/15/1, note of 15 July 1940 on Association.
132 PRO HO 213 1744 204/15/6, recruitment letter for the FGB, no date (July/August 1940?).
133 *Ibid.*
134 PRO HO 213 1744 204/15/6, Les Français de Grande Bretagne, 'Historique de l'Association, 19 September 1940'.
135 PRO HO 213 1744 204/15/6, letter of Passy to Guéritte, 11 September 1940.
136 PRO HO 213 1744 204/15/6, letter of Pierre Fontaine to Guéritte, 14 September 1940.
137 CCC NBKR 4/261, FGB pamphlet, 'Pour la Resurrection de la France'.
138 Copy of the letter supplied to the author by Professor Martin Alexander.
139 PRO FO 371 28459 Z8173/709/17, letter of Bessborough to Mack, 16 October 1941.
140 PRO HO 213 1744 204/15/6, Sullivan, Spears Mission, to Williamson, HO, 21 October 1940.

141 PRO FO 371 31990 Z897/231/17, note of 27 January 1942.

142 PRO FO 371 28365, Report of French Welfare, 'The French Community in the United Kingdom', to the CFR, 5 February 1941.

143 PRO FO 371 24359 C9172/7736/17, letter of Maurice Vignon, vice president of the Société de Bienfaisance, to Brennan, French Welfare, 23 August 1940.

144 PRO FO 371 28459 Z709/17, note of 14 January 1941. On the history of the Chamber, see Goiran, Les Français à Londres, pp. 232–6.

145 PRO HO 213 1744 204/15/6, Les Français de Grande Bretagne, 'Historique de l'Association, 19 September 1940'.

146 PRO FO 371 28365, Report of French Welfare, 'The French Community in the United Kingdom', to the CFR, 5 February 1941.

147 PRO FO 371 28443 Z3055/411/17, 'Alliance Française in England and Free French Cultural Propaganda', 19 April 1941.

148 Goiran, Les Français à Londres, pp. 238–9 for a history of the Institut.

149 PRO FO 371 28472, Memorandum on the Institut Français, 18 December 1941.

150 Ibid.

151 Mengin, No Laurels, passim.

152 PRO FO 371 28472, Minute by Speaight, 20 December 1941.

153 RUL The Astor Papers.

154 PRO FO 371 24345 C12621/7328/17, letter of Law to Morton, 10 December 1940.

155 PRO FO 371 28367 Z6153/123/17, Minute by W. H. B. Mack, 17 July 1941.

156 PRO FO 371 28459 Z8173/709/17, letter of Bessborough to Mack, 16 October 1941.

157 PRO FO 371 28459 Z7482/709/17, note by Mack, 26 August 1941.

158 Ibid.

159 PRO HO 213 1744 204/15/6, Les Français de Grande Bretagne, 'Historique de l'Association, 19 September 1940'.

160 PRO HO 213 1744 204/15/6, War Cabinet Committee on Foreign (Allied) Resistance, Corrigenda to Record of the Fifty-Ninth Meeting, Wednesday, 2 October 1940.

161 PRO HO 213 1744 204/15/6, letter of P. O. Lapie, Chef du Service des Relations Extérieures et Coloniales, FFF, to Colonel S. A. Hibbert, 1 October 1940.

162 PRO FO 371 28365 Z1205/123/17, Extract from the Minutes of a Meeting of the CFR, 27 January 1941.

163 PRO FO 1055 8, letter of Miss Davies, Home Office, 15 March 1941.

164 PRO FO 371 28365 Z1205/123/17, letter of Cooper, Home Office, to Secretary of the Committee on Foreign (Allied) Resistance, 25 January 1941.

165 PRO FO 1055 8, letter of E. M. Cooper, Home Office, 24 February 1941.

166 PRO HO 213 1744 204/15/6, letter of Morton to Newsam, Home Office, 4 October 1940.

167 PRO HO 213 1744 204/15/6, War Cabinet Committee on Foreign (Allied) Resistance, Corrigenda to Record of the Fifty-Ninth Meeting, Wednesday, 2 October 1940.

168 PRO FO 1055 5, Newsletter of the AVF, 15 February 1941.

169 *Ibid.*

170 PRO FO 1055 5, 'Report of the General Committee for the Year Ended September 30th 1943 (AVF)'.

171 *Ibid.*, and PRO FO 1055 5, *They Fight On*, AVF brochure of 30 October 1941, p. 4.

172 PRO FO 1055 5, letter of Ivor Spencer Churchill to Vere, 4 September 1941.

173 PRO FO 1055 5, letter of H. Randall Lane, legal officer, British Council, to Captain Williams, French Welfare, 29 February 1944.

174 PRO FO 1055 5, 'Report of the General Committee for the Year Ended September 30th 1943 (AVF)'.

175 PRO FO 1055 5, AVF Newsletter, August 1944.

176 PRO FO 1055 5, AVF Newsletter, January 1945.

177 CCC SPRS 1/134, contains the relevant correspondence.

178 PRO FO 371 41912 Z6969/129/17, 'Memorandum on AVF by Lord Bessborough, 17th October 1944'.

179 *Ibid.*

180 CCC SPRS 1/135, 'Report on Senior French Naval Personnel at Blackpool', no date.

181 PRO FO 1055 1, 'Memorandum of visits paid to French camps in the Neighbourhood of Liverpool, 5 September 1940'.

182 CCC SPRS 1/134, letter of Morton to Spears, 24 July 1940.

183 T. Torrès, *Une française libre. Journal, 1939–45* (Paris, Phébus, 2000), p. 80.

184 On this legislation, see W. D. Halls, *Politics, Society and Christianity in Vichy France* (Oxford, Berg, 1995).

185 *L'Osservatore Romano*, 8 July 1940.

186 PRO FO 371 24344 C11619/7328/17, telegram of High Commissioner to Canada, 4 November 1940.

187 Carpenter, *Refugees*, p. 157.

188 See R. Griffiths, *Fellow Travellers of the Right* (Oxford, Oxford University Press, 1981).

189 G. White, 'The Fall of France', in *Studies in Church History*, 20, 1983, p. 438.

190 *NS & N*, 5 October 1940, p. 326.

191 See especially T. Moloney, *Westminster, Whitehall and the Vatican. The*

Role of Cardinal Hinsley, 1935–1943 (Tunbridge Wells, Burns & Oates, 1983); O. Chadwick, *Britain and the Vatican during the Second World War* (Cambridge, Cambridge University Press, 1982); White, 'Fall of France'; S. Mews, 'The Sword of the Spirit: A Catholic Cultural Crusade of 1940', *Studies in Church History*, 20, 1983, pp. 409–30; J. Keating, 'British Catholics and the Fall of France', in F. Tallett and N. Atkin (eds), *Catholicism in Britain and France since 1789* (London, Hambledon, 1996), pp. 27–42; and her 'Roman Catholics, Christian Democracy and the British Labour Movement, 1910–1960', unpublished Ph.D. thesis, University of Manchester, 1992.

192 On Maritain, see especially B. Williams Smith, *Jacques Maritain. Anti Modern or Ultra Modern?* (New York/Oxford, Elsevier, 1986).
193 Moloney, *Westminster, Whitehall and the Vatican*, p. 176.
194 PRO FO 371 28358 Z2200/95/17, letter of Oliver Harvey, Ministry of Information, to Strang, Foreign Office, 20 March 1941, and letter of John Pollock to Major Hamilton, 14 March 1941.
195 PRO FO 371 24341 C8949/7328/17, letter of Bernanos to Sir George Knox, 11 July 1940.
196 PRO FO 371 36056 Z7063/371/17, 'Notes of a Meeting in the Minister's Room, 16 June, 1943, to Discuss Question of the French Press'.
197 F.-L. Closon, *Le Temps des passions* (Paris, Presses de la Cité, 1974), p. 29.
198 *FL*, vol. 2, no. 11, 15 September 1941, pp. 400–6.
199 J. Rochelle, 'Epreuve du catholicisme français', *FL*, vol. 3, no. 18, 17 April 1942, pp. 490–7.
200 *Westminster Cathedral Chronicle and Diocesan Gazette*, vol. XXXIV, August 1940, no. 8, p. 153.
201 PRO FO 371 24360 C13565/7736/17, Minutes of the CFR, 23 August 1940.
202 Goiran, *Les français à Londres*, p. 224, in which he remarks that the Church was 'gardienne de nos traditions et un centre de ralliement et de cohésion national'.
203 Torrès, *Une française libre*, p. 84.
204 WDA Bo 1/92, letter of Father L— to Cardinal Hinsley, 28 August 1940.
205 PRO FO 371 28470 Z1159/17, letter from Edward Muir, Ministry of Works and Buildings, to French Department, Foreign Office, 17 February 1941.
206 PRO FO 371 28470 Z1159/17, letter of Speaight to Muir, 28 February 1941.
207 Torrès, *Une française libre*, p. 165.
208 CCC NBKR 4/259, 'Memorandum on the Activities of Undesirables Still at Large in England', no date.
209 PRO FO 371 28470 Z1159/17, Minute by Hankey, 27 February 1941.

210 Interview with Léon Wilson, 22 March 2002, London.

211 PRO FO 371 24344 C11414/7328/17, letter intercepted on 10 September 1940.

212 PRO FO 371 24344 C11414/7328/17, note of 23 October 1940.

213 PRO FO 371 24344 C11414/7328/17, letter of Morton to Speaight, 24 October 1940.

214 PRO FO 1055 1, letter of Grace Peel to Oliver Harvey, Ministry of Information, 9 August 1940.

215 PRO FO 371 24360 C7763/17, letter of Castellane to Makins, FO, 10 July 1940.

216 G. Blond, *L'Angleterre en guerre. Récit d'un marin* (Paris, Grasset, 1941), p. 166.

217 PRO FO 1055 1, letter of Father M— to Lady Peel, September 1940.

218 PRO FO 1055 1, letter of Grace Peel to Aidan Baillie, 20 September 1940.

219 M. Larkin, *Religion, Politics and Preferment in France since 1890. La Belle Epoque and its Legacy* (Cambridge, Cambridge University Press, 1995), p. 176.

220 B. Wasserstein, *Britain and the Jews of Europe, 1939–1945* (Oxford, Oxford University Press, 1979), p. 83, and for much that follows in this paragraph, as well as M. Kochan, *Britain's Internees in the Second World War* (London, Macmillan, 1983), p. 18.

221 PRO HO 213 1724 200/271/1, letter of Newsam, HO, to W. R. D. Robertson, WO, 1 August 1940.

222 PRO HO 213 1724 200/271/1, letter of Newsam, HO, to Major Morton, 22 September 1940.

223 PRO HO 213 1724 200/271/1, letter of Morton to Newsam, HO, 24 September 1940.

224 *Ibid.*

225 PRO HO 213 1724 200/271/1, handwritten note from Clayton to Newsam, HO, 4 October 1940.

226 PRO FO 371 28365 Z508/123/17, letter of Speaight, 1 February 1941.

227 MO TC25 Box 1 25/1/E, letter of Strong & Co Solicitors to Home Office, 27 July 1940.

228 PRO FO 371 28365 Z774/123/17, CFR, 18 January 1941.

229 PRO FO 371 28365 Z862/123/17, letter of Spears to Mack, 8 February 1941.

230 PRO FO 371 28365 Z862/123/17, Minute of 8 February 1941.

231 PRO FO 371 28365 Z1621/121/17, letter of Chartier to the Foreign Office, 3 March 1941.

232 PRO FO 371 28365 Z1621/121/17, letter of Speaight to Cooper, 15 March 1941.

233 PRO FO 371 28366 Z2541/123/17, letter from H. R. Hotchkiss, Home Office, to Speaight, 31 March 1941.

234 PRO FO 371 28367 Z6740/123/17, recommendation of the Lindley Committee.
235 Cases in PRO FO 371 31990 Z3342/231/17.
236 PRO FO 371 28365 Z1003/123/17, letter of 7 January 1941.
237 PRO HO 214 39, Case of Robert Frank, 19 November 1941.
238 PRO FO 371 28366 Z2549/123/17, letter of Cooper to Hankey, 3 April 1941.
239 PRO HO 214 39, Case of Pierre Henri Frank, 19 November 1941.
240 PRO FO 371 24346 C12952/7328/17, contains all the correspondence.
241 PRO FO 371 28367 Z6766/123/17, press cutting.
242 PRO FO 371 28367 Z6481/123/17, letter of Nicole to Griggs, 3 July 1941.
243 PRO FO 371 28367 Z6766/123/17, letter from British consulate, Tangier, 29 July 1941.
244 PRO FO 371 28368, press cutting.
245 PRO FO 371 28365 Z346/123/17, note of 13 January 1941.
246 PRO FO 371 28365 Z1501/123/17, draft letter to Miss Warner, British Red Cross, March 1941.
247 PRO FO 371 28366 Z2038/123/17, various correspondence, March 1941.
248 PRO FO 371 28367 Z6766/123/17, note, 15 August 1941.
249 PRO FO 371 28367 Z5014/123/17, note, 11 June 1941.
250 PRO FO 371 28368 Z7320/123/17, telegram from Sir Samuel Hoare, Madrid, 22 August 1941.
251 PRO FO 371 28365 Z822/123/17, CFR, Memorandum by Major-General Spears, 28 January 1941.
252 PRO FO 371 28365, Report of French Welfare, 'The French Community in the United Kingdom', to the CFR, 5 February 1941.
253 PRO FO 371 28365 Z1205/123/7, CFR Sub-Committee on Welfare and Security, 7 February 1941.
254 PRO FO 1055 8, letter of Major le Mesurier to Brennan, Foreign Office, 25 February 1941.
255 There remains no satisfactory biography of Weygand; the best guide to his policy remains R. O. Paxton, *Parades and Politics at Vichy. The French Officer Corps under Marshal Pétain* (Princeton, Princeton University Press, 1966) and P. C. F. Bankwitz, *Maxime Weygand and Civil-Military Relations in Modern France* (Cambridge, MA, Harvard University Press, 1967).
256 PRO FO 371 28365 Z1205/123/17, CFR Sub-Committee on Welfare and Security, 12 February 1941.
257 PRO FO 1055 8, various correspondence rehearses these possibilities.
258 PRO FO 1055 8, letter of French Welfare to Davies, HO, 3 March 1941.
259 PRO HO 213 1724 200/271/5, Newsam to Chief Constables, 5 June 1941.
260 PRO HO 213 1724 200/271/5, contains the many replies.
261 PRO FO 371 28365 Z1205/123/17, Minutes of the CFR Sub-Committee on Welfare and Security, 12 February 1941.

262   PRO FO 371 28365 Z822/123/17, Report of the Sub-Committee on Welfare and Security to the CFR, 13 February 1941.

263   PRO FO 371 28365 Z1726/123/17, 'Frenchmen in the UK', report by the Chairman of the CFR Sub-Committee on Welfare and Security, 26 February 1941.

264   PRO FO 371 28365 Z822/123/17, 'The French Community in the United Kingdom', report to the CFR, 18 February 1941.

265   PRO FO 371 28365 Z1726/123/17, letter of Butler, Foreign Office, to Viscount Swinton, 11 March 1941.

266   PRO FO 371 28365 Z1988/123/17, extracts from minutes of the 29th meeting of HD(S) Executive held 12 March 1941, 'Frenchmen in the UK'.

267   PRO FO 371 28365 Z1726/123/17, Minutes, 11 March 1941.

268   PRO FO 371 28366 Z4298/123/17, Minutes of the 36th meeting of the HD(S) Executive, 21 May 1941.

269   PRO FO 371 28366 Z3780/123/17, letter of Cassin to Major Watson, Spears Mission, 7 May 1941.

270   PRO FO 371 28367 Z5020/123/17, letter from Semet to Captain Williams, French Welfare, 10 June 1941.

271   PRO FO 371 28367 Z5020/123/17, draft letter of Hankey, FO, to Captain Williams, FO, '20 June 1941 – job of not giving over names given over to the Ministry of Labour'.

272   PRO FO 371 24339 C7903/7328/17, contains correspondence on this matter.

273   PRO HO 213 2097, 'Exemption of French and Danish Nationals from certain of the restrictions upon aliens', 14 July 1942.

274   CCC SPRS 1/134, letter to Newsam of 17 July 1940, in which the Cardinal's office made known that the Free French had offered to help the nuns so long as they adhered to the general.

275   CCC SPRS 1/137, letter of 8 July 1940.

276   PRO HO 213 2098 411/3/16, letter of Mack, Foreign Office, to Newsam, HO, 11 August 1944.

277   PRO HO 213 2098 411/3/16, 'Aliens Restriction on Allied nationals: The French', 22 August 1944.

278   PRO HO 213 2098 411/3/16, press cuttings from *The Times*, *Western Mail*, *Daily Express*, *Daily Mirror*, *Evening News*, *Manchester Guardian*, all of 24 August 1944.

6

Conclusion

Certes, j'aurai pu vivre dans un autre pays, en Grande Bretagne ou aux
Etats Unis, et m'y conduire en bon citoyen. Mais sans y trouver une patrie
de substitution.   Raymond Aron[1]

If, since the 1970s, an ever-growing body of historians has carefully
disassembled the Gaullist notion of France as a 'nation of resisters',
revealing the complex and subtle ways in which public opinion
responded to the occupier, reactions often determined by time, place
and circumstance, the myth that the French in Britain were at least
supporters of de Gaulle and resolutely opposed to Vichy has remained
more or less intact. It is a myth that has remained untouched by the
huge literature that has carefully scrutinised the general's every move
throughout the war years, from Bordeaux to London, from London to
Algiers, and from there, via London again, to Normandy and Paris.
Admittedly, something of the intellectual opposition to de Gaulle,
fronted by Labarthe and Aron, has been noted, as have the quarrels
within the Free French movement itself. Nonetheless, it is still the
general and his supporters who command centre stage. In his memoirs,
de Gaulle claimed that in making his stand in June 1940 he was entering 'an adventure like a man thrown by fate outside all frames of
reference'.[2] It was his achievement as a myth-maker that he soon
erected those 'frames of reference' through which all histories of the
French in wartime Britain have been written since.

There is strong irony that Britain, a country which in his incarnation
as president of the Fifth Republic, de Gaulle denounced as a threat to
both French and European interests, constitutes the refuge of one of
the last remaining elements of the right-wing 'resistancialist' mythology carefully elaborated in the 1950s and 1960s. This is evidence not
only of the general's skill in projecting his own particular reading of

history, but also of the impact that he had on the British consciousness. Although Mass-Observation surveys reveal that public opinion soon tired of the quarrels that broke out among the Free/Fighting French and while government officials despaired of the arrogance and obduracy of the general himself, the man who would insist on using Hampstead tube station even though there was an unexploded bomb nearby,[3] his individuality and his courage appealed to a nation that had to confront recurrent bad news about the war effort in 1940–41. In this sense, his call of 18 June 1940 drew on the same wellsprings as the 'myth of the Blitz': in neither case could any weakness in morale be acknowledged. Instead, both de Gaulle and the British people drew comfort from the heroic image of their unflinching and lonely resistance against Nazism.

Factors other than de Gaulle's consummate ability as a myth-maker and the memories of wartime have also contributed to the notion that all French residents in Britain were supporters of his cause. The fact that the French were not a numerous body, nor an especially conspicuous one, despite the explosive arguments between Carlton Gardens and Downing Street, have ensured that other exiled groups – notably the Germans, Jews, and Poles – have received the lion's share of attention. When French communities-in-exile have been studied in depth, attention has naturally focused on the USA and Canada, where their numbers were always greater than in Britain, and where French artists and writers unquestionably bequeathed a more enduring legacy. Whatever de Gaulle might have claimed for his movement, even he could hardly assert that London was the French cultural capital in exile. That honour must unquestionably be shared between Montréal and New York. Other than the recently erected statue of de Gaulle in Carlton Gardens and the half-pint glasses served in the York Minster, now the French House, in Dean Street there are few reminders of the French presence in Britain. No plaque adorns the houses in Pembury Road in Tottenham or the racecourses in the North-West. The consulate in Bedford Square is now just another office.

This study has demonstrated that we can no longer speak of the French community in Britain in the singular. Aside from the Gaullist forces, there were several other communities – the 'forgotten French'. Initially their numbers were larger than the recruits for de Gaulle's fledgeling forces, and it should be remembered that support for the Free/Fighting French largely grew abroad, principally in those colonies tired of the treachery and shenanigans of Vichy. While it is undeniable

Figure 5   The statue of de Gaulle in Carlton Gardens – one of the few
reminders of the French wartime presence in London

that many of the French communities in Britain intermixed making it
extremely difficult to tell them apart – the image of MI5 officers,
disguised as continental refugees, intermingling in the bars and restaurants of Soho, attempting to identify fugitive French sailors and
Gaullist deserters among the colonist and overseas communities,
springs to mind – they nonetheless retained distinctive identities, reinforced by the circumstances of their arrival.

    Unless they had wealthy friends or relatives to offer them shelter, or
active bank accounts to dip into, refugees lived a peripatetic existence,
shunted out from the refugee centres to various lodgings in London, a
life of austerity in which the task of keeping body and soul together

remained paramount. Their plight was not all that dissimilar from that of the asylum seekers of today, marked out by their clothes, inability to speak English and the stigma of measly state handouts. As Mass-Observation observed, they were especially conspicuous in shops where the French habit of prodding food to test its freshness before purchase was seen as evidence of greed and 'wanting a lot for their money'.[4] French servicemen likewise retained a separate identity, arrested in ports at the time of the Armistice, and soon gathered together in make-shift camps, principally in the north of England where they were visited by Vichy consular officials, another group whose identity was readily apparent. And, there remained from pre-war times, an extensive French community, based in London and the Home Counties, that was well assimilated into British culture. To be sure, its numbers shrank with the onset of war yet, if anything, this process provided these colonists with an even stronger identity as those who remained were principally expatriates of long standing, with strong roots in Britain, and well accustomed to avoiding unwelcome attention. The paradox was that, with the defeat of France and arrival of de Gaulle, they could no longer preserve their preferred anonymity.

The diversity of the French communities raises a further observation: few of these men and women had chosen to be in Britain. These were not 'resisters of the first hour', who had rallied to the *appel* of 18 June, undertaking a hazardous exit from France by travelling across the Pyrenees to Spain or taking their chance on foreign-registered steamers to Glasgow or Liverpool. Refugees were in Britain by happenstance, driven across the Channel along with retreating British and French troops at Dunkirk. Most other refugees who had participated in the *exode* had retreated inland, making their way southwards to lands that they might have encountered as a result of the Popular Front's holidays, but all determined to escape the rush of German armour. As we have noted, those civilians who arrived in Britain emanated from the Nord-Pas-de-Calais, the territories that were squeezed by the claw-like movement of Guderian's tanks. Servicemen were similarly in Britain by chance, either veterans of Narvik or Dunkirk, or more likely sailors resting in British ports at the time of the Armistice.

Given these circumstances, it is not difficult to understand why several refugees and servicemen sought early repatriation, as would the large London-based diplomatic staff, which had grown significantly in the course of 1939–40. While such luminaries as Cambon and Corbin were too closely associated with Britain to seek immediate repatriation, and indeed Cambon would remain *in situ* throughout the war, other high-ranking diplomats and their families quickly arranged their passage back home, well ahead of those soldiers and sailors who would have to wait until the close of 1940, and whose plight served the needs of Vichy anti-British propaganda. Those diplomatic officials that remained, members of the missions and the consuls, must have bemoaned their luck, being left in a country, a former ally, now more or less at war with France, with no particular jobs to do other than to perform tedious administrative chores and fend off the snide asides of Foreign Office and Gaullist officials, not to mention the acidic observations of those expatriates who had aligned themselves to the Allied cause. The image of the Glasgow consul de Curzon, taking furtive notes, and rebutting the jibes of his countrymen, comes to mind. Unquestionably, these Vichy officials were anxious to book their return home; only as the war developed, and the prospects of the Pétain government deteriorated, and no doubt the opportunities for pensions and career advancement worsened, did the prospect of resettling in France appear less attractive. Even among the expatriates there was discomfort. Although some were fugitives from religious persecution across the Channel, descendants of seventeenth-century Huguenots or members of the religious orders that had been originally booted out by the legislation of Waldeck-Rousseau and Combes, the majority were settled in Britain not because of any particular ideological reason; rather Britain, and most likely London, had become the source of their income, whether as merchants in luxury goods, whether as bankers or industrialists, or whether as waiters and waitresses serving in the capital's hotels. No doubt it was reassuring that Britain, despite its odd habits and customs, was a country, in many respects, similar to France. It was after all only a short boat ride away, and had proved tolerant of the strange ways and customs of foreigners – even if, in the 1930s, it had not proved to be the welcoming haven for Jews and others that some historians and commentators would have us believe.

The very fact that a majority of the 'forgotten French' were in Britain by chance, and not out of any desire to oppose either Nazism or Vichy, points to the fact that their attitudes were remarkably similar to those of their countryfolk who remained on metropolitan soil. None took any satisfaction in the defeat of their nation, and most looked forward to the day of liberation, although few believed that this would be achieved by Britain whose cause looked pretty dire in the aftermath of the Armistice. Those who had fled across the Channel, especially the refugees, must have thought they had jumped out of the frying pan into the fire, especially when the Blitz began in earnest. Exiled sailors and soldiers also gave Britain little chance, and considered that it would not be long before 'perfidious Albion' witnessed the inexorable march of Blitzkrieg. It is also striking that few of the 'forgotten French' shed any tears for the departed Third Republic. As in France itself, most believed that the regime, unloved for so long, had been hopelessly discredited by the speed and overwhelming nature of the German victory. Significantly, there was a particular grudge felt towards the Popular Front, notably among affluent business elements of the colony, even though their livelihoods had not been directly affected by the introduction of paid holidays and compulsory collective bargaining. It is of further significance that nearly all of the 'forgotten French' accepted that Vichy was the legitimate government of their country, as indeed it was. Whatever René Cassin said about the unconstitutionality of the vote of 10 July 1940, it was manifest that the National Assembly had observed legal procedures to the best of its ability, and it had hardly needed the machinations of Laval to ensure that Pétain received absolute powers; indeed, the notion of a Pétain-Laval plot to overthrow the Republic remained popular only among a small number of intellectual exiles and the ever-mistrustful Free French. That said, there was no particular enthusiasm for the values of Vichy's National Revolution. When this did become evident, it was principally among the consular officials and high-ranking naval officers, traditionally conservative in their outlook, who now spoke of important work needing to be done. *Les catholiques avant tout*, notable among isolated elements of the clergy, also threatened to become disciples of the National Revolution, yet their numbers were few and their influence was curtailed by the swift action of the Catholic hierarchy, the propaganda of the Ministry of Information, the containment strategy of French Welfare and the absence of any prominent spiritual figures who might have whipped up trouble. No doubt had any of these right-wing sympathisers, Catholics, high-ranking military men and Vichyite officials, been resident on metropolitan soil, they would have gravitated towards the Pétainist veterans' organisation, the Légion Française des Combattants, or would have become Vichy *notables*, those predominantly bourgeois supporters of the Vichy state who manned the town halls and the general administration of the regime. Perhaps the only other potential band of supporters for the National Revolution was among those Maurrassian-leaning volunteers for de Gaulle, men whose hatred of the

Boche was fractionally stronger than their allegiance to reactionary values.

So it was that few of the 'forgotten French' were what could be best described as 'active' Pétainists in that they readily subscribed to his political values. Most were 'passive' in their support, convinced that the old man had France's best interests at heart and would do his utmost to protect his people from further suffering. Always viewed as supremely pragmatic in his decision-making, and known to be contemptuous of self-interested politicians, it was difficult to avoid the conclusion that, in the summer of 1940, he had acted out of any motive other than that of patriotism. The Armistice was the logical result of his actions and, as Kedward suggests, to argue against this step was to fly against reason and to invite ridicule.[5] Viewed from the precarious position of Britain, seemingly the next state to fall in Hitler's unstoppable game of conquest, this impression must have been even more pronounced, especially among such vulnerable and anxious groups as refugees and soldiers. It was only as the war progressed that it was possible to deconstruct Pétainist mythology, although the rumour that the marshal was a prisoner of Laval or the Germans was just as prevalent among the 'forgotten French' as it was on metropolitan soil; it did not need Isorni, the marshal's most able trial lawyer, to invent the 'double-game' or shield arguments. These were implicit in the cult of Pétainism and the circumstances of the Occupation. How far the various French groups in Britain eventually came to disassemble Pétainist mythology remains decidedly unclear. The fact that, after Montoire, neither the British nor the French press in London chose to make personal attacks on the marshal, regarding these as counter-productive, preferring instead to highlight his impotency and shortcomings of judgement, may well have facilitated this deconstruction process. In this way, it was possible for the French in Britain to express a loyalty both to Pétain and de Gaulle.[6]

That support for the general was slow in forthcoming is not in doubt. It is striking that most members of his entourage came from within France itself, and that support for the Free/Fighting French grew principally in the colonies. All the various groups in Britain had reason to be suspicious of this two-star general: he was an unknown figure whose prestige compared badly to Pétain's; he was rumoured to have dubious elements among his entourage, whether left-wingers such as Cot or extremist Cagoulards such as Passy, and maybe even Republican anti-clericals; his politics were similarly vague and soon smacked of a

Bonapartism that pleased neither right nor left; his personal manner was marked by an arrogance and short temper which was let loose on his fellow countrymen just as much as it was on the British; he had disobeyed the legitimate government of France; he was seemingly unable to offer any protection against Vichy or German retribution against relatives in France; he appeared almost entirely dependent on British support; he was unable to offer good rates of pay to his supporters; and his overall position seemed hopeless as did the whole Allied cause in 1940. It is perhaps significant that those of the 'forgotten French' who did rally to de Gaulle stemmed largely from the ranks of the colonists, maybe because these men and women were the most secure financially and socially, and understood how he was perhaps their greatest hope, especially when it became clear that his politics were not of the left. Even so, it is worth remembering that only two-thirds of London-based colonists enlisted in the Français de Grande Bretagne, a movement that was never truly Gaullist in the first place. It is highly significant that when, in November 1941, the FGB organised a rally for the general in the Albert Hall it was worried, in the words of Lennon and McCartney, lest it could not fill the '4,000 holes' with French supporters.

Although backing for the general unquestionably grew, it is striking that Britain never witnessed the 'Gaullist juggernaut' that Colin Nettelbeck describes in the USA,[7] an unstoppable takeover of existing French exile institutions. To be sure, the Free French and their supporters in the FGB did their very best to colonise all existing French organisations in Britain, whether they were welfare clubs for refugees in Manchester or prestigious cultural outposts such as the Institut Français in London. Ultimately, this campaign had chequered results. This was partially because of the suspicion of de Gaulle described above, and the success of individuals such as Aron and Labarthe in retaining an intellectual independence. Credit must also be extended to Bessborough's French Welfare. It is commonly said that, in 1941, the Foreign Office became ever more sympathetic to de Gaulle after recognising that Vichy was a hopeless case and that there was a need to curtail Churchill's pro-American enthusiasms. Yet French Welfare was one part of the Foreign Office that was exceedingly wary of de Gaulle, maybe because it regularly saw at close quarters the harm his men did whenever they came into direct touch both with British citizens and with French exiles. The number of occasions when British officials withdrew their support after making contact with Carlton Gardens is truly astonishing. The 'Gaullist juggernaut' was also resisted by other bodies, eventually the Spears Mission in 1941, but also the CEAF. The British tradition of female *bourgeois* philanthropy, widely practised by the likes of Lady Warwick and Lady Reading, was not going to crumble before the maladroit advances of de Gaulle and his supporters, especially the smart-uniformed ladies of the Assistance Sociale who were no match for the 'women in green' of the WVS.

With so much infighting going on, it is not surprising that the 'forgotten French' found it hard to settle in Britain. Refugees were very much a group apart, often 'apathetic',[8] powerless to shake off the unpropitious circumstances of their arrival, and unable to integrate easily in British life. Their poverty, partially enforced by a government that had no wish for them to take up their pre-war jobs lest they upset the indigenous workforce and that was further reluctant to pay much out in the way of welfare relief, further dictated their existence, as did the nature of the lodgings in the suburbs of the capital. Servicemen, kept apart in camps well away from intelligence centres and London itself, always excepting those at Crystal Palace and White City, also thought they had reason to grumble, although in retrospect their ordeal might well have been exacerbated by their own officers who seemingly cared little about their men other than to exacerbate anti-British feelings by destroying food, holding back radios and exerting little discipline. Seemingly embarrassed by their anomalous positions, the Vichy consuls led a furtive life, discovering that diplomatic charm cut little ice with Foreign Office officials; the fact that they were constantly suspected of fifth-columnist activities, even though few if any were truly dabbling in espionage, only hardened their discomfort. Even the expatriates, used to keeping their heads down and their quarrels to themselves, found life increasingly difficult. The arrival of new exiles, the busy-body activities of the FGB and the dilemmas posed by the enemy occupation of their mother country, brought them to the attention of the authorities and threatened their traditional reticence.

Their failure to assimilate, their disparate nature, their frequent squabbles, their lingering sympathy for Pétain, and their occasional antagonism towards Carlton Gardens did little to endear the 'forgotten French' to their British hosts, who were already attempting to reach a conclusion about de Gaulle. Whereas the general eventually won round the public, partially because of the manifest courage of his stand, the 'forgotten French' continued to arouse suspicion. While they escaped the fifth-column scare of May–June 1940, the reluctance of those abandoned soldiers and sailors to embrace the Allied cause and their tendency to insist upon repatriation tarred the reputation of all the French in Britain, even those belonging to de Gaulle. Their position was further weakened by the contrasting manner in which other exiled nationalities, especially the Poles, rushed to take up arms against the Axis powers. According to Mass-Observation studies of 1940–42, the British public no longer thought a future Anglo-French friendship desirable and viewed the French as among the most exasperating of allies, their popularity lagging behind that of the Americans, Norwegians and Poles. It was this latter group that most frequently earned sympathy, both for their courageous defiance of Hitler and the appalling manner in which the Nazis had treated their homeland.[9] It was to the credit of the British population at war that many acts of kindness were nonetheless displayed towards French exiles, especially those in impecunious circumstances. It was a charity that contrasted markedly with the attitudes of government bodies, few of which showed any real goodwill. Refugees, even the small numbers involved, were never wanted by the Ministry of Health, which soon relinquished them to local committees and relief agencies. The Admiralty and War Office lacked any enthusiasm for those sailors and soldiers, viewing these men as poorly motivated, difficult to train and fundamentally ill-disciplined. Only the RAF, desperate for recruits at the height of the Battle of Britain, was free of such scruples. Meanwhile, the Foreign and Home Offices, together with the security services, regarded the Vichy consular and Mission officials with disdain, a sentiment that was not altogether absent in the dealings with the colony. The ever-shifting nature of Vichy foreign policy in 1940–41, especially the prospect of a fragmenting of power between a Laval government in Paris, a Pétain regime in Vichy and a Weygand authority in North Africa, meant that a careful watch had to kept over the activities of the *colons*. Their general internment was seriously considered although it was obvious that few were overt admirers of the marshal, and that even these managed to combine this stance with sympathy for the Allied cause. The many shades of political opinion among the 'forgotten French' clearly irritated government bodies, and were not readily understood even by seasoned watchers in Bessborough's department.

Exile in Britain was not, then, a particularly happy episode for either the 'forgotten French' or the British. As Ministry of Information officials had forecast in 1939, while the two nationalities maybe shared the same fundamental values, the differences in temperament and outlook were profound, and these were vividly exposed by the peculiar circumstances of wartime, especially the anomalous position of the Vichy government, which was alone in Hitler's Europe in that it retained a sizeable measure of autonomy. It would have been much easier for the 'forgotten French' if their government had accompanied them into exile as did those of the Norwegians, Belgians and Poles. De Gaulle was no substitute. It would also have been easier if they had been able to set aside their love of their homeland. Throughout history, the French have generally made unhappy exiles, and the events of 1940–44 only highlighted their inability to adapt. In this respect, perhaps the last words should be left with Tereska Torrès, a genuine Anglophile and truly courageous figure who fled France to continue the struggle. In January 1942, on leaving the Belgian restaurant Chez Rose in Greek Street, where she had eaten horsesteak and chips, she went out into the streets of Soho, walking to Piccadilly Circus, and up along lower Regent Street, before heading home to her barracks. It was then that Big Ben struck two in the morning, and as she gazed towards St James's Park, and Westminster Cathedral, she tried to fathom in which direction France lay.[10] As elsewhere in the world, the 'forgotten French' of wartime Britain were 'forever French', even if they were not always 'fighting French'.

Notes

1 R. Aron, *Mémoires* (Paris, Juillard, 1983), p. 191. 'Certainly, I would have been able to have lived in another country, Great Britain or the United States, and leading a life there as a good citizen. But without discovering there a country which was a substitute.'

2 C. de Gaulle, *The Call to Honour* (London, Collins, 1955), p. 89.

3 Private letter to the author, Douglas Johnson, 24 April 1994.

4 M-O TC25 Box 1 25/1/H, report of 15 May 1941 on comments of woman, aged 35.

5 H. R. Kedward, *Occupied France. Collaboration and Resistance, 1940–1944* (Oxford, Blackwell, 1985), p. 19.

6 PRO FO 371 24346, Spears memorandum, January 1941.

7 C. Nettelbeck, *Forever French. Exiles in the United States 1939–1945* (Oxford, Berg, 1991).

8 M-O TC25 Box 1 25/1/D, Refugees, 13 May 1940.

9 M-O FR 523B, 'Attitudes to Other Nationalities', Report of 10 December 1940.

10 T. Torrès, *Une française libre. Journal, 1939–1945* (Paris, Phébus, 2000), p. 153.

Appendix 1

Reception centres for war refugees: nationalities and admissions to 29 October 1940

Algerian	1	Latvian	5
American	19	Lithuanian	8
Arabian	2	Luxembourger	7
Argentinian	4	Moroccan	46
Armenian	3	Norwegian	53
Austrian	9	Palestinian	50
Belgian	5,852	Panamayan	1
British	2,861	Persian	4
Chinese	1	Polish	3,243
Cuban	7	Portuguese	5
Czech	653	Roumanian	36
Danish	12	Russian	24
Dutch	1,209	Slovak	1
Egyptian	5	Spanish	277
French	2,905	Stateless	163
German	21	Swedish	6
Greek	9	Swiss	8
Hungarian	23	Turkish	37
Iraquian	1	Uruguayan	1
Irish	12	Yugoslav	5
Italian	12		

Source: LCC We/M (1) Box 9

Appendix 2

Statistics for the year ended 31 December 1941
Immigration Office, Royal Victoria Patriotic School, London, SW18

Code	Belg.	Czech.	Da.	Dutch	Fr.	Greek	Norw.	Pol.	Yug.	Various	Total
1A							2,416				2,416
1B	5			66	52						123
1C	2		2	6	9						19
1D							147				147
2A	203	37	13	49	204	5	39	302	8		860
2B	15	21	35	6	48	76	124	66	3		394
2C	2				118						120
2D	1		3		842			49			895
2E					3		264	2			269
2F	2	1	1	42			81	14			141
3A										1,565	1,565
Total	230	59	54	169	1,276	81	3,071	433	11	1,565	6,949

Direct from enemy occupied territory to the UK: 1A By small boats to the Shetlands &
east of Scotland ports; 1B By small boats from France to south coast ports or by small
boats from Holland and Belgium to east & south-east ports; 1C By stolen planes from
occupied countries to landing grounds in east & south England; 1D From raids on
occupied countries – rescued by British forces.

Through neutral countries or British territory abroad: 2A From, France, Belgium and
Holland via Spain and Portugal and thence by sea from Lisbon to UK ports, or by air
from Lisbon to Bristol airport or Poole airport, or via Spain and Gibraltar to UK ports;
2B From Vichy-controlled North Africa in small boats or stolen planes to Gibraltar and
thence to UK ports or from Dakar in small boats to Bathurst, Gambia and Freetown and
thence to UK ports; 2C From Vichy-controlled territory in North and South America
and the East to nearest British territory; 2D From France in Vichy-controlled ships to
neutral ports in America and the East and thence with the help of the nearest British

consul, to UK ports and members of crews of captured Vichy ships who have volunteered to serve in Free French Forces; 2E   From Norway and Sweden and thence via Russia, Turkey and the Middle East to India or Africa for embarkation to British ports; 2F From Norway on foot to Sweden or from Holland or Germany as seamen to Swedish ports (where the ship is deserted) and thence from Stockholm airport to Leuchars airport, Fifeshire; 3A   Non-escapees, volunteers for allied forces, seamen arriving in the UK for time since outbreak of war; evacuees from Gibraltar, stow-aways, volunteers for war industry, general cases etc.

Appendix 3

Note from Robertson, HO, B3, to L. W. Clayton, HO, February 1941
List of all detainees who have been at RPS for more than a week
Weekly return of refugees

	Nationality	Arrived from	Date of arr.	Destination
B—, B. T.	Moroccan	Dover	15.1.41	Discharged FFF, disciplinary grounds
C— J.	French	Liverpool	15.1.41	Discharged FFF, medically unfit
F—, E.	French	Plymouth	11.1.41	Waiting for a ship
G—, A.	Polish	Oratory School	11.1.41	In hospital, wishes to join FFF
L— R—, P.-M.	French	Southampton	28.1.41	MI5 case pending
M-G, L. J.	French	Weymouth	22.1.41	MI5 case pending
Z—, S.	Algerian	Dover	15.1.41	Discharged FFF, disciplinary grounds

Source: PRO HO 213 1978 203/2/107

20 names on list: 4 Poles; 4 'ex-Austrians'; 1 Belgian; 4 French; 1 Moroccan; 1 Czech; 1 Hungarian; 1 Norwegian; 1 Dane; 1 Dutch; 1 Algerian.

Appendix 4

Extracts from the Diary of C— F— L— G—

(Senior naval officer belonging to one of the sailors' camps in the Liverpool area. This diary had been seized and translated by the British.)

23 June: Sad Sunday. In the evening we learn of the Armistice conditions, much harder than 11.11.18 and dishonouring two countries, and which does not even put an end to the war and is subject to the laying down of arms and the acceptance of the Armistice imposed by Italy who has no military success even when, with all her forces, she attacked a country already beaten.

The English hope that like the Poles, Dutch and Norwegians, we will continue to fight. They show themselves full of strength.

24 June: The proclamation of Gen de Gaulle is widely discussed. Some who desire at all costs to finish with the whole business treat it offhandedly. Others, who place no reliance on German promises, ask themselves where their duty lies towards France. This dilemma boils itself down to an appreciation more or less exact of British chances. What about Russia and the USA?

5 July: Some of our officers still believe in maintaining friendly relations with the English, in spite of the assassination at Oran.

8 July: The English are having typed a *Journal du Camp* full of lies and false news, just like their 'VICTORY' over unarmed ships.

9 July: Commandant G— refutes the declaration of Gen de Gaulle that the English were right in destroying our fleet, and doubtlessly to kill our comrades.

10 July: Capitaine de Vaisseau L— told us after lunch that an honourable solution was on the point of being arranged between Admiral Cayol and Admiral Dunbar Nesmith by leaving small French parties aboard the ships to guard them, when the incident of the *Surcoeuf* occurred.

14 July: We receive some hogheads of our own wine with the compliments of the Admiralty. Lunch so insufficient that I have to complete it with purchases at the canteen.

17 July: The propaganda of de Gaulle grows. They offer our men cigarettes, women, and wine, 45/- per week for seamen.

18 July: Two lieutenants of Gen de Gaulle's legion came to the camp to invite us to go to Liverpool to listen to Gen de Gaulle. As one of their colleagues had previously said that those of us who did not join them were 'cunts', they were very badly received. Commandant S... took them by their coat lapels and gave them the order to 'fuck off' if they did not want their faces bashed. Thereupon Commandant L— C— intervened and led them quietly away. He negotiated with them the return of young R— and young O—, who allowed themselves to be enrolled.

19 July: I go to de Gaulle's recruiting centre to enquire who are the officers, I am well received by the sailors and we chat for about a quarter of an hour in a friendly manner, when a Lieutenant arrives who asks me to get out. I follow him out but ask the seamen to witness and pitying them. Two hours later a representative of the Legion and a seaman come and beg me to return in order to receive the excuses of the Lieutenant.

26 July: The English informed the French government that repatriation was beginning, but without notifying the hour or the route of the ship. Torpedoing took place at 10 pm. The Germans had moreover said that owing to the use of our flag by General de Gaulle they would torpedo any ship flying the French flag.

27 July: The English decide to intern at Oxford the two Admirals. They send into the camp a car with loudspeakers and an armed guard to protect it. An officer photographs it. They try in vain to seize the camera. Finally, more than 100 armed men surround the car, which beats a retreat to the tune of the Marseillaise. Muselier informed of the state of mind postpones his recruiting tour.

28 July: Commandant G— is also taken away to Oxford. Gen Spears makes a very able speech, but it seems that the officers will be separated from their men in the hope of converting them to Gen de Gaulle, or at least so as not to make an admission before the British public of the errors of Churchill's politics.

31 July: The English have decided that we will not be given our pay. Only those who join de Gaulle will be paid. At the Aintree camp all remain faithful to the French Gov. In other camps sentiment is divided and defections must be foreseen.

7 August: At Doddington the starving men have had to kill and eat the swans. A crime of lese majesté ...

9 August: The Gaullists attempt to debauch our men by standing the drinks and offering to get women for them.

12 August: This afternoon I discussed with the camp commandant and the naval Liaison officer the internment of de T—. Great pressure is being

brought to bear on us and the sailors to join de Gaulle. This evening they
decided that we must get back to camp an hour earlier and we will no
longer be supplied with drink. What undignified meanness on the part of
a strong people.

15 August: Two Gaullist sailors bring me an order from Admiral Watkins
authorising their entry into the camp without me giving permission to
contradict their propaganda. The German attack seems to intensify.
Numerous special boats gathered in Norway and Holland. Numerous
aerial attacks on the Channel Coast. Gun fire in the Dover region.
Parachutes found in Scotland.

16 August: Numerous aerial attacks. New Gaullist effort. Admiral Watkins has
repeated through the camp commandant the order to allow Gaullist
propaganda in the camp. As I do not give it any importance I expect to be
kidnapped.

20 August: I learn that as a result of a provocative speech by Gen Spears the officers protested, and as a punishment L. V. B— has been interned in a
barracks until the end of the war. At Oulton when this same general
showed himself the colours were lowered half mast.

21 August: Today I have been worrying about M— (wife). Have she and the
children got enough to eat. The bombardments of Brest etc with all the
British lack of precision which we discovered at Dunkirk and Calais, must
worry her terribly. How happy we would be without this war, which I
foresaw coming with anguish. What will be the physical state of the children after this inhuman blockade. The adventure of de Gaulle is full of
uncertainty. What a utopia to believe one can serve one's country in
receiving orders from a stranger who annoys the race!

23 August: A Gaullist Lieutenant, who like many other Gaullist officers, has
never fought, confirms to me that they have asked the English to shut up
a number of French officers, because they advised their men to remain in
the path of duty. Also they hoped shortly to land in Morocco and start a
civil war, to which the German would put a quick ending.

26 August: The bombardments of Ramsgate, Dover, London and Birmingham
become serious. The English multiply their bombardments of our coasts
and aerodromes from Boulogne to Vannes. At Cherbourg the sea front
has suffered a great deal.

28 August: I learn that six officers of Oulton Camp, including D— B— and de
B—, who were on the repatriation list with me, have been kidnapped.
Every day they come with lorries to the camps to take away the men who
lower themselves by joining de Gaulle.

Source: PRO FO 371 24353 C10327/7407/17

Appendix 5

List of officers, officials and staff of French missions in UK

Air Mission A	22
Air Mission B	21
Allied Military Committee Personnel	15
Anglo-French Coordinating Committee	11
Armaments Mission	22
Civil Air Mission	6
Coal Mission	39
Delegation to the Shipping Executive	6
Economic Warfare Mission	14
Food Mission	9 (plus staff of 12)
French Military Mission	13 (not complete)
Naval Mission	59
Oil Mission	6
Scientific Mission	1
Sea Transport Mission	62 (mainly British)
Textiles Mission	17
Timber Mission	2

Source: CCC SPRS 1/134

Appendix 6

French in London (1933), consulate figures

	Male	Female	Total
Coiffeurs	167	15	182
Cuisiniers, hôteliers, chefs, garçons	879	—	879
Divers, artistes	121	198	319
Domestiques	37	558	595
Employés banque, commerce, industrie, mode	977	850	1,827
Enfants de moins de 15 ans	518	392	910
Etudiants, Etudiantes	376	673	1,049
Gouvernantes, dames de compagnie	—	616	616
Industriels, directeurs de compagnies, de banques	95	14	109
Négoçiants, commerçants, agents	388	160	548
Ouvriers, ouvrières	244	390	634
Professeurs, institutrices	131	482	613
Religieux, religieuses	183	613	796
Sans profession	20	1,389	1,409
Totals	4,136	6,350	10,486

Source: H. Goiran, *Les Français à Londres* (Pornic, Editons de la Vagne 1933), p. 220.
Figures are missing for approximately one-third of French-based Londoners.

Appendix 7

Census of French subjects over the age of 16 registered in the UK and NI on 6 February 1941

	Male	Female	Total
Metropolitan Police District	3,252	3,224	6,476
England and Wales (provinces)	1,697	3,087	4,784
Scotland	113	160	273
Northern Ireland	17	26	43
War refugees	352	607	959
Totals	5,431	7,104	12,535

Source: PRO FO 371 28365 Z1753/123/17

Appendix 8

Detailed figures of French residents in districts having 50 or more residents (6 February 1941)

District	Male	Female	Total
England and Wales			
Berks	85	69	154
Bucks	42	99	141
Cardiganshire	38	30	68
Cheshire	22	35	57
Devonshire	45	172	217
Dorset	15	73	88
Glamorgan	29	22	51
Gloucestershire	12	60	72
Hants	61	120	181
Herts	41	102	143
Kent	25	109	134
Lancs	63	64	127
Monmouthshire	17	74	91
Somerset	17	128	145
Surrey	67	117	184
E. Sussex	17	65	82
W. Sussex	25	67	92
Isle of Wight	29	29	58
Yorkshire – West Riding	38	37	75
Birmingham	36	54	90
Brighton	15	80	95
Bristol	11	41	52
Dover	48	4	52
Hove	13	37	50
Liverpool	15	52	67

District	Male	Female	Total
Manchester	33	35	68
Reading	17	33	50
Southampton	23	31	54
Wolverhampton	17	38	55
Scotland			
Glasgow	32	32	64

Source: PRO FO 371 28365 Z1753/123/17

Bibliography

Archival sources

Archives Nationales, Paris (AN)

Archives de la Musée Pédagogique
AJ 40 63 Papiers d'André Philip

BBC Written Archives, Caversham, Reading (BBC)
E1/702 France

Churchill College, Cambridge (CCC)

Spears Papers
1/134 France. De Gaulle
1/135 France. French infantry. French navy
1/136 France. Correspondence, telegrams, papers
1/137 France. Personal, confidential correspondence, general files
1/140 Friends of the French Forces Fund
1/154 Correspondence, 1933–40
1/182 Jewish refugees
1/235 Ministry of Information Correspondence, 1939–40
2/6 Diaries and enclosures, 30 August 1940–26 October 1940
2/7 Diary 29 October 1940–17 November 1940

Papers of Lord Vansittart of Denham
VNST II 2/25 Printed papers and correspondence on Germany and on Britain
    and France (1940)

Papers of Lord Noel Baker
NBKR 4/258 Correspondence on France

NBKR 4/259 Notes and cuttings on France
NBKR 4/261 Correspondence on France
NBKR 4/579 Correspondence on refugees, T, 1939–50
NBKR 4/585 Correspondence on internees and refugees in Britain named T–Z,
    1940–46
NBKR 4/586 Correspondence on refugees named J–K, 1940–46
NBKR 4/587 Correspondence on refugees named L, 1940–46
NBKR 4/588 Correspondence on refugees named M–O, 1940–46
NBKR 4/589 Correspondence on refugees named R, 1940–46
NBKR 4/590 Correspondence on refugees and internees in Britain, named R–S,
    1940–48
NBKR 5/591 Correspondence on refugees and internees in Britain, named R–S,
    1940–48
NBKR 4X/10 France, 1940–41

Foreign Ministry Archives, Berlin (PA–AA)

Buro des Staatssekretars, 1940–44
R29570–4 Relations with England
R29585–606 Relations with France

German Embassy, Paris
1106 French government in Vichy: personalities, collaboration, etc.
1120b Political relations with France and England
1158b Correspondence exchanged between the Paris embassy and its office in
    Vichy
1158c Correspondence exchanged between the Paris embassy and its office in
    Vichy
1228–31, and 1295 Relations between France and countries other than Germany
1296 Diplomatic and consular representatives of France and other countries in
    Germany and other countries
1361 Political files: England
2483 French diplomatic and consular representatives in Germany and in other
    countries

Imperial War Museum, London (IWM)

Department of Documents
63/34/1 Miss M.-L. Touchard
Con Shelf Toutain (Part II) Miss C. E.
97/7/1 Diary of M. Vila

London Metropolitan Archives, Faringdon, London (LMA)

London County Council
LCC We/M (1) Box 8 1940. Reception of French merchant seamen and others
LCC We/M (1) Box 9 1940. Reception of French merchant seamen and others
LCC We/M (1) Box 10 1940. Reception of French merchant seamen and others
LCC We/M (1) Box 11 1940. Reception of French merchant seamen and others
LCC We/M (1) Box 12 Crystal Palace. Admission forms for French seamen
LCC We/M (1) Box 13 Crystal Palace. Admission forms for French seamen

Middlesex County Council
MCC/WE/PA/2/36 War refugees administration
MCC/WE/PA/2/37 1940–41. War refugees scheme
MCC/WE/PA/2/38 1940–45. War refugees
MCC/WE/PA/2/39 1940. War refugees mainly from abroad
MCC/WE/PA/2/40 1940–41. War refugees mainly from abroad
MCC/WE/PA/2/41 1940–41. War refugees, official circulars
MCC/WE/PA/2/58 1940–41. War refugee statistics
MCC/WE/PA/2/84 1940. Rehousing of war refugees. Tottenham.

British War Refugees Fund
A/FWA/C/J8/1 British war refugees

London School of Economics (LSE)

Dalton papers
7/2 Ministry of Economic Warfare papers
7/3 Special Operations Executive papers
8/1 Political and General Correspondence
18/1 SOE papers, 1940–41
18/2 SOE papers, 1941

Mass-Observation Archives, University of Sussex (M-O)

File reports
Report 201 French surrender
Report 238 June 1940 Refugees: questioning refugees about their reasons for leaving their country
Report 245 Refugees: questions about leaving the country
Report 262 Third and Main Report on the refugees
Report 276 Supplementary report on public opinion about allies
Report 288 June 1940 Anglo-French lecture by Professor Saurat: 'Civilians in wartime': audience reaction to talk delivered at the Queen's Hall, French Institute

Report 461 Refugees in Worcester
Report 523B December 1940 Attitudes to other nationalities: replies from the volunteer panel of observers
Report 541 December 1940 Feelings about various racial groups: analysis of replies from panel of observers
Report 566 February 1941 Public opinion about the French: opinion trends, 1939–41
Report 713 Report 713 Feelings about Vichy France
Report 1669Q April 1943 Attitudes to foreigners: analysis of panel replies with comparisons to questions asked previously
Report 2023 February 1944 Feelings about the French (GM)
Report 2131 The invasion of France

Topic collections
TC 25 Box 1 Aliens, Refugees and internment, 1939–43
TC 25 Box 2 Countries. Reactions to war events and attitudes to other nationalities, 1939–44

Ministère des Affaires Etrangères, Paris (MAE)
ZV 291 Guerre, 1939–45 Rupture des relations diplomatiques avec la France
ZV 292 Guerre, 1939–45 Corps diplomatiqes et consulaire britannique, août 1940–juillet 1944

Public Records Office, Kew, London (PRO)
It would be otiose to list all the file names consulted at the PRO; hence only the series and numbers are named.
AST II Public Assistance – wartime functions: 6; 29–40; 45–6; 65–72; 75–6; 79–80; 82–5; 88–90; 94–9
BW2 British Council. Registered files, GB series: 228; 233–4; 236–42
BW31 British Council. Registered files, France: 2–7; 14–5; 23
BW68 British Council. Governing Board and Executive Committee, Minutes and Papers 2–3
CAB 65 Minutes of War Cabinet meetings
FO 371 Political Central – France: 22367; 24338–47; 24352–61; 28166–75; 28184–9; 28212–4; 28240–2; 28261–2; 28317; 28336–41; 28358; 28362–8; 28419–26; 28443; 28448; 28452–3; 28457–60; 28466; 28470; 28472; 28482–3; 284989; 28507; 28517; 28519; 28529; 28531; 28535; 28545–6; 28561; 28563–4; 28580; 28582; 28584–5; 28592–3; 28598; 28606; 28608; 31877–8; 31924; 31932; 31936; 31948–50; 31959–62; 31974–5; 31983–5; 31987; 31990–1; 31994; 31996; 31992; 32001; 32003–6; 320133–4; 32025; 32027–8; 32039; 32041; 32047; 32071; 32075; 32099; 32101A; 32114; 32117; 32160; 32170; 32181; 36004–6; 36027; 36031; 36040; 36042; 36044–7; 36051; 36053–4; 36056; 36064–5; 36069; 36069; 36084; 36091; 36093; 36101;

41870–5; 41908–9; 41912; 41919; 41934; 41982; 41985; 41989–93; 41995; 41998; 42005; 42031–2; 42041; 42044; 42048; 42071–3; 42095; 42112; 42115–6; 49059–62; 49115; 49171–2; 49195; 49220; 49245.

FO 371 Refugees: 29158–9; 29173–92; 29196–207; 29217–19; 29222; 25244–9
FO 1055 French Welfare: 1–14
HO 213 Home Office Aliens Department: 56; 67; 89; 276–7; 303; 314–5; 447; 451; 462–8; 474–5; 556–7; 589–90; 828–31; 1724; 1731; 1739; 1744; 1756; 1760; 1781; 1931; 1934; 1937; 1977–81; 2046–7; 2096–8
HO 214 Internment: 12; 39
HO 215 Internment: General Files: 23; 42; 485–9; 505–11
INF 1 Ministry of Information 181; 264; 529; 858–9; 877; 970.
MAF 74 Ministry of Food Central Registry. Correspondence and papers: 16
MH 76 Emergency medical services: war refugees: 519
PREM 3 Prime Minister's papers: 174/2
PREM 4 Prime Minister's Papers: 66/1; 66/2; 66/4; 66/6 A

Reading University Library (RUL)
The Astor Papers
The War and Us, the unpublished diary of J. W. Dodgson

Westminster Diocesan Archives, London (WDA)
Hi 2 1934 1939–40 Catholic Women's League
11 b (Cardinal Griffin's papers) Catholic Committee for Refugees, 1938–51
G2 81 France, 1944–46
Bo 1/92 French Church

Women's Royal Voluntary Service, Abingdon, Oxfordshire (WRVS)
Box 12 FC42 French welfare, 1938–47
Box 12 FC42 French welfare, 1945–79
Box 30 RFG 1A Regional refugees, 1941–46
Box 31 RFG 25/1 War Refugees committee, correspondence, 1940–46 (parts 1/2)
Box 197 miscellaneous memoranda, WVS wartime activities, 1938–45, evacuation, food, French visitors
Box 198 Miscellaneous memoranda, WVS wartime activities, 1938–45, refugees, refugees and repatriates, salvage, school volunteer schemes, Scotland, shelters

Published primary sources

Collections of documents

Barbas, J.-C., *Philippe Pétain. Discours aux français, 17 juin 1940–20 août 1944* (Paris, Albin Michel, 1989)

Bulletin Officiel des Forces Françaises Libres, 1940
Census of England and Wales, 1931, vol. 1, *Preliminary Report Including Tables of Population* (London, HMSO, 1931)
Documents on British Foreign Policy, Series D, vols, 1940–45
Journal Officiel de la France Libre de la France Combattante, January 1941–September 1943
London County Council, *Minutes of Proceedings, 1940–1942*
Middlesex County Council, *Minutes of Proceedings, 1940–1944*
Ophuls, M., *The Sorrow and the Pity* (London, Paladin, 1971)
Veillon, D., *La Collaboration. Textes et débats* (Paris, Livre de Poche, 1984)

Pamphlets and contemporary accounts of France
Bois, E. J., *Truth on the Tragedy of France* (London, Hodder & Stoughton, 1941)
Dejean, M., *Free France, Its Leader. Its Nature. Its Aims. Lecture Given at Caxton Hall*, Westminster on April 15th 1941 (London, Dent, 1941)
Jacques, 'A Free Frenchman Speaks', *Nineteenth Century*, vol. 128, 1940, pp. 500–8, 604–15, and vol. 129, 1940, pp. 92–104, 276–82
Maillaud, P., *France* (London, Oxford University Press, 1942)
Michael, *France Still Lives* (London, Lindsay Drummond, 1942)

French and other overseas memoirs
Aglion, R., *De Gaulle et Roosevelt. La France Libre aux Etats-Unis* (Paris, Plon, 1984)
Alphand, H., *L'Etonnement d'être* (Paris, Fayard, 1977)
Andrieux, J., *Le Ciel et l'enfer. France Libre, 1940–1945* (Paris, Presses de la Cité, 1965)
Aron, R., *Mémoires* (Paris, Juillard, 1983)
——, *Chroniques de guerre. La France Libre, 1940–1945* (Paris, Gallimard, 1990)
Astier, E. d', *Sept Fois sept jours* (Paris, Editions de Minuit, 1947)
——, *Les Dieux et les hommes, 1943–1944* (Paris, Juillard, 1952)
Billotte, P., *Le Temps des armes* (Paris, Plon, 1972)
Bloch, J.-P. *Le Vent souffle l'histoire* (Paris, SIPEP, 1956)
——, *De Gaulle ou le temps des méprises* (Paris, La Table Ronde, 1969)
——, *Londres, capitale de la France Libre* (Paris, Editions Carrère/Michel Lafon, 1986)
Blond, G., *L'Angleterre en guerre. Récit d'un marin français* (Paris, Grasset, 1941)
Boisseau, Gén. de, *Pour combattre avec de Gaulle* (Paris, Plon, 1981)
Bret, P.-L., *Au feu des événements. Mémoires d'un journaliste. Londres-Alger, 1929–1944* (Paris, Plon, 1959)
Cassin, R., *Les Hommes partis de rien* (Paris, Plon, 1975)
Charbonnières, G. de, *Le Duel Giraud–de Gaulle* (Paris, Plon, 1984)

Chevalier, J., 'Un témoignage sur deux points d'histoire', in *Ecrits de Paris*, juillet 1953, 83–7

Christol, F., *Comme au temps de nos pères. Ceux de la France Libre* (London, Hamish Hamilton 1946)

Ciano, G., *Ciano's Diaries* (London, William Heinemann, 1947)

Closon, F.-L., *Le Temps des passions* (Paris, Presses de la Cité, 1974)

Coulet, F., *Vertu des temps difficiles* (Paris, Plon, 1967)

Crémieux-Brilhac, J.-L., 'Avec de Gaulle, les Français libres de Londres', in *L'Histoire*, no. 233, juin 1999, 48–50

Delavenay, E., *Témoignage d'un village savoyard au village mondial, 1905–1991* (Aix-en-Provence, Diffusion Edisud, 1992)

Dronne, R., *Carnets de route d'un croisé de la France Libre* (Paris, Editions France-Empire, 1984)

Gaulle, C. de, *The Army of the Future* (London, Hutchinson, 1940)

_____, *War Memoirs*, 3 vols, vol. 1 *The Call to Honour 1940–1942* (London, Collins, 1955); vol. 2 *Unity, 1942–1944* (London, Weidenfeld & Nicolson, 1959); vol. 3 *Salvation, 1944–1946* (London, Weidenfeld & Nicolson, 1960)

Gillois, A., *De la résistance à l'insurrection* (Lyon, Sève, 1946)

_____, *Histoire secrète des français à Londres de 1940 à 1944* (Paris, Hachette, 1972)

Girard, L.-D., *Montoire. Verdun diplomatique?* (Paris, André Bonne, 1947)

_____, *Mazinghen ou la vie secrète du maréchal Pétain, 1856–1951* (Paris, privately published, 1971)

Gombault, G., *Un journal, une aventure* (Paris, Gallimard, 1982)

Henery, M., *An Exile in Soho* (London, Dent, 1952)

Ingold, G., *Un matin bien rempli ou la vie d'un pilote de chasse de la France Libre, 1921–1941* (Paris, Charles-Lavauzelle, 1969)

Lapie, P.-O., *Les Déserts de l'action* (Paris, Flammarion, 1946)

Marin, J., *Petit Bois pour un grand feu. La Naissance de la France Libre* (Paris, Fayard, 1994)

Maritain, J., *Messages, 1941–1944* (New York, Fayard, 1945)

Mengin, R., *No Laurels for de Gaulle* (London, Michael Joseph, 1967)

Miribel, E. de, *La Liberté souffre violence* (Paris, Plon, 1981)

Monnet, J., *Mémoires* (Paris, Fayard, 1976)

Morand, P., *Londres* (Paris, Plon, 1933)

_____, *Chroniques de l'homme maigre* (Paris, Bernard Grasset, 1941)

Muselier, E., *De Gaulle contre le gaullisme* (Paris, Editions du Chêne, 1946)

_____, *Jean Oberlé vous parle* (Paris, La Jeune Parque, 1945)

Oberle, J., *Images anglaises ou 'L'Angleterre occupée'* (London, Hachette, 1943)

Palewski, G., *Mémoires d'action, 1924–1974* (Paris, Plon, 1988)

Queuille, H., *Journal de guerre. Londres-Alger, avril 1943–juillet 1944* (Paris, Plon, 1995)

Raczynski, E., *In Allied London* (London, Weidenfeld & Nicolson, 1962)

Rémy, *Mémoires d'un agent secret de la France Libre* (Paris/Monte Carlo, Raoul Solar, 1947) 3 vols

_____, *Dix Ans avec de Gaulle* (Paris, Editions France-Empire, 1971)

Robet, C., *Souvenirs d'un médecin de la France Libre* (Paris, SIDES, 1994)

Rougier, L., *Mission secrète à Londres.* (Paris, La Diffusion de Livre, 1948)

Schumann, *La Voix du couvre-feu. Cent allocutions, 1940–1944* (Paris, Plon, 1964)

_____, *Un certain 18 juin* (Paris, Plon, 1980)

Simon, J., *Pétain, mon prisonnier* (Paris, Plon, 1978)

Sonneville, P., *Les Combattants de la liberté. Ils n'étaient pas 10,000* (Paris, La Table Ronde, 1968)

Soustelle, J., *Envers et contre tout* (Paris, Robert Laffont, 1947–50) 2 vols

Thierry d'Argenlieu, G., *Souvenirs de guerre, juin 1940–janvier 1941* (Paris, Plon, 1973)

Torrès, T., *Une française libre. Journal, 1939–1945* (Paris, Phébus, 2000)

Vallès, J., 'La Rue à Londres', in Beller, R. (ed.), *Oeuvres*, Vol. 2, *1871–1885* (Paris, Gallimard, 1989)

Villefosse, L. de, *Les Iles de la liberté. Aventures d'un marin de la France Libre* (Paris, Albin Michel, 1972)

Wieviorka, O. (ed.), *Nous entrerons dans la carrière de la Résistance à l'exercice du* pouvoir (Paris, Seuil, 1993)

British memoirs

Bessborough, Lord and Aslet, C., *Enchanted Forest. The Story of Stanstead in Sussex* (London, Weidenfeld & Nicolson, 1984)

Bryant, A., *The Turn of the Tide, 1939–1943* (London, Collins, 1957)

Cadogan, A., *Diaries* (London, Cassell, 1971)

Churchill, W., *The Second World War* (London, Collins, 1949) 6 vols

Cobb, R., *Promenades* (Oxford, Oxford University Press, 1980)

Colville, J., *Footprints in Time* (London, Collins, 1976)

_____, *The Fringes of Power. Downing Street Diaries* (London, Hodder & Stoughton, 1985) 2 vols

Duff Cooper, *Old Men Forget* (London, Rupert Hart-Davis, 1953)

Eden, A., *Memoirs* (London, Cassell, 1965) 3 vols

Graves, R., *Goodbye to all that* (London, Penguin, 1960 edn)

Harvey, J. (ed.), *The Diplomatic Diaries of Oliver Harvey, 1937–1940* (London, Collins, 1970)

Hodgson, V., *Few Eggs and No Oranges. A Diary Showing how Unimportant People in London and Birmingham Lived Through the War Years, 1940–1945, Written in the Notting Hill area of London by Vere Hodgson* (London, Dobson, 1976)

Knight, F., *The French Resistance, 1940–1944* (London, Lawrence & Wishart, 1975)

Koestler, A., *Scum of the Earth* (London, Eland, 1991 edn)

Long, H., *Change into Uniform. An Autobiography, 1939–1946* (Lavenham, T. Dalton, 1978)

____, 'Hero on the Home Front', *The Times*, 23 June 1993

Lyttelton, O., *The Memoirs of Lord Chandos* (London, Bodley Head, 1962)

Lytton, N., *Life in Occupied France* (London, Macmillan, 1942)

Mortimer, J., *Summer of a Dormouse* (London, Penguin, 2000)

Nicolson, H., *Harold Nicolson's Diaries* (London, Flamingo, 1996)

Orwell, G., *The Collected Essays, Journalism and Letters of George Orwell*, vol. 2, *My Country. Right or Left, 1940–1943* (London, Secker & Warburg, 1968)

Panter-Downes, M., *London War Notes, 1939–1945* (London, Longman, 1971)

Pimlott, B. (ed.), *The Second World War Diary of Hugh Dalton, 1940–1945* (London, Jonathan Cape, 1986)

Spears, E., *Assignment to Catastrophe* (London, William Heinemann, 1954) 2 vols

____, *Two Men who saved France* (London, Eyre and Spottiswoode, 1969)

____, *Fulfilment of a Mission. The Spears Mission to Syria and Lebanon, 1941–1944* (London, Cooper, 1977)

Tree, R., *When the Moon was High. Memories of War and Peace, 1897–1942* (London, Macmillan, 1975)

Newspapers

British Press, 1940–44

Daily Express
Daily Herald
Daily Mail
Daily Mirror
Daily Sketch
Daily Telegraph
The Times
Times Educational Supplement
Daily Worker
Manchester Guardian
News Chronicle
Observer

French Press, 1940–44

Je Suis Partout
Les Cahiers Français
Les Documents
Les Documents Français
France
La France Libre

La Marseillaise
La Volontaire pour une Cité Chrétienne

Journals, 1940–44

The Economist
Listener
New Statesman and Nation
Tablet
Westminster Cathedral Chronicle and Diocesan Gazette

Interviews/correspondence

Georges le Poittevin, London, February 2002
Helen Long, London, 19 April 1994
Pierre Veydert, Paris and Mauthausen, March 1994
Léon Wilson, London, 22 March 2002

Novels

Sartre, J.-P., *Iron in the Soul* (London, Hamish Hamilton, 1950) vol 3
Wesley, M., *The Camomile Lawn* (London, Macmillan, 1984)

Secondary sources

Books

Abac-Epezy, C. d', *L'Armée de l'air des années noires* (Paris, Economica, 1997)
Abbey, W. (ed.), *Between Two Languages. German-Speaking Exiles in Great Britain, 1939–1945* (Stuttgart, Verlag Hans-Dieter Heinz, 1995)
Accoce, P., *Les Français à Londres* (Paris, Balland, 1989)
Ackroyd, P., *London. The Autobiography* (London, Chatto & Windus, 2000)
Agulhon, M., *The French Republic, 1879–1992* (Oxford, Basil Blackwell, 1993)
Ambrose, T. (ed.), *Hitler's Loss. What Britain and America Gained from Europe's Cultural Exiles* (London, Peter Owen, 2001)
Amouroux, H., *La Grande Histoire des français sous l'occupation* (Paris, Robert Laffont, 1976–99) 10 vols
____, *Le 18 juin 1940* (Paris, Fayard, 1982)
Anson, P. F., *The Religious Orders and Congregations of Great Britain and Ireland* (Worcester, Stanbrook Abbey Press, 1949)
Ashton, R., *Little Germany. German Refugees in Victorian Britain* (Oxford, Oxford University Press, 1989)
Atkin, N., *Pétain* (London, Addison Wesley Longman, 1997)
Bankwitz, P. C. F., *Maxime Weygand and Civil-Military Relations in Modern France* (Cambridge, MA, Harvard University Press, 1967)

Barker, E., *Churchill and Eden at War* (New York, Macmillan, 1978)

Bell, P. M. H., *A Certain Eventuality. Britain and the Fall of France* (London, Saxon House, 1974)

_____, *France and Britain* (London, Longman, 1996–97) 2 vols

Bellanger, D. A., *The French Exiled Clergy in the British Isles after 1789* (Bath, Downside Abbey, 1986)

Bennett, E. G., *In Search of Freedom. The Story of some Refugees and Exiles who Found a Haven in Bournemouth and District* (Bournemouth, Bournemouth Local Studies Publications, 1988)

Berghahn, M., *German-Jewish Refugees in England. Continental Britons* (Oxford, Berg, 1988)

Berthon, S., *Allies at War* (London, Collins, 2000)

Blaxland, G., *Destination Dunkirk* (London, Military Book Society, 1973)

Blond, G., *Pétain* (Paris, Presses de la Cité, 1966)

Bond, B., *France and Belgium, 1939–1940* (London, Brassey's 1990)

Bramwell, A. C. (ed.), *Refugees in the Age of Total War* (London, Unwin Hyman, 1988)

Bridges, S., *The Home Front. War Years in Britain, 1939–1945* (London, Weidenfeld & Nicolson, 1975)

Briggs, A., *The History of Broadcasting in the UK*, Vol. 3 (London, Oxford University Press, 1972) 5 vols

Briggs, S., *The Home Front. War Years in Britain, 1939–1945* (London, Weidenfeld & Nicolson, 1975)

Brooks Richards, S., *Secret Flotillas. Clandestine Sea Lines to France and French North Africa, 1940–1944* (London, HMSO, 1996)

Brown, F., *Zola. A Life* (New York, Macmillan, 1996)

Burrin, P., *La France à l'heure allemande* (Paris, Seuil, 1993)

Burrus, M., *Paul Morand, voyageur du Xxe siècle* (Paris, Séguier, 1987)

Cahalan, P., *Belgian Refugee Relief in England during the Great War* (New York/London, Garland, 1982)

Calder, A., *The Myth of the Blitz* (London, Jonathan Cape, 1991)

_____, *The People's War. Britain 1939–1945* (London, Pimlico, 1992)

Caron, V., *Uneasy Asylum. France and the Jewish Refugee Crisis, 1933–42* (Stanford, Stanford University Press, 1999)

Carpenter, K., *Refugees of the French Revolution. Emigrés in London, 1789–1802* (Basingstoke, Macmillan, 1989)

Carpenter, K. and Mansel, P. (eds), *The French Emigrés in Europe and the Struggle against Revolution, 1789–1814* (Basingstoke, Macmillan, 1999)

Cesarani, D. (ed.), *The Internment of Aliens in Twentieth-Century Britain* (London, Frank Cass, 1993)

Cesarani, D. and Fulbrook, M. (eds), *Citizenship, Nationality and Migration in Europe* (London, Routledge, 1996)

Chadwick, O., *Britain and the Vatican during the Second World War*

(Cambridge University Press, 1982)

Chaline, E. and Santarelli, P., *Historique des Forces Navales Françaises Libres* (Vincennes, Service Historique de la Marine, 1989)

Christienne, C. and Lissarague, P. *Histoire de l'aviation militaire. L'Armée de l'air* (Paris, Charles Lavanzelle, 1981)

Cointet, J.-P., *La France Libre* (Paris, Presses Universitaires de France, 1976)

Cointet, J.-P. and M., *La France à Londres. Reassissance d'un état* (Brussels, Editions Complexe, 1990)

Collier, R., *The Sands of Dunkirk* (London, Collins, 1961)

Cordier, D., *Jean Moulin. L'Inconnu du panthéon* (Paris, Lattès, 1989) 3 vols

Cras, H., *Dunkerque* (Paris, Editions France-Empire, 1960)

Crémieux-Brilhac, J.-L., *Les Français de l'an quarante* (Paris; Gallinard, 1989) 2 vols

____, *La France Libre de l'appel du 18 juin à la liberation* (Paris, Flammarion, 1995)

Crisham, W., *Divided Island. Faction and Unity of Saint Pierre* (Cambridge, MA, Harvard University Press, 1969)

Dejonghe, E. and Le Maner, Y., *Le Nord-Pas-de-Calais dans la main allemande, 1940–1944* (Lille, Presses Universitaires de Lille, 1999)

Destrumau, B., *Weygard* (Paris, Perrin, 1989)

Divine, D., *The Nine Days of Dunkirk* (London, Faber and Faber, 1959)

Doughty, R., *The Breaking Point. Sedan and the Fall of France* (Hamden, Archon, 1990)

Durand, Y., *Vichy 1940–1944* (Paris, Bordas Poche, 1972)

Duroselle, J.-B., *L'Abîme. Politique étrangère de la France, 1939–1944* (Paris, Imprimerie Nationale, 1982)

Eck, H. (ed.), *La Guerre des ondes* (Paris/Lausanne, Armand Colin, 1986)

ENSTA, *Les Armées françaises pendant la deuxième guerre mondiale, 1939–1945* (Paris, Institut Charles de Gaulle, 1986)

Egremont, M., *Under Two Flags. The Life of Major General Sir Edward Spears* (London, Weidenfeld & Nicolson, 1997)

Faber, R., *French and English* (London, Hutchinson, 1925)

Ferro, M., *Pétain* (Paris, Fayard, 1986)

Fishman, S., Downs, L. L., Sinanoglou, I., Smith, L. V. and Zasetsky, R. (eds), *France at War. Vichy and the Historians* (New York, Berg, 2000)

Fondation Charles de Gaulle, *Le Rétablissement de la légalité républicaine, 1944* (Paris, Plon, 1996)

Foot, M. R. D., *SOE in France, 1940–1944* (London, HMSO, 1966)

Footit, H. and Simmonds, J., *France, 1943–45* (Leicester, Leicester University Press, 1986)

Funk, A., *The Politics of TORCH* (Lawrence, University Press of Kansas, 1974)

Gardiner, J., *'Overpaid, Oversexed and Over Here.' The American GI in World War II Britain* (London, Abbeville Press, 1992)

Gelb, N., *Dunkirk. The Incredible Escape* (London, Joseph, 1990)

Gilbert, M., *The Second World War* (London, Collins, 1991)

Gildea, R., *Marianne in Chains. In Search of the German Occupation, 1940–1945* (London, Macmillan, 2002)

Girard, L.-D., *Mazinghem ou la vie secrète de Philippe Pétain* (Paris, privately published, 1971)

Glees, A., *Exile Politics during the Second World War. The German Social Democrats in Britain* (Oxford, Clarendon, 1982)

Graves, C., *Women in Green. The Story of the WVS* (London, Heinemann, 1948)

Griffiths, R., *Pétain* (London, Constable, 1970)

____, *Fellow Travellers of the Right* (Oxford, Oxford University Press, 1981)

Goiran, H., *Les Français à Londres. Etude historique, 1544–1933* (Pornic, Editions de la Vague, 1933)

Gough, H. and Horne, J. (eds), *De Gaulle and Twentieth-Century France* (London, Edward Arnold, 1994)

Guitard-Auviste, G., *Morand (1888–1976). Légendes et vérités* (Paris, Hachette, 1981)

Gunsburg, J., *Divided and Conquered. The French High Command and the Defeat of the West* (Westport, Greenwood Press, 1979)

Gwynn, R., *The Huguenot Heritage. The History and Contribution of the Huguenots in Britain* (London, Routledge & Kegan Paul, 1985)

Hale, E. R. W. and Turner, J. F. (eds), *The Yanks are Coming* (Tunbridge Wells, Hidus, 1983)

Halls, W. D., *The Youth of Vichy France* (Oxford, Clarendon, 1981)

____, *Politics, Society and Christianity in Vichy France* (Oxford, Berg, 1995)

Harman, N., *Dunkirk. The Necessary Myth* (London, Hodder & Stoughton 1980)

Hartley, A., *De Gaulle* (London, Routledge & Kegan Paul, 1972)

Hay, I., *Peaceful Invasion* (London, Hodder & Stoughton, 1946)

Hinsley, F. H., *British Intelligence in the Second World War* (London, HMSO, 1978–88) 4 vols

Hirschfeld, G. (ed.), *Exile in Great Britain. Refugees from Hitler's Germany* (Leamington Spa, Berg, 1984)

Holman, V. and Kelly, D. (eds), *France at War in the Twentieth Century. Propaganda, Myth and Metaphor* (Oxford, Berghan, 2000)

Holmes, C., *John Bull's Island. Immigration and British Society, 1871–1971* (Basingstoke, Macmillan, 1988)

____, *A Tolerant Country. Immigrants, Refugees and Minorities in Britain* (London, Faber & Faber, 1991)

____ (ed.), *Immigrants and Minorities in British Society* (London, Macmillan, 1978)

Horne, A., *To Lose a Battle* (London, Macmillan, 1969)

Hurstfield, J., *America and the French Nation, 1939–1945* (Chapel Hill, University of North Carolina Press, 1986)

Hytier, A., *Two Years of French Foreign Policy, 1940–1942* (Westport, Greenwood Press, 1974)

Jackson, J., *Charles de Gaulle* (London, Cardinal, 1990)

____, *The Dark Years. France, 1940–1944* (Oxford, Oxford University Press, 2001).

Kedward, H. R., *Resistance in Vichy France. A Study of Ideas and Motivation in the Southern Zone*, 1940–1942 (Oxford, Oxford University Press, 1978)

____, *Occupied France. Collaboration and Resistance, 1940–1944* (Oxford, Basil Blackwell, 1985)

Kersaudy, F., *Churchill and de Gaulle* (London, Collins, 1981)

____, *Norway 1940* (London, Collins, 1990)

Knowlson, J., *Damned to Fame. The Life of Samuel Beckett* (London, Bloomsbury, 1996)

Kochan, M., *Britain's Internees in the Second World War* (London, Macmillan, 1983)

Kushner, T. and Knox, K., *Refugees in the Age of Genocide. Global, National and Local Perspectives during the Twentieth Century* (London, Frank Cass, 1999)

Laborie, P., *L'Opinion publique sous Vichy* (Paris, Seuil, 1990)

Lacouture, J., *The Rebel* (London, Harper Collins, 1986)

Larkin, M., *Religion, Politics and Preferment in France since 1890. La Belle Epoque and its Legacy* (Cambridge, Cambridge Univesity Press, 1995)

Ledwidge, B., *De Gaulle* (London, Weidenfeld & Nicolson, 1982)

Levisse-Touzé, C., *L'Afrique du Nord dans la guerre, 1939–1945* (Paris, Albin Michael, 1998)

London, L., *Whitehall and the Jews, 1933–1948. British Immigration Policy and the Holocaust* (Cambridge, Cambridge University Press, 2000)

Longmate, N., *How We Lived Then. A History of Everyday Life during the Second World* War (London, Hutchinson, 1971)

____, *The GIs. The Americans in Britain, 1942–1945* (London, Hutchinson 1975)

Mack, J. and Humphries, S., *The Making of Modern London, 1939–1945. London at War* (London, Sidgwick & Jackson, 1985)

Maga, T. P., *America, France and the European Refugee Problem, 1933–1947* (New York/London, Garland, 1985)

Maguire, G. E., *Anglo-American Relations with the Free French* (Basingstoke, Macmillan, 1995)

Marrus, M., *The Unwanted. European Refugees in the Twentieth Century* (Oxford, Oxford University Press, 1985)

Marrus, M. and Paxton, R. O., *Vichy France and the Jews* (New York, Basic Books, 1981)

Martel, A. (ed.), *Histoire militaire de la France*, Vol. 4 (Paris, Presses Universitaires de France, 1994) 4 vols

Masson, P., *La Marine française et la guerre, 1939–1945* (Paris, Tallandier, 1991)

Mauriac, C., *The Other de Gaulle* (London, Angus & Robertson, 1973)

Michel, H., *Histoire de la France Libre* (Paris, Presses Universitaires de France, 1980)

Moloney, T., *Westminster, Whitehall and the Vatican. The Role of Cardinal Hinsley, 1935–1943* (Tunbridge Wells; Burns and Oates, 1983)

Nettelbeck, C., *Forever French. Exiles in the United States, 1939–1945* (Oxford, Berg, 1991)

Oddone, P., *Dunkirk 1940. French Ashes, British Deliverance. The Story of Operation Dynamo* (Stroud, Tempus, 2000)

Ollier, N., *L'Exode sur les routes de l'an 40* (Paris, Robert Laffont, 1970)

Paillole, P., *Services spéciaux, 1939–1945* (Paris, Laffont, 1975)

Panayi, P. (ed.), *Germans in Britain since 1500* (London, Hambledon, 1996)

Paxton, R. O., *Parades and Politics at Vichy. The French Officer Corps under Marshal Pétain* (Princeton, Princeton University Press, 1966)

_____, *Vichy France. Old Guard and New Order, 1940–1944* (New York, Alfred A Knopf, 1972)

Péan, P., *Vies et morts de Jean Moulin* (Paris, Fayard, 1998)

Pierre-Bloch, M., *De Gaule on le temps des méprises* (Paris, La Table Ronde, 1969)

Poirier, F. (ed.), *Londres, 1939–1945. Riches et pauvres dans le même élan patriotique*, derrière la légende (Paris, Autrement, 1995)

Proudfoot, M. J., *European Refugees, 1939–1952* (London, Faber and Faber, 1957)

Reynolds, D., *Rich Relations. The American Occupation of Britain, 1942–1945* (London, Phoenix Press, 2000)

Rousso, H., *The Vichy Syndrome. History and Memory in France since 1944* (Cambridge, MA, Harvard University Press, 1991)

Schoenbrun, D., *The Three Lives of Charles de Gaulle. A Biography* (London, Hamish Hamilton, 1966)

Schom, A., *Emile Zola* (London, Queen Anne Press, 1987)

Servent, P., *Verdun, ou le mythe des tranchées* (Paris, Payot, 1988)

Shennan, A., *Rethinking France. Plans for Renewal* (Oxford, Oxford University Press, 1989)

_____, *De Gaulle* (London, Longman, 1993)

Sheppard, F., *London. A History* (Oxford, Oxford University Press, 1998)

Sherman, A. J., *Island Refuge. Britain and the Refugees from the Third Reich, 1933–1945* (London, Frank Cass, 1994, 2nd edn)

Sims, G. R. (ed.), *Living London* (London, Cassell, 1901) 3 vols

Smith, G., *When Jim Crow met John Bull. Black American Soldiers in World War 2 Britain* (London, Tauris, 1987)

Snowman, D., *The Hitler Emigrés. The Cultural Impact on Britain of Refugees from Nazism* (London, Chatto and Windus, 2002)

Stafford, D., *Britain and European Resistance, 1940–1945* (London, Macmillan,

1980)

Sweets, J., *Choices in Vichy France* (New York, Oxford University Press, 1985)

Sword, K., Davies, N. and Ciechanowski, J., *The Formation of the Polish Community in Great Britain, 1939–1950* (London, SSEES, 1989)

Thibault, P., *L'Allure de Morand. Du modernisme au Pétainisme* (Birmingham, AL, University of Birmingham, 1992)

Thomas, M., *The French Empire at War, 1940–1945* (Manchester, Manchester University Press, 1997)

Thomas, R. T., *Britain and Vichy, 1940–1942* (London, Macmillan, 1979)

Thomson, D., *Two Frenchmen. Pierre Laval and Charles de Gaulle* (London, The Cresset Press, 1951)

Titmuss, R., *Problems of Social Policy* (London, HMSO, 1950)

Tournoux, R., *Pétain et de Gaulle* (Paris, Plon, 1966)

Tute, W., *The Reluctant Enemies. The Story of the Last War between Britain and France, 1940–1942* (London, Collins, 1990)

Vidalenc, J., *L'Exode de mai-juin 1940* (Paris, Presses Universitaires de France, 1957)

Vinen, R., *France, 1934–1970* (Basingstoke, Macmillan, 1996)

Waites, N. (ed.), *Troubled Neighbours. Franco-British Relations in the Twentieth Century* (London, Weidenfeld & Nicolson, 1971)

Wasserstein, B., *Britain and the Jews of Europe, 1939–1945* (Oxford, Oxford University Press, 1979)

Werth, A., *De Gaulle* (London, Penguin, 1965)

Wheeler-Bennett, J. W., *John Anderson, Viscount Waverley* (London, Macmillan, 1962)

White, J., *London in the Twentieth Century. A City and its People* (London, Viking, 2001)

White, R. and Bell, P. M. H., *Our Gallant Ally* (London, Longman, 1994)

Williams, C., *The Last Great Frenchman. A Life of General de Gaulle* (London, Little, Brown, 1993)

Williams Smith, B., *Jacques Maritain. Anti-Modern or Ultra Modern?* (New York/Oxford, Elsevier, 1986)

Wilson, F. M., *They Came as Strangers. The Story of Refugees to Great Britain* (London, Hamish Hamilton, 1959)

Winfield, P., *Bye Bye, Baby. The Story of the Children the GIs Left Behind* (London, Bloomsbury, 1992)

Young, R., *In Command of France. French Policy and Military Planning, 1933–39* (Cambridge, MA, Harvard University Press, 1979)

Ziegler, P., *London at War, 1939–1945* (London, Sinclair Stevenson, 1995)

Articles

Atkin, N., 'De Gaulle et la presse anglaise, *1940–1943*', *Espoir*, no. 71, juin 1990, 39–45

_____, 'Une communaute héteroclite. Les Français', in Poirier, F. (ed.), *Londres,*

1939–1945. Riches et pauvres dans le même élan patriotique, derrière la legende (Paris, Autrement, 1995), pp. 83–90

____, 'France in Exile'. The French Community in Britain, 1940–1944', in Conway, M. and Gotovich, J. (eds), *Europe in Exile. European Exile Communities in Britain, 1940–1945* (New York/Oxford, Berghahn Books, 2001), pp. 213–18

____, 'L'Accueil des réfugiés français en Grande Bretagne', in Vaïsse, M. (ed.), *Mai–juin 1940. Défaite française, victoire allemande sous l'oeil des historiens étrangers* (Paris, Autrement, 2001), pp. 113–25

Bell, P. M. H., 'The Breakdown of the Alliance in 1940', in Waites, N. (ed.), *Troubled Neighbours. Franco-British Relations in the Twentieth Century* (London, Weidenfeld Nicolson, 1971), pp. 200–27

____, 'L'Evolution de l'opinion publique anglaise à propos de la guerre et de l'alliance avec la France', in *CNRS, Français et Britanniques dans la drôle de guerre* (Paris, CNRS, 1979), pp. 51–80

____, 'Shooting the Rapids. British Reactions to the Fall of France', *Modern and Contemporary France*, no. 42, July 1990, 16–28

____, 'L'opinion publique en Grande Bretagne et le général de Gaulle', *Guerres Mondiales et Conflits Contemporains*, 190, 1998, 79–101

Bellanger, A., 'France and England. The English Female Religious from Reformation to World War', in Atkin, N. and Tallett, F. (eds), *Catholicism in Britain and France since 1789* (London, Hambledon, 1996), pp. 1–11.

Branca, E., 'Les Oreilles de 18 juin', *Espoir*, no. 71, juin 1990, 11–13.

Buck, M. 'Feeding a Pauper Army. War Refugees and Welfare in Britain, 1939–1942', *Twentieth Century British History* 10 (3) 1999, 310–44.

Carpenter, K. 'London. Capital of the Emigration', in Carpenter, K. and Mansel, P. (eds), *The French Emigrés in Europe and the Struggle against Revolution, 1789–1814* (Basingstoke, Macmillan, 1999), pp. 49–61.

Charlot, J. and M., 'Le Général de Gaulle dans la mémoire des Britanniques', in Institut Charles de Gaulle, *De Gaulle en son siecle. Sondages et enquêtes* (Paris, Institut Charles de Gaulle, 1992), pp. 297–319

Cornick, M., 'Interview with Emile Delavenay. The BBC and the Propaganda War against Occupied France', *French History*, September 1994, 316–54

____, 'Distorting Mirrors. Problems of Anglo-French Perceptions in the *fin de siècle*', in Crossley, C. and Cornick, M. (eds), *Problems in French History. Essays in Honour of Douglas Johnson* (London, Palgrave, 2000), pp. 125–48

____, 'Fighting Myth with Reality. The Fall of France, Anglophobia and the BBC', in Holman, V. and Kelly, D. (eds), *France at War in the Twentieth Century. Propaganda Myth and Metaphor* (Oxford, Berghahn, 2000), pp. 65–87.

Debouzy, M., 'L'amical invasion', in Poirier, F. (ed.), *Londres, 1939–1945. Riches et pauvres dans le même élan patriotique, derrière la légende* (Paris, Autrement, 1995), pp. 108–19

Flonneau, J.-M., 'L'Evolution de l'opinion publique', in Azéma, J.-P. and

Bédarida, F. (eds), *Vichy et les français* (Paris, Fayard, 1992), pp. 506–22

Frank, R., 'Vichy et les britanniques, 1940–1941. Double Jeu ou double langage?', in Azéma, J.-P. and Bédarida, F. (eds), *Vichy et les français* (Paris, Fayard, 1992), pp. 144–61

Foot, M. R. D., 'De Gaulle et les services secrets pendant la guerre', *Espoir*, no. 71, juin 1990, 46–52

Halls, W. D., 'Catholicism under Vichy. A Study in Ambiguity', in Kedward, H. R. and Austin, R. (eds), *Vichy France and the Resistance. Culture and Ideology* (London, Croom Helm, 1985), pp. 133–46

Harvey, A. D., 'Gide, Forster and HMG. French Writers in the Public Records Office', *Times Literary Supplement*, 8 November 1996

Hutchins, S., 'The Communard Exiles in Britain', *Marxism Today*, March 1971, April 1971, June 1971

Hutt, M., 'Refugees, exiles and émigrés', in Johnson, D., Bédarida, F. and Crouzet, F. (eds), *Britain and France. Ten Centuries* (Folkestone, Dawson, 1980), pp. 130–6

Jackson, J., 'General de Gaulle and his Enemies. Anti-Gaullism in France since 1940', in *Transactions of the Royal Historical Society*, 6th series, vol IX, 1999, pp. 43–65

——, 'Etrange défaite française ou étrange victoire anglaise', in Vaïsse, M. (ed.), *Mai-juin 1940. Défaite française, victoire allemande sous l'oeil des historiens étrangers* (Paris, Autrement, 2001), pp. 177–213

Johnson, D., 'Les Britanniques et les gaullistes', in Fondation pour les Etudes de Défense, *Les Armées françaises pendant la seconde guerre mondiale* (Paris, FNED, 1986), pp. 81–91.

——, 'Aragon and the British', *Times Literary Supplement*, 10 December 1999

Keating, J., 'British Catholics and the Fall of France', in Atkin, N. and Tallett, F. (eds), *Catholicism in Britain and France since 1789* (London, Hambledon, 1996), pp. 27–42

Kedward, H. R., 'Patriots and Patriotism in Vichy France', *Transactions of the Royal Historical Society*, 5th series, 32, 1982, 175–92

——, 'The French Resistance', *History Today*, Special Supplement, June 1984

Lesourd, J.-A., 'Refugees, exiles, émigrés', in Johnson, D., Bédarida, F., and Crouzet, F. (eds), *Britain and France. Ten Centuries* (Folkestone, Dawson, 1980), pp. 117–29.

Martel, A., 'De Gaulle et la France Libre. L'Appel du soldat', in Martel, A. (ed.), *Histoire militaire de la France*, vol. 4 (Paris, Presses Universitaires de France 1994), pp. 771–30

Mews, S., 'The Sword of the Spirit: A Catholic Cultural Crusade of 1940', *Studies in Church History*, 20, 1983, 409–30

Moore, F., 'Les Engagés de 1940. Des hommes qui, en 1940, se sout engagés à vingt ans dans les FFL, se souviennent,' *Espoir*, no. 71, juin 1990, 14–26.

Raes, F., 'Female Belgian Refugees in Britain during the Second World War. An

Oral History', in Conway, M. and Gotovitch, J. (eds), *Europe in Exile. European Exile Communities in Britain, 1940–1945* (New York/Oxford, Berghahn Books, 2001), pp. 67–80

Reavell, F., 'The French Chamber. A Bit of History', *Info*, vol. 24, Jan–Feb 2002, 28–9

Roberts, A., 'Hitler's England. What if Germany had invaded Britain in May 1940?', in Ferguson, N. (ed.), *Virtual History Alternatives and Counterfactuals* (London, Papermac, 1997), pp. 281–320

Snowman, D., 'How Germany's Loss was Britain's Gain', *History Magazine*, vol. 1, no. 4, August 2000, 42–5

White, G., 'The Fall of France', *Studies in Church History*, 20, 1983, 431–41

Unpublished theses

Carswell, R., 'The British Press and France, 1940–1944', paper written in preparation for Reading University Ph.D., January 2000.

Clausard, M.-L., 'De Gaulle et la presse anglaise en 1940. Du ministre inconnu au célèbre homme d'Etat', *Mémoire de maîtrise*, Université de Paris X-Nanterre, 1997

Delin, J., 'L'Opinion britannique et les français en Grande-Bretagne pendant l'année 1940', *doctorat*, Université de Lille III, 1993

Dombrowski, N., 'Beyond the Battlefield: The French Civilian Exodus of May–June 1940', New York University Ph.D., 1995

Keating, J., 'Roman Catholics, Christian Democracy and the British Labour Movement, 1910–1960', University of Manchester Ph.D., 1992

Martinez, P. K., 'Paris Communard Refugees in Britain 1871–1880', University of Sussex D.Phil., 1981

Merrett, K., '*La France Libre*, 1940–1944: Resistance and Exile Journalism', University of Alberta MA, 1992

Reavell, F., 'The British Press and Pétain in 1940', University of Reading BA dissertation, 1999

Smith, D., 'La Perfide Angleterre. *Je Suis Partout* and Britain, 1941–44', University of Reading MA thesis, 2002

Index